Judith M. Lieu is s... at
Macquarie University, Sydney, a... r in
New Testament Studies at King's College, ...n.

The jacket illustration is of the Torah shrines in the synagogue at Sardis. (Author's private photograph).

T&T Clark
59 George Street Edinburgh EH2 2LQ

IMAGE AND REALITY

IMAGE AND REALITY
The Jews in the World of the Christians in the Second Century

JUDITH M. LIEU

T&T CLARK
EDINBURGH

T&T CLARK LTD
59 GEORGE STREET
EDINBURGH EH2 2LQ
SCOTLAND

First published 1996

ISBN 0 567 08529 5

British Library Cataloguing-in-Publication Data
A catalogue record for this book is available from the British Library

Typeset by Trinity Typesetting, Edinburgh
Printed and bound in Great Britain by Hartnolls Ltd, Bodmin

CONTENTS

PREFACE

A new interest in and understanding of the changing relationship between Judaism and Christianity during the first centuries CE has been a major feature of recent scholarship. This has owed much both to new methods, including the social scientific study of early Christian texts, redaction criticism which recognises the concerns of their writers and communities, and a fresh approach to both Palestinian and diaspora Judaism, as well as to a much needed and painful awareness of the terrible legacy of the Christian 'teaching of contempt' towards her Jewish heritage and partners. Study of individual texts, of the historical situations and development behind them, and of the theological questions within the debate has made fruitful progress without exhausting either the subject or the contemporary theological problems it poses. The present exploration owes much to such studies, yet it seeks to pose the question in a different way. What is the *rhetorical* function of Jews and Judaism in the early texts, after those of the New Testament but before the increasingly stereotypical polemic and diatribe of third- and fourth-century authors? How does this rhetorical function relate to the historical, theological and social frameworks within which these texts arose and functioned? How, in turn, did they help constitute the framework for later texts? If the question is multifaceted so will be the answer, but this is better than a simple or globalised explanation of what is too easily labelled Christian antisemitism. Without devaluing the gravity of the latter, in content, animus and consequences, or suggesting that to seek to interpret is to condone, only by understanding the tangled skein of the past can we hope to weave a more wholesome pattern for the future.

Much of the initial work was done during a year, 1989–90, spent at the Institutum Iudaicum, Evangelisch-theologisches

Seminar, Universität Tübingen, with the support of a *Stipendium* awarded by the Alexander von Humboldt Stiftung. I owe much to the initial invitation by Professor Martin Hengel, to the warm hospitality shown to our family by himself and by Frau Hengel, and to his continued support and interest. Many others made their contribution during that year, among whom I would particularly thank Professor Otto Betz and Professor Peter Stuhlmacher.

A much needed further impetus was given by a term, January to April 1994, spent at the Tantur Ecumenical Institute, Jerusalem, as the first Woods–Gumbel Fellow. I am deeply grateful to the British Trust for Tantur for the award of that fellowship, to the staff at Tantur for their friendship and support, and to the students whom I taught and with whom I shared so much.

In the interim teaching and other commitments meant that the project has taken longer than I first hoped, but interaction with many colleagues and friends on the way has been a source of great enrichment. My colleagues at King's College, London, particularly Graham Stanton and Francis Watson, deserve special mention, as too do those in Ancient History and Jewish Studies from whom I have learnt much, among others Martin Goodman, John North and Tessa Rajak. There are, as always, many others, too numerous to name, who, by the odd comment, question or answer, or by what they have written, have stimulated the ideas for which I alone take full responsibility.

My family have shared the various stages of learning and writing; my husband, Samuel, has shown his support in innumerable ways, while it is to Esther, who has cheerfully made the adventures of Tübingen and of Jerusalem her own, that I dedicate this book.

London, 1995

ABBREVIATIONS

AAR	American Academy of Religion
AGAJU	Arbeiten zur Geschichte des antiken Judentums und des Urchristentums
AJA	*American Journal of Archaeology*
AnatStuds	*Anatolian Studies*
AnBoll	*Analecta Bollandiana*
ANRW	*Aufstieg und Niedergang der römischen Welt*
ATR	*Anglican Theological Review*
AUSS	*Andrews University Seminary Studies*
BASOR	*Bulletin of the American Schools of Oriental Research*
BETL	Bibliotheca ephemeridum theologicarum lovaniensium
BFCT	Beiträge zur Förderung christlicher Theologie
BHT	Beiträge zur historischen Theologie
BibNot	*Biblische Notizen*
BJRL	*Bulletin of the John Rylands University Library of Manchester*
BJS	Brown Judaic Studies
B.TAVO	Beiheft zur TAVO
BullLitEccl	*Bulletin de littérature ecclésiastique*
BZNW	Beiheft zur *ZNW*
CBQ	*Catholic Biblical Quarterly*
CC.SA	Corpus Christianorum Series Apocrypha
CIG	*Corpus Inscriptionum Graecarum*
CIJ	*Corpus Inscriptionum Iudaicarum*
CPJ	*Corpus Papyrorum Iudaicorum*
CQR	*Church Quarterly Review*
CRAIBL	*Comptes rendus de l'Academie des inscriptions et belles-lettres*
CSCO	Corpus scriptorum christianorum orientalium
EJ	*Encyclopaedia Judaica*

ErFor	Erträge der Forschung
EtBib	Études bibliques
FoC	Fathers of the Church
FRLANT	Forschungen zur Religion und Literatur des Alten und Neuen Testaments
Fs.	Festschrift
FZPhT	*Freiburger Zeitschrift für Philosophie und Theologie*
GRBS	*Greek, Roman and Byzantine Studies*
HSCP	*Harvard Studies in Classical Philology*
HTR	*Harvard Theological Review*
HUCA	*Hebrew Union College Annual*
HUT	Hermeneutische Untersuchungen zur Theologie
JANES	*Journal of the Ancient Near Eastern Society of Columbia University*
JbAC	Jahrbuch für Antike und Christentum
JBL	*Journal of Biblical Literature*
JECS	*Journal of Early Christian Studies*
JEH	*Journal of Ecclesiastical History*
JQR	*Jewish Quarterly Review*
JJS	*Journal of Jewish Studies*
JMedStuds	*Journal of Mediterranean Studies*
JRH	*Journal of Religious History*
JRS	*Journal of Roman Studies*
JSHRZ	Jüdische Schriften aus hellenistisch-römischer Zeit
JSJ	*Journal for the Study of Judaism in the Persian, Hellenistic and Roman Period*
JSNT	*Journal for the Study of the New Testament*
JSNT.SS	*JSNT* Supplement Series
JSS	*Journal of Semitic Studies*
JTS	*Journal of Theological Studies*
LCL	Loeb Cassical Library
LXX	Septuagint
MBTh	Münsterische Beiträge zur Theologie
MGWJ	*Monatsschrift für Geschichte und Wissenschaft des Judentums*
NAWG	*Nachrichten des Akademie der Wissenschaften in Göttingen*
nf.	neue Folge
ns.	new series

NT	*Novum Testamentum*
NTAb	Neutestamentliche Abhandlungen
NTOA	Novum Testamentum et Orbis Antiquus
NTS	*New Testament Studies*
NT.S	*Novum Testamentum* Supplements
NTT	*Nederlands theologisch tijdschrift*
OECT	Oxford Early ChristianTexts
OTL	Old Testament Library
PAAJR	*Proceedings of the American Academy of Jewish Research*
PTS	Patristische Texte und Studien
PW	Pauly-Wissowa, *Real-Encyclopädie der classischen Altertumswissenschaft*
RAC	*Reallexikon für Antike und Christentum*
RBib	*Revue biblique*
REAug	*Revue des études augustiniennes*
REByz	*Revue des études byzantines*
RechSR	*Récherches de science religeuse*
REJ	*Revue des études juives*
REL	*Revue des études latines*
RevSciRel	*Revue des sciences religeuses*
RGG	*Religion in Geschichte und Gegenwart*
RHPhR	*Revue d'histoire et de philosophie religeuses*
SBLDS	Society of Biblical Literature Dissertation Series
SC	Sources chrétiennes
ScriptHier	*Scripta hieroslymitana*
SHAW	*Sitzungsberichte der heidelbergen Akademie der Wissenschaften*
SJLA	Studies in Judaism in Late Antiquity
SJOT	*Scandinavian Journal of the Old Testament*
SJT	*Scottish Journal of Theology*
SNTSMS	Society for New Testament Studies Monograph Series
SPB	Studia Postbiblica
SR	*Studies in Religion/ Sciences religeuses*
StTh	*Studia theologica*
TAVO	Tübinger Atlas des Vorderen Orients
TLZ	*Theologische Literaturzeitung*
TRE	*Theologische Realenzyklopädie*
TRu	*Theologische Rundschau*
TS	*Theological Studies*

TU	Texte und Untersuchungen
TzF	Texte zum Forschung
UM	University Microfilms
VC	*Vigiliae Christianae*
VT	*Vetus Testamentum*
WUNT	Wissenschaftliche Untersuchungen zum Neuen Testament
ZKG	*Zeitschrift für Kirchengeschichte*
ZNW	*Zeitschrift für die neutestamentliche Wissenschaft*
ZPE	*Zeitschrift für Papyrologie und Epigraphik*
ZThK	*Zeitschrift für Theologie und Kirche*
ZWT	*Zeitschrift für wissenschaftliche Theologie*

1

INTRODUCTION

It has, in recent years, become something of a truism to assert that in order to construct *her own* identity, early Christianity had to construct for herself the identity of the '*other*', of Judaism within which she was born, of 'paganism' from which before very long most Christians came. Whereas the latter exercise has caused little anxiety, the process by which the former becomes synonymous with Christian anti-Judaism or antisemitism[1] has justifiably provoked searching analysis. Recognition that the constructed 'identity' of Judaism, which has continued to form part of the 'knowledge' of many in both church and academy, is at best a distorted reflection of the reality of both past and present, has demanded a number of responses. One response has been the careful description of that reality through a new encounter with the sources;[2] another has been to trace the development of Christian–Jewish debate and polemic in the early period. The fruits of this have been manifold: a clearer sense of how the multiform theological needs of the nascent church shaped that polemic against Judaism, and of how often the latter hid continuing contacts and interaction between Jews and Christians. Just as the mono-lithic and uniform 'late Judaism' of earlier scholarship has given place to a more nuanced, varied and changing 'early Judaism', so too the – tardy and necessary – discovery of a relentless and endemic Christian anti-Judaism has been succeeded by the detailed mapping of the complex interplay of individual per-sonalities, situations, theological traditions and literary forms which make up the early Christian responses to and construc-tions of Judaism.[3] Such mapping must play an essential role in responding to the hermeneutical challenge the whole enter-prise has posed; how is Christianity to respond theologically

to the exposure of this history; how far can she construct a
self-identity which does not maintain so destructive a construction of the identity of the 'other', Judaism? It is a challenge which has been made the more urgent by the
recognition that this process of construction is already
beginning within the New Testament with its historical priority and canonical authority.

To say this is to recognise that 'anti-Judaism' is at its heart
not a statement about the Jews but one about those who held
and articulated such views.[4] Yet it is also to recognise the interplay between image – for what else is identity-construction? –
which moves towards the universal or absolute, and the
particular in the writing of the individuals from which the
image is drawn. This is why what follows is a study not of 'anti-
Judaism' but of the ways in which Jews and Judaism are
presented in particular authors and contexts. At the same time,
it does not, like many recent studies, concentrate on the theological arguments in Jewish–Christian debate, their precursors
and successors. Although it is impossible to exclude totally the
theological arguments, they are peripheral to the task of
exploring 'presentations' of Jews and Judaism. Instead, such
'presentation' has to be seen both as belonging to the literary
construction of the text and as grounded in the text's social
context and function. Clearly, literary presentation cannot
automatically be taken as directly mirroring external reality but
frequently meets particular needs, internal or external to the
literature itself; it is also the case that the particular situation
may often shape the presentation, even when that situation is
not being directly addressed. Therefore we shall speak of 'image and reality', while recognising that *neither* of these is static
or accessible free of interpretation: the image is the presentation, that which each text projects concerning Jews or Judaism;
the reality is the actual position of Jews and Jewish communities in the context from which the literature comes, both in
themselves and in relation to their Christian contemporaries.
It is a reality which may sometimes be recovered from other
sources, literary or material, sometimes by a form of mirror
reading of the texts themselves. So, in an effort to hold together
the variables and the constants, the chapters which follow take
a fixed period – **the second century** – a (slightly less) fixed geo-

graphical area where it is possible to recover something of Christian and Jewish life within the pagan context – **Asia Minor** – and a cross-section of the emerging and formative **Christian literature**, and explore there **the presentation of Jews and Judaism**.

Second Century

For most of the NT writings the Jews are still a major point of reference for the identity of the new faith. In the Gospels this is hardly surprising for, as recent scholarship has repeatedly emphasised, that faith is rooted in 'Jesus the Jew' whose story had to be told within its Jewish matrix. However, there is little doubt that the Gospel authors also tell the story of Jesus in the light of their own experience, and that on their pages Jesus's encounters with *his* contemporaries reflect more than a little about the early Christians' own encounters with theirs. Using a variety of conflict models, contemporary scholarship has seen a recurring and dominant current in that interpretative experience as the worsening relations between Judaism or local Jewish communities and the Christian communities who are perhaps in, or near the end of, the process of 'separating' from their Jewish origins. It is a current particularly clear in the Fourth Gospel where the different groupings – crowds, Pharisees, scribes, elders, Sadducees – of the earlier tradition are becoming absorbed into the undifferentiated and alienating terminology of 'the Jews', leaving a sense that neither Jesus nor his true disciples are counted among 'the Jews'.[5] Each of the other Gospels reveals something of the same tensions expressed in different ways and makes it possible to debate whether 'the ways have parted' – are the Christians still 'within the synagogue', how do they view the future fate of the still unbelieving Jews, have they been thrown out, separated themselves or simply established new and independent groups? – questions which would be meaningless in the case of Jesus himself.[6]

Paul's letters deploy a very different rhetoric, reflecting all the contradictions in one who could claim he was 'a Hebrew of the Hebrews', that to him had been entrusted the Gospel to the uncircumcised, and that he *became* 'as a Jew to the Jews' (Phil.

3.5; Gal. 2.7; 1 Cor. 9.20). He too speaks of the Gospel and of those who live in response to it, who are 'in Christ', in contradistinction to both Jews and Greeks (1 Cor. 1.22–24; Gal. 3.28); yet for him both the 'claims' of Judaism on gentile Christians, which he rejects, and the continuing claim of the Jewish people, to whom belong the covenants and the promises (Gal. 3.21–22; Rom. 9.1–5), are issues of utmost urgency.

Looking ahead, by the third century we find the systematised collection of arguments and proof texts *Against the Jews*, in Tertullian, Cyprian, Hippolytus and their successors.[7] While it would be wrong to deny any contact between these authors and contemporary Judaism,[8] the arguments they used quickly become standardised and predictable, following well-established themes, and extend from explicit polemic to homiletic, exegetical and liturgical rhetoric.[9] Most of the foundations for these arguments were laid in the second century, particularly in Justin's *Dialogue with Trypho* and its immediate precursors, such as the lost *Dialogue of Jason and Papiscus*, or in the *Epistle of (Ps.)Barnabas*. This makes these authors particularly important as we ask of them how far their arguments were born out of genuine encounters with Judaism, how far the Judaism they denounce is already either a 'straw figure' or the creation of some other needs.

This immediately provokes further questions. If we date Justin's *Dialogue* in the middle of the second century, or even give its supposed setting soon after 134 CE some credence, we are left with a generation gap since the last explicit concern with the Jews, perhaps in John's Gospel. The Apostolic Fathers, whose writings approximately fill that gap (together with some of the later writings of the New Testament), appear to have no genuine concern with or about the Jews and Judaism. What has happened? It is not enough to dismiss the problem by saying that these writers were more concerned with the internal needs of the churches than with external polemic, that they write as pastors and not as apologists or polemicists;[10] the same could be said of some of the NT writers for whom 'the Jews' are still a fundamental model for dealing with these very needs. When the issue returns in the latter part of the century, are we to speak of the revival of anti-Jewish polemic or merely of its reappearance to our view, and in either case what has provoked this new situation?[11]

The answer to this question is unlikely to be simple; we need to be aware of factors internal to Christianity – its thought, literature, structures and composition – and to Judaism, but we also need to recognise them as components within the wider Graeco-Roman world of which all were part. This is, then, but a part of the broader problem of understanding the growth of Christianity in the second century, both numerically as well as in terms of the inner structures which shaped her total identity. Christian literature or 'discourse' played an inalienable role in that growth, and recent study has demonstrated the degree to which 'certain of the most characteristic features of Christian discourse in fact fitted the circumstances of society at large extremely well'.[12] This was a period not only of apparent growing pagan literary interest in Christianity,[13] but also of a burgeoning 'religious' literature which could become the vehicle of competition and of choice between different claimants to divine power.[14] Contrary to earlier accounts of decline and sterility, the second century was marked by the vitality of religious life and choice,[15] a vitality within which Christian–Jewish interaction must be set.

The very different conditions of the third century, provoked by invasions, by economic crisis and by changes in the organisation of the cities, warn against drawing simple lines of continuity or of development towards later Christian attitudes, which now must have been shaped by a different social context, something which would have been particularly true of Asia Minor.[16] These uncertain links with what precedes and with what follows make the creativity of the second century particularly challenging.

Asia Minor

Choosing a limited historical area has obvious advantages when looking for common patterns or concerns, or for their absence. Asia Minor in particular experienced both a literary and cultural vibrancy and 'une vie religieuse intense' in the second century;[17] at the same time it can claim the advantage of being the home to a variety of Christian groups and literature, as well as to thriving Jewish communities which in recent years have become much more visible to us through the excavation of their material remains – synagogues, inscriptions and epitaphs.

As we shall see, these communities could look back on a long history, and claim the support or protection of Roman and of local authorities. Josephus preserves a series of charters which record that protection and which give a valuable insight into the concerns and 'pressure points' of these diaspora communities.[18] The series comes to an end in the time of Augustus, leaving the continuing history of those communities shrouded in obscurity until the increasing range of archaeological evidence offers a new perspective. It is often supposed that the failure of the Jews of Asia Minor to become involved in any of the revolts against Roman power in 66–70, 115–17 or 132–5 CE, the lack of evidence for any continuing need to appeal against infringements of their rights, and their later apparent self-confidence point to a long period of peaceful coexistence with their gentile neighbours, although this is as insecure as any argument from silence.[19]

Earlier accounts of their Judaism tended to depict these communities as markedly syncretistic, even while maintaining an isolationism which earned them such opprobrium from pagan literary observers.[20] This picture was drawn from the assumed consequences of their absence from 'the centre', the Temple and the 'Land', and of their presence in the midst of the pagan world; from presuppositions that the Judaism of the later rabbinic sources represented a historical and theological norm; and from archaeological, often inscriptional, remains which appeared 'Jewish' but which decisively contradicted that 'norm'; as well as from deviant movements within Christianity which were presented as originating in 'Jewish' counter-influence. The influence of such accounts, even when their often explicit anti-Judaism is repudiated, is still to be seen in studies of 'judaising' within Christian groups. However, more recently a growing consensus has appealed to the archaeological evidence to depict the Judaism of Asia Minor as self-confident, neither syncretistic nor so introverted and isolationist as to have no real interaction with the cities in which they lived; involvement in city life and culture and the influence of local tendencies are equal parts of the self-identity of these communities, with sizeable synagogues, reading of Torah, and faithfulness to its precepts.[21] The fundamental work here was that of A. T. Kraabel – who must be able to claim one of most cited unpublished theses (1968) – and has been built on by others.[22] What is particularly important is that this attention to the non-literary evidence has revealed a very different picture of the Judaism contemporary with the rise of early Christianity from that popularly culled from the rabbinic literature, a picture of obvious greater relevance when we consider that the new faith's most fertile growth was in the Diaspora, away from the home of rabbinic literature.[23]

Certainly we have no evidence that the Jewish communities of Asia Minor suffered anything like the trauma and violent conflict which assailed those of Alexandria, and, to a lesser degree, the Jews of Antioch or of mixed cities in Palestine in the first century. However, sensitivity to the 'new' evidence prohibits generalising statements not just about 'diaspora Judaism' but even about 'Asia Minor Judaism'. It is obvious that there were enormous differences between the various locations and times in the size of the communities, their social status, integration into their immediate context, expression of religious or political identity...[24] Were literary evidence available from these same communities the picture might be yet more kaleidoscopic, for instance if the sharp polemic against Asia in the second century *Fifth Sibylline* (ll. 286–327) originated from that province before being incorporated into its Egyptian framework.[25] Yet this too would have to be balanced by the evidence for a growing respect for the Jewish God, betrayed by the oracle of Apollo at Claros who declared Iao to be the god above all gods,[26] whether or not Jewish communities were concerned for such recognition.

Obviously, it would be attractive if we could locate independent evidence of a Jewish community and of a Christian perception of Judaism in a known context in the same place and at the same time. As we shall see, at one time this seemed possible:[27] within a quarter of a century the city of Sardis came to dominate scholarly awareness both as the home of an unparalleled polemic against 'the Jews' in Melito's homily *On the Pascha*, first published in 1940,[28] and as the site of a synagogue unparalleled both in size and in apparent self-confident integration in the city, first discovered in 1962 with publication starting a year later.[29] The temptation to correlate the two in order to explain the former was irresistible.[30] However, further reflection has revealed the methodological problems involved in assuming simple correlations, and, more seriously, has also shown that the correlation is chronologically flawed: Melito cannot be any later than the last third of the second century, the traceable synagogue cannot be any earlier than a similar point in the following century.[31] Too much happened in that period to ignore; the example is a salutary reminder of the caprice of survival, and a warning against broader generalisations.

If we may suspect that the Judaism of Asia Minor was diverse, that was undoubtedly no less true of Christianity. Already within the New Testament period the range of literature and articulations of the Christian faith which can be reasonably associated with Asia Minor is staggering: the Pauline tradition including its later developments – Colossians, Ephesians, the Pastorals – Acts, the Apocalypse and the Johannine tradition; in most cases a specific link with one location, Ephesus, can be or has been claimed! In the second century, the fate of Pauline Christianity is shrouded in obscurity,[32] while the uncertainty surrounding the 'John' traditions has been one of the major arguments against the later consensus that the literature now associated with that name came from 'John' circles in Ephesus. The literature studied in the following chapters itself witnesses to the continuing variety of Christianity in the area, particularly when we add the silenced or echoed voices of the 'others': Montanism, Marcionism, gnostic movements, and forms of 'Jewish Christianity', represented at least by Cerinthus (Irenaeus, *Adv. haer.* IV.14), all found a home, and in some cases were born here.[33]

Archaeological evidence, such as we rely on for our picture of Judaism, only really emerges and is still very uneven in the third century – an epigraphic reticence at odds with open literary apologetic.[34] Yet there is enough to lead many to see the third century as a period of rapid expansion of Christianity, even though the literary remains suggest Asia Minor no longer played the focal role in Christian (or imperial) life that she had a hundred years before.[35] The epigrahic survivals from before Constantine, however, confirm the sense of continuing diversity, while also reminding us that the assumptions or expectations of the literary or structural élite often fail to reflect the reality of day-to-day living. Detailed studies, for example of epigraphic conventions, formulae or tendencies, have shown far more interaction between Christians and both their pagan and their Jewish neighbours than the literary sources would lead us to expect.[36] Such overlapping, which often leaves scholars debating whether particular inscriptions are Jewish or Christian, finds some parallel in the literary sources which suggest the continuing influence of Judaism on Christianity in this area.[37] It would be false to conclude from the fact that only two Christian writers of the third century from Asia Minor refer to the Jews,[38] that the second century had effectively severed all links between the two groups.

Such evidence reminds us too that neither Jews nor Christians, nor indeed their interaction with each other, should be seen in isolation. They were part of the religious life and activity of that corner of the Roman Empire, a life marked both by the ubiquity of paganism and also by discernible regional variations and local loyalties. In particular terms, this can be seen where distinctive elements of the 'religious world-view' of Asia Minor seem to have influenced or to have found a natural affinity in characteristic aspects of Judaism and/or of Christianity there – in the relatively independent role available to women, in the drive towards a form of monotheism, or in the attitudes which gave birth to Montanism. In more general terms, as already implied by the development of apologetic literature in this period, neither Christianity's self-understanding in relation to her Jewish roots, nor her self-justification in the encounter with Jewish neighbours took place in the proverbial ivory tower or in a vacuum.[39] Even where active missionary activity or defence in the face of attacks or persecution were not explicit, the arena was that of the (pagan) Graeco-Roman world. Choosing a specific geographical area, even though its contours may not always be clearly visible through the literature, is an important reminder of this. It also underlines that our concern is not with the development of theological arguments from their earlier roots, but with the elusive interplay between the reality which was part of the particular context of each of these writings, and the image they project, which transcends the particular.

Literature

In the second century the creative use of a range of literary genres, which seems to have been characteristic of the early Christians from the very beginning, is continued and extended. The 'biographical' mode of the Gospels does not disappear, although most of what survives seems derivative, and perhaps exploited particularly by those whom the church was to label 'heretical'. In fact, only the *Gospel of Peter*, which most frequently has been located in Antioch or in Asia Minor,[40] will occupy us at any length, although other allusions to the story of Jesus, whether or not drawn from our canonical Gospels, also reflect the developing tradition. However, the 'biographical' apocryphal *Acts* of the Apostles, an apparently flourishing genre from the second century which gave ample scope for elaborations of the hero's triumph over the forces of opposition, do seem to have had their birth in Asia Minor, for it was here, according to Tertullian (*De baptismo* 17), that the *Acts of Paul* was written. With these we have a firm base for asking how far the progressive antagonism towards the Jews, usually traced in the New Testament Gospels and Acts, is further developed, or what new narrative functions they fill.

Letter writing continues, with some conscious awareness of the Pauline precedent, in Ignatius and in Polycarp of Smyrna. Here that precedent will encourage us to look for the tension between the local or particular and the universalising tendency which if not fully present in the undisputed Paulines is clearly there in Ephesians – and whose impact is to be felt in the *Martyrdom of Polycarp*. The tendency towards the abstract or universal is not irrelevant: the problem of believers' relations with the Jewish roots of their faith and identity is a recurring and fundamental issue for Paul; however, a sensitivity to the specific situations behind and reflected in the individual letters and to the rhetoric and strategies of Paul's response has enabled us to gain a rich picture of the conflicting currents in the early communities, and this will be equally true of his successors.

However, the second century also witnesses the emergence of new genres, although, as we shall see, these have some precedent already in the New Testament and even more so in Jewish literature. Most notable are *Apologies*, ostensibly addressed to the secular authorities, explicit polemical literature 'In answer to' or 'Against the Jews' and, eventually, against those perceived or branded as heretical, and *Martyr Acts*. Whether or not the apologetic literature was read, or was seriously expected to be read, by outsiders,[41] its use by Christian writers reflects a new self-awareness in relation to the outside world, and possibly a new class of Christian thinker, well typified by Justin Martyr, who both felt the need and possessed the ability to explore the Christian faith within the framework of and by adopting the conventions of contemporary thought.[42] The other genres, whose expected readership is no less open to discussion, reflect a similar self-awareness as well as being a response to the historical situation in which the Christians found themselves as they became increasingly, for good or ill, in the public eye in the second century. They provide the beginnings of the development of a characteristic and 'world-creating' rhetoric which was both distinctive to Christianity and fundamental to its eventual effectiveness in the Graeco-Roman world.[43]

The literature chosen here represents a cross-section of these characteristic and creative genres of the second century, allowing us to explore both their debt to their predecessors and their innovative contributions, particularly as these are expressed through the presentation of Judaism.

'Image and Reality'

All we have said so far implies that when it comes to references in Christian writers to Jews and Judaism there was a 'reality'. This does not simply mean that there were Jewish communities, often very significant ones, in the cities and settings where Christian communities grew and produced these literary remains – that has never been in real doubt, even if often ignored. It means that the Christians continued to be acutely aware of their Jewish neighbours and to interact with them, whether on friendly or on more hostile terms. This has more often been denied; it has been argued that by the second century the Christian church was, and was content to be, a gentile one, while the Jewish communities had lost all interest in or anxiety about their erstwhile 'offspring'. Any real knowledge of contemporary Jewish life by Christian writers has been said to be minimal; instead 'the Jew' of their literature is a creation born out of their own needs, predominant among which was the need to justify the continuing retention of the 'Old Testament' without a continuing literal observance of its precepts. Christian authors undoubtedly tend to define and describe Jews in terms and imagery drawn from the Old Testament, while there is an unmistakable overlap between arguments supposedly directed 'against the Jews' and those directed against Marcion who sought to reject this continuing retention of the 'Old Testament'; such observations give strong support to an interpretation which might be succinctly summed up in the words of A. Harnack, that the Jew of the literature is 'the Jew whom they feared'.[44]

However, to the material evidence for Jewish–Christian interaction from Asia Minor already cited can be added many examples of Christian knowledge of Jewish practice and particularly exegesis, which cannot be explained as merely an inheritance from the past.[45] Pagan writers who still confused the two religions may have been representative of some popular perception even among adherents of the two religions.[46] Contemporary, and not just 'Old Testament', Judaism continued in the second century to be part of the immediate religious, literary and social world of early Christianity.

Recognition both of the stereotyping and of evidence of real contact, even in the same author, means we must speak about 'image and reality' in some form of interaction. When this literature speaks of Jews and Judaism there is a contemporary reality, one of which, in differing degrees, its authors are aware. Yet their own needs, the logic of their own argument, and the tradition they draw on, especially the 'Old Testament', help create and mould the terms in which they speak – to create an 'image'. Neither can we see these two components in simple opposition; part of the social reality or world of the early Christians was the Old Testament as read by them in the light of their conviction that it had been fulfilled, or its true meaning revealed, in the person and story of Jesus. While they draw on and maintain such earlier traditions, they also create new ones through the 'image' they project, which in turn becomes part of the 'reality' for the next generation.

Although the image they create can assume an independent existence, helping constitute the symbolic universe of later generations, it starts life within the particular piece of literature. We, then, have to begin by suspending historical judgement and by tracing how the Jew(s) or Judaism function within the overall strategy of each of the documents concerned. This is akin to what in New Testament study has come to be called 'narrative criticism', even when, as in the case of Ignatius's letters, we are not dealing with overt narrative. More important, even in the case of the *Martyrdom of Polycarp*, which, understandably, has often been treated as a historical source and been investigated for precise details of dating,[47] all this literature has a clear rhetorical function, and its details serve that rhetoric – and nowhere is this more true than in the roles played by Jews and Judaism. Recognition of this function means that our primary question regarding the presentation of Judaism must be the elucidation of its rhetorical role; investigation of the historical reality can only then follow, always remembering the interaction between the two just described.

The Texts

Each of the texts chosen in the chapters which follow allows us to explore this construction of Jews and Judaism as it takes place through different literary genres and in different contexts, but broadly – as we shall see, a necessary qualification – within the parameters already outlined.

Ignatius, bishop of Antioch, wrote seven letters, six of which were to the churches of Asia Minor, during his journey through that province to trial in Rome; in these he tackles the tensions and issues which, either from direct experience or from report, he sees as besetting these churches. He is a prime example of one whose concerns were pastoral, hardly glancing outside the boundaries of the churches except in anticipation of his death. Yet if as letters they address particular situations and varying specific issues, including what he calls 'Judaism', Ignatius perceives these through the lens of his own concerns for his church at Antioch and his intense desire for martyrdom. The letters reflect and were agents within a rhetoric of charism and persuasion; before long, collected together, they became part of the tradition-reality of subsequent Christian ideology and literature in Asia Minor, notably helping shape the *Martyrdom of Polycarp*.

Yet if Ignatius's letters mark some degree of continuity with the Christian epistolary genre established in the first century, the *Martyrdom of Polycarp* also heralds a new development, although one with roots both in the Christian and in the Jewish tradition. Within this tradition accounts of persecution and martyrdom meet the needs of the community, whether making sense of their experience, offering a model for others, defining their values in opposition to those of 'the world', or claiming legitimacy against alternative responses. Here the account takes the form of a letter from the church of Smyrna where Polycarp was bishop and where he was martyred. As such it is not just informative but paraenetic, and this purpose shapes the telling of events including the deliberately highlighted role assigned to the Jews. Yet its immediacy and local detail also bear out its own claim to have been written soon after the event, not long after the middle of the second century, while memories were fresh. It helped shape the image of the martyr for the future, while Eusebius used it as exemplary in his telling of the second century.[48]

The most explicit engagement with Judaism in the second century, at least that which survives, is Justin Martyr's account of his *Dialogue with Trypho*, a two-day marathon, often a monologue, with a Jew whom he encounters, according to Eusebius, in Ephesus. Justin too draws on earlier tradition, and hammers out many of the exegetical and theological arguments which were to become standard in later polemic against the Jews. The long scholarly debate as to whether Trypho is drawn from life, as suggested by the authentic ring of much of the exegetical debate, or is rather a creation of Justin's own rhetorical needs, further shaped by the literary 'dialogue' form with its Socratic roots, illustrates well the process explored here. The *Dialogue* is more than a literary artifice, yet its present form undoubtedly owes at least something to Justin's subsequent sojourn in Rome, where it was written, and to his arguments against Marcionism. Yet his stay and experiences in Asia Minor too have shaped Justin's theology.[49] The *Dialogue* arguably looks back on more than one encounter with Jewish protagonists, whether or not with an individual named Trypho, and whether or not Justin was as successful in keeping the upper hand as he here reports: it is that familiar image-drawing exercise of 'setting the record straight'.[50]

Asia Minor seems to have been a fruitful seed-bed for the development of the apologetic literature; here too Christianity was treading in the footsteps of the Jewish communities of the area who had collected the charters to which Josephus appeals for apologetic purposes,[51] but Christians were also responding both to the new political situation in which they found themselves as they came to the notice of the wider public and secular authorities,[52] as well as to their developing self-awareness as a distinct 'people' on the stage of 'world' affairs and culture. Quadratus, Melito of Sardis, Apollinarius of Hierapolis and, a little later, Miltiades all submitted *Apologies* from Asia Minor. Justin, who wrote his in Rome, also had earlier connections with the province. Unfortunately, except for the last named, their works are for the most part lost, leaving only tantalising hints. It is, therefore, necessary to call on the *Apology of Aristides*: although Aristides is more usually associated with Athens, he does betray contacts with other sources from Asia Minor.[53] His explicit and in some ways positive representation of Judaism shows the variety of 'images' still possible in the second century, while the sustained way in which he identifies the Christians as a 'third' or 'fourth race' alongside the others[54] provides a focus for exploring Christian strategies in the process of self-definition through apologetic literature.

If an Apology is ostensibly directed to outsiders, worship is for those present, for the committed. Melito of Sardis, as we have seen, has (again) become famous for the vivid rhetoric of his *Peri [On the] Pascha*, a liturgical interpretation or homily focusing on the Christian celebration of Christ's 'passion' as the goal or reality to which the Exodus/Passover deliverance pointed. At all times, and perhaps particularly on the solemn occasion of Paschal commemoration, worship helps to define boundaries and to sharpen the sense of inclusion for those who participate. The *Peri Pascha* is not the first Christian 'liturgical' text we possess – there may even be fragments or echoes of such material in the New Testament – but it does belong to a fixed point in the

Christian calendar, reflecting the development of stable patterns
of worship in the second century. Calendar had long distinguished Jewish groups from their pagan neighbours, giving
social expression to their distinctive self-identity; Christians were
following a similar path but with the added similarity/contrast
with the Jews. Yet Melito's *Peri Pascha* does more than define
and differentiate, for it has become notorious for the passion of
its accusations against 'Israel', addressed as if present, and particularly for the ominous charge of 'deicide'. These, when read
against the backdrop of a flourishing Jewish community supposedly reflected in the large synagogue now excavated at
Sardis, seemed to offer a powerful example of an image shaped
by the reality it sought to deny. Although now the claimed correlation cannot be sustained, the reminder that social context
has to be part of understanding a text and its images must be;
yet Melito's rhetoric and its later 'post-history' also remind us
that the image cannot be reduced to being a product of its
context: it acquires its own life as a very creative, or destructive, reality.

There are other voices from Asia Minor, although for the most
part we hear these through the mouths of others. Arguably
chronologically prior, but placed here for that reason, are the
'Elders of Asia Minor'. This shadowy group, known to us through
the reported words of Papias of Hierapolis, who may be included
among their number, and particularly through their own words
as reported by Irenaeus, were seen by later generations as the
bridge between the age of the Apostles and the known 'luminar-
ies' of the second century. Irenaeus himself came from Asia
Minor before going first to Rome and then to Lyons, where he
was to become bishop, and he does not seem to have lost his
contacts with or his loyalty to his home province. Although
Irenaeus quotes the Elders for his own purposes, we can still
recover at least the gist of their own words, and we should not
be surprised if the place of the Jews numbered among their concerns. Our real knowledge of the identity and location, and even
of the period, of the 'Elders' is hazy, clouded too by the suspicion that Irenaeus is largely responsible for shaping them into a
fixed group to meet his own need for a continuity of tradition
and authority. The recovery of any part of their 'reality' is fraught
with difficulties; they themselves are part of the 'image' projected

by the early church in its need for this secure continuity of tradition and authority, and we can only guess at the perhaps very different world from which they come.

Equally shadowy are the worlds which gave birth to the re-telling of the story of Jesus, as by the *Gospel of Peter*, or of the Apostles, in the *Acts* which bear their names, or, accepting these as post-Pauline, through the Pastoral Epistles. Inevitably the apocryphal *Acts* of the Apostles are creating an image, in the case of the Apostles often a very different one, in very different social contexts, from that of the New Testament. In the displays of apostolic miracle-working they share the self-advertisment of the Apologies, in the trials of the Apostles they share the understanding of Christian identity of the martyr accounts. Despite all their links with popular novelistic literature, they create a world in sharp conflict with contemporary social structures, rejecting marriage and family life, anticipating and valuing suffering and death.[55] Yet because in its New Testament form the story they tell demands the presence of the Jews, the latters' virtual disappearance here, as also in the Pastoral Epistles, another form of 'story-telling', displays again the unstable relationship between symbolic universe and social reality.

The most striking example both of the contended place of the Jews in the Christian symbolic universe and of the creative variety of second-century Christianity in Asia Minor was perhaps Marcion, who came from Pontus. As with most deemed 'heretics', we can encounter him only through the reports and charges of those who rejected him and the path that he took. He was rejected by the early church for his attempt to sever the God of the Old Testament from the Loving Father of the New, and so to deny any consanguinity between Judaism and Christianity. This puts him in the peculiar position of appearing both as an ally of the Jews, whose integrity he could maintain, and as their enemy, whose God he vilified. The church, which defended both that God and his past revelation, turned the vilification upon the Jews, using Marcion to attack them, them to attack Marcion. Yet before we can wrestle with the theological challenge this presents, we need to ask again the genesis of the image and whether it can still reveal a different reality.

Other Texts

It would not be difficult to suggest other texts which would further enrich our picture. Irenaeus came from Asia Minor originally, and belongs to the second century, but his voluminous refutation 'of all heresies' (*Adversus haereses*) is so extensive and encompasses such a range of arguments that to focus on the role of the Jews or Judaism would be very difficult without losing any sense of proportion in relation to the whole work. Moving more firmly outside Asia Minor could add the *Embassy* of Athenagoras of Athens as well as the *Apology* (*To Autolycus*) of Theophilus, bishop of Antioch – the home of Ignatius and a city with a known vibrant Jewish community – whose writing betrays many links with and sympathies for the Jewish people. Among fundamental writings in the development of anti-Jewish polemic are the *Epistle to Diognetus* and the *Epistle of Barnabas*; both may belong to the second century and are of disputed geographical origin. Asia Minor, however, seems to have little claim to them and they have been well treated elsewhere. Despite attempts to associate other apocryphal 'apostolic' literature or 'gnostic' writings, such as the *Epistle of the Apostles* or *Gospel of Philip*, with Asia Minor, other locations probably have stronger claims.[56] Lastly (or first), the trajectory of 'the Jews' in the Johannine tradition, which probably belongs to Asia Minor and may be at least close to the second century, will be left as meriting (and, for the Gospel, having) detailed study in its own right.[57]

No doubt inclusion of these or of other texts would have resulted in a more detailed and yet more nuanced picture. Yet we must recognise that the firm location of any literature is often much more tentative than many who reconstruct historical settings acknowledge, and that the survival of Christian literature from this period is even more haphazard – as Eusebius's references to lost works make evident. This cannot then even attempt to be an account of Christian attitudes to Judaism in Asia Minor. Instead it is an exploration into how, even within a relatively restricted time and place, an image could be constructed from the projection of multiple perceptions, expectations and needs; or, better, multiple images, sometimes overlapping, sometimes contradictory. The way these feed into subsequent images, or are fed by earlier ones, can only in part be traced. Yet a recurring theme has been that this was not a purely abstract process; there was always, and there is for us, albeit in too fragmentary a state, the 'control' presented by the actual Jewish communities as whose neighbours Christians lived. What is their role in this process? Where are they to be seen? How does image become reality, reality succeed in denying the image?

Notes

[1] There is a proper and active debate regarding the appropriateness of these terms, with or without hyphens or capitals, which need not be entered at this point.

[2] E.g. E. P. Sanders 1992.

[3] The importance of the impact of the earlier picture (e.g. Ruether 1974) should not be overshadowed by its weaknesses (see A. Davies 1979); for examples of individual studies see de Lange 1976; Wilken 1971; 1983; Wilson 1986c.

[4] This is well emphasised by Langmuir 1990: 65–6.

[5] The bibliography on this is vast; see Ashton 1994: 36–70.

[6] See, for example, on Matthew, Stanton 1992a: 113–281; on Luke, J. Sanders 1987; on John, Brown 1979; and the essays in Dunn 1992.

[7] See A. Williams 1935; Wilde 1949.

[8] Simon 1986 was fundamental in undermining this common claim.

[9] These have often been traced; see Ruether 1974.

[10] So Harakas 1967.

[11] According to Blanchetière 1973: 356, 364 – this is a fundamental question.

[12] Cameron 1991: 45. The whole of this chapter (pp. 14–46) is important for this discussion.

[13] E.g. by Lucian, Galen and others.

[14] The writings of Lucian; the Life of Apollonius of Tyana, etc.; see Anderson 1994, and on the literature pp. 18–27.

[15] See Wardman 1982: 118, 'Religion was therefore a major form of spending on leisure'; Lane Fox 1986; North 1992.

[16] Although Mitchell 1993: I. 227–40 also points to important continuities. However, a failure to recognise such changes in context has allowed false assumptions about simple continuity or development in Christian relations with Judaism or in the position of Judaism itself (for example, see below, pp. 203, 228, on Sardis).

[17] Blanchetière 1981: 30–2, quotation from p.32.

[18] See on this and what follows pp. 158–9, 200–1 below.

[19] See below, p. 201. I have not seen E. Faust, *Pax Christi et Pax Caesaris* (Freiburg and Göttingen, 1993), which, according to the review by A. T. Lincoln (1995), argues for conflict between the Jews and Greeks of Asia Minor (?in similar terms to that in Alexandria) as part of the background to Ephesians.

[20] Most infamously, Kittel 1944.

[21] Kraabel 1968.

[22] See especially Trebilco 1991 and the succinct but invaluable comments by Mitchell 1993: II. 31–7; for Kraabel's articles see the bibliography in Overman and MacLennan 1992: 359–61.

[23] See further Rajak 1992, but note the cautions of Goodman 1994b.

[24] See Kraabel 1981.

[25] Schürer 1973–87: III. 645 raises the possibility that some non-Egyptian material may be included in *Sib. V.*

[26] Apud Macrobius, *Sat.* I. 18.18–21 (Stern 1974–84: II. 411–12); Parke 1985: 163–4, also 104–5.

[27] And was the original inspiration of extending the attempt in this study.

[28] Bonner 1940.

[29] Hanfmann 1963; 1983; Robert 1964; Seager and Kraabel 1983.

[30] See Kraabel 1971; and below, p. 184.

[31] See Bonz 1993; Botermann 1990; below, pp. 201–3.

[32] See Lindemann 1979.

[33] See Blanchetière 1981: 114–222.

[34] Mitchell 1993: II. 37–43.

[35] Mitchell 1993: II. 63; Blanchetière 1981: 346–7, 399.

[36] Mitchell 1993: II. 40–51; Rutgers 1992.

[37] Mitchell 1993: II. 98–9.

[38] So Blanchetière 1981: 322–3, 381–2: *Mart. Pionius* (see below, p. 62), and Firmilian of Caesarea in Cyprian, *Epist.* 75.17, 19 simply as a point of comparison. It was the fourth-century panegyrist who had Gregory Thaumaturgus in the mid-third century in miraculous competition with Jews and pagans; see Lane Fox 1986: 531 and below, p. 93.

[39] Mitchell 1993: II. 48 speaks of the 'melting pot of Phrygia'.

[40] See below, pp. 259–60.

[41] See below, pp. 163–4.

[42] See Droge 1989: 11.

[43] See Cameron 1991: 6 '... a large part of Christianity's effectiveness in the Roman Empire lay in its capacity to create its own intellectual and imaginative universe, and ... its own literary devices and techniques in turn related to changing contemporary circumstances'.

[44] Harnack 1883: 63–74; see among others Efroymson 1979; Barnes 1971 – both on Tertullian; below, pp. 105–6.

[45] See below, pp. 108–9, and above, n. 8.

[46] Lieu 1994c.

[47] See below, pp. 72–3, and Buschmann 1994: 11, 65–7, 320–7 for a rejection of this approach to *M. Poly.*

[48] For the argument that Eusebius's version, while briefer, is not more original, see below, p. 69.

[49] So Osborn 1973: 8.

[50] See Lim 1995: 4–5, who suggests that Tertullian was doing this in the *Adversus Iudaeos* when in fact the public disputation ended with victory for the Jew: Tertullian says 'truth was obscured by a cloud' (I.1).

[51] So Freudenberger 1967: 11–13.

[52] Something which apparently happened earlier in Asia Minor than elsewhere: Blanchetière 1981: 69.

[53] See below, pp. 170–2.

[54] See below, pp. 166–7, on the textual uncertainties regarding the number of 'races'.

[55] See Perkins 1985: 219–22.

[56] Daniélou 1969: 90–1 notes parallels between the *Gospel of Philip* and the theology of second-century Asia Minor, but Syria is a more probable home: on this *Gospel*'s interesting use of Jewish categories see Siker 1989. Syria may also be the home of the *Acts of John* while an Alexandrian origin is more probable for the *Epistle of the Apostles*.

[57] The Apocalypse should in this context be included in 'the Johannine' tradition. For the continuity of part of that trajectory in Polycarp, *Philipp.* and elsewhere see pp. 243, 256–7.

2

IGNATIUS AND THE WORLD OF HIS LETTERS

That Ignatius should have no knowledge of Judaism seems hard to conceive. Antioch, the city of which he was bishop, had a substantial Jewish community, perhaps representing a significant percentage of the population.[1] Josephus singles it out as a community which attracted sympathisers or adherents, even if his language of 'constantly attracting to their observances a large number of Greeks' seems more than a little exaggerated (*B.J.* VII.3.3 [44–5]). In the second half of the first century relations with the gentile population had become strained and efforts had been made to reduce the Jews' status, efforts rejected by Titus despite his recent victory over the Jewish rebellion centred on Jerusalem (*B.J.* VII.5.2 [100–11]). The story of the Jewish apostate, Antiochus, son of an *archon*, who sought to implicate the Jews in a supposed attempt to set fire to the city and who also stood behind the imposition of a test of loyalty by sacrifice (VII.3.3 [47–61]), may reflect internal conflicts within the Jewish community, perhaps fired by differing ideas as to the degree of participation in city life compatible with Jewish faith and practice. Such internal conflicts may have had repercussions for the Christians; Matthew's Gospel, often associated with Antioch, implies that the community has suffered or could expect to suffer at the hands of the synagogue authorities (Matt. 10.17). Although we know little of the Jewish community in Antioch over the next two centuries, there is nothing to suggest that it had suffered an appreciable decline by the time of Ignatius only forty years after the events described by Josephus.

Antioch also appears as the (or a) highly significant centre for the development of the separate self-identity of Christianity over against Judaism. Antioch was the location of the dispute between Paul and Peter over the permissible degree of social intercourse between Jews and gentiles within the church, a crucial issue for that separate identity (Gal. 2.11–14). It was here too, according to Luke–Acts, with some credibility, that the name 'Christians' was first used (Acts 11.26), almost certainly as an epithet by outsiders.[2] If Luke had a source particularly associated with Antioch, this may point to the church's self-awareness shortly before his time of writing.

The later history points to the continuing importance of Judaism for Christianity, whether as a source of ideas or as a threat to the distinctive self-identity of Christianity. Evidence of the former is there still, despite himself, in Ignatius's own thought and language,[3] and continues in a long series of writers starting with Theophilus of Antioch. For the latter, of more significance for us, it is natural to think of Chrysostom's sermons *Against the Jews*, which imply that at least some ordinary members of the church saw nothing out of order in attending the synagogue services, joining in other Jewish festivities, regarding the synagogue as a sacred place appropriate for the taking of oaths, and respecting the supernatural powers of the teachers.[4] Probably towards the end of the fourth century, Ignatius's letters were expanded and interpolated producing a form commonly called 'the long recension'.[5] This new edition reflects a number of the theological concerns of the time, and, in contrast to the original (middle) recension, a heightened polemic against the Jews now appears in nearly every letter: the Jews are those who fight God and killed the Lord and the prophets (*Trall.* 11; cf. *Tars.* 3; *Smyrn.* 2; *Hero* 2), and any commonality with them is bitterly denounced (*Magn.* 8; *Philipp.* 13–14).[6] Yet even if the long recension occasionally takes its cue from the original letters of Ignatius, as at *Magn.* 8 where the authentic letter already refers to Judaism, the contrast between the tone and concerns of the two recensions shows we cannot imagine a simple continuity from the beginning of the second century to the end of the fourth. The interpolator, like Chrysostom, was writing on the other side of the establishment of Christianity as the official religion of the Empire by Constantine as well as of the attempt by Julian to rebuild the Temple at Jerusalem; Judaism too had changed its profile during that period and had perhaps experienced something of a revival during the fourth century.[7]

We, however, are concerned not with the fourth century nor with its continuity with the second, but with Ignatius, travelling from Antioch to Rome where he was to be martyred some time around 114 CE.[8] During his journey he wrote letters to various churches of Asia Minor, as well as one to his destination at Rome. Some of these churches he had visited personally, from others he had received delegations *en route*, so that we naturally turn to his letters to learn more about the churches in this obscure period. Our efforts, however, are hampered by the considerable opacity created by Ignatius's intense preoccupation with his own journey to Rome and to martyrdom which overshadows all his thinking. The dominant theme of his letters is the unity of the church, which he unflaggingly both celebrates and urges, but which, even more, he sees as ever threatened. Yet this is a theme which refuses any attempt to separate it from his own personal and spiritual concerns, leading many scholars to see it as a projection of the troubled situation he left behind him in Antioch. The peace which he celebrates in *Smyrn.* 11.2 as having come upon the church in Antioch may well be not respite from persecution but the achievement of harmony after bitter division, divisions which perhaps had more than a little to do with his own sentence to death in Rome.[9] So his desperate concern for the unity of the church centred round the bishop reflects the ambivalences or anxieties surrounding his own status; his dread of the threat offered by a docetic interpretation of the incarnation and, even more, of the death of Jesus is rooted in the fear that it would make a mockery of his own martyrdom which he both eagerly awaits and yet faces with anxious concern about his steadfastness. Small wonder that through his letters breathes an intensity that overshadows any attempt to reconstruct the reality behind his own personal situation, either that at Antioch or that in the churches to whom he writes; for each of these concerns he creates in his letters a world whose distance from reality is the source of continual debate – what authority did he hold, what patterns of ministry were exercised in the churches to whom he wrote, what patterns of belief were in the ascendant?[10] Yet some of the extravagance of language which alienates the modern reader may only belong to the familiar rhetoric of his time and place.[11] Therefore, to say that he has lost touch with reality, as portrayed by S. Laeuchli in a poetic and perceptive piece,[12] may be to go too far; but we must expect to find at least something of a gulf between the reality he creates in his letters and that experienced by the churches.

There may be a further gulf: Ignatius writes to the churches of Asia Minor purportedly about their own internal situation; yet he repeatedly disclaims any personal knowledge of disruption or of schism, and indeed knew of some of the churches only through the reports of their delegates. This, combined with the tensions just discussed, prompt the supposition that it is in fact the situation in the church of Antioch which he describes in his exhortations and warnings to the churches of Asia Minor. Yet another level at which Ignatius's own preoccupations may confuse us is that of the 'heresy' (he uses the word with connotations of schism and wrong belief) against which he writes. The recurring issue is that of the reality (or unreality) of the human body and experiences of Jesus; in two letters, as we shall see, the problem is that of 'Judaism'. Were there two separate (heretical) patterns of belief or do they represent a single 'judaising docetism'? These questions are fundamental to any account of Ignatius and have been repeatedly discussed; yet they are but aspects of the essential issue of the relation between the world of the letters and that of 'reality', and so belong to the conclusions and not to the introduction of this exploration.

To explore the position of Judaism in and behind the letters of Ignatius we need to separate three levels: first, the way Ignatius himself perceives Judaism; secondly, what relationship between Judaism and Christianity is suggested by his argument, and, thirdly, the actual situation he reflects. Inevitably these three areas show considerable overlap but they are not identical, and confusion between them can result in misleading interpretations.

Ignatius's View of Judaism

Perhaps the most striking feature of Ignatius's letters for our purposes is, with the exceptions we shall discuss, the absence of any awareness of 'the Jews'. The term itself appears only once: in his opening expression of praise in *Smyrn*. Ignatius speaks of Jesus raising 'an ensign [Isa. 5.26; 49.22; 62.10] to the ages through his resurrection for his saints and faithful ones whether among the Jews or among the Gentiles in one body of his church' (1.2).[13] The whole passage is semi-credal, and Ignatius is clearly taking over traditional formulae, in this case one which he significantly fails to develop in his understanding of the church. However, in the light of developments after him we should perhaps note a positive element in this reticence: despite his repeated references to Jesus's death, and even his explicit timing of it 'under Pontius Pilate and Herod the tetrarch' (*Smyrn.* 1.2; cf. *Magn.* 11), he nowhere assigns responsibility for that death to the Jews.[14]

Only in two of his letters does Ignatius explicitly introduce the question of 'Judaism' in relation to Christianity, in those to Magnesia and to Philadelphia. When he wrote to the church at Magnesia Ignatius was staying at Smyrna and had been visited by their bishop, two elders and a deacon (*Magn.* 2). As elsewhere in his letters, but perhaps following rhetorical convention,[15] he denies any personal knowledge of credal disunity in the church and claims only to be forewarning them (11); yet alongside the concerns we find repeated in most of the letters – that they act in unity with one another and, most important, with the bishop and elders (6–7), and that they acknowledge the reality of Jesus's human experience (11) – there come more specific notes of caution. One of these concerns the youth, probably in age rather than in ecclesiastical or episcopal experience, of the bishop (3); the other is introduced abruptly after the appeal to unity and concerns what Ignatius labels 'Judaism':

> Do not be led astray by false opinions nor by fables which are old and profit nothing. For if even now we live according to Judaism,[16] we confess that we have not received grace.For the most divine prophets lived according to Jesus Christ... (8.1–2)

The language of being **led astray** belongs to the rhetoric regarding schismatic and false belief in Ignatius as well as elsewhere (*Eph.* 10; *Smyrn.* 6.1;[17] cf. 1 John 4.6; 2 John 7), as too does that of **false opinions** (ἑτεροδοξία) (*Smyrn.* 6.2;[18] cf. 'empty opinion', κενοδοξία, in *Magn.*11). Characteristically, and to some extent innovatively, Ignatius does think in terms of true and false belief ('orthodoxy and heresy'), and what he goes on to say about 'Judaism' belongs within this scheme even though it is not the faith content of Judaism which he elaborates; however, this continuity of language does not in itself mean we are meeting the same 'heterodoxy' in Magnesia as in Smyrna.

The dismissal of **fables** (μύθευμα) belongs to the rhetoric of polemic in the pagan but also in the Jewish world. Dependency on myths or fables was probably a common accusation against Judaism: thus Philo repeatedly denies that myths are to be found in the Jewish scriptures (*De Opif. mundi* 1.2; *Quod Deus* 155; *Quod det.* 125) and pours scorn on the pagan and, particularly, the Egyptian, fondness for them (*De cher.* 91; *De post. Cain* 2; *De migr.* 76).[19] Similarly, Josephus dismisses the dependence by Greek historians and by the detractors of Judaism on myths, and shows how Moses stands out among other legislators by not following fables (*C. Apion.* I.25, 229, 287; II.120; *Ant.* I.Proem.4 [22]). For these apologists myths are human creations, tied to the worship of idols and opposed to the truth (Philo, *De dec.* 7; 157; *De spec. leg.* I.51; Josephus, *C. Apion.* II.256). Two hundred years later the pagan philosopher Porphyry characterises Judaism by its 'myths'.[20] To produce or to rely on myths is to mislead and take advantage of the gullibility of others such as children and old women – a theme not only of anti-Jewish argument (Celsus in Origen, *C. Cels.* IV.33f.; 51) and later anti-Christian polemic (Minucius Felix, *Octavius* 11.2, 23), but also of the polemic between philosophical schools (Lactantius, *Inst.* V.1.26).[21] Thus Ignatius draws on stock vocabulary of denigration, perhaps familiar to his readers from popular dismissal of Judaism but not from that alone. We cannot then build too much on the parallels with the Pastoral Epistles where the author warns his congregations against godless and silly or Jewish myths or disputes and genealogies and conflicts about the law which profit nothing (1 Tim. 1.4; 4.7; Tit. 1.14; 3.9).[22] Ignatius is not identifying the 'Judaism' he opposes as concerned with cosmologies or angelologies;[23] he is dismissing its claim to serious consideration, particularly in a Christian context for those who have left what is old to share in what is new (cf. *Magn.* 9.1; 10.2 below; 1 Cor. 5.7).

Yet Ignatius does not intend merely to denigrate a system he opposes; he simply excludes it. To continue to **live according to**

Judaism is not just to misunderstand the implications of the Gospel, it is to put oneself outside the compass of the salvation it offers (cf. *Magn.* 10.1). Ignatius opposes not law and grace but *Judaism* and grace. To understand this we must add what he says later in the same letter (10.1, 3):

> Therefore, having become his disciples, let us learn to live according to *Christianism*. Whoever is called by another name more than this is not of God... It is impossible to speak of Jesus Christ and to judaise. For *Christianism* did not put its faith in Judaism, but Judaism in *Christianism*.

A similar contrast, discussed below, appears in his letter to the church at Philadelphia (6.1): 'If anyone expounds Judaism to you, do not listen to him. For it is better to hear *Christianism* from a man with circumcision than Judaism from an uncircumcised one.' **Christianism** (χριστιανισμός) appears first in Ignatius and is not otherwise found in the Apostolic Fathers, suggesting that it is his own coinage; certainly he shows a predilection for Christ- compounds and has probably coined '*Christomathia*' (χριστομαθία: discipleship of Christ), '*Christonomos*' (χριστόνομος: observing the law of Christ) and '*Christophoros*' (χριστόφορος: bearing Christ).[24] He seems to have formulated '*Christianismos*' in a different way, on the analogy of and in conscious opposition to **Judaism**, ιουδαισμός.[25] Yet, although derivative in formulation, conceptually 'Christianism' is not dependent for its content on 'Judaism'; in *Rom.* 3.3 Ignatius uses it again without any conscious contrast: 'For *Christianism* is not a matter of persuasion but of greatness, when it is hated by the world.' This is typical: in the same way, the epithet 'Christians' (and so also the other Christ- compounds) is not a nickname given by outsiders, as perhaps it was in origin (Acts 11.26 at Antioch; 26.28; Tacitus, *Annal.* XV.44.2; see also 1 Peter 4.16), but has become his most favoured name for believers and a designation of honour which represents the goal of their individual and corporate existence.[26] One must *be* and not simply be *called* 'Christian', and for Ignatius himself this will be most truly demonstrated or even achieved in his martyrdom, just as it is only then that *Christianism* exercises its true force (*Rom.* 3.2–3; cf. *Magn.* 4).

Yet even here Ignatius's independence is more apparent than real; when put in this context *Christianism* does carry some of the original overtones of 'Judaism'. The latter term seems to have been a Hellenistic Jewish coinage – there is no precise contemporary Hebrew equivalent – and appears first in the Maccabean context (2 Macc. 2.21; 8.1; 14.38; 4 Macc. 4.26). As a single term encompassing life, belief and practice, it reflects a self-consciousness of the people as a corporate entity living in an inner region marked by clear boundaries within the wider world. Yet in the setting in which it occurs first, the Maccabean revolt, it inevitably not only carries both religious and national overtones but also suggests the total life commitment which might even include the readiness to die: 'those who for the sake of Judaism emulated one another in acting the man' (2 Macc. 2.21).[27] Even in its single NT occurrence it is exemplified by Paul's persecution of the church and his zeal for the traditions of his fathers (Gal. 1.13–14).

That Ignatius should be heir to some of these sentiments need cause no surprise, for other parallels have been noted between his language and that of 4 Maccabees, which is usually associated with Antioch.[28] Yet, if so, the positive connotations of commitment even to death have been transferred to *Christianism*; what, then, of Judaism? According to Ignatius, one can, but should not, **live according to Judaism**, just as one should 'learn to live according to Christianism'; perhaps again he is adopting a Jewish phrase, for it appears as a designation of honour in the third-century inscription of C. Tiberius Polycharmus, the 'father of the synagogue' at Stobi, who conducted his whole public life 'according to Judaism'.[29] However, given the time and geographical gap between the two men, we may need look only to Ignatius's propensity for speaking of 'living according to' ($\zeta\tilde{\eta}\nu$ $\kappa\alpha\tau\acute{\alpha}$), whether it be 'the Lord's day(?)', 'the truth', 'man', or, as here, 'Jesus Christ' (*Magn.* 9.1; *Eph.* 6.8; *Trall.* 2.1; *Rom.* 8.1; *Philad.* 3.2). We may note too that the prophets also apparently did not 'live according to Judaism' since they 'lived according to Jesus Christ' – a point to which we shall return. For the moment, however, Ignatius does not expand further on what 'living according to Judaism' might involve, other than its incompatibility with 'having received grace', 'living according to Jesus Christ' or, of course, 'living according to Christianism'. It is not, then, for him, simply the adoption or maintenance of particular, isolated practices which do not stand up to closer scrutiny in the light of the Gospel; it is a life-system.

Judaism is also something that can be expounded, probably being the end result rather than the content or object of an exposition, and so also can be heard (*Philad.* 6.1):

> If someone interprets Judaism to you, do not listen to him. For it is better to hear *Christianism* from a man with circumcision than Judaism from an uncircumcised man. But if neither speak concerning Jesus Christ, they are stones and graves of the dead on which are written only human names.

Again Ignatius's language hints at a belief or credal context – he also talks of 'speaking' and 'hearing' in connection with the threat posed by the docetic heretics (*Trall.* 10.1; *Eph.* 16.2) – yet any credal content is left unspecified. We know only from *Magn.* 10.3 (above) that to '**judaise**' is incompatible with *speaking* of Jesus Christ. 'To judaise' (ἰουδαΐζειν) has a less honourable pre-history and usually refers to behaviour rather than confession. In the LXX of Esther 8.17 it is applied to pagans who were circumcised and adopted Judaism 'out of fear of the Jews'; in Josephus, too, it is used of non-Jews adopting Jewish life even to the point of circumcision and perhaps not from the best of motives (see also Gal. 2.14).[30] Most naturally this would point not to Christians of Jewish origin maintaining their earlier practices but to non-Jewish Christians adopting such a lifestyle; however, Ignatius may not have made the distinction, finding both equally unacceptable and meriting the negative resonances of the description.

If we ask what content 'living according to Judaism' had for Ignatius, only two characteristics appear. To the Philadelphians he says that **it is better to hear Christianism from a man with circumcision than Judaism from an uncircumcised man**. Since the former can be readily illustrated, whether by the first disciples who were Jews, by Paul in particular,[31] or more generally by the Christians of Jewish descent who founded the church at Antioch and no doubt were still to be found there, the latter –

the uncircumcised from whom, apparently in a Christian context, Judaism might be heard – has been eagerly analysed as a representative of forms of Judaism or of judaising Christianity current at the beginning of the second century. When we investigate the relation between the world of Ignatius's letters and the real world we shall need to return to this, but as far as Ignatius is concerned he is not describing anything that could bear the name 'Christianism': he would not say, as do some interpreters, that such a person was teaching Jewish or judaising Christianity.

In contrast to his need to expose and refute the beliefs of the 'docetics' because of the threat they posed to his own Christian- and self-understanding, circumcision has no theological role for Ignatius. We cannot transfer to him Paul's need to deal repeatedly with circumcision because of his recognition of its place within God's promises to Israel (Rom. 3–4 etc.), nor even suppose he is taking up the Pauline affirmation 'in Christ Jesus neither circumcision is of any force, nor uncircumcision' (Gal. 5.6; cf. Col. 3.11). Nothing in the context suggests that circumcision is an issue raised by any opponents, and it is not 'circumcision' that is being taught:[32] the terms are introduced by Ignatius to characterise polar opposites. For most pagan observers at the time circumcision was the defining characteristic of the Jew even though other nations observed the same practice; thus Horace speaks as if proverbially of 'the circumcised Jews'.[33] Ignatius simply reflects this stereotyping, although in the contrasted 'uncircumcised man' (ἀκροβύστος) he is following biblical, and specifically Pauline, terminology.[34] Ignatius is caught in his own rhetoric and in his conviction that if there is to be any relationship between Judaism and Christianity it can only be a one-way passage: one can move from Judaism to Christianity – a circumcised person can preach Christianity – but one cannot move the other way, from Christian uncircumcision to Judaism. It is perhaps in recognition of the complexities into which his rhetoric has led him that he characteristically drops the argument and declares that if either fails to speak about Jesus Christ they are like graves or gravestones.

Thus Ignatius is saying no more than he says to the Magnesians, that **Christianism did not put its faith in Judaism but Judaism in Christianism** (*Magn.* 10.3). This image is also an odd one and has prompted the suggestion that he is referring to the first Jewish Christians who moved from Judaism to Christianity;[35] while we may not need to be so precise, this does show that whereas Ignatius sees no connection between Christianism and 'docetism', he does recognise one between Judaism and Christianity, even while denying the possibility that any relationship might be reciprocal. Yet he may be uneasy about the connection; there is something grudging in his '*it is better* to hear "Christianism" from a man with circumcision', and in the implicit suggestion that such a man might not 'speak about Jesus Christ'.

The second characteristic of Judaism is apparently the sabbath, although here the connection is not so explicit. Having warned the Magnesians against living according to Judaism, and having appealed to the example of the prophets (8.2 above), he continues (9.1):

> If then those who lived within old conditions came to newness of hope, no longer sabbathising (σαββατίζοντες) but living according to the lord's [day?], on which our life also rose through him and his death, which thing some deny – how are we able to live without him...?

Again Ignatius's fondness for schematised contrasts makes precise interpretation difficult. Are those who made this radical change the prophets of whom he has just been speaking, who in the light of polemic like that of Isaiah 1.13 perhaps could be said not to have 'sabbathised', or are they the first Christians who were converted from their Jewish background, or are they a more recent group of Jewish Christians who gave up their judaising practices, becoming 'strong' in terms of Romans 14.1–6?[36] For Ignatius's conception of Judaism this need not bother us; more important is the meaning of **sabbathising** and of its opposite, **living according to the lord's**. The former term (σαββατίζω) does not come in the NT or Philo, but in its few LXX occurrences means observing the sabbath rest.[37] For the second, the text read by most modern editions following Lightfoot supplies no noun with the feminine adjective 'lord's' (κυριακήν), but interprets it as 'the Lord's day' (understanding ἡμέραν). This as a designation of Sunday comes first in Revelation 1.10, although some have stressed the eschatological overtones of 'the Lord's day' in that context, but appears here for the first time without the qualifying 'day'; it comes again in *Did.* 14.1, 'On the lord's [day] of the Lord come together, break bread, and hold eucharist', although some have preferred to see an Easter reference there.[38] A minority opinion, however, favours the text of the Greek middle recension which reads 'life' (ζωήν) after 'lord's'.[39] Both readings merit consideration, although ultimately the difference may not be so great for our purposes as it is for those debating the origins of Sunday observance.

Following the more widely received text suggests at first that Ignatius is characterising Judaism and Christianity by sabbath and Sunday observance respectively, but in what way? The context and the contrast with 'living according to the lord's [day]' do not suggest he is rejecting the strict observance of the sabbath rest from work. If indeed he is rejecting what some 'Christians' are doing, it may be that we should interpret it in the light of his repeated urging in these and other letters that the Christians meet together regularly and his considerable anxiety that some are holding separate eucharists (*Magn.* 4.1; *Philad.* 4.1; *Eph.* 13). If so, it is meeting for worship on Saturday (possibly rather than or as well as on Sunday) which disturbs him. Again we meet the collision of the world Ignatius creates in his letters and the one that he is meeting in the churches. Whether or not the reality is that some are meeting or holding eucharists on Saturday, for whatever reason, in his world it is a matter of slogans, 'sabbathising' as opposed to 'living according to the lord's'. Indeed, the slogans, or at least the former, are suggested perhaps not so much by what was happening, or by the motivation of the participants, as by standard characterisations of Judaism. Along with circumcision, sabbath was for the pagan world the fundamental mark of the Jew: Persius need speak only of 'the circumcised sabbath' (*Sat.* V.184), and observance of the sabbath was enough to indicate a dangerous association with Jewish practices.[40] However, the focus here is on a practice no longer followed, and Ignatius does not dwell on 'sabbathising', but instead moves swiftly from the lord's day or life to his more dominant preoccupation with Jesus's death 'which some deny' (*Magn.* 9.1); Christianity too is characterised by its own alternative marker.

Judaism, for Ignatius, is a system, as also is Christianity (-ism). Both of them are characterised by typifying features, and faithfulness to these is gaining priority over matters of underlying theological principle and debate.[41] Yet even if described in the language of contemporary pagan perception and polemic, Judaism, the system, is only of interest in its proper relationship with Christianity. There is no awareness of 'the Jews' nor of *their* Judaism. This is particularly noticeable when compared with those whom Ignatius accuses of 'mingling Jesus Christ with themselves' (*Trall.* 6.2), but who are never labelled doce*tism.* They are to be shunned (*Eph.* 7.1; *Trall.* 7.1; 9.1; 11.1; *Smyrn.* 4.1; 7.2), they represent a mortal threat (*Eph.* 7.1; *Smyrn.* 5.1), they seek to infiltrate the community with their false teaching (*Eph.* 9.1; *Poly.* 3.1), they abstain from eucharistic meetings and from social concern (*Smyrn.* 6.2–7.1), they, rather than complete outsiders, are 'unbelievers' (*Eph.* 18.1; *Trall.* 10.1; *Smyrn.* 2.1); they, we feel, are an alternative grouping, whether within or outside the Christian community. This, Judaism is not.

Models of the Relationship

The apparently *ad hoc* provocation of Ignatius's remarks about Judaism means that the next level of enquiry is implicit rather than explicit. How did Ignatius understand the relationship between Judaism and Christianity, particularly when compared with writers before and after him? It has already become clear that for Ignatius the relationship between the two is a necessary one but only permits a one-way traffic, from Judaism into Christianity and not vice versa. Moreover, it was 'Judaism', not some differentiated group or remnant, nor even '(the) Jews', which put its faith (aorist) in Christianity (*Magn.* 10.3); there is no concern for any unbelieving residuum. The obvious conclusion must be that, subsequent to the coming of Christianity, Judaism has for Ignatius no valid existence,[42] although the absence of any theological rationale means that this is not argued through in the way it would be by later writers.

In the light of other writers, we may wonder whether Judaism did have a preparatory function; whether living according to Judaism was acceptable earlier but belongs to what is 'old' (*Magn.* 8.1, 'old fables'; 10.2, 'put aside the evil leaven which has grown old'), so that it is only doing so still, 'if we are living *even now* according to Judaism' (μέχρι νῦν: *Magn.* 8.1), that is excluded? Ignatius would probably answer in the negative;[43] after all, the prophets did not live according to Judaism but 'according to Jesus Christ'; they even, perhaps, did not 'sabbathise' but lived according to the Lord's day. Unlike those who 'live according to Judaism' and so demonstrate that they 'have not received grace', the prophets 'were inspired by his grace' (*Magn.* 8.2); just as the goal of Christian existence is to be 'disciples' of Jesus Christ (and so to live according to 'Christianism'), 'the prophets were his disciples by the spirit and looked forward to him as teacher' (*Magn.* 9.2 cf. 10.1), an interpretation similar to that in 1 Peter 1.10.

Perhaps countering claims that he disparaged them, or more probably trying to match their high evaluation by his opponents, Ignatius assures the Christians of Philadelphia that he also loves the prophets, but immediately he interprets them entirely christocentrically – 'because they also preached with the Gospel as their goal, and put their hope in him and waited for him, and having believed in him were saved' (*Philad.* 5.2). This does not mean that the prophets were 'Christians before Christ'; their being numbered in the Gospel or sharing in the unity of Jesus Christ is grounded in his testimony to them, and even more in his raising them from the dead (*Magn.* 9.2, an apparent reference to the descent to Hades).

The relationship of the prophets to their contemporaries is of less interest to Ignatius. Although he says the task of the prophet was 'to fully convince the unbelievers', these are probably the people (?Jews) at the time of Christ and the first preaching of the Gospel, or more particularly Ignatius's own opponents who fail to acknowledge that 'there is one God who manifested himself through Jesus Christ' (*Magn.* 8.2). In the only other letter to refer to the prophets, that to Smyrna, Ignatius claims that a proper attention to the prophets would refute the docetics' claims (*Smyrn.* 5.1; 7.2). Certainly he assumes that they were disregarded in their own time, for he speaks of their persecution, although avowedly as consequent upon their living 'according to Jesus Christ' (*Magn.* 8.2), which for him is supremely characterised by persecution and martyrdom. Yet this only confirms the tenor of the continual future reference of his language about the prophets: they have no true significance except in the light of Jesus Christ.

Although Ignatius holds that proper attention to the prophets (and also to the Law of Moses, *Smyrn.* 5.1 discussed below) would lead to a true estimation of the Christian message, he is not working primarily within a scheme of prophecy and fulfilment, and even less within one of salvation-history.[44] In fact the prophets appear in Ignatius, like the Apostles (*Philad.* 5.1), much more as people with a message, who could be persecuted, believe and be saved, than as 'scriptural' or written authorities. Ignatius's response to the written scriptures is more than a little ambiguous and, despite a number of allusions, he does not use proof texts and rarely quotes the Old Testament explicitly. Although he knows a number of its images, particularly Temple-related imagery, these could have come to him through tradition; even when he says 'the priests are good, but better is the high priest to whom is entrusted the holy of holies' (*Philad.* 9.1), despite the echo of Hebrews, there is no typological development of a scriptural model.

In another difficult passage he records a dispute about scripture in which he himself was involved while visiting the church at Philadelphia (8.2). His opponents ('some people saying') had declared, 'If I do not find it in the archives, I do not believe in [it as part of] the Gospel (ἐν τῷ εὐαγγελίῳ οὐ πιστεύω)'. That the second clause should be expanded with the words in brackets is widely accepted; not only does it fit the parallelism better, it is hard to conceive how anyone within the church would at that point refuse to believe in the Gospel unless it was to be found in the scriptures, and would remain unconvinced that it was to be found there.[45] Ignatius simply replied 'It is written' (γέγραπται), a regular way of introducing biblical quotations (*Eph.* 5.3; *Magn.* 12, and frequently in the NT), asserting that he did have the support of scripture. While they remained unconvinced that that had been established, replying only 'that is the question', Ignatius refused, or refuses, to pursue the argument further, taking refuge instead in the higher authority of 'the cross, the death and the resurrection of [Jesus], and the faith made possible through him': ' for me this is the inviolable archives' to which all others are subject. The logic of the passage clearly indicates that 'the archives' are the Old Testament scriptures;[46] the epithet, which carries a note of antiquity and reliability, was that used by Ignatius's opponents, and arguably reflects an estimation of their significance also found in Hellenistic Judaism.[47] Ignatius neither questions the epithet nor the propriety of arguing from the Old Testament, but he will not accord it the ultimate authority.

Another sign of ambivalence towards scripture may be seen in his warning against anyone 'interpreting Judaism' (*Philad.* 6.1). Perhaps, particularly in the light of the later dispute about 'the archives', it was the Old Testament which was being interpreted – ἑρμηνεύειν comes only here in Ignatius. What concerned him was that the result of an exposition would be 'Judaism' rather than 'Christianity', even when offered by someone who was not himself circumcised. Again Ignatius judges the exercise by its end result and is not concerned to establish a right hermeneutic except as is implied when he claims the prophets for the Gospel.

Ignatius's own understanding of the scriptures/Old Testament is difficult to gauge. He has been forced by his opponents – perhaps at Philadelphia – to consider it: they have supplied the terminology of 'archives' and perhaps even taken the initiative in arguing from scripture; he himself uses few explicit quotations from scripture, and the allusions to the prophets and psalms probably come from tradition. Even his references to the prophets appear only in the letters already concerned with 'Judaism', *Magn.* and *Philad.*, and in *Smyrn.* Despite his assumption that the prophets belong to Christianity while sabbath and circumcision belong to Judaism, Ignatius has no interest in 'the Law', a word conspicuous by its almost complete absence,[48] and, unlike Paul or Justin, he does not define either Christianity or Judaism in relation to it. When he, exceptionally, denounces those (docetics) 'whom neither the prophets nor the Law of Moses have persuaded, nor even now the Gospel nor our human sufferings' (*Smyrn.* 5.1), we may note the priority given to the prophets but also suspect that here he is adopting a traditional formula which contributes little to his own theology.

Of course, Ignatius still understands Jesus in terms indebted to the scriptures. His appeal for unity to the one altar (-court) (ἓν θυσιαστήριον: *Philad.* 4)[49] in idea and vocabulary is thoroughly biblical and not obviously polemical. A similar concern for unity comes in another passage with a more obviously polemical edge, but again it relies more on christocentric affirmation than on any felt need to make sense of past scripture:

> The priests are good, but superior is the high priest to whom is entrusted the holy of holies, who alone is entrusted with the secret things of God. He is the door of the father, through which enter Abraham and Isaac and Jacob and the prophets and the apostles and the church. All these lead to the unity of [given by] God (*Philad.* 9.1).

The place and the interpretation of the 'Old Testament' were to play a central role in Christian self-definition over against Judaism and so in Christian–Jewish debate; at the heart of that debate lay the question 'to whom do the scriptures belong?'. Ignatius reflects the importance of that question, but almost in spite of himself or not of his own choosing; he also anticipates the path by which the messianic interpretation of prophecy reinforced the Christian expropriation of the prophets and by which Jesus Christ was to become the central hermeneutical key. Yet what is surprising is both the intensity of Ignatius's concern about 'the prophets' in the very contexts where he is attacking 'Judaism', and his failure to make any explicit connection between that Judaism and the question of scripture. For him it is not the dividing issue that lies at the boundary between Judaism and Christianity. On the other hand, even if forced to confront the issue by others or by more mundane considerations (see below), the path he begins to map out is one of considerable significance for its future development.[50]

Judaism and Christianity in the Time of Ignatius

Given the paucity of our evidence for this period in the church's development, any insight into the pattern of relations between Judaism and Christianity is important, and it is hardly surprising that Ignatius has featured frequently in scholarly reconstructions of these. Moreover, other sources suggest a significant presence of Jews in the cities to which Ignatius wrote: Smyrna and Ephesus will reappear in later chapters,[51] while

there is archaeological evidence of Jews at least in Tralles and
Philadelphia as well.[52] Yet, as we have suggested more than once,
Ignatius's interpretation of the relationship may often fail to
coincide with that occurring in the churches. This is most clear
when we ask about the boundaries of the church. For Ignatius,
Judaism and Christianity share no common ground and it is
inconceivable that anyone should participate in both. Yet the
very force of his argument demonstrates that this was precisely
what was happening, or perhaps what was happening was that
his clear definition of Judaism and Christianity did not match
the life of the churches.

It was apparently within a normal church gathering that
Ignatius had his dispute about the 'archives' with opponents who
were equally accepted there (*Philad.* 8.2). Significantly, he
introduces his account of the event with the exhortation, 'Do
nothing in [according to] strife but in discipleship of Christ.' In
a similar vein he reports a prophetic outburst when he urged
the Philadelphians to avoid divisions, provoking the suspicion
from some present (perhaps those who he says had tried to
deceive him) that he had been forewarned (*Philad.* 7.2). This
concern for unity is found also in *Magn.* but is rather more forceful in *Philad.*, 'Do not be deceived, my brethren, if anyone
follows a schismatic (σχίζων) "he will not inherit the kingdom
of God" [1 Cor. 6.9f.]' (*Philad.* 3.3). It is admittedly a regular
theme in all Ignatius's letters, and can be countered by his
repeated avowals that he is forewarning rather than betraying
knowledge of existing failings (*Magn.* 11.1; *Philad.* 3.1; 7.2). Yet
his actual experience at Philadelphia implies that there were
there what Ignatius perceived as divisions, most sharply visible
in their failure to gather together for worship and for a single
eucharist, and also in their lack of 'proper' submission to the
bishop (*Philad.* 4.1), although he may have read this experience
into the situation at Magnesia (*Magn.* 4.1; 7.2) when writing to
them a little later.[53]

There is a certain ambivalence in Ignatius's response to the
situation: first he urges on them a single-minded unity in these
respects as if the problem were an internal one; yet he also por-
trays the sources of division as coming from outside like wolves
attacking the flock, and as sources of deception to be avoided
(*Philad.* 2; 3.1).[54] Both responses are part of a policy of drawing

boundaries more firmly, binding together those who are inside and excluding more clearly those who are outside, for whom there is no hope of salvation (cf. *Trall.* 7.2).[55] They imply in reverse that the real situation was one of much more poorly defined boundaries – which makes it difficult to say that the threat was coming *only* from inside and not from outside. If conflict within the church at Antioch had been partly responsible for Ignatius's own arrest and sentence to be sent to Rome to die, this too would colour his view of whether opposition was as dangerous from within as threatening from without, particularly when that conflict repeated itself in the mixed reception he and his envoys enjoyed (*Philad.* 11). However, his offer of repentance and redemption in *Philad.* 3.2; 11.1 suggests that there even Ignatius recognised that the divisions were not insurmountable.

If the meeting for separate eucharists was part of a conscious policy by those involved, grounded in a lack of mutual recognition, we would need to speak of separate groups within the churches, perhaps centred on different 'houses'; but it is perhaps more probable that Ignatius gives higher value to the eucharist, or at least to its function as a symbol of unity under the authority of the bishop, than do members of the churches: in this case, he is polarising a situation which could include within itself differing and even conflicting tendencies.[56] The frequency in early Christian writings of the call to meet together more regularly implies that the issue was not unique to the churches of Asia Minor but played an important part in conflicting understandings or religious expectations, particularly perhaps of gentile Christian communities who had little background in the weekly rhythm of Judaism (cf. Heb. 10.25; *2 Clem.* 2.17; *Barn.* 4.10). However, when in the context of his summons to live 'according to Christianism' Ignatius denounces anyone who wishes to be called 'by another name more than this' (*Magn.* 10.1), we may wonder whether at least one of these 'tendencies' was sufficiently self-conscious to adopt a specific label, perhaps evoking the 'Judaism' which he proceeds to exclude.

Yet it was, surely, Ignatius much more than the churches to whom he wrote who saw the situation in terms of coherent systems, *-isms*, and we have continually to counter his schema by the much more fluid picture he unwittingly betrays. Moreover, his tendency to subordinate everything he meets to the necessi-

ties of a unity based on bishop and common worship, and of a
proper estimation of Jesus's real humanity, constitutes a prism
through which we also encounter the Judaism he sees and
rejects. Yet, while he may ignore any other reality outside the
world whose axis he thus constructs, we need not. In which prior
or contemporary currents in Christian or Jewish life in Asia
Minor did the 'judaising' he found so 'monstrous' belong?

Reconstructions which attempt to answer this question are
notoriously diverse, as are the potential other pieces in the jig-
saw. Ignatius's own language of 'judaising', circumcision and
even 'Judaism' invites comparison with Paul's letter to the
Galatians, although indebtedness to the language does not
demand a parallel or continuing situation, and Ignatius has
no interest in law or justification.[57] Colossians, geographically
and perhaps culturally closer to Philadelphia and Magnesia,
opposes patterns of teaching involving sabbath, as well as matters of food and drink, and other festal observances, including
perhaps circumcision, apparently combined with some forms
of 'cosmic' speculation (Col. 2.11, 16–23). Revelation 'knows'
that the churches of Smyrna and Philadelphia are threatened
by 'those who say they are Jews and are not, but are the synagogue of Satan', while also attacking in Old Testament terms
patterns of teaching castigated as involving immorality and
eating food sacrificed to idols (Rev. 2.9; 3.9; 2.14, 20–21). The
Pastorals reject 'Jewish myths' along with patterns of thought
which move towards cosmic speculation and/or towards ex-
cessive concern for the Law (Tit. 1.14; 1 Tim. 1.4–7).[58]

Labelling such tendencies 'judaising' or 'Jewish Christianity'
does little to help define or to interpret them. There is sufficient variety in the language to caution against seeing a single
or coherent movement, still less an orchestrated one; sufficient
commonality to qualify an atomising approach which sees each
situation independently. Yet the sources also do little to determine whether such tendencies owed much, if anything, to the
Judaism of Asia Minor. There is little, if any, evidence external
to these Christian sources to support the assumption that Judaism
here was prone to syncretising Hellenistic or oriental influences,
or to the development of speculative scriptural interpretation,
which might lie behind these shadowy charges.[59] The argument
that 'Jewish Christianity', once settled on the soil of Asia Minor,

might develop its own momentum, in independence of contemporary Judaism, allowing a combination of gnosticising tendencies with an emphasis on Law-observance or owing increasing debt to other Hellenistic influence, is equally an attempt to explain the sources by creating a single picture out of them.[60] Thus it is that docetism, at first glance alien to Jewish patterns of thought, has often been readily absorbed into such a reconstruction.[61]

It is easy to see how Ignatius might be assimilated, and also contribute, to a picture of this type. The unity of threat which he constructs can then be taken at face value: there was a single heresy in the churches of Asia Minor (or Antioch), namely a 'judaising docetism', with the judaising elements most clearly seen or at least encountered in Magnesia and Philadelphia.[62] Yet to adopt this picture is to be persuaded by Ignatius's own harmonising rhetoric, which is undermined by the detail of his argument. Given the short period during which the letters were written and Ignatius's evident extreme anxiety about the state of the churches, a degree of standardisation of language and rebuttal is hardly surprising; hence *Philad.* and *Magn.* inevitably include the regular appeals to unity and submission to the bishop, and the warnings against division or false teaching, but the so-called antidocetic passages are stylised in *Magn.* (9.1, 'which some deny'; 11) and carry no note of urgency, while they are even fainter in *Philad.* where Ignatius reports an actual dispute in which he was involved. The myths or fables of *Magn.* 8.1 belong more to a tradition of polemical rhetoric than to evidence for 'gnosticising', cosmological speculations perhaps based on the early chapters of Genesis such as found in later gnostic texts. If there is any link between the 'Judaism' and docetism, it is arguably one created by Ignatius himself.[63]

That the one exception to this may be the situation at Smyrna only confirms the unsystematic pattern in the churches. Although there are no references in this letter to 'Judaism' as a threat, at three points we may detect a broadly 'Jewish' note. As we have already seen, Ignatius's opening thanksgiving climaxes with 'his saints and faithful whether among the Jews or among the Gentiles in the one body of his church' (*Smyrn.* 1.2) – the only use of 'Jews' in his letters. After an extended argument against docetism, the overriding concern of this letter, he speaks of those who so

deny Jesus as having being persuaded by neither 'the prophets
nor the Law of Moses' (5.1): Ignatius does not otherwise refer
to the latter; the former we have already met in the letters concerned with 'Judaism', and they appear again when Ignatius urges
avoidance of all who thus refuse to recognise the eucharist as
the flesh of Jesus Christ, and appeals for proper attention 'to
the prophets and supremely to the Gospel' (7.2). Here we should
probably see a reflection of the specific situation at Smyrna.[64]
There also appears to have been some sort of appeal to the 'heavenly powers and the glory of the angels and the rulers, seen and
unseen' who Ignatius says must either believe in the blood of
Christ or come under judgement (6.1): they may have acted as
authorities behind claims to ecstatic or visionary experience (cf.
Col. 2.18), a claim not beyond Ignatius himself (*Trall.* 5).[65] Thus
at Smyrna Ignatius himself does not see 'Judaism', but from
our perspective there seems to be a docetic Christology, combined with, in Ignatius's eyes, an inadequate grasp of the
eucharist, an interest in 'heavenly' experiences and perhaps a
reliance on – for Ignatius a blindness towards – the Law and the
prophets; such a combination may merit the epithet 'judaising',
although this raises as many questions as it answers.[66] However,
there are few grounds for reading this situation into the churches
at Magnesia and Philadelphia.[67]

An alternative hypothesised trajectory still speaks of 'judaising',
but reasonably starts from Ignatius's own references to 'Judaism',
and specifically from 'the uncircumcised' from whom Judaism
might be heard (*Philad.* 6.1): here, apparently, we have a Gentile – it seems unlikely that Ignatius would so label an
uncircumcised Jew – who advocates Jewish belief and practice in
some form.[68] On one reading such a man may have been a former
adherent of Judaism, a so-called 'God-fearer', or even an
'uncircumcised proselyte'. Indeed, this passage has been claimed
as supporting evidence that certain Jews accepted proselytes, at
least in theory, without the requirement of male circumcision,
and perhaps even gave up circumcision for themselves (or their
sons) while continuing to consider themselves as Jews. For Philo
the ethical significance of circumcision as the excision of pleas-
ures expresses the real meaning of circumcision (*Quaest. in Exod.*
22.20); although he himself probably felt that the true proselyte
must none the less also be bodily circumcised in obedience to

the Law, he does know of those who allegorised this and other Jewish observances to such an extent that they would dismiss their external observance as unnecessary, and while he condemns them he does not seem to count them apostates (*De migr. Abr.* 86–93). According to Josephus's account, King Izates of Adiabene, when first converted to Judaism by the merchant Ananias, was persuaded that he need not be circumcised since this would provoke political unrest among his subjects; only later, under the instruction of a stricter Jew, Eleazar, did he have himself circumcised (Josephus, *Ant.* XX.2.3–4 [34–48]).[69]

However, Philo's allegorists also dismissed the external observance of sabbath rest as well as of festivals and the sanctity of the Temple. While it is very unclear what else the 'Judaism' of Ignatius's opponents involved, he does seem to see it as characterised by 'sabbathising'. More important, Ignatius is writing at the other side of the destruction of the Temple in 70 CE, of the imposition of the *fiscus iudaicus* payable by every Jew, of its severe exaction under Domitian and regularisation under Nerva. It seems probable that this would have necessitated a much clearer definition of categories of adherence to Judaism and of what constituted conversion. While this is often not at all clear before these landmarks – for example, what was Izates' status, and in whose eyes, and what other practices did he observe (presumably without upsetting his subjects) – after them conversion must have had clearly measurable consequences in the eyes of both outsiders and insiders.[70] This did not of course prevent the attraction of non-Jews to Judaism, whether passively or in response to active missionary activity, but, if they did not accept male circumcision (and also, from about the time of Ignatius, immersion for both sexes) and the other consequences of being a Jew, they remained non-Jews. It is unlikely that in Philadelphia uncircumcised converts were seeking to bring others into the fold of the synagogue on the same terms as themselves.

By 'Judaism' Ignatius does not mean joining the synagogue, something that would surely provoke a much fiercer denunciation than 'interpreting Judaism'. This also disproves the suggestion that Christians are being attracted into the synagogue in order to avoid the pressures of the imperial cult;[71] given the supreme value Ignatius assigns martyrdom, he would hardly have passed over such a motive in silence. Yet neither, whether or not the disturbances in the Pauline congregations were the work of 'gentile judaisers', can we draw a simple line from these to Philadelphia, meeting there also one who, in continuity with the God-fearers, adopted 'selected Jewish practices' and attempted 'to impose them upon others as a means of self-justification'.[72] Likewise, these are not the heirs of Peter, accepting gentile Christians but according to them a lower status than Jewish Christians, or bringing Christians back under 'the yoke of the Law'.[73] Although the two issues which are highlighted, in separate letters, are sabbath and circumcision, it is unlikely that this is a 'Judaising movement ... [which] works for the reinstitution of the observance of the old law, the replacement of Sunday by the Sabbath, and the readoption of the Jewish name', which celebrates a separate eucharist 'in compliance with the dietary laws' and which is supported by those not born as Jews and not circumcised and yet 'in favour of keeping the whole ritual law'.[74] As we have seen, the Law is not at issue, and nothing in the way Ignatius focuses on sabbath observance and on the (un)circumcised suggests that these practices were being actively advocated as signs of obedience to God's Law.

The contrast between 'the man with circumcision' and 'the uncircumcised man' belongs largely to the rhetorical trajectories of pagan polemic and of Pauline argument. Despite Ignatius's inclusive language at the beginning of *Smyrn.*, it is perhaps likely that by the beginning of the second century most Christians in Asia Minor were uncircumcised, including those whom Ignatius accuses of interpreting Judaism, but this is hardly central to his argument or to an understanding of the situation, which turns more on the identity of the Judaism being interpreted.[75]

His reference in *Magn.* to sabbathising is more ambiguous, belonging as it does to the pagan rhetoric of Jewish caricature, and yet also apparently having a practical dimension when set against 'living according to the lord's [day]' and after an appeal to common meeting. It would be consonant with Ignatius's concerns elsewhere if some were meeting on the sabbath, whether as a 'Christian' group but celebrating their eucharist separately,[76] or participating in something additional, perhaps attending the synagogue as did some later Christians in the time of Origen and again in the time of Chrysostom.[77] Either would fit the sense in the letter that it is not yet a matter of division or schism, although this is a potential threat (6.2), and would also fit Ignatius's failure to articulate the problem more clearly. If the regular, but not yet normative, Christian celebration was held at night, probably the night from Saturday to Sunday,[78] either a sabbath daytime meeting for those with the leisure, or attendance at the very different synagogue service, could be both attractive for some and seen as a threat by others. Yet Ignatius refers only to those who had abandoned such a way of life and expresses the real danger as 'living without him' (*Magn.* 9.1–2): 'sabbathising' may be only a caricature for what Ignatius perceives as 'living according to Judaism' or 'judaising', something which certainly disturbs him deeply but for which he has no other language.

We are, then, left with the problem of scriptural interpretation and perhaps particularly an appeal to 'the prophets'. Only in his account of his abortive debate at Philadelphia do we actually hear the voice of his opponents: 'If I do not find [it] in the archives, I do not believe in [it as part of] the Gospel!'[79] Exactly what they did not find is less clear. Ignatius's defensive retort that the immutable 'archives' are for him the cross, death and resurrection of Jesus, and faith through him, in effect 'the Gospel' as self-authenticating, either deliberately clouds the problems or betrays his failure to handle them. Given his general overriding concern that these articles of belief 'truly' took place in the flesh and not just in semblance, some have argued that Ignatius' opponents were affirming a docetic Christology on the basis of their exegesis of the Septuagint.[80] Certainly whether the scriptures prophesied the suffering and death of the coming Messiah was a central feature of later Jewish–Christian debate,[81] yet the absence of any real anti-docetic polemic in *Philad.* makes it unlikely that this was the issue. Similarly, while later Christian writers do label particular patterns, usually literalistic, of scriptural interpretation 'Jewish', even when propounded by Christians,[82] this would not fit Ignatius, with his background in Antioch, or the situation at the beginning of the second century.

In Philadelphia Ignatius met dissidents who apparently were both more interested in scriptural exegesis and more skilled at it than he was.[83] Certainly he saw their sophism as a threat to unity, and perhaps to his christological focus; to this, as we have seen, he can only respond with avowals: similarly, following the description of the unsatisfactory exegetical battle, Ignatius asserts, 'the priests are good, but better is the high priest to whom is entrusted the holy of holies' (*Philad.* 9.1). Yet there is nothing to indicate whether their (undue) regard for Jewish priests was merely an antiquarian interest, reflected an exegetical focus on particular Old Testament themes, or resulted in contrasting ecclesial or theological structures.[84]

Ignatius himself does not directly link his disputes about 'the archives' with his rejection of 'Judaism', but his warning against *interpreting* (ἑμηνεύειν) Judaism (*Philad.* 6.1) invites such a connection. His reticence allows him to distinguish between his ambivalent experience of a significant current at Philadelphia and a less compromising warning against a threat he can compare with 'the deadly arts and snares of the ruler of this age' (*Philad.* 6.2). However, this suggests that more is at stake than a competition over skill in Old Testament exegesis and that more is meant by 'Judaism' than this: the issue cannot be reduced to the threat constituted by such exegetical competition to Ignatius's own authority, and by an equally threatening tendency to separatism.[85] The urgency which breathes through the letter, and through this section in particular, is inspired not merely by the fact of the appeal to the scriptures but by the conclusions reached and by the strife and divisions occasioned.

A clear characterisation of the 'Judaism' Ignatius opposes is continually obscured by its refraction through the prism of his own concerns and anxieties, not least because these combine the theological (the reality of Jesus's humanity) with what to the modern reader appear the structural (submission to the bishop and unity of action). He undoubtedly shows a, perhaps regrettable, 'tendency to attach questions of doctrine to matters of order and even of calendar',[86] while it often appears to be his own self-identity as Christian and as authority-holder (bishop) which is at stake in his concern for structure and unity.[87] In many ways this is even more true of his rejection of 'Judaism' than of the docetism, which is never labelled as an '-ism' but as certain people saying 'that...'; consequently the 'Judaism' easily appears to be far less real, and in recent scholarship has often been reduced to a disagreement over exegetical priorities. Yet even if

Ignatius does not represent the consensus, nor the churches the unity he would like to assume, the writing, the urgency and also the preservation of the letters imply that the questions of doctrine and the issues of structure and unity were real issues; that many in the churches shared his outlook is shown by the considerable efforts they made to send delegations to meet him or to Antioch in response to his urging.[88]

A final picture of these churches of Asia Minor in the time of Ignatius must be one of considerable variety, certainly excluding blanket judgements about developments of doctrine or heresy or about the situation in the region as a whole. Ignatius himself, although from Antioch, encapsulates something of that variety, reflecting in his own thought both affinities with gnosticising trends and also (perhaps less consciously) the Jewish roots of the traditions to which he is heir.[89] Different tendencies were at work within the churches, often peacefully coexisting although in some cases resulting in virtual separation. A docetic understanding of Jesus was the commonest tendency, and one we find also outside these letters, but may not have been a visible threat in the churches of Magnesia or Philadelphia. In Smyrna at least there were possibly 'Jewish' elements in that docetism, probably in the use of the scriptures as a base for speculation, less certainly in the Jewish background of some of its proponents. However, there was in that church nothing that Ignatius saw as 'Judaism' in the behaviour of his opponents. The situation was different in Magnesia and Philadelphia. In the former there is little sign of real divisions; some were continuing to 'live according to Judaism'. They may have been former Jews or adherents of the synagogues who continued to attend synagogue worship alongside Christian meetings;[90] they seem to have taken very seriously the scriptures, particularly the prophets, for their own self-understanding – more seriously than Ignatius was able to do either by inclination or by expertise. They may too have wished to affirm this allegiance in some open way, thus incurring the charge of wanting to be called by an additional name. Yet they held no beliefs to be condemned and probably did not exclude themselves from fellowship with other Christians. Such dual loyalty would have been particularly repugnant to Ignatius if the troubles in the Antiochene church or his own sentence were in any way related to the power of the Jewish community in Antioch and its own history of conflict.

At Philadelphia the issue appears both more urgent and dangerous and yet also more obscure. Here there is a mood of debate, of argument and of attempts to persuade others. The images are of attack from without and even of the machinations of 'the ruler of this age' (2.2; 6.2, cf. *Eph.*17.1; 19.1; *Magn.* 1.2), but the disputes are between those who meet together (7.1; 8.2). Even more than elsewhere, personal issues are involved – Ignatius must defend himself against charges of having burdened anyone, or having a secret system of informers within the church (6.3; 7.2), and was involved in a debate he failed to win (8.2). His hope for the repentance of some may not have been met by a felt need for repentance (8.1)! Yet there is little trace of any serious doctrinal problems that can be spelt out and denied; only a sense that in some way the clear proclamation of Jesus Christ is being obscured. There are perhaps hints that differing styles of authority are involved – in particular the claims of those adopting a more charismatic style against the episcopal model supported by Ignatius, or, more probably, a different understanding of charism.[91] Ignatius's response is his defence of the bishop's divine appointment and of his own spirit-inspired outburst, as also of Jesus Christ's sole insight into the secret things of God (1.1; 7.2; 9.1); perhaps he too sees the need to correct a focus on the prophetic model by seeing the prophets' activity as pointing to and fulfilled in Jesus (5.2). It is possible that the styles of authority he opposes could appear to smack of 'Judaism' to Ignatius, either because of their scriptural base or because of the patterns of meeting and life-style they encouraged. It is then a conflict over practice or structures; one where appeal to the scriptures plays a significant role and perhaps too an interest in the authority or mediating role of the priests. That an 'unhealthy' fascination with the allegorical exegesis of scripture alone is involved does not explain all these various threads. If, however, access to texts of the scriptures, which Ignatius did not have,[92] involved some sort of association or dialogue with the synagogue, he might have seen his opponents as implicated in 'Judaism'.

Ignatius then offers us only uncertain help in the search for Jewish–Christian relations in the early second century. The impact of the synagogue on local communities, particularly in 'ownership' and interpretation of scripture, may still be being felt. On the other hand, Ignatius supplies no evidence about the syncretism or readiness to make concessions of the Jews of Asia Minor, or for their readiness to capitalise on the protection they could offer against the demands of the imperial cult. Equally, he adds little to the uncertain history of Jewish Christianity or of its contribution to the development of docetism and gnosticism. What he does show is how Judaism could become a slogan, a way of defining Christianity against a significant alternative, even against its roots. He shows too how the creation of that slogan or counter-image is dependent on a mix of contemporary reality, popular image and internal needs. Yet it is not only a matter of negative attack. Differentiation against what he has labelled 'Judaism' and has put outside the church goes hand in hand with clear insistence on a distinguishing Christian lifestyle, practice ('living according to the lord's day'), and an understanding of the methods and limitations of scriptural authority.[93] Indeed, that the problem focuses on scriptural interpretation and on the authority to interpret seems to be one of the few points of agreement in reconstructions of Ignatius's background. All this suggests that he represents not a period when the 'Jewish question' was absent or temporarily settled, awaiting its revival half a century later, but one where seeds of the future were sown.

Notes

[1] See Kraeling 1932; Meeks and Wilken 1978: 1–13.

[2] See J. Taylor 1994 and below, p. 29.

[3] See Grant 1963.

[4] Harkins 1977, who gives them the more eirenic title 'Against Judaising Christians'; Wilken 1983.

[5] On the problem of the different recensions see Schoedel 1985: 3–7; 1993: 286–92; C. Bammel 1982: 62–5. The collection of seven letters generally accepted as authentic is variously known as the 'short recension' or as 'the middle recension' in contrast to the Syriac which contains only the letters to the Ephesians, Romans and Polycarp.

[6] On the nature of the 'long recension' see Smith 1986, who sees the attacks against Judaism as part of the backlash against the Jews, following Julian's support of them.

[7] So Wilken 1983: 55.

[8] The date is disputed; see S. Davies 1976 and Essig 1986 for independent attempts to correlate Ignatius's martyrdom with contemporary events; both of which, contrary to Eusebius, set it after Pliny's correpondence with Trajan.

[9] This represents a growing consensus in scholarship: see C. Bammel 1982: 87–97; Schoedel 1985: 10–11.

[10] Questions well articulated by Bauer 1971: 67–9, even if his interpretation of the reality is equally insecure.

[11] Riesenfeld 1961.

[12] Laeuchli 1972.

[13] 'Gentile' (ἔθνος) only appears here and in *Trall.* 8.2, where it appears to mean 'outsiders'.

[14] Even *Magn.* 8.2 does not explicitly say the persecution of the prophets was at the hands of their Jewish contemporaries.

[15] Schoedel 1985: 129; see *Smyrn.* 4.1; *Trall.* 8.1.

[16] On the text here see n. 48 below.

[17] Although Ignatius can also use it generally: *Magn.* 3.2.

[18] Neither noun nor verb comes in the NT or in the LXX; the verb is also not found in Josephus or Philo.

[19] See also Mendelson 1988: 136–7.

[20] *Adv. Christ.* apud. Eusebius, *Prep. Evang.* I.2.3, cf. Stern 1974–84: II. 447–9.

[21] Opelt 1980: 107. See also Pindar, *Olymp. Od.* I.29: myths lead astray because they are decked with lies.

[22] See pp. 258–9 below. Cf. Irenaeus, *Adv. haer.* IV.26.1, 'When the law is read by the Jews in the present time it is like a myth.'

[23] Ctr. Lightfoot 1889: II.2, 124; see further below, pp. 42–3.

[24] *Philad.* 8.2; *Rom.* Praef.; *Eph.* 9.2, cf. Bommes 1976: 33.

[25] So Schoedel 1985: 126. The transliteration is used here rather than the translation 'Christianity' to accentuate the parallelism of form. Dörrie 1971: 285–6 argues that most words ending in '-ismos' carry a pejorative note but excludes from this 'Christianismos', which also exceptionally has no prior '-izein' verb form (cf. below, n. 30). He suggests that 'Christianismos' is derived from the non-Greek 'Christianos'. However, it seems that 'Judaismos', which he does not discuss, also carries no pejorative tone.

[26] Bommes 1976: 30–8; van Damme 1976: 295–7; Staats 1986: 246. See also J. Taylor 1994 for the argument that the term started in Antioch as a term of opprobrium.

[27] On this and what follows see Hengel 1966: 178f.; Amir 1982.

[28] Perler 1949; Asia Minor is also possible, see van Henten 1986; 1993: 713 and below, pp. 80–1.

[29] *CIJ* 694: Hengel 1966; see Rajak 1985a: 247–8, who accepts the interpretation that this refers to Polycharmus's public life; cf. *CIJ* 537.

[30] *B.J.* II.17.10; 18.2 [454, 463]; see also Plutarch, *Cic.* 7 in polemical disparagement of Caecilius as suspected of Jewish practices and called contemptuously by Cicero 'a Jew'; Dörrie 1971: 285–6 argues that '-ize' (-ιζειν) verbs of this sort are often pejorative or ironical, implying the adoption of an alien model of life or behaviour.

[31] Niebuhr 1994: 229 sees Paul as the primary model for Ignatius.

[32] So also Schoedel 1985: 203; Sumney 1993: 357, both of whom suggest Ignatius introduced it on the Pauline model.

[33] 'Curti Iudaei': *Serm.* I.9.70 in Stern 1974–84: I. 325; see also Stern index ad loc. Pagan authors are of course aware that the Jews were not alone in being circumcised, and some claim that the Jews adopted the practice from the Egyptians (so Herodotus, *Hist.* II.104.1–3 etc. = Stern 1974–84: I. 2).

[34] The LXX and NT (Acts 11.3 and Paul) only use the noun ἀκροβυστία (uncircumcision); although not found in the LXX, ἀκρόβυστος is found in the other Greek versions; it also appears in Justin, *Dial.* 19.3. Neither term is found in classical Greek.

[35] Schoedel 1985: 126.

[36] Schoedel 1985: 123 holds that they are the first Christians; Molland 1954, the prophets, and, more unusually, Rordorf 1966: 138–40, recent Jewish-Christian converts.

[37] Exod. 16.30; Lev. 23.32; 26.35; 2 Chr. 36.21; 1 Ez. 1.38; 2 Macc. 6.1.

[38] On this and for the arguments in favour of Sunday in each case see Rordorf 1966: 205–15.

[39] So Guy 1964, although he acknowledges that 'life' may then be an internal accusative going with 'living' rather than the noun accompanying 'lord's', i.e. 'living a life according to the lord's'. He is followed by Kraft 1965: 27–8, and, more forcefully, by Lewis 1968.

[40] Persius: 'Recutita sabbata', in Stern 1974–84: I. 436–7; in Juvenal's well-known satire, the son who converts follows his father who 'feared the sabbath' (*Sat.* XIV.96), while Seneca also fixed on the evils of the Jewish sabbath (*De superstit.* apud Augustine, *De civ. Dei* VI.11; *Epist. moral.* XCV.47) (Stern 1974–84: II. 102–3; I. 431–3).

[41] See Barrett 1976: 243–4, to whose insights I owe much.

[42] So Klevinghaus 1948: 94 '"Judentum" seit Christus eigentlich nicht mehr existiert.'

[43] So also Schoedel 1985: 126.

[44] Bartsch 1940: 43–4 suggests that the community tradition Ignatius takes over may have used a prophecy and fulfilment scheme, as in *Philad.* 5.2; 9.2, but that this is not Ignatius's scheme. Klevinghaus 1948: 88–94 stresses that Ignatius would not support a salvation-history perspective. Similarly, he has no room for a covenant scheme. Ctr. Meinhold 1979b, who argues that for Ignatius Christian history does begin in the old covenant with the prophets.

[45] See Lightfoot 1889: II.2. 271–2. Molland 1954 holds that in the heat of the argument, or through the prism of Ignatius's reporting, they may have asserted something like that. On this whole section see Schoedel 1978. C. Bammel 1982: 74 suggests that 'in the Gospel' may be a gloss.

[46] Against those, e.g. Klevinghaus 1948: 100, who sees them as private revelation books of the opponents against which Ignatius sets the scriptures.

[47] So Schoedel 1978 with reference to Josephus, *C. Apion.* I.37–8; 143.

[48] Besides *Smyrn.* 5.1, discussed below, it comes only in *Magn.* 2, 'subject to the presbytery as to the law of Christ' (cf. *Rom.* Praef. where the text is disputed, 'observing the law of Christ' or 'named after Christ'). Lightfoot 1889: II.2, 124–5 is surely right in seeing νόμον as a gloss in the Greek text of *Magn.* 8.1, κατὰ Ἰουδαϊσμὸν νόμον.

[49] For θυσιαστήριον, which is drawn from the LXX (and NT) and not classical Greek, see also *Eph.* 5.2; *Magn.* 7.2; *Rom.* 2.2; *Trall.* 7.2.

[50] See Meinhold 1979b; Barrett 1976: 238, 242–3.

[51] Smyrna in the *Martyrdom of Polycarp*, and Ephesus in Justin.

[52] Tralles: Josephus, *Ant.* XIV.10.20 [241–3]; Brooten 1982: 157–8; Philadelphia: *CIJ* 754. Schürer 1973–87: III. 22, 24.

[53] Ignatius wrote to Magnesia from Smyrna following his stay at Philadelphia. His letter to that church was written later from Troas. On the formative effect of his experience of the Philadelphian church see Speigl 1987.

[54] The language of avoidance is even stronger in *Smyrn.* 4.1; 7.2

[55] On Ignatius's strategy see H. Maier 1991: 174–81. It is not clear whether those for whom prayer is urged in *Eph.*10 are unbelievers (so Lightfoot 1889: II.2, 57–9) or 'insiders' who are the source of hostility and threat, as perhaps suggested by the use of 'error', blasphemy or slander (βλασφημία), and the call to be 'their brothers'.

[56] On the centrality of the eucharist for Ignatius see Bartsch 1940; on the situation as one of coexisting tendencies Meinhold 1979a; Barrett 1976: 244.

[57] For Ignatius's indebtedness to Paul's language see Niebuhr 1994; for a demonstration that there is no parallel to Galatians see Molland 1954: 2.

[58] See below, p. 259.

[59] Georgi 1967 argues for the latter leading to 'a theology of great speculative power' but appeals to Philo and Wisdom, neither from Asia Minor.

[60] See Koester 1959; 1965.

[61] See U. Müller 1976: 11–12, 78; Prigent 1977; more restrained, Barrett 1976: 235; Schweizer 1976 sees the Jewish influence as secondary to movements with an origin in Pythagorean and similar tendencies.

[62] E.g. Lightfoot 1889: II.2, 103, 242–3; Koester 1965: 310; 1959: 19; U. Müller 1976: 78; Prigent 1977.

[63] See Schoedel 1985: 118, 125, 200.

[64] See Barrett 1976: 238–9, and above, pp. 36–7.

[65] See Goulder 1994 on claims to visionary experience as characteristic of his reconstruction of Jewish Christianity.

[66] Thus Schweizer 1976: 255 speaks in Colossae of 'a kind of Pythagorean philosophy, embellished with rites borrowed from both Hellenistic mystery religions and Judaism ... [which] may have grown out of a Jewish Christianity that adapted itself more and more to its Hellenistic environment'.

[67] It would be over-interpreting to see the claim in *Philad.* 9.1 that Jesus Christ alone is entrusted with 'the secret things of God' as a polemic against supposed visionary experience.

[68] On this and what follows see Wilson 1992.

[69] Borgen 1987a and b and elsewhere has developed this argument. He also appeals to rabbinic discussion as to what is the crucial act in conversion of a proselyte. According to Borgen, this material provides part of the vital background for a proper understanding of Paul's conflicts with those who questioned his teaching about circumcision.

[70] On the issue in general see the clear discussions by Collins 1985 and Goodman 1992; 1994a: 67, 81–2; on the significance of the actions of Domitian and Nerva in relation to the *fiscus iudaicus* as marking a watershed see Goodman 1989b; 1994a: 121–6.

[71] So Hemer 1986: 9, 169.

[72] Gaston 1979: 58; but there is little evidence that a legalism of 'self-justification' was the motivation of God-fearers outside Christianity.

[73] Donahue 1978; Tarvainen 1967: 27–32.

[74] Simon 1986: 267.

[75] See above pp. 31–2 for the argument that Ignatius is caught in his own rhetoric; Wilson 1992: 608 argues the reverse, that the first clause is rhetorical, the second factual, indicating 'gentile Judaizers', but still sees the main problem as identifying their 'Judaism'. Sumney 1993: 357 argues that Ignatius has introduced the language of circumcision, but that the problem was the interpretation of scripture.

[76] So even Gaston 1986: 38, who otherwise thinks largely in terms of scriptural exegesis; similarly and tentatively Schoedel 1985: 123–5.

[77] Origen, *Hom. in Lev.* V.8; Chrys. *Hom. adv. Jud.* I.5. See Wilken 1983: 75 and Lieu 1992: 89.

[78] So convincingly Staats 1975.

[79] *Philad.* 8.2; see above, p. 37.

[80] So Lightfoot 1889: II.2, 72; also Molland 1954; Prigent 1977: 7; Gaston 1986: 37; U. Müller 1976: 78.

[81] Justin, *Dial.* 72–3; 89–90.

[82] See de Lange 1976: 105–6 on Origen.

[83] Possibly through allegorical exegesis: so Schoedel 1978; 1985: 209.

[84] Corwin 1960: 61–4 uses this, together with their interest in calendar (sabbath), exegesis and teachers, as evidence that the 'Judaizers' in (Antioch) had an Essene background; she finds in Ignatius's assertion that the prophets looked forward to Jesus as teacher, just as he is the only teacher of the disciples of Jesus (*Magn.* 9.1–2), 'an implication that some teacher of special eminence has influence' and compares the Teacher of Righteousness. Schoedel 1978, 1985: 210 notes the interest in priests as guarantors of tradition in Hellenistic Judaism (esp. Josephus).

[85] Schoedel 1985: 201–5; Schoedel allows for a 'mild judaising' at Magnesia which may have involved sabbath 'observance' but which beyond that is difficult to define. Even more sharp is the position of Slatter 1985, who appears to see the focus of the problem as the question of the succession to the bishop at Antioch; those who appealed to the OT depended on a model of God as shepherd. Bartsch 1940: 40 over-interprets the verbs 'to do' (πράσσειν, ποιεῖν), which come in this context, 'do nothing out of strife, but according to discipleship of Christ', cultically and argues it is a matter of separate meetings established by scriptural exegesis.

[86] Barrett 1976: 243.

[87] See Schoedel 1980 ; Laeuchli 1972: 97–102, 108–11.

[88] So H. Maier 1991: 158.

[89] See Corwin 1960: 52–65 on Ignatius as occupying a mediating position between the two extremes he rejects; for the gnostic affinities of Ignatius's thought see Bartsch 1940, for its Jewish roots, Grant 1963.

[90] It would be as well here to affirm that nothing suggests that the *birkath ha-minim* would have resulted in the immediate exclusion of all Christians from all synagogues in the diaspora as sometimes portrayed.

[91] On the opponents as appealing to 'charism' see Meinhold 1979a and Trevett 1983; 1989b; H. Maier 1991: 156–87 analyses Ignatius's own authority

in terms of charism; Hann 1987 sees in Ignatius a re-emergence of charismatic authority from a new base in gentile Christianity at Antioch.

[92] See above, p. 37, for the suggestion he was dependent on 'Testimonies'.

[93] Schoedel 1980: 32.

3

THE *MARTYRDOM OF POLYCARP*

With the *Martyrdom of Polycarp* we meet, apparently for the first time, the beginning of a new and highly significant[1] genre in Christian literature, the literary account of a Christian martyrdom. While there were influential precedents – most obviously the death of Stephen in Acts 7 and the Gospel passion narratives – these are incorporated within more extensive literary sources of a different kind. The sole purpose of the letter written by the church at Smyrna to that at Philomelium, the form taken by the *Maryrdom*, is to relate 'the things concerning those who bore witness, in particular the blessed Polycarp' (1.1) in order that glory might be given to 'the Lord who makes election from among his servants' (20.1).[2] As we shall see, much of the imagery, the vocabulary, and the interpretation and presentation of martyrdom has antecedents not only in the accounts of the deaths of Stephen and of Jesus but also in other Christian and non-Christian sources; for the literary genre itself, however, there is little to which we can appeal to suggest existing conventions of form, method, motive or *Sitz im Leben*.

Although the letter claims to be a response to a request from the church of Philomelium (20), the opening prescript betrays an awareness that this is more than an occasional letter: 'The church of God sojourning at Smyrna to the church of God sojourning at Philomelium and all the sojourning ones of the holy and catholic church in every place'. The language of sojourning, which follows earlier models (*1 Clem.* praes.; cf. 1 Peter 1.17; 2.11), reflects the self-awareness of living in an 'exile' situation, while the extended address, together with the closing instruction to forward the letter to the brethren elsewhere (20), acknowledges its more than parochial significance. The authority for this must lie not in that held by the authors, unlike most earlier Christian letters going back to those of Paul, but in the charism of martyrdom itself. Recognising these elements, and the 'Jewishness' of their ideology and of the language, C. Andresen, following the work of E. Peterson, argued that the *Martyrdom of Polycarp* is a 'diaspora' or community letter following the pattern of earlier Jewish diaspora letters.[3] However, evidence for Jewish diaspora letters which might provide a model for the Christian version is sparse, and certainly cannot explain the combination of letter form and martyrdom account. We should probably see *M. Poly.* as a genuine letter, although written in a developing tradition of Christian epistolography with a wider audience and with a clear didactic and kerygmatic purpose in view, but also decisively shaped by the events it describes and by the embryonic 'veneration' of Christian martyrs.[4]

The account claims to be near contemporary – written within a year of the events and when the community were still looking forward to celebrating the first anniversary of Polycarp's martyrdom (18.2) – and to be based on the reports of actual witnesses 'who had been preserved to proclaim to the rest what had happened' (15.1; cf. 9.1). A further chapter, possibly added later since it follows the closing doxology and greetings (20.2), provides the support of an apparently precise dating 'on the second day of the month Xanthikos, seven days before the Kalends of March, on a great sabbath, at the eighth hour', and of named personnel, 'Herod, who arrested him, Philip of Tralles as highpriest, and Statius Quadratus as proconsul' (21).[5] Yet the ultimate pinnacle of this chain of dates and people is not the emperor and the year of his reign (which we would dearly like to know) but 'and as King reigning for ever our Lord Jesus Christ'. The author's kerygmatic and theological perspective is not limited to comments such as 'so we should be most pious and ascribe authority over all affairs to God' (2.1), but provides the framework within which the whole is described and understood.

It is against this background that we should understand the role of the Jews in the events, and in particular what Musurillo has called 'the author's undisguised anti-semitism'.[6] While the early date of the account makes *M. Poly.* a precious historical source, the theological factors at play in the presentation of the Jews and of their role *vis-à-vis* both Christians and pagans need to be separated from the contentious question as to their historical role in early Christian persecution, discussion of which has so often started from Polycarp's death in Smyrna.

The Jews of the Narrative

The Jews appear explicitly at three distinct points in the narrative; for the rest of the time there is nothing but silence to suggest that their presence was pervasive. At each of these three points their presence fulfils an unmistakably dramatic, and to that extent 'theological', role within the argument of the narrative.

a) *M. Poly. 12.2*

.... When the herald had said this, the whole crowd of gentiles and Jews dwelling in Smyrna with uncontrollable anger and in a loud cry shouted, 'This is the teacher of Asia [*or* of impiety],[7] the father of the Christians, the destroyer of our gods, the one who teaches the masses to neither sacrifice nor worship'.

In the initial account of the persecution which broke out at Smyrna no mention is made of the Jews; when the bravery of the earlier martyrs astounds the crowd (το πλῆθος) and drives them to cry 'Away with the godless (ἄθεοι); let Polycarp be sought!' (3.2), there is no hint that Jewish voices were added to (never mind loudest in) that cry. It is only when the narrative focuses on Polycarp that they appear. He, although at first persuaded to find refuge outside the city, is arrested and brought before the proconsul, but remains unmoved by all attempts at persuasion to renounce his Christian confession; the herald is then sent into the stadium or amphitheatre to announce to those who had been waiting that 'Polycarp has confessed three times that he is a Christian.'[8] It is at this that **the whole crowd of gentiles and Jews** (ἅπαν τὸ πλῆθος ἐθνῶν τε καὶ ʾΙουδαίων) **dwelling in Smyrna** respond in uncontrollable anger. The drama of the moment is inescapable; on the one side, the solitary witness who has made his clear confession, 'I am a Christian', on the other, the opposing forces against whom the Christians must ever stand and argue, the gentiles and the Jews. There is irony, too: those forces, in spite of themselves, make their own confession of Polycarp's significance – **This is the teacher of Asia [impiety],**

**the father of the Christians, the destroyer of our gods, the one
who teaches many to neither sacrifice nor worship** – in terms to
which the Christian author could only assent and add little more;
his own description of Polycarp, given later, is that he was an
'apostolic and prophetic teacher, bishop … in Smyrna' (16.2;
cf. 19.1).

In this framework it is, therefore, irrelevant, albeit true, that
the words are unlikely to have been found on Jewish lips – they
would not have claimed the city gods as 'theirs', nor ventured to
accuse someone else of avoiding their worship, without running
the risk of having the same charge turned against themselves, as
apparently happens to Alexander in Acts 19.34. There is for the
same reason little point in allocating the cries to the groups
involved, so that the Jews contribute only the first two affirmations
– even though it is true that these would fit a Jewish context
well.[9] From the point of view of the narrative what matters is
their common and unanimous, albeit unwitting, witness to the
truth.[10]

The significance of the moment is underscored by the fact
that elsewhere *M. Poly.* thinks primarily in terms of the contrast between the Christians and 'the rest'. As we have seen,
the crowd (πλῆθος) has already been mentioned with no suggestion that it comprised both Jews and gentiles (3.2). When
Polycarp is invited by the proconsul to make the anti-Christian
cry, 'Away with the godless', he groans and repeats it with ironic
feeling as he gazes around at the crowd of 'lawless *gentiles*'
(ἀνόμων ἐθνῶν) who fill the amphitheatre (9.2). Later (16.1),
it is again the 'lawless people' (ἄνομοι) who realise that the
flames will not burn Polycarp and demand his death by the
sword. Despite this hostility, the author asserts that Polycarp's
posthumous fame was such that it 'was spoken of even by the
gentiles (ἐθνῶν) in every place' (19.1). Although, as we shall
see, the Jews play a distinctive part at two further points in the
narrative, the underlying thread of events pictures only an
undifferentiated crowd of gentiles (ἔθνοι). Theologically, too,
it is a bipartite scheme which dominates the author's thinking:
when the sword-thrust releases a flow of blood which quenches
the flames and miraculously preserves Polycarp's body, all are
amazed at the great distinction thus shown 'between the unbelievers and the elect' (16.1).[11]

The presence of the Jews alongside the pagans at 12.2, therefore, must be quite deliberate. While it prepares for their more active involvement later in the narrative, it does not only anticipate their presence then. It has been suggested that they are picked out here as part of the 'imitation of Christ' theme which is undoubtedly so important for *M. Poly.*[12] Polycarp's martyrdom was 'according to the Gospel' (1.1; 19.1),[13] and the parallelism between his path to death and that of Jesus in the Gospels is well marked. So just as the Jews shouted loudly demanding Jesus's death (Luke 23.18, 21, 23), here their voices are to be heard in the demand that Polycarp be put to death. Yet if this was the intention of the author we would have expected him to make the point far more clearly, if not by cross-reference (which is rarely explicit), then by the use of allusion and parallel formulation.

This is not to deny possible scriptural echoes at this point in the narrative. It is notorious that whereas the language of *M. Poly.* is predominantly 'biblical', actual quotations are rare and it is near impossible to determine when deliberate allusions are intended and which books are known.[14] However, the description of **the whole crowd of gentiles and Jews dwelling in Smyrna** – an apparently superfluous elaborateness at this mid-point in the narrative when we already know of the crowd's presence in the stadium – not only draws attention to the comprehensive audience, 'universal' in a local sense, who will witness Polycarp's confession and add their own, but also recalls the language of the Acts of the Apostles where the word of the Lord becomes known to 'all those dwelling in Asia ... Jews and Greeks' (Acts 19.10; cf. 19.17, 'all the Jews and Greeks dwelling in Ephesus'; 14.5, 'gentiles and Jews'). It is also worth noting that it is in Ignatius's letter to the church at Smyrna, and only in this letter, that he speaks of 'his saints and faithful ones, whether among the Jews or among the gentiles' (Ignatius, *Smyrn.* 1.2).[15]

This theme of the universality of the audience of the Christian witness – and a martyr is a witness – may be a traditional one. According to Hegesippus's account of the martyrdom of James, the brother of Jesus, James was invited to persuade those who had come to Jerusalem for the Passover, namely 'all the tribes together with the gentiles' (Eusebius, *H.E.* II.23.11).[16] After his death and burial James is declared to be a true witness 'to both Jews and Greeks that Jesus is the Christ' (*H.E.* II.23.18).[17] However, whereas in James's case the focus of the testimony is christological, in this it is Polycarp as teacher and as martyr. The third-century *Martyrdom of Pionius*, which both contains much authentic tradition and is explicitly rooted in the theological and literary tradition of *M. Poly.*, marks a further development when it identifies the crowd witnessing Pionius's testimony as comprised of 'Greeks and Jews and women' (*M. Pionius* 3.6).[18]

The narrative does not pause to note the significance of the moment; even as they say this, 'they' cry out demanding that Polycarp be given to the lion, and, when that proves impossible, 'agree with one accord to shout out that he be burned alive' (12.3). Their concerted (ὁμοθυμαδόν) 'decision' is, however, but the necessary means of fulfilling Polycarp's prior prophecy of his manner of death; three days earlier he had had a vision that he *must* be burned (δεῖ) and had told this to 'the believers with him'. It is hard to ignore the echo of the 'divine must (δεῖ)' of the Gospel passion predictions and more particularly of John 18.32, where the Jews' inability to carry out a capital sentence fulfils Jesus's earlier prediction (12.32–3) of the manner of his death. Again this crowd are unwitting tools of the truth and of the divine purpose, to which Polycarp is both privy and conformed.

b) *M. Poly.* 13.1

> …the crowds immediately gathering from the workshops and baths wood and firewood, with the Jews assisting at this particularly enthusiastically, as is their custom.

In the author's own words, what follows 'happens faster even than can be told'; yet, now ourselves privy to the divine purpose, we are impressed with how the initiative remains with Polycarp in obedience to God: he prepares himself for the flames, removing his own garments, and, refusing the 'security' they offer of the nails, offers himself to be bound, trusting that God will enable him to remain steadfast in the fire (13.2–3).

First, underlying by its contrast Polycarp's calm preparation of himself, comes the frenzied activity of the crowds (ὄχλοι) collecting wood and fuel for the fire from the neighbouring workshops and the baths (13.1). Here, the Jews not only share in the activity but do so **particularly enthusiastically** (μάλιστα Ἰουδαίων προθύμως…);[19] the point is underlined when the author adds **as is their custom**. Inasmuch as this comment is unnecessary to the story – and, in the light of our later discussion, of questionable veracity – it may merit the epithet 'antisemitic'. Certainly it takes us a stage further than the first more neutral mention of the Jews and betrays a deliberate focusing of attention and blame on them. Yet the comment is also characteristic of the author and is not limited to the activity of the Jews. The troops and cavalry set out to arrest Polycarp 'with their customary weapons' (7.1), the centurion burns Polycarp's body in public 'as is their custom' (18.1), while the proconsul tries to persuade Polycarp to recant out of consideration of his age and with other such arguments as follow 'their custom' (9.2). In contrast to this 'typical' and largely futile activity – for none of it achieves anything other than was already bound to happen – Polycarp spends the days preceding his arrest ceaselessly 'praying for all people and for the church throughout the world, as was *his* custom' (5.1).

On one level these appeals to custom may be an apology for the summary nature of the account when the Christians of Philomelium had asked for rather more detail (20.1). On another, they highlight the contrast between the behaviour of the martyr and that of those who oppose him: thus they come armed to arrest him 'as against a brigand' (7.1, quoting Matt. 26.55), while he offers them whatever food and drink they desire (7.2); he asserts traditional Christian respect for the powers and authorities ordained by God (10.2), while those same authorities appear to be little more than organs of the mob.[20] All this suggests that these appeals are not primarily to what is already known but are creating models of behaviour and expectation. Christians may be treated as dangerous criminals but this is not how they are to react, but rather are to return aggression with hospitality; city authorities may give way to popular pressure, although personally being rarely antagonistic, but Christians are to respect them as ordained by God. Despite hostility from all sides, the commitment to prayer for all people is never rendered void. So, too, it is unlikely that the Christians of Smyrna and those of Philomelium were already well aware of regular Jewish enthusiastic participation in building fires for the burning of Christians, but rather they are being warned that even at this point of crisis, or perhaps especially at this point of witness, the fiercest competitors will be the Jews.

The sources of this image are probably complex. The historical reality, of course, must be a major issue and will be discussed later. How far Jewish participation in the persecution of Christians was common is a much disputed question; that it was both proverbial – Tertullian's oft-quoted description of the synagogues as the 'fount-heads of persecution'[21] – and biblically rooted needs little demonstration. Christians could, and regularly did, appeal not only to Jewish responsibility for the death of Jesus and of the first martyr Stephen, but also to dominical predictions of Christian suffering at their hands (John 16.2; Matt. 10.17–21; cf. 1 Thess. 2.14–16). In a martyrdom which, as we have noted, proceeds 'according to the Gospel', where Polycarp prays before his arrest, is betrayed by one of his own household, and is arrested by a 'Herod', it is not surprising to find the Jews, although not legally responsible, active in ensuring the carrying out of the death sentence. Yet the imitation theme is hardly likely to have created the Jewish presence nor is it sufficient explanation of the highlighting of their contribution to the mob action at this point. For that we shall need to look more deeply at the motives and setting of this document.

c) *M. Poly. 17.1 – 18.1*

> And this with the Jews inciting and urging, who also kept watch, as we were about to take him from the fire. For they did not know that we would never be able to abandon the Christ... When the centurion saw the contentiousness of the Jews that took place, he placed him in the midst and burnt him...

With the final appearance of the Jews in the drama we reach a climax of hostility. Here, however, neither the text nor the pattern of events are entirely clear, suggesting either later editorial activity or an artificial attempt to work into the narrative a number of themes and issues. Certainly in this section the author's (or later editor's) theological concerns are more transparent than in the preceding chapters.

Polycarp has offered his final prayer, the fire has been lit, and yet the martyr is not consumed but encircled by the flames, baked like bread or refined like gold or silver (15). Frustrated by this miracle and by the sweet odour of incense rather than the stench of burning flesh,[22] the 'lawless men', ἄνομοι – most naturally only used of pagans – demand that Polycarp be pierced with the sword – again there is an umistakable Gospel echo: John 19.34. This done, the flow of blood quenches the flames, demonstrating, as we have seen, 'the distinction between the unbelievers and the elect, among whom was the most wonderful Polycarp' (16.1–2). After this triumphant and eulogistic conclusion,[23] it is no surprise to meet the forces of opposition seeking to have the last word.

The ultimate source of all this opposition is not the proconsul nor the mob nor even the Jews, although we shall return to them, but the devil.[24] Already at the beginning of the account the colourful variety of tortures endured by the earlier martyrs was recognised as the devices of the devil, trying by many means to subvert them to denial (2.4 – 3.1). At that point he appeared merely as 'the devil',[25] but in opposition to 'the greatness of Polycarp's martyrdom, his blameless life and the crown of immortality he has now won', his true identity is manifested; as 'the jealous and envious and evil one, the one who opposes the race of the righteous' (17.1), he determines that the Christians will be deprived at least of the 'poor body' of the martyr. To this end he incites Nicetas, the father of the police chief Herod and, incidentally, brother of a certain Alce, to request the magistrate that the body not be handed over on request, as was usually possible, 'lest abandoning the crucified one, they begin to worship this man'.

At this point (17.2) 'the Jews' are introduced in a subordinate (genitive absolute) clause as **inciting and urging** – although the absence of a main verb obscures the connection; Eusebius offers a better sequence – 'they [i.e. those who were behind Nicetas's action] said these things when the Jews incited and urged' – but the smoothness of his account is probably secondary.[26] Showing his hand ever more clearly, the author continues, 'they also kept watch as we were about to take him from the fire, not realising [presumably still referring to the Jews although the motive which follows has just been attributed to Nicetas][27] that we shall never be able to desert the Christ, who, for the sake of the salvation of the whole world of the saved, suffered blameless for sinners, and so to worship some other one. For him we worship as being son of God, but the martyrs as disciples and imitators of the lord we love deservedly because of their unsurpassed loyalty to their king and teacher.'

At this, the centurion (and not the magistrate), seeing **the contentiousness of the Jews**, apparently on his own initiative takes the body and, 'as is their custom[!]', publicly burns it, presumably first reigniting the fire quenched by Polycarp's blood (18.1)! However, the Christians are not prevented from later gathering 'the precious bones' and putting them in an appropriate place (18.2).

The inconsistency as to the active players in the action and the patent concern about the validity and status of any veneration of the martyrs and their mortal remains invite theories of a later adaption or expansion of the text, although, in contrast to a number of the points where redaction has been postulated, here the text given by Eusebius is almost identical to that of the independent manuscript tradition.[28]

At the most basic level the account explains why Polycarp's mortal remains, despite his miraculous protection by and from the flames, were only such as could be rescued from the fire. Yet within this a number of themes have been woven. Most obvious is the concern about the veneration of the martyr's remains in relation to the worship of Christ. It is certainly possible that the beginnings of a cult of the martyrs is to be traced to near the time of Polycarp's death at Smyrna and from there travelled to Africa where it is next to be found, only developing later in Rome.[29] The elements contributing to its origins are obscure but the possibility of misunderstanding or of confusion with pagan parallels could naturally lead to the careful distinction made here between the worship offered to Jesus as son of God and the love accorded to the martyrs.[30] A related but separate problem is tackled in the account of the persecution at Lyons and Vienne where the 'martyrs' are described as deliberately avoiding that term, reserving it for Christ alone (Eusebius, *H.E.* V.2.1–4). Both accounts also reflect concerns related if not to Montanism itself then to the piety which gave birth to it – thus *M. Poly.*

rejects deliberately seeking martyrdom (4).[31] This means that
the chapter is in fact reflecting an inner-Christian debate
under the guise of objections made by Jews or pagans. It is
after all improbable that either group would fear that or be
worried whether Christians desert Jesus in favour of Polycarp.[32]
The grammatical unevenness may suggest that this issue has
been introduced by a later editor, although the general agreement of Eusebius indicates that any redaction was early.

A second element in the story is the role played by Nicetas,
who requests the magistrate that the body not be surrendered.
His sister, Alce, should probably be identified with the Alce who
receives a special greeting in Ignatius's letters to the church at
Smyrna (13.2) and to Polycarp (8.3); although this could be
interpreted as evidence of later (redactional) hagiographical
personal interest,[33] it is more likely to be an authentic reminiscence, for a redactor would hardly celebrate that a renowned
Christian of the church had a brother who could be suborned
by the devil! That it is Nicetas and not his ominously named, as
explicitly pointed out in 6.2, and presumably more influential
son, the police chief Herod, who is set up by the devil also points
to genuine tradition. However, when we are reminded for the
second time (cf. 8.2) that he is the father of Herod, this is not
just for biographical interest, nor evidence that one passage or
the other is redactional, but recalls us to the role played by Herod
in the (Lukan) passion narrative. The highlighting of the role
of Herod appears to be a characteristic of Asia Minor tradition
and is also found in Melito (*Peri Pascha* §93, l. 686).[34] That a
'Herod', even if not a Jew, should be closely related to the activity of the Jews should against this background cause no surprise.
An important question is whether this relationship has any historical base.

Finally we come to the role of the Jews themselves. Here they
are no longer one group within the crowd but initiators of the
attempt to thwart the influence of Polycarp even after his death.
Their activity is even parallel to, or perhaps the earthly counterpart of, that of the 'evil one who opposes the race of the righteous'; just as he 'incited' (ὑπέβαλεν) Nicetas, so they too are all
the while **inciting** (ὑποβαλλόντων) these things. This connection
is lost in Eusebius's account where 'certain [unidentified] people' incited Nicetas and in giving their fears were themselves

incited by the Jews, but the use of the same verb favours its originality.[35] That it is the Jews and not the earthly authorities carrying out the persecution who are the agents of the devil, although here more implicit than explicit, is an important step. In the New Testament it is Judas who is suborned by Satan (Luke 22.3; John 13.2, 27), although John can speak of the Jews as stemming from their father the devil who was 'a murderer from the beginning' (8.44); particularly significant is the letter to the church at Smyrna in Revelation 2.8–11 which speaks of the slanders 'of those who call themselves Jews but are not, being rather the synagogue of Satan' (v. 9), and in the next verse warns of the suffering to come when the 'devil' (διάβολος, as in *M. Poly.* 3.1) will cast some of them into prison. Not only does this raise the question of the historical relation between Jews and Christians in Smyrna, but also that of the theological tradition of language and models.

There are also biblical echoes in the Jews **keeping watch** as the Christians seek to take the body of Polycarp from the fire. The same verb (τηρέω) is used in Matthew 28.4 of the guards posted by the tomb of Jesus lest 'his disciples steal him and say to the people, "He is risen from the dead", and the final deception is greater than the initial one' (Matt. 27.64). It may be this parallel which has facilitated a motive for the Jews which historically seems highly improbable: the death of Polycarp 'according to the Gospel' imitates that of his master even beyond death.[36] However, we shall suggest below that contemporary polemical concerns are also at play.

When the centurion[37] finally takes action and publicly burns the body of Polycarp, it is in response to the visible **contentiousness** of the Jews. Here the confusions of chapter 17 and in particular the role of Nicetas are ignored, and the more straightforward explanation inspires less suspicion of editorial activity.[38] The term 'contentiousness' (φιλονεικία) suggests elements of rivalry and ambition, and as it led to immediate action we may suspect that more than verbal complaints were involved. The same word is used by Josephus (*B.J.* II.13.7 [267]) of the conflict between the Greeks and Jews at Caesarea in 66 CE and would fit the sort of internal city rivalries which were not uncommon at the time. This means that while the description serves the author's theological purposes, granted a historical nucleus to the whole narrative, it could also carry historical plausibility. If, then, the opposition of the Jews was a foundational element in the explanation of why Polycarp's body was, despite its earlier miraculous protection, burnt, the references to the Jews in chapter 17 cannot be totally rejected as later reworking.[39] As just noted, *in the author's presentation* their unjustifiable hostility and rivalry extends even beyond the death of the martyr, ensuring, as they think, its finality. However, their rivalry is misplaced and thwarted; the Christians' love of the martyrs and veneration of their memory and example is undiminished and an annual celebration is eagerly anticipated. At the same time, the part played by elements of rivalry and competitiveness between Jewish and Christian groups, and the accompanying threat of disorder, cannot be dismissed as purely the theological creation of the author.

The question of theological interpretation and historical events in *M. Poly.*, as in so many early Christian texts, is complicated by the possibility of layers of subsequent reworking in the light of ongoing concerns. Theories of detectable stages of literary redaction of the text extending beyond the date of Eusebius's inclusion of an account in his church history have largely failed to win wide support. In particular the imitation of Jesus in his passion, which according to Campenhausen's foundational argument belongs to a later redaction of the account, has been shown to be integral to it as a whole and not foreign to its late second-century date.[40] Nevertheless, the hostile role of the Jews, which even on Campenhausen's presentation belongs to the early stage, cannot be explained by the imitation theme alone. In fact, as we shall see, the imitation theme leads to a highlighting of certain events or individuals rather than to their creation. Certainly, biblical images and language have been used to paint the picture of the Jews; moreover, that picture fits into a tradition of hostility that already appears in the New Testament period and continues long after. At the same time the immediate and more general historical circumstances of relations between the Jewish community and the Christians undoubtedly played a crucial role. Only so can we explain the rarity of Jewish presence in other pre-Decian authentic martyr acts.[41] Since even in *M. Poly.* the Jews are not (except at the end) presented as instigating action, why was there felt a need to draw attention to them in particular?

The recognition of the theological significance of the presentation of the Jewish role in the martyrdom of Polycarp, whether or not it is helpfully labelled 'antisemitic', demands rather than replaces a historical interpretation.

Jewish Framework and Jewish Influence

Alongside its hostility to the Jews *M. Poly.* betrays considerable influence of Jewish ideas and language, including but going beyond its 'biblicism'.[42] This need cause no surprise: the same phenomenon can be found many times over in early Christian literature from the Gospels of John and Matthew onwards. At certain points, however, the contacts are far more specific than can be assigned to 'tradition' or 'thought-world', and demand some explanation within the historical setting of the document.

a) *The 'Great Sabbath' and the Passover*

The most striking and probably the most intractable of these 'links' is the dating of Polycarp's martyrdom to a 'great sabbath' (σαββάτος μεγάλος), a dating where the Jewish resonances are hard to ignore and as hard to explain.

This dating is given twice, in two very different contexts, both of which provoke problems of interpretation. The first occurs during the narrative describing Polycarp's arrest: having been found at his refuge outside the city itself, he is given time to pray 'for everyone he had ever encountered, small and great, notable and ignoble, and for the whole catholic church throughout the world'. Having ceased his prayer, 'the hour having come for him to leave, sitting him on a donkey, they led him into the city, *it being a great sabbath*' (8.1). There he is met by the eirenarch Herod, with his father Nicetas, who together try to persuade him to sacrifice to Caesar as Lord. Only after they fail in this is he brought, or rather he makes his own way with determination, into the stadium which is already filled with a tumultuous and very noisy crowd (8.3).

The contribution made by the reference to the great sabbath is not immediately clear. Since the encounter with Nicetas and Herod separates it from the description of the crowded stadium it cannot merely explain why so many people were at leisure to respond to the rumour of Polycarp's arrest which they had been demanding a short time before. The long sentence which it closes, as a genitive absolute, is loaded with deeper significance. First and most elaborately, there is Polycarp's comprehensive and universal prayerful concern not merely for the church of which he is bishop but for the whole universal church, and indeed not merely for the church but for all people of whatever status with whom he has had contact. If there are biblical echoes they are not of Jesus's prayer in Gethsemane but of the so-called 'high priestly' prayer in John 17. As there, the effect is to stress that Polycarp, like Jesus, is not the victim of events but is in control both of them and of himself. Indeed, he is not led passively into the city until he has ceased his prayer and 'the hour has come'. Here too Johannine echoes are hard to avoid, particularly the words with which Jesus opens that prayer, 'Father, the hour has come, glorify your son' (John 17.1), but also the theme which runs throughout the Fourth Gospel that Jesus's hour is only fully come in his death; we should perhaps think too of John 13.1, 'Before the feast of Passover, Jesus, knowing that his hour had come to go from this world to the father, having loved his own who were in the world, loved them to the end.'

While Polycarp's entry into the city on a donkey is not improbable as a historical detail, it is hard to exclude any echo of Jesus's entry into the city of Jerusalem on a donkey, although this was several days before his arrest and crucifixion. Any allusion would be closer in wording to Matthew's version (21.2–11) where the same word for the donkey is used (ὄνος),[43] although in John's account (John 12.12–16) we are less aware of the time gap which separates the entry from the arrest and trial. Moreover, just as Polycarp is encouraged by 'a voice from heaven' as he enters the stadium, no one seeing the speaker but the Christians present hearing it (9.1), so Jesus too was answered by 'a voice from heaven', the words of which the evangelist can report although to the crowd it seemed to be but a clap of thunder (John 12.28–29).

Against this background it is natural to look for a symbolical, 'Gospel' significance in the mention of 'a great sabbath', without necessarily denying its historical reference. However, whereas the evangelists differ as to the dating of Jesus's death they are all agreed that it took place not on the sabbath but on the preceding day. John's account of the entry into Jerusalem opens with a reference to the crowds who have come 'for the feast'; during the trial, we are told, the Jews avoided defilement from entering the praetorium 'so that they might eat the Passover', and the day on which Jesus was crucified was 'the preparation (παρασκευή) of the Passover' (John 18.28; 19.14). The following day, the sabbath, in preparation for which the bodies of the victims had to be removed from the cross, was 'great' (μεγάλη ἡ ἡμέρα ἐκείνου τοῦ σαββάτου: John 19.31), but this is because, according to John's dating, it was also the Passover.[44] However, since the party coming to arrest Polycarp arrived 'on the preparation' (i.e. Friday) (τῇ παρασκευῇ: 7.1),[45] a conscious attempt to draw parallels with the passion of Jesus even where the actual historical details were somewhat recalcitrant seems likely.

Other, contemporary, parallels suggest *M. Poly.* may reflect a wider Asia Minor tradition: Melito of Sardis in his *Peri Pascha* accuses the Jews of having 'killed your lord on the great feast' (ἐν τῇ μεγάλῃ ἑορτῇ: *Peri Pascha* §79, l. 565), probably meaning the Passover in accordance with the Johannine dating of Jesus's death on 14 Nisan,[46] while Apollinarius opposes those who, adopting the Synoptic dating, fix Jesus's death on 'the great day of Unleavened Bread'.[47] Within such a tradition Jesus's death could be seen as falling on 'the great day' according to the Jewish calendar – although this would still not be a sabbath.

However, the 'imitation of Christ' does not explain the second reference to Polycarp's martyrdom 'on a great sabbath'. In chapter 21, possibly an appendix but probably not a late one,[48] Polycarp's martyrdom is dated by the Asiatic and Roman calendars as the second day of Xanthikos, seven days before the Kalends of March, and as on a great sabbath and at the eighth hour. It is further fixed by the personnel involved, Herod who arrested him (cf. 6.2; 8.2), the high priest Philip from Tralles, who as Asiarch refused to make room for Polycarp to be 'fed' to the lions (12.2), and the proconsul, who is only named at this point as Statius Quadratus. The references to Philip of Tralles and to Statius Quadratus, which can be approximately fixed, demand that the dating be taken seriously and that the 'great sabbath' be given more than a 'theological' explanation.

Although the problem of the precise dating of the martyrdom of Polycarp and in particular of the 'great sabbath' appears so far to have defied any totally satisfactory resolution, its importance in a number of proposed solutions for the question of Jewish–Christian relationships means some exploration of these is unavoidable. We shall for the moment ignore Eusebius, who dates the martyrdom to the time of Marcus Aurelius, and those scholars who have also rejected the evidence of this paragraph.[49] The accuracy of the names is more probably genuine tradition than the work of a later, erudite, author who added a semblance of historical veracity from his knowledge of local inscriptions,[50] while the identification of Philip as Asiarch in 12.2 but as high priest here in 21 parallels other individuals who are separately recorded with each title, and at the very least conforms to the confusion surrounding the relationship between them and their attendant duties which continues to bedevil modern scholarship.[51] More generally, the language of the chapter and the contrast between the secular rulers and Jesus Christ's eternal kingship can be seen as characteristic of a second-century date and as balancing the image of the churches as sojourning in the opening prescript.[52]

The first two dates by month point, unless it was a leap year which could account for a day's variation, to 23 February, a date also supported by the liturgical tradition. Philip of Tralles is known as Asiarch in 149 CE, although there is some dispute as to whether and for how long he would continue to hold that title or the related(?) one of high priest.[53] The proconsulship of Statius Quadratus is also disputed, although a date around 156/7 CE seems possible if he is correctly identified as the consul of 142 CE.[54] All this points to the mid/late 150s, and any further precision is to be gained by determining in which year 23 February fell on a Saturday, and, for our purposes, a Saturday of some significance for at least one of the groups involved, Jews, pagans or Christians.

The most natural assumption must be that the reference is to the Jewish sabbath.[55] A condemnatory gibe at the Jews' use of the sabbath – in the same mood as that in which Jesus asks those who condemn his sabbath healing and go on secretly to plot to kill him, whether it is lawful on the sabbath to do good or harm, to save life or kill (Mark 3.1–6) – is probably too subtle and does not explain the 'great'. In this case, in the light both of the imitation theme and of the actual language,[56] the Jewish Passover or (?and) the Christian Easter must have first claim for consideration. Leaving aside any calculation as to in which year 23 February or thereabouts was both a Saturday and a full moon, an obvious objection will be that 23 February is impossibly early for Passover, a spring festival, unless the Jews, followed by the Christians, of Smyrna followed a highly idiosyncratic calendar which made so early a Passover possible.

That this must have been the case could, as we have seen, be supported by the language, by the parallels in the other Asia Minor witnesses, Melito and Apollinarius, and by the echoes of the New Testament, all of which point to a Passover reference. Pointing to the same association is the fact that Polycarp was remembered as an outstanding advocate of the Quartodeciman practice, according to which it was the Jewish Passover, 14/15 Nisan, rather than Easter Sunday which provided the focus of the Christian Paschal celebrations.[57] Not only did the church which wrote the account of his martyrdom follow Quartodeciman practice,[58] but a generation later Polycrates could appeal to the 'martyrs' of Asia Minor who supported this position, including Polycarp, perhaps implying a link between the testimony of their martyrdom and the dating (Eusebius, *H.E.* V.24.4).[59]

Yet could the Jewish Passover fall so early in Smyrna? In the century following the destruction of the Jerusalem Temple in 70 CE and before the re-establishment of a central, recognised authority at Usha, the communities of the Diaspora were left very much on their own to determine matters of calendar. It would be a natural solution for them to adopt the local spring month as a starting-point. In Syria the closest equivalent to the Jewish month Nisan was the month Xanthikos, and Josephus identifies the two in his account of the Passover (*Ant.* III.10.5 [248]);[60] the Jews of Smyrna, it is argued, have simply adopted the month of the same name although according to the Asian calendar it fell considerably earlier. Lacking independent guidelines and not thinking to question the Jewish computations, the Christians followed their dating even though it entailed Easter falling well before the spring equinox.[61]

The historical significance of this view, if correct, is obvious, both for our understanding of the Jewish communities in Asia

Minor and for the relationships between them and Christianity. Without the central authority of the Temple which had earlier ensured that the streams of pilgrims to Jerusalem knew when Passover fell, the Jews of Smyrna maintained the celebration of Passover and Unleavened Bread,[62] but devised their own method of determining its date. The Christians were not so hostile to or distant from the Jewish community that they could not borrow their calendar.

This solution is important because it reaffirms the theological dimensions of the issue. It is, however, open to a number of objections. While it seems true that the rabbinic authorities in Palestine exercised very little control over the diaspora Jewish communities, the one area where we would expect a degree of voluntary acceptance of guidance would be in matters relating to the calendar. Even without the possibility of pilgrimage to Jerusalem, we should envisage sufficient contact between Jewish communities for radical divergence soon to become self-evident and a matter of concern. In fact the little evidence we do have of letters sent out from Jamnia to the Diaspora concerns matters of calendar.[63] Moreover, unless all Jews, followed by all Christians, observed this calendar we would expect to find considerably more polemic about the disunity between Christian churches thus occasioned than the questions of permissible degrees of variety in practice which are a feature of the Quartodeciman debate.

If the date is impossibly early for Passover an alternative Jewish festival must be found, the most obvious one being Purim. This has been a popular solution[64] and would fit later evidence that Purim could become the occasion of anti-Christian feeling.[65] However, such evidence mostly post-dates the establishment of Christianity under Constantine and is clearest in the Theodosian legislation of 408 CE forbidding Jews setting fire to Aman or mocking the form and shape of the cross.[66] The story that when R. Meir visited Asia (Minor) he found no copy of Esther may even suggest that the Jews of Asia Minor did not celebrate Purim, perhaps in repudiation of its nationalistic mood.[67] We must therefore be cautious in using this as evidence that already in the middle of the second century Jewish hostility against Christians was expressed through the religious calendar. More important, this suggestion does not explain why the dating is given without elaboration; it may explain why the Jews were on holiday, but the sabbath alone could account for this, and, as we have seen, this does not appear to be the function of the reference, not least because it would not explain why the rest of the crowd, the gentiles, were also at leisure.

This last could be solved if the reference had as much a pagan as a Jewish significance: thus a number of scholars have suggested there was a coincidence of a Jewish sabbath or even festival and a pagan one. A fixed holiday would also ensure that Christians would be able to observe the 'memorial' each year (*M. Poly.* 18.3). *M. Pionius* perhaps supports this explanation by explicitly saying that on the same date nearly a century later 'Greeks, Jews and women ... were on holiday because it was a great sabbath' (3.6); however, the fact that this document undoubtedly contains much authentic tradition does not absolve it from the possibility that at some points the narrative is shaped by conscious imitation, and in this case clarification, of *M. Poly.*[68] Given the frequency of potential festivals in the Roman calendar – which means that not every one could have been a holiday[69] – the identification of the pagan festival is bound to be more tentative: the Dionysia, an imperial festival and the Terminalia have all been suggested.[70] While this solution would suggest that pagan rather than Jewish conventions are now the most natural framework for the early Christians, and even that 'sabbath' has lost its polemical associations,[71] it too has its problems: why is there no explicit mention of the celebrations, or advantage taken of the setting to indulge in the usual Christian condemnation of the worship of the Graeco-Roman gods – such as is found in *M. Pionius*?[72] Most important, the first mention of the date in 8.1 then only serves to explain why the stadium was so crowded and falls out of the symbolical significance and parallels which we have discovered in the other details of this long and loaded sentence. When we remember that *M. Poly.* is concerned not only to answer our question 'what happened', but to encourage the reader to hear and respond to the description, we must feel that such solutions are too reductionist.

That a final solution seems as elusive as ever is probably as much a reflection of the complexity of layers of meaning in this text as of its redaction. Yet, despite the historical problems involved, the Passover associations of the term seem most convincing. As well as the NT echoes, those in Melito and Apollinarius, who also come from Asia Minor, are important. So too is the comment preserved in Eusebius, *H.E.* IV.26.3, that Melito's discussion of the Pascha was prompted by the dispute concerning it which arose when Bishop Sagaris was martyred, 'Passover falling about that time'. Both Melito and Sagaris as well as Polycarp are among the martyrs to whom Polycrates appealed in his defence of Quartodeciman practice. The association between Passover, martyrdom and witness to Quartodeciman practice, however difficult to unravel, seems firmly fixed in the tradition. Passover associations with martyrdom, independently of Quartodecimanism, are also well established. In addition to the debate whether 1 Peter with its concern about suffering is a Paschal liturgy or homily, there is the timing of James's martyrdom to the Passover.[73] That there is a literary and theological tradition at work seems highly probable.

A further link with Passover traditions may be found in the presentation of Polycarp as martyr which is achieved more by the imagery used than by any explicit reflection on the theme.[74] The description in 14.1 of the bound (προσδέθεις) Polycarp – he had refused the nails – as 'a splendid ram (κριὸς ἐπίσημος) from a great flock for sacrifice (προσφορά), prepared as a burnt offering (ὁλοκαύτωμα) acceptable to God' is particularly notable. In his prayer which follows, and which probably shows the influence of contemporary Christian liturgical and eucharistic language,[75] Polycarp speaks of his death as a sacrifice, although using different terms: 'the martyrs ... among whom may I be received before you today in a rich and acceptable sacrifice (θυσία)' (14.2). The use of sacrificial imagery in the contexts of suffering and martyrdom is found widely in both Jewish and Christian literature before Polycarp.[76] The absence here of any hint of atoning efficacy means that the apparent allusion to the 'ram for a burnt offering (κριὸς εἰς ὁλοκαύτωμα)' in Leviticus 16.3, 5; 9.2 is only one of language and not of context. A more striking parallel comes in surviving fragments by Melito of Sardis which draw parallels between the story of Isaac in Genesis 22 and the death of Jesus, under the influence too of Isa. 53 – a theme we shall explore in fuller detail later. Without adopting any consistent typology, Melito likens Jesus both to Isaac and to the ram which was sacrificed in his place.[77] Jesus was 'bound like the ram ... and as a sheep led to the slaughter (Isaiah 53.7)'; as the ram freed Isaac so the Lord 'slain saved us, bound freed us and sacrificed redeemed us'.[78] Isaac carried the wood on his shoulders (Gen. 22.6), was himself bound (Gen. 22.9) like the ram and yet remained silent, opening not his mouth (Isa. 53.7);[79] he feared neither sword nor fire nor suffering, and was offered 'in the middle' bound like the ram. So he both was a 'type' of Christ, and yet was not – for Christ suffered, Isaac did not (Frag.9). That *M. Poly.* and Melito share a common tradition of exegesis of Genesis 22 is suggested by the language of the **bound ram**, particularly the word 'bound' which, although not that used in Genesis 22 LXX, Melito also uses in the *Peri Pascha* itself where he says that Jesus was 'bound in Isaac' (§69. l. 482).[80] This may lead us to see other allusions to the Genesis 22 tradition, in Polycarp's silence before Herod and Nicetas (8.2, possibly also an echo of Mark 14.61), in his lack of fear of the fire (11.2; 13.3), in the use of the sword to kill him (16.1), and in his placing 'in the middle' where he was burnt (18.1) – all themes in Melito's exegesis of the story. Although not developed in the surviving fragments of Melito, the ram was offered (as had been intended for Isaac) as a burnt offering (ὁλοκάρπωσις) (Gen. 22.13, cf. 3, 7, 8), just as Polycarp is presented as a burnt offering acceptable to God (14.1).[81]

As we shall see, in these fragments, and in less detail in the *Peri Pascha* itself, Melito probably reflects the use of the Isaac story within Jewish–Christian interaction or polemic. The story of Isaac in Genesis 22 had been developed by the beginning of the second century to portray him as going willingly to his death – the prototype of the martyr;[82] at what point his offering was also seen as effecting atonement is a matter of intense debate. The most cautious assssment would conclude that rather than the Christian use of the story being adopted from and used in polemic against a fully fledged earlier Jewish doctrine, the two developed in some form of interaction with each other, probably during the second century.[83] At some stage in this development the Isaac story became associated with the Passover, an association we find in the Targums and also in Melito, but again it is a matter of debate how far this was a Jewish response to Christian understanding of the death of Jesus, whose Passover links were fixed, rather than part of its inspiration. It was a dialogue which was to continue; rabbinic elaboration of the tradition becomes increasingly detailed with surprising echoes of Christian ideas, while Christian authors also used the story in their own interests, as when Apollinarius describes Jesus as the true Pascha, 'the bound one, who bound the strong' (cf. Matt. 12.29).[84] Chilton and Davies, whose position is here in part adopted, see this interaction as polemical, a stance inevitably conveyed by the literature. Other evidence of continuing influence on Christians of Jewish exegetical traditions – and why should not the process have also been reversed? – suggests that it may sometimes have been less explicitly so.

Although any hints of an Isaac typology are more implicit than explicit in the case of Polycarp, this itself may suggest the model was a familiar one. They too, particularly in the light of Melito's use of the same typology, reinforce the Passover associations of Polycarp's martyrdom. Any further discussion of their rooting in the Quartodecimanism of both Polycarp and his community and of their possible polemical edge against the Jewish understandings will have to await our analysis of Melito.[85] Yet if, as suggested above, the exegesis of Genesis 22 developed in dynamic interaction between the two groups, and given the other concerns with the Jews in *M. Poly.*, it becomes clear that even if *M. Poly.* is not itself a polemical document, it reflects a setting where polemic or counter-claims were a living part of thought, preaching and liturgy.[86]

b) *Suffering and Martyrdom in Judaism and M. Poly*

The common ground between *M. Poly.* and Jewish literature in the understanding of suffering and martyrdom is much more extensive than the use of the figure of Isaac. The Jewish experience of persecution and suffering, particularly since Antiochus IV's persecution in the early second century BCE, was expressed in distinctive literary accounts and helped shaped a self-understanding, to which the Christians were heirs.[87] The echoes in *M. Poly.* of Jewish martyrological traditions, and in particular of 2 and especially 4 Maccabees, although rarely if ever implying direct quotation or allusion, are stronger than their common biblical roots might explain. They are also far stronger than the echoes often noted in Ignatius's understanding of his forthcoming martyrdom,[88] to which *M. Poly.* is also heir.

General themes are held in common:[89] so Polycarp's death brings an end to the persecution (1.1) as does that of the seven brothers in 4 Maccabees 18.4; the endurance of the martyrs is expressed in their refusal even to groan and in their apparent freedom from pain (*M. Poly.* 2.2; 13.3; 4 Macc. 6.9; 9.21; 11.26), in their joy (*M. Poly.* 12.1; 2 Macc. 7.10; 4 Macc. 9.31; 11.12) and in their despising of death since their eyes were fixed rather on the hope to follow (*M. Poly.* 2.3; 4 Macc. 9.5–9; 13.1; 2 Macc. 7.36) – for them the fire is cool (*M. Poly.* 2.3; 4 Macc.11.26);[90] the authorities urge the martyrs to take heed of their youth or their advanced age as appropriate (*M. Poly.* 3.1; 9.2; 4 Macc. 5.12, 33; 8.10, 20); however, they refuse to anul, by a single act, a lifetime of faithful living (*M. Poly.* 9.3; 2 Macc. 6.24–28; 4 Macc. 5.31–38; 6.17–23); the martyr is granted a final epiphany or vision (*M. Poly.* 5.2; *M. Isa.* 5.7–16). There are also closer parallels of language and technique: the rhetorical question, 'who would not be amazed' at the nobility of the martyrs (*M. Poly.* 2.2; 4 Macc. 17.16); the imagery of the athlete or combatant with their manifest nobility of character, contending and winning the prize (or crown) in a contest which is part of the contest between God and the devil (*M. Poly.* 3.1; 17.1; 18.3; 4 Macc. 11.20; 16.14, 16; 17.12–15);[91] the final prayer with its use of sacrificial language, in which the martyr acknowledges God as creator as the foundation of his hope (*M. Poly.* 14; 2 Macc. 7.23, 28; 4 Macc. 6.27–30; Dan. 3.39–40); here Polycarp recalls the 'noble' Eleazar who also reached old age after a life 'adorned' with virtue, but whose prayer to God as creator and Father prompted the divine intervention which brought confusion and conversion upon the enemy (3 Macc. 6).[92]

Although 4 Maccabees offers the most parallels, there are also significant differences which make it difficult to argue for any literary dependence, particularly the absence from *M. Poly.* of the Stoic themes fundamental to 4 Maccabees of the triumph of reason and of victory over, and of distance from the body. Yet the common material and themes are so extensive and broadly based as to suggest more than parallel but separate developments from a shared Jewish and biblical base. Thus the development of athletic and combatant imagery marks a distinctive response to the ideals and values of contemporary society precisely in a period when games were acquiring an increased significance:[93] those ideals are being adopted and re-evaluated, even reversed, neutralising mockery of a religion that led to the death of its adherents.[94] Even on a late dating of 4 Maccabees it seems improbable that it could be influenced by Christian martyr acts or understandings of martyrdom known to us.[95] Rather we should think of a common tradition base but also of a shared thought world, perhaps in the same geographical area.[96] Given a range of shared presuppositions, some of its common expression may be only expected – for example, the despising of death in the light of future hope. The development of a self-understanding, to which we shall return, might be another example. Yet other common elements in the telling of the story point to a process similar to that in the interpretation of the story of Isaac in Genesis 22: an interpretation of martyrdom and a way of describing the events – perhaps even the impetus to describe the events focused on particular individuals – evolving in dynamic interaction of claims and counter-claims by Christians and Jews.

It is perhaps against this background that the Jews are credited with the fear that the Christians would turn to reverence Polycarp, abandoning Jesus 'who suffered for the salvation of the whole world of the saved, blameless for sinners'. Although they have kept themselves pure, the Maccabean martyrs acknowledge that they suffer on account of their own sins (2 Macc. 7.32, 40); yet they also hope that by their death God will forgive the sins of the nation (2 Macc. 6.12–17; 4 Macc. 6.28–29; 17.20–22). The sacrificial language of Polycarp's final prayer is not developed in the direction of atonement, neither does he at this point intercede for others; however, he has done so at earlier stages (5.1; 8.1), and the description of his 'anniversary' celebration as a 'memorial' (μνήμη) may suggest that he and other Christian martyrs were already being seen as intercessors.[97] Such intercession is an important feature of the Maccabean accounts where, in virtue of the coming martyrdom, those who have committed themselves totally are able to intercede for the sins of the nation (2 Macc. 7.37f.).[98] There may be an undercurrent of criticism against a perceived Jewish evaluation of their martyrs' deaths, appropriately expressed by dismissing the same evaluation as attributed to the Christians by the Jews; a certain caution about a parallel development in Christian attitudes (above, pp. 66–7) would sharpen rather than blunt the argument. However, this interaction between Jewish and Christian understandings – which would also involve development on the Jewish side under Christian influence – has not taken place in a vacuum but in the context of living within the Graeco-Roman city. Both Jewish and Christian attitudes to martyrdom are influenced by ideals of voluntary death in Cynic–Stoic philosophy and possibly by Roman ideas of *devotio* and of death for the fatherland;[99] both, as we have seen, also explicitly set themselves up in competition with the city's values focused in the stadium and amphitheatre. The city context is reinforced by Lucian's account of Peregrinus's self-immolation which shares some common motifs, although whether this is deliberate is less certain; the spectators of that event are not spared the foul smell of burning flesh (*Pereg.* 37), but they too are keen to find some 'relic' of the event, and are even ready to believe the apparition of a bird, a vulture, rising from the burning corpse (39, 40), as perhaps also accompanied the flow of blood from Polycarp's side (*M. Poly.* 16.1).[100]

Martyrdom and Self-definition

Both martyrdom itself and the account of martyrdom have an inherent relationship with group identity and self-definition.[101] Thus it can be said both for the martyr and for the observers that martyrdom 'is an ultimate statement of commitment to the group and what the group represents'.[102] The martyrdom account then continues to have this function even when persecution or the possibility of martyrdom is not an ever-present possibility.

The telling of the story of a martyrdom inevitably leads to setting the martyr over against those who oppose him or her. In *M. Poly.*, as in all the martyr acts, however, it is not only the individual who stands alone, attacked for what s/he has taught, as in the deaths of Jesus, Stephen or James. The confession 'I am a Christian' (10.1; 12.1) binds the martyr with all Christians everywhere; Polycarp dies not for his beliefs alone or because of his refusal to sacrifice to Caesar, but because he makes and sustains that confession. Whatever the historical problems of the legal base for persecution, in terms of the telling of the story this is the key to its understanding and the grounds for its sharing with 'all the sojourners of the holy and catholic church everywhere' (1.1). It is all the more important because the churches are 'sojourning' – they are joined together by the fact that they are only temporarily identified with the place where they are to be found. This awareness of the church in every place infuses the story at the same time as its, perhaps innovatory, focusing on the witness of one named individual: 1.1; 5.2; 8.1; 16.2; 19.2; 20.1.[103] Although not all may have to die, Polycarp's death is an election by the Lord 'from among his own slaves' (20.1).

As we have seen, the miraculous quenching of the flames by the blood from Polycarp's body serves to witness to the crowds 'the distinction between unbelievers and the elect' (16.1). Here the elect must be all Christians, for whom Polycarp is a representative; they are, as it were, defined by his confession, martyrdom and experience of divine support. Opposed to them are **the unbelievers**; unlike the term 'the lawless men' (ἄνομοι) used in 9.2 and immediately before in 16.1 of those who demand the fatal sword-thrust, this is an undifferentiated term including Jews and pagans alike. There is a tension within *M. Poly.* here; when the author needs a polemic against the Jews, he differentiates between the Christians and the pagans and the Jews, although the pagans have no real identity as a third group and there is no independent polemic against their beliefs or behaviour. However, although, at the crucial moment of Polycarp's confession of himself as a Christian, the crowd separates out into 'Jews and gentiles' (12.1–2), the more fundamental model is of Christianity against 'the rest'.[104]

Despite the use of terms like 'lawless', 'unbelievers', 'elect', these make little contribution to the definition of Christianity over against the other group(s). No use is made of the opportunity for characterisation and polemic – instead Polycarp considers the crowd not worthy of any apologetics (10.2). However, it is precisely with Christian apologetics that *M. Poly.* shares some common terminology of self-definition.[105] Just as the quenching of the fire led to amazement by the whole mob at the distinction between unbelievers and the elect, so Germanicus's 'encouragement' of the wild animal to help him leave this life leads the whole crowd to amazement at 'the nobility of the God-loving and God-fearing race of Christians' (3.2). The language of **race** (γένος) occurs again in Polycarp's prayer where he addresses God as 'God of angels and powers and all creation and the whole race of the righteous who live before you' (14.1),[106] and once more in 17.1 where the devil is described as the one who 'opposes the race of the righteous'. The description of Christianity as a race does not feature in the earlier Apostolic Fathers but does become part of Christian self-perception in the second century. The *Epistle to Diognetus* describes Christianity as a 'new race or custom'; as we shall see, the *Apology* of Aristides, which predates *M. Poly.*, divides the world into three or four races (2.1),[107] of whom the race of Christians are particularly blessed (17.2). The use of 'race' (γένος) as a term of opprobrium by the opponents of Christianity (Tertullian, *Scorp.* 10) and with confidence by its defenders suggests that it developed in the context of attack and persecution.[108]

The description of Christians as 'God-fearing' or 'righteous' belongs in a similar context; again, 'God-fearing' is characteristic of the apologetic literature, of Aristides, Quadratus and Melito, and of other authors.[109] 'Fear of God' (θεοσέβεια) would have been particularly effective against the common charge of impiety (ἀσέβεια) – which may have been laid against Polycarp.[110] Yet it also appears in a polemic denying the epithet to the Jews: the *Epistle to Diognetus*, which takes as its starting-point Diognetus's enthusiasm to learn more about the 'religion [*fear of God*] of the Christians' (1.1), firmly rejects Jewish claims to 'fear of God', reserving it for the Christians alone (3.1, 3; 4.5, 6; 6.4). In Justin, too, the term encompasses in a single word the Christian religion to which pagans turn from idolatry but which can also be affirmed against Jewish counter-claims (*Dial.* 92.3; 110.2; 118.3 etc.).[111]

It is not surprising to find a similar development of language in Jewish literature in the same period. The theme of the Jewish people as a 'nation' (ἔθνος) or race (γένος) is particularly clearly developed in the Maccabean literature. Their suffering and their celebration of deliverance is as a nation (2 Macc. 10.8; 11.25, 27; 4 Macc. 4.19) or race (2 Macc. 6.12; 12.31; 14.8); in particular the martyrs pray on behalf of the whole race who, through their death, will soon experience the mercy of God (2 Macc. 7.16, 37, 38).[112] Similarly, Judith's prayer – perhaps consciously echoed by Polycarp – acknowledges God's protection of 'the race of Israel' (9.14),[113] and implies a contrast with all the other nations who give way to the oppressor's demands.[114] Here too the claim to be God-fearing is a proud claim, as too is that to be righteous. For 4 Maccabees the 'fear of God' is that for which the martyrs suffer and which in them conquers and wins a crown of victory (4 Macc. 7.22; 17.15).[115] In a less obviously polemical setting the *Sybilline Oracles* speak of the Jews as a 'race of the most righteous' or 'pious men' (III.219; 573; cf. IV.135–6).[116]

The same setting prompted the creation of the term 'Judaism' (ἰουδαϊσμος) as encompassing the life and beliefs for which the battle was fought: 2 Maccabees 2.21 includes in its brief 'the appearances which came from heaven to those who fought bravely on behalf of Judaism' (cf. 8.1; 14.38; 4 Macc. 4.26).[117] Perhaps inevitably, bound up with the threat of martyrdom, there developed an understanding of Judaism and of the Jewish people set over against a hostile world which was bent on its destruction. Judaism demanded a loyalty of belief and life that could lead to death itself and set the Jewish people apart from all other peoples. It provided a citizenship or city life of its own, even when circumstances gave this no political reality. Language drawn from the city is common: the Jewish way of life is a 'citizenship' (πολιτεία; πολιτεύεσθαι) which is defined by its opposition to alien, or Greek, practices (2 Macc. 4.11; 8.17; 4 Macc. 5.16; 8.7; 17.9).[118] When Razis, who 'risked body and soul for Judaism' and finally committed suicide, is named 'father of the Jews' (2 Macc. 14.37), or when the martyrs are called 'father' or 'mother' (4 Macc. 7.1, 9; 15.29), this is a civic not a familial title, echoing the Roman title 'father of the Roman people' or, more immediately, the epithet given the emperor which would have been familiar from decrees and inscriptions, including some at Smyrna, in this period, 'father of the fatherland'.[119]

M. Poly. reflects a similar self-understanding. Christians too are a 'race'; Polycarp can look back on a lifelong faithful 'citizenship' (13.2; 17.1),[120] and is rightly called 'the father of the Christians' (12.2) by the crowd of pagans and Jews. Brought before the proconsul, he is urged to swear by the Fortune of the Emperor; this he refuses to do, for he is a Christian, and if the proconsul wants to understand what that means he will teach him 'the message of Christianity' (Χριστιανίσμος) (10.1). In the context of refusal to swear by the emperor's 'fortune', this clearly means a pattern of belief and practice and is that for which Polycarp will die. Since the term only previously occurs in Ignatius's letters, perhaps coined, as we have seen, by himself, that was probably its source for *M. Poly.* For Ignatius it is characterised by an explicit contrast with 'Judaism' (*Magn.* 10.1, 3; *Philad.* 6.1), but also by anticipated suffering and martyrdom (*Rom.* 3.3). The epithet 'Christian', so important for *M. Poly.*, is also central to Ignatius's self-identity of suffering, alone of the Apostolic Fathers.[121] Inevitably, that 'name' is equally important for the other martyr acts and for the apologists who both claim it as a self-designation and defend it against outsiders' use of it as a basis for attack.[122]

In the context of persecution the Christians are defining themselves in a parallel fashion to the Jews. The degree of Jewish influence in this is not explicit but can hardly be ignored. Some of it is already well established in Christian thought before Polycarp – the language of citizenship; but some suggests continuing opportunities for such influence and, indeed, that the influence moved in both directions. Yet even where there was mutual influence, the process of self-definition involved inevitably meant a distancing: the Jews were numbered among the opposition and so in antagonism to them. In what ways was this 'theological' process acted out on the 'historical' stage?

The Historical Setting

Despite the uncertainties about its dating of the death of Polycarp, *M. Poly.* undoubtedly throws valuable light on the situation of the Christians in one city of Asia Minor and on their relations with other members of that city, particularly the Jews. These can be briefly sketched and laid alongside our other information.

Little can be gathered about the size and organisation of the Christian community at Smyrna. Despite the vivid language describing the attacks of the devil and the nobility of the martyrs, only twelve martyrs, including those from the neighbouring town of Philadelphia, are celebrated (19.1) – a number which may be symbolic but hardly a substantial reduction on the true numbers. That the devil did not 'prevail over all' (3.1) has been taken as evidence that a considerably larger number than the solitary Quintus of ch. 4 gave way under persecution and apostasised.[123] This is probably to push the language too hard – it is just as probable that the crowd's amazement at the nobility of the 'race of Christians' (3.2) points to a larger number of martyrs than Germanicus, who alone is named at this point.[124] However, clearly the majority of the church were not implicated, for they were able to be present at the proceedings, to report what had happened and to anticipate future celebration of Polycarp's death.

Although a crucial step is being taken here in the development of Christian attitudes to the martyrs, and particularly of a cult involving their intercession, and, although the Jewish sources of that cult are often argued,[125] it would be hazardous to assume that the Jewish presence at Smyrna provides the necessary link in this process. In contrast to such an innovatory spirit, there appears to be a more 'primitive' and conservative structure of church life. Polycarp is indeed bishop of the church in Smyrna (16.2), but it is more fundamental that he is 'apostolic and prophetic teacher' (διδάσκαλος ἀποστολικὸς καὶ προφητικός: 16.2; cf. 19.1; 12.2). Although prophetic charisma is often associated with the martyr in both Jewish and Christian sources,[126] and the only supportive evidence in the narrative itself is the fulfilment of Polycarp's vision as to the manner of his death (5.2; 12.3), it is likely that both epithets, apostolic and prophetic, acknowledge Polycarp's status as one whose discipleship went back to the earliest period of the church – which need not mean that he knew personally any of the Apostles – and whose personal authority was accepted far outside the church of Smyrna.

It is not only within Christian circles that Polycarp was treated with such respect. Admittedly the theme of the Roman authorities' concern to offer the Christians every opportunity to recant without rushing them to the lions, in contrast to the hostility of the crowd, is a regular one in the martyr acts and may reflect apologetics as well as historical reality. However, as a mark of his proper respect towards earthly authorities Polycarp is willing to teach the proconsul, but considers the crowds not worthy of any public apologetics (10.2). He has, too, the initial support of the police chief Herod, despite his ominous name and earlier enthusiasm to play a role in Polycarp's arrest (6.2), and of his father Nicetas (8.2). The latter name is not a rare one and may represent a well-known family at Smyrna: in the time of Nero a famous Sophist of Smyrna was so called, and in the oft-quoted subscription list of *c.*124 CE a Claudia, daughter of Nicetas, joins with others in making a subscription of 10,000 denarii.[127] Whether the Nicetas of *M. Poly.* belonged to the same family is a matter of speculation, but in any case the office of 'police chief' (εἰρηνάρχης) was a *leitourgia,* requiring due financial and social status both within the city, which proposed the list of potential names, and in the eyes of the proconsul who made the final selection.[128] Polycarp, therefore, had connections with a leading family, connections which are reinforced by the fact of Nicetas's sister, Alce, being a member of the church.

Whether or not the country dwelling to which Polycarp fled was his own property is not certain (6.1), although he was able to give instructions that food be prepared for the party who came to arrest him. He did possess at least two slaves, one of whom betrayed his new hiding-place; since the latter did so under torture, the comparison with Judas may seem something of an exaggeration (6.2), unless the author shared a perception that slaves owed absolute loyalty to their owner. The overall impression remains that Polycarp himself was of some social standing, with connections among leading families. Of course, this says nothing about the status of the majority of his flock; it does reflect a tradition by which it was those who were heads of a family and owners of a suitable house in which to meet who also held office in the church.[129]

M. Poly. adds little distinctively new to, but does seem to support our existing information concerning the Jewish community at Smyrna. As elsewhere in Asia Minor, the Jewish community was probably well established by this period and had long developed a pattern of living within the city, no doubt with various concessions such as are explicitly witnessed for other cities in the area by Josephus, including freedom to maintain sabbath observance. The few extant inscriptions imply the existence of a well-defined community with a scribe and a 'ruler of the synagogue': the latter, a woman arguably holding the office in her own right and not as wife,[130] instructs that if her grave is usurped fines are to be paid not only, as regularly, to 'the most sacred treasury', but also to the 'nation' (ἔθνος) of the Jews;

assuming that the city treasury is intended, this implies a degree
of integration, which is counter balanced by the interesting use
of 'nation'.[131] Since the grave was for the use of her freedmen
and children born in the house, she must have been a woman of
some wealth. Both her social standing and the respect given her
by the Jewish community are echoed by the inscription from
Kyme, not far north, where a certain Tation was honoured with
a seat of honour and with a golden crown in recognition of her
gift of a sizeable building to the Jews:[132] a very different crown
from that Polycarp received. Perhaps we should compare with
these women the Christian Alce, who also came from a significant family and was well enough known to be separately mentioned.

   The scribe (γραμματεύς), apparently a Roman citizen whose
name Justus is the Latin equivalent of 'Zadok', describes himself as scribe of the 'people (λαός) – a characteristic term for the
Jewish community – in Smyrna'; the phrase parallels the Christian 'the church in X'.[133] A later fourth- or fifth-century inscription records a contribution to the building or decoration of a
fairly elaborate synagogue by Eirenopoios, who is a presbyter
and son of a presbyter by the name of Jacob, and who also
describes himself as 'father of the stemma [?]':[134] the phrase may
be parallel to the 'father of the synagogue', a fairly common
title found not far away at Elaia, which recalls the description of
Polycarp as 'father of the Christians'.[135] The addition of a closing 'shalom' to Eirenopoios's inscription testifies to the revival of
Hebrew in this later period.

   The one discordant note in this picture of a self-conscious
Jewish community continuing over a long period has been seen
in the subscription list described earlier where a further contribution of 10,000 denarii is made by 'the former Jews'. This has
been taken by some as evidence of the apostasy of this group, by
others as witnessing to their change in political status after the
destruction of Jerusalem in 70 CE, or even as referring to pagans
who having once converted to Judaism were now advertising their
return to their previous way of life.[136] More recently it has been
understood simply as indicating that these people had recently
come to Smyrna from Judaea, and, although this is an unusual
use of the term 'Jews' in this period, it remains the most likely
explanation;[137] such movements would not be unlikely in this

period, and probably increased after the Bar Kochba revolt which
came between the date of this inscription and the death of
Polycarp, since the communities of Asia Minor do not appear to
have suffered the upheavals experienced in Palestine or elsewhere in the revolt under Trajan. We can hardly say how such
an influx would have affected relations between Jews and Christians. Perhaps more significantly, these Jews are taking an active
part in city life, making their financial contribution alongside a
number of highly placed individuals, including those who held
various religious offices. On the other hand, their name comes
fairly well down on the list and they alone appear as a group and
not as named individuals. Thus we have a group who are not
isolated from the city and who are willing and able to contribute
a reasonable sum, but who retain their self-identity.

There is nothing in *M. Poly.* to contradict this picture. The
Jews are a defined group – although this is also the result of the
author's own presentation – but are to be found joining with
the gentiles. The confused chapter which leads to the burning
of Polycarp's corpse may suggest that the Jews were in a position
to seek the support of Nicetas, father of the 'police chief' and
perhaps a member of a well-placed family. That together with
the gentiles they can gather wood from the neighbouring workshops and baths may imply a similar situation to that in Sardis
where Jewish and non-Jewish workshops were to be found in
close proximity to each other and to the synagogue.[138]

The question of the 'great sabbath' discussed earlier is rather
more problematic. We have already considered the difficulties
in suggestions that it provides evidence of a distinctive Jewish
calendar involving an unusually early Passover. More particularly, the mere fact that the Jews are represented as attending
the stadium and as carrying wood for the fire on the sabbath has
been seen as pointing either to their 'non-orthodox' character
or to the theory that this 'was in no way an official Jewish manifestation' but 'the action of Jewish "lewd fellows of the baser
sort", such as once persecuted Paul'.[139] Setting aside the literary
and theological tendencies of *M. Poly.* and the public mood which
is envisaged, such claims wrongly impose supposed rabbinic
conceptions of 'orthodoxy' on the diaspora Jewish community
of this period. So, too, it is difficult to see what is entailed in the
denial that their participation was 'official'; certainly it is purely

local, relying on no directives concerning Christianity from outside, nor is there any suggestion that Christians are perceived as a problem relating to Jewish law and rights (ctr. Acts 18.12–17), but in both cases this is only to be expected at this period. Moreover, if Nicetas has been 'persuaded' by the Jews this is most likely to have been through the intervention of leading members of the Jewish community. We cannot say that the Jews who participated in Polycarp's martyrdom were fanatics on the extreme wing of the synagogue, but neither can we say that their participation permits any certain conclusions about the pattern of Torah observance in Smyrna.

More certain is the impression of rivalry between the two groups. Here, this is expressed as the one-sided hostility of the Jews against the Christians in contrast to Polycarp's universal prayerful concern, and also in contrast to the later *M. Pionius*'s invective against the Jews (13–14). The involvement of the Jews here has led to wide generalisations about the active participation of the Jews in the persecution of Christians: 'In the persecutions which were to wrack Asia Minor in the reign of Marcus Aurelius the Jew was often in the background. For nearly another century he continued to stir up trouble wherever he could.'[140] Such assertions can appeal to their prototypes in the writings of the Church Fathers, particularly Tertullian's description of the synagogues as the fountheads of persecution (*Scorp.* 10.90), and Justin's repeated assertion that the gentile persecution of Christians and Jewish cursing of them are inextricably linked (*Dial.* 96.2; 131.2). Yet Justin acknowledges despite himself that to kill Christians is what Jews (and proselytes) would *like* to do but can only effect whenever they get the authority, which was rarely, if ever, the case in the Diaspora (*Dial.* 14.4; 122.2; 133.6), whereas Tertullian is concerned firmly to place the heretic who denies the value of martyrdom alongside all who oppose Christianity – the synagogues where the Apostles were persecuted (past) and the heathen of the present with their cry of a third race against the Christians. Moreover, the theme of Christian imitation of Christ brought Jewish participation in persecution into the theological tradition. As study of the texts has shown, actual evidence of Jewish instigation of persecution ('stirring up trouble') is hardly to be found.[141]

This is separate from the question whether Jews shared in the spreading of calumnies against the Christians, some of which were those earlier levelled against the Jews,[142] something for which conclusive evidence is also lacking. Yet it would not be surprising if rivalry and competition could sometimes lead to outbreaks of disturbance and that such disturbances would provoke measures which led to or were seen as 'persecution'; sometimes Jews and Christians may have been the players in such rivalry. Already Revelation 2.9 warns the church of Smyrna against those who say they are Jews but are not; if indeed the Jewish community is in view here, the author is taking the initiative in denying the self-legitimation of the synagogue. How and whether such language would be transmuted into public behaviour is a matter of guesswork; Revelation may well reflect the response of a powerless minority but its formative ideological power would then be so much the greater. The account of the martyrdom of Pionius under Decius (*c*.250 CE), although in its literary form reflecting later conventions, continues the theme of antagonism against the Jews. Here this takes the form of a strong invective against the Jews by Pionius while in prison and of warnings against being seduced into the synagogues or being persuaded by Jewish accounts of Jesus;[143] since these are characteristic of the later period, they indicate that in *M. Pionius* we do not have only the literary development of a theme found in *M. Poly.*, but a reflection of real continuing tensions with the Jewish community of Smyrna.

In what we have suggested may be a genuine historical reminiscence, the public burning of Polycarp's body by the centurion is in response to the 'contention' of the Jews (18.1), which, if it provoked such a decisive act, was probably not limited to a war of words. Why such public wrangling should be provoked particularly by the Christian desire to have possession of Polycarp's body is not clear. We have seen that the reason given – fear of Christian veneration of the martyr – reflects both inner Christian concerns and anti-Jewish polemic. The late (? fourth-century) and fictional *Life of Polycarp* celebrates the various miracles he performed, in particular those in which he was in competition with and inevitably proved superior to the Jews – in healing the chief magistrate's servant from possession, in quenching a dangerous fire and later in bringing rain to the drought-stricken city (*Vita Poly.* 28). While devoid of all historical value,[144] this may reflect Jewish–Christian relations of that period and the place of magical skill or effective access to the divine within the rivalry between the two groups, in propagandic claim if not in actual reality; the fourth-century Life of Gregory Thaumaturgus similarly records his triumph over Jews and pagans in miracle-working, while John Chrysostom rails against those who turn to the synagogues and their leaders for healing or amulets.[145]

While such a very different framework for understanding religious rivalry is attractive,[146] it would be hazardous to read back such Christian literary anxieties to the time of Polycarp's death and to suppose that possession of the body of the martyr, who was even 'spoken of by the gentiles in every place' (19.1), would be seen by the Jews, even in Christian imagination, as constituting an unfair advantage and posthumous victory for the Christians. The confused state of chs. 17–18 can hardly sustain such a view in the absence of any contemporary supporting evidence. We cannot get far beyond the issue of contention or rivalry, which itself makes good sense in the city context of the time. Responding to the recent outbreak of persecution, Melito invited the Emperor Marcus Aurelius to determine whether the 'workers of this contention' (φιλονεικία) are rightly worthy of death or of release (Eusebius, *H.E.* IV.26.6). Internal wrangling was nothing strange in the cities of Asia Minor – Apollonius of Tyana wrote to Sardis highlighting their internal strife.[147] City disturbance also played its part in the history of Christian persecution from the ejection from Rome under Claudius of certain Jews 'impulsore Chresto', to the rescript of Hadrian to Minucius Fundanus which discourages 'trial' by public outcry.[148] As we have seen, Ignatius's sentence to Rome to die may have been associated with troubles within the church which led to public disorder;[149] we may think too of Clement of Rome's references to the jealousy (ζῆλος) that led to the deaths of Peter and of Paul.[150] The Jews too could look back on rivalries and conflict which had led to outside intervention, from the bitter conflicts at Alexandria which were settled by Claudius's instruction that they be content with what they had and not infiltrate the gymnasium, to the troubles at Antioch over their city rights, including too the fateful 'contention' between Jews and Greeks at Caesarea.[151] Nothing so violent is envisaged for Smyrna, which as part of Asia

Minor appears to have avoided these violent conflicts, yet the issues involved of rights, privilege and influence remained there too.

In exploring the understanding of martyrdom we have seen how the Christian imagery of *M. Poly.* and contemporary documents betrays not only its Hellenistic Jewish roots but also a continuing pattern of competing legitimation. Such competition probably implies closer interaction and possibilities for influence than the documents would have us realise. It suggests that where matters of doctrine and belief were involved they were such as touched most closely on legitimacy – the sense of being a people, the claim to be 'God-fearers', the efficacy of Passover, death of Jesus or sacrifice of Isaac. Since martyrdom was for both sides the ultimate demonstration of legitimacy, it is too the ultimate point at which the illegitimacy of the rival is to be demonstrated – on a literary and perhaps on a historical level too.[152] Yet we sense too conflicting claims to influence, and here meet the pervading importance of the city. Jewish–Christian rivalry was played out in no theological ivory tower. Polycarp wins the intervention of Nicetas, they are perhaps of comparable status – something which *M. Poly.* both acknowledges and yet downgrades in the rough response of Nicetas and his son when they fail to sway Polycarp. But the Jews too can claim access to him – again acknowledged by *M. Poly.*, but condemned by paralleling it with the influence of the devil. However, the maintenance of influential contacts and the display of loyalty to the city, whether through suitable donations or declarations of due respect, were important measures of security and hardly to be dismissed so lightly.

The world of the document is not identical with the world of the events it purports to describe; yet in seeking to recover the latter we are continually drawn back into the former. This is both inevitable and important: the text is in the end all to which we have direct access, but it itself created a reality or 'universe of meaning' for its readers, while also being itself the product of another reality.[153] The result of our exploration into the two worlds is to move beyond simplisitic descriptions *either* of the antisemitism of the document *or* of the pervasive presence in second-century Asia Minor of the Jew bent on persecution.

Notes

[1] This is not to deny both Jewish and pagan partial precedents: see Rordorf 1977: 36; Dehandschutter 1979: 175–87.

[2] The account, in part paraphrased, given by Euesebius, *H.E.* IV.15 also starts with the letter prescript.

[3] Andresen 1965; Peterson 1958. In contrast to the Pauline greeting, the 'mercy and peace ... be multiplied' here is closer to Jewish precedent.

[4] For the letter form see Dehandschutter 1979: 157–75, and on the 'kerygmatic' goal Buschmann 1994. On *M. Poly.* and the development of Christian veneration of martyrs see Rordorf 1977.

[5] The validity of the claims and the problem of dating will be discussed later, see below, pp. 72–3.

[6] Musurillo 1972: xiv.

[7] Dehandschutter 1979: 91–2 accepts the reading of all the Greek manuscripts except M(oscow), 'teacher of impiety'; 'of Asia' has the support of M, Eusebius and the Latin translation but Dehandschutter argues reasonably that a conscious scribal change to 'Asia' from 'impiety' is more credible than the reverse; so also Robert 1994: 109. See further below, p. 84.

[8] It fits the drama of the moment as well as historical probability (Pliny, *Epist.* X.96.3) that the 'three times' goes with Polycarp's confession and not with the herald's (i.e. threefold) proclamation: see Boeft and Bremmer 1985: 112.

[9] Musurillo 1972: 11 n. 16 allocates the cries to the two groups. On Jewish parallels to 'father' and 'teacher' see below pp. 89, 205.

[10] Surkau 1938: 130 compares John 11.50; 19.7.

[11] See Richardson 1969: 24–5, and below pp. 83–4.

[12] Schoedel 1967: 67; Buschmann 1994: 259, 312.

[13] A key argument in Campenhausen 1963 for the priority of the Eusebian version over the more heavily redacted *M. Poly.* is that the imitation theme is only found in the latter. The passage here discussed appears in Eusebius without alteration. However, it has been shown that the imitation theme is also there in Eusebius's version: see Barnard 1970.

[14] See Guillaumin 1975 who estimates that only 6.3 per cent of the vocabulary of *M. Poly.* is absent from the Greek Bible.

[15] See pp. 27, 43–4.

[16] It is not clear whether 'gentiles' (ἔθνοι) here are non-Jews or Jews from the Diaspora.

[17] Beyschlag 1965 and 1966 argues for a common tradition underlying the martyrdom of James, that of Polycarp, and other Christian martyr traditions; see below p. 77.

[18] On the authenticity of *M. Pionius* see Robert 1960: 262, dramatically developed by Lane Fox 1986: 460–92, and now Robert 1994.

[19] It has been suggested to me that the 'enthusiastically' is to be seen historically in the light of Paul's zealous persecution in Gal.1.13; however, the word is used elsewhere by *M. Poly.* (8.3) and should not be overstressed.

[20] See Surkau 1938: 130.

[21] *Scorp.* 10.9. See below, p. 91.

[22] Contrast the foul stench in Lucian, *Peregrinus* 32.

[23] Schoedel 1967: 73 follows Campenhausen in seeing 16.2 as a later editorial addition because of the use of 'catholic' (= 'orthodox') of the local church at Smyrna – as well as an apostolic and prophetic teacher Polycarp as 'bishop of the catholic church in Smyrna'. This problem would be avoided if, with Lightfoot and following M and the Latin, we read 'holy'. However, even without the addition of 16.2, the conclusion with its contrast between unbelievers and the elect remains a triumphant one.

[24] This is a standard theme in martyr accounts, compare the martyrs of Lyons in Eusebius, *H.E.* V.1.16.

[25] And possibly as 'the tyrant' (ὁ τύραννος) which is read in 2.4 by the majority of Greek MSS (except the M) but which is not accepted by Lightfoot or Dehandschutter. However, it is not a common term in Christian martyrologies but is used of the earthly opponent and persecutor in Jewish martyr stories (4 Macc. 9.1, 10 etc.) and so perhaps should be preserved.

[26] Eusebius, *H.E.* IV.15.41; i.e. Eusebius adds the word 'they said' referring back to where he has not the devil but unnamed persons inciting Nicetas, and uses the aorist rather than present participles. Schoedel 1967: 75 accepts this as giving the right sense but see below, pp. 67–8.

[27] If we were to accept or understand the reading 'they said' (see previous note) the participle could refer back to those who said these things.

[28] See above, n. 26.

[29] On this and what follows see Saxer 1982: 996–7; on the cult of the martyrs, Rordorf 1972; 1977.

[30] Rordorf 1972: 329.

[31] Buschmann 1994 sees this as a major motivating force behind *M. Poly.*

[32] So Saxer 1982: 992–5.

[33] So Campenhausen 1963: 276–7.

[34] Herod also has a key role in the death of Jesus in the *Gospel of Peter*, the provenance of which has been assigned to Syria or Asia Minor; see Perler 1964.

[35] See n. 26 above.

[36] There may be another echo of Matthew's Gospel in Polycarp's words before his arrest, 'The will of God be done' (7.1), recalling both the Lord's Prayer and Jesus's words in Gethsemane (Matt. 6.10; 26.42).

[37] κεντυρίων: this Latinism occurs only here, Mark 15.39 and *Gospel of Peter* 8.31 in early Christian literature. At this point Eusebius uses the more common ἑκατοντάρχης.

[38] So Schoedel 1967: 74.

[39] So also Campenhausen 1963: 277.

[40] Campenhausen 1963 countered by Barnard 1970 and Dehandschutter 1979.

[41] Musurillo 1972: liii, lv–lvi finds 'an early anti-Semitism' only in the martyrdoms of Polycarp and of Pionius, which is related both in location and in literary heritage to that of Poycarp (see below, pp. 91–2). In his collection of the most reliable Acts the Jews only otherwise appear in the Martyrdom of Conon. Parkes 1934: 121–50, 402–4 shows that even in the spurious martyrdom accounts active involvement by the Jews largely disappears after the first century. See further below, pp. 91, 257–8.

[42] See above, n. 14.

[43] John uses ὀνάριον.

[44] John also speaks of the last day of the Feast of Tabernacles as 'great' (John 7.37).

[45] The word 'preparation' (παρασκευή) is already used in *Didache* 8.1 as a Christian designation for Friday.

[46] So Hall 1979: 43 although Perler 1966: 181 and Huber 1969: 44 take it as a reference to 15 Nisan, the first day of Unleavened Bread; see p. 219 below.

[47] In *Chron. Pasc.* quoted by Perler 1966: 244.

[48] See above, p. 58.

[49] Eusebius, *H.E.* IV.15.1; he dates Pionius's martyrdom, which was certainly under Decius, to the same period (15.47): Brind' Amour 1980 (167 CE) and Grégoire 1951; 1964 (177 CE) follow Eusebius in putting the martyrdom under Marcus Aurelius. Marrou 1953 and Campenhausen 1963: 265 followed by Conzelmann 1978: 53 and Schoedel 1967: 61, 79 conclude from the problems that the reference to the 'great sabbath' cannot be original.

[50] This is the argument of Grégoire 1951; 1964: 26f., 108–14, who uses this as part of his argument that Polycarp's martyrdom took place in 177 CE. However, this renders impossible Polycarp's link with Ignatius and leads to the questioning of the authenticity of Ignatius's letters: for a critique see Meinhold 1952: 1676–80. On the historical evidence see Barnes 1967.

[51] Rossner 1974 argues that the titles refer to the same post but are used in different contexts; Kearsley 1987 disagrees, arguing that the 'archiereus' served in the imperial cult on the provincial level, while the asiarch was concerned with internal affairs relating to the city. Both agree that the asiarch's term of office was not used for dating purposes, something followed by *M. Poly.* See also Friesen 1993: 92–113.

[52] So Merkelbach 1975; Frend 1964 (who favours a date *c.*166 CE).

[53] Cf. Barnes 1967; 1968; Rossner 1974: 133 is less precise; see also Friesen 1993: 101 and above n. 51 for the two offices.

[54] Barnes 1967; 1968.

[55] Hilgenfeld 1879: 154–5 suggests that the sabbath might not be a real sabbath; the term could be used of 15 Nisan (cf. Lev. 23.11, 15f. and the use of 'the great feast' of 15 Nisan in Apollinarius). Cf. also the next note.

[56] Although it is only later that the term is used in Jewish circles of the Saturday before Passover and in Christian of Easter Saturday; see already Lightfoot 1989: II.1, 709–10. Lateness of other attestation does not prevent Brind' Amour 1980 from seeing a reference to Sunday as 'the greater sabbath'. However, this usage implies a development of 'sabbath' theology uncharacteristic of the second century.

[57] On the problems of determining the details of Quartodeciman practice and the probable variety within it see Hall 1984.

[58] Hence any reference to 'Easter Saturday' is not only anachronistic but highly improbable. Hilgenfeld 1879: 145 describes *M. Poly.* as 'an important document of early Quartodeciman practice'.

[59] So Strobel 1977: 32.

[60] A confusion arising from the different place of this month is part of the argument both of Grégoire 1951 that the late redactor had in mind his own Easter Saturday which regularly fell in 'his' Xanthikos, and added 'great' to the 'sabbath' of the tradition, and of Hilgenfeld 1879 that the

identification with February is secondary via the same but reverse process.

⁶¹ So E. Schwartz 1963: 11; Strobel 1977: 245–53, 362. As Schwartz notes, during the later fourth-century Easter controversy the Jews were accused of celebrating Passover at the end rather than the beginning of the year; however, this is related to the argument about the importance and dating of the spring equinox in calculating Easter, and none of the Easter dates quoted by Schwartz falls as early as 23 February. On this later controversy as independent from the Quartodeciman issue and as involving much more explicit polemic against the Jews see Grumel 1960.

⁶² We may leave aside the question whether 'the great sabbath' refers to Passover or Unleavened Bread; see above, n. 54.

⁶³ The letters of Gamaliel in *jSan.* 18d; see Alexander 1984: 581, 592f. On the issue see Thornton 1989.

⁶⁴ Lightfoot 1989: II.1, 711–13. Lane Fox 1986: 485–6 accepts a Purim reference for *M. Pionius* where again it is said to be 'a great sabbath' (2.1; 3.6) and this is explicitly given as the reason why the 'Greeks, Jews and women' are on holiday.

⁶⁵ See Thornton 1986 citing the tradition (supported by the LXX) that Haman, the Jews' arch-enemy in the story of Esther, was crucified, and references from the end of the fifth century onwards.

⁶⁶ *Cod. Theod.* 16.8.8; see Linder 1987: 236–8.

⁶⁷ See Seager and Kraabel 1983: 183; Kraabel 1992: 232.

⁶⁸ See above, nn. 18, 41.

⁶⁹ So Nikolai 1963.

⁷⁰ Dionysia + Purim: Lane Fox 1986: 485–6; the *dies imperii* of Antoninus Pius: Colin 1964: 136; more generally, an imperial festival: Price 1984: 124; the Commune of Asia's Games: Lightfoot 1889: II.1, 713–15; Terminalia (cf. Ovid, *Fasti* II. 639ff.) + ordinary sabbath: Rordorf 1980 followed by Buschmann 1994: 125. Rordorf's argument, the most elaborately developed and based on external parallels and a number of possible allusions in the text, is undermined by the absence of any evidence of this festival outside Rome: see Boeft and Bremmer 1991: 107–8.

⁷¹ So explicitly Rordorf 1980.

⁷² So, in *M. Pion.* it is the Temple of Nemesis which is in the foreground as the expression of the city's religious life which Pionius rejects (6.3; 7.2; 18.13).

⁷³ See above pp. 61–2, n. 17 and Beyschlag 1965: 172f.

⁷⁴ On what follows see Kretschmar 1972: 292–9.

⁷⁵ See Barnard 1970: 199–203.

⁷⁶ See especially Dan. 3.39–40 LXX; also 2 Macc. 1:24–26; 4 Macc. 6.29; 17.22; Ign., *Eph.* 21.1; *Smyrn.* 10.2; Schoedel 1967: 71.

⁷⁷ See the fragments in Perler 1966 (translation in Hall 1979) and the discussions by Lerch 1950: 27–38; Nikolasch 1963: 25–7; below, pp. 225–7. The parallel with *M. Poly.* 14.1 was already noted by Lightfoot 1889: II.iii. 386.

⁷⁸ The first quotation comes from Frag. 9, the second from Frag. 10.

⁷⁹ An alternative to Isaac's silence is found in traditions which allow him a reaction: see Ps.Philo, *Bib. Ant.* 18.5.

⁸⁰ See also New Fragment II.l. 88 (Hall 1979: 89) 'and the one who freed the tied was bound'. In *M. Poly.* the verb is προσδέω, in Melito δέω; in the

LXX the ram is caught in the bush and not 'bound', while Isaac was earlier tied by the feet (Gen. 22.9, συμποδίσας used by Melito in *Peri Pascha* §59. l. 417).

[81] LXX uses a different word (ὁλοκάρπωσις). Kretschmar 1972: 297 n. 21 notes that the donkey is also to be found in Gen. 22.

[82] In the light of the discussion below the use of this theme in 4 Macc. 16.20 is important.

[83] So Davies and Chilton 1978; P. Davies 1979 sees the Passover association as secondary and as not developing until the end of the second century, but see pp. 226–7 below and Harl 1986: 471–2; Levenson 1993: 176–83.

[84] Fragment in Perler 1966: 244, l.17; the allusion is to Matt. 12.29. On the development see Davies and Chilton 1978: 538–40.

[85] See below, pp. 232–3.

[86] Kretschmar 1972 also remains agnostic about the actual date of Polycarp's martyrdom but sees the Passover themes as firmly fixed and as highlighting the contrast with the Jewish Passover celebration.

[87] See Surkau 1938; Frend 1965; Baumeister 1980. On what follows see in particular Baumeister 1980: 295–306; Kellermann 1989: 71–5.

[88] See Perler 1949; van Henten 1993: 711–13 does not find literary dependence.

[89] For what follows see Kellermann 1989: 1971–5; van Henten 1993: 714–23.

[90] ὑπομένειν *M.Poly.* 2.2,3,4; 3.1; 13.3; 19.2; 4 Macc. 17.11; on the resurrection hope see Kellermann 1989.

[91] γενναῖος and related terms: *M.Poly.* 2.1,2; 2 Macc.6.28; 4 Macc. 6.10; 8.3; 17.3 etc (26 times in 1–4 Macc. and not elsewhere in LXX). 4 Macc. 6.10; 17.15,16 uses ἀθλῆτης (here only in LXX), *M.Poly.* 18.2 προαθλητέω; the crown in *M.Poly.* 17.1; 19.2; 2 Macc. 14.4; 4 Macc. 17.15; on the devil as 'tyrant' in *M.Poly.* 3.1 as in the Maccabean literature see above n. 25.

[92] Both Eleazar and Polycarp are described as ἐπίσημος (3 Macc. 6.1; *M. Poly.* 14.1; 19.1), both are said to have been 'adorned' (κοσμέω) by their virtue (3 Macc. 6.1; *M. Poly.* 13.2), both address God as παντοκράτωρ and πάτερ (3 Macc. 6.2–3; *M. Poly.* 14.1, cf. also 19.2; 2 Macc. 3.22, 30; 5.20; 6.26 etc. and below p. 84).

[93] See Mitchell 1990 for this increased significance in the second century.

[94] See Merkelbach 1975; Stewart 1984, in both cases concentrating on this as a Christian phenomenon, although Stewart notes the Jewish parallels.

[95] Raised as a question in van Henten 1989: 253. On the date of 4 Macc. see van Henten 1986 (*c.*100 CE) and Klauck 1989: 668–89 (90–100 CE). Perler 1949 argued against any late date of 4 Macc. on the grounds that it is known not only by *M. Poly.* but also by Ignatius. However, the parallels he stresses establish only a common linguistic and stylistic thought world and not literary dependence.

[96] See Beyschlag 1966 who overstresses the idea of a common martyrological literary tradition as responsible for parallels between 2 and 4 Macc., *M. Poly.*, *M. Lyons* and Hegesippus's account of the martyrdom of James (see above, pp. 61–2, nn. 17, 73). Baumeister 1980: 295–8 speaks more convincingly of 2 and 4 Macc. contributing to the thought world about martyrdom in Asia Minor at the time of *M. Poly.* and perhaps Ignatius. Ignatius's contribution to this thought-world should not be ignored – a number of the terms he shares with

4 Macc. come in his letters to Smyrna and to Polycarp (eg. ἀθλῆτης, *Poly.* 1.3; 2.3; 3.1 only; ἀντιψύχον, *Poly.* 2.3; 6.1; *Smyrn.* 10.2; *Eph.* 21.1; 4 Macc. 6.27f.; 17.20f. but not in *M. Poly.*).

[97] So Rordorf 1990: 69.

[98] See Kellermann 1980; Le Deaut 1970 also notes that according to the Targums Isaac offered intercession before offering himself for sacrifice. However, on the problem of whether such traits go back to this period see n. 83 above.

[99] See further van Henten 1989: 146–8; on the 'noble death' in pagan thought, Seeley 1990:113–41.

[100] In Polycarp's case the bird was a dove, but in the absence of Eusebius's support, its presence may be redactional. J. Schwartz 1972 argued for dependency by *M. Poly.* on *Peregr.*, but the parallels do not suggest a literary relationship.

[101] See generally Weiner and Weiner 1990.

[102] Ibid. 51.

[103] Conzelmann 1978 suggests that the original text may have described rather more about the other martyrs who are only alluded to in its present form (2–3; 19.1: eleven others from Philadelphia). In 16.2 the description of the local church at Smyrna as 'catholic' seemingly reflects later use of the term and so should either be attributed to redaction or replaced with the alternative reading 'holy', n. 23 above.

[104] See above pp. 60–1 and Richardson 1969: 24–5, although he underestimates the significance of 12.1–2.

[105] On what follows see Lieu 1995b: 485–93.

[106] The closest parallel appears in Judith's prayer (Judith 9.12, 14) where God is described as 'master of heaven and earth, creator of the waters, king of all creation … God of all power and might, there is none other than you who shield the race of Israel'.

[107] The Greek has Jews, Greeks and Christians, while the Syriac and Armenian speak of four, adding the barbarians. According to Eusebius, *Chronicon*, Aristides' *Apology* was entitled 'Concerning the fear of God'. See further below pp. 166–8.

[108] See further below p. 168 and also Melito's *Apology* in Eusebius, *H.E.* IV.26.5. 'Race' is also used of Christians in *Hermas*, Sim. IX.17.5; 30.3 in describing apostates as losing their place in the 'race of the righteous'.

[109] Athenag., *Supplic.* 4.2; 12.2; 14.2; 37.1; Tatian, *Oratio*, 13.3; 17.3. See below pp. 187–8 and Lieu 1995b: 489–90, 498–9.

[110] 12.2; see above p. 59, n. 7 for the text here.

[111] Justin does not use 'fear of God' in the *Apology*, whereas the more common 'pious' comes six times. Although in the *Dialogue* 'pious' is still more frequent than 'God-fearing' (18 vs. 13), the 'Jewish' context of the latter is notable.

[112] On this theme see van Henten 1989: 142–3.

[113] See n. 106 above. See also Dan. 1.6; Judith 6.2, 19; 8.20, 32; 16.17; 3 Macc. 1.3; 7.10.

[114] Van Henten 1989: 127–8.

[115] This is in contrast to its limited use earlier in the Jewish tradition: see Job 1.1; Gen. 20.11. In Baruch 5.4 the name 'Peace of righteousness and glory of "fear-of-God"' will be given to Jerusalem. However, 'pious/piety' is still the more important term for 4 Macc. (60+ vs. 6 occurrences).

[116] See Lieu 1995b: 495.

[117] See Amir 1982 and above p. 30.

[118] 2 Macc. 6.1; 11.25; 13.14; 3 Macc. 3.4, 21, 23; 4 Macc. 2.8, 23; 3.20; 4.23; Esther 8.13. See Hengel 1966: 180–1.

[119] Livy, VI.14.5; see van Henten 1989: 143–4. *CIG* 3176 = *ISmyrn* (Petzl 1982–7): no. 600, in a letter of Marcus Aurelius dated to the same period (157/8); see also *CIG* 3187 = *ISmyrn* no. 591 where a decree of the Commune of Asia speaks of the divinised emperor as 'father of the fatherland and saviour of the whole human race' (? time of Nero). See also Robert 1966: 85–6 for the (at first honorary) title 'father/mother' of a city or association, to which must also be compared the diaspora title 'father of the synagogue' (below, n. 135).

[120] This terminology was by now a regular part of Christian discourse coming frequently in *1 Clem.* and also in Justin.

[121] Otherwise it comes only in *Did.* 12.4 and the apologetic *Epistle to Diognetus*.

[122] See Bommes 1976: 32, n. 35.

[123] So Campenhausen 1963: 267.

[124] So Conzelmann 1978: 50–1.

[125] See Rordorf 1990 who judiciously assesses the evidence.

[126] See Fischel 1947; Holl 1928 stressed the prophetic role of the martyr but did not relate it to the Jewish tradition.

[127] *CIG* 3148 (= *ISmyrn.* (Petzl 1982–7): no. 697, where Petzl notes that Boekh identified Claudia's father with the Sophist but that the further link with the Nicetas of *M. Poly.* cannot be proved). On this inscription see below, pp. 89–90.

[128] See Schulthess 1918.

[129] See Kretschmar 1972: 300–1.

[130] See Brooten 1982: 5–11.

[131] *ISmyrn.* no. 295 (=*CIJ* II. 741): second (Brooten) or third (Petzl) century.

[132] *CIJ* II. 738; see Brooten 1982: 143–4; White 1987: 143; third century.

[133] *ISmyrn.* no. 296; see Robert 1960: 260–2.

[134] *ISmyrn.* no. 884 (= *CIJ* II. 739); the synagogue appears to have an inner hall separated by a grille and is laid with a mosaic.

[135] *CIJ* I. 190, 281; see above, n. 119.

[136] Cadoux 1938: 348 who rejects the two former explanations as inconsistent with the 'complimentary' tone of the mention.

[137] See Kraabel 1968: 30–1; Solin 1983: 649 notes that this would be an unusual use.

[138] See Kraabel 1983: 185–6.

[139] Parkes 1934: 137; also Simon 1986: 121–3.

[140] Frend 1965: 259; see also 270–2. The words of Harnack 1904: 66 'wherever bloody persecutions are afoot in later days the Jews are either in the background or the foreground' are often quoted. On what follows see Lieu 1996.

[141] See Parkes 1937: 121–50; Simon 1986: 115–25; Hare 1967: 66–79.

[142] So Henrichs 1970: 22–4.

[143] On Jewish parallels to the charges against Jesus see Gero 1978.

[144] See Lightfoot 1889: II.iii. 423–31 and the text on 432–65; Cadoux 1938: 306–10 argues unconvincingly for the Pionian authorship and early third-century date for the *Vita* and so accepts its information as broadly trustworthy. Reinach 1885 argues, also unconvincingly, that older local traditions reflecting second-century Smyrna are being used.

[145] Gregory of Nyssa, *De vita beati Gregorii: PG* 46: 893–953, 940c–41c; Chrysostom, *Adv. Iud.* VIII.5.6; I.7.5–6.

[146] See Lightstone 1984: 125–52; although Lightstone is concerned to trace the importance of 'non-Rabbinic' patterns of access to the divine, including magic and veneration of the dead, as early as possible and makes heavy use of Chrysostom, he does not refer to *M. Poly.* or the *Vita*.

[147] Apollonius of Tyana, *Ep.* 75; 76.

[148] Suetonius, *Claud.* 25.4; Hadrian's rescript in Eusebius, *H.E.* IV.9.1–3. Doubts about the reference of the former to Christians and about the authenticity of the second do not invalidate the basic point!

[149] Above pp. 25, 41.

[150] *1 Clement* 5.

[151] Claudius' Letter in *CPJ* II. 153; for the troubles at Antioch see above, p. 23, and at Caesarea, *B.J.* II.13.7 [267].

[152] The same is true of Justin's denial of Marcionite readiness for martyrdom in *Apol.* I.58 despite the evidence to the contrary (Eusebius, *H.E.* IV.15.46).

[153] See Weiner and Weiner 1990 and above, pp. 82–3, on the role models.

4

JUSTIN MARTYR'S
DIALOGUE WITH TRYPHO

Justin Martyr's *Dialogue with the Jew Trypho* marks a turning-point in Christian literary presentations of Judaism; here the Jews, or a Jew, are being addressed directly, at least within the narrative setting, and are presented with the argument from scripture not only for Jesus as Messiah but also for the status of the church as the New People of God and for the Jews' corresponding loss of that status. While the polemic remains far less bitter than future examples of the 'Adversus Iudaeos' literature,[1] and the note of openness as well as of courtesy is never totally lost, many of the characteristics as well as many of the explicit arguments of that literature are already to be found here.

By Justin's own admission, the *Dialogue* was written after his *Apology* (*Dial.* 120.6), and therefore in Rome where he spent the last period of his life, probably between 155 and 160 CE. Yet the actual debate it claims to describe takes place some twenty or twenty-five years earlier, when the Bar Kochba revolt (*c.*132–5 CE) is still a matter of active discussion (9.3). The text as we have it – there was perhaps an introduction now lost – gives no hint of the location, but it seems reasonable to follow Eusebius in setting the debate in Ephesus (*H.E.* IV.18.6), even though his additional information, that Trypho was one of the leading Hebrews of the day, is contradicted by the latter's evident ignorance of Hebrew and dependence on the Jewish teachers.[2]

Several scholars, noting the consciously constructed literary form of chapters 1–9 which describe Justin's philosophical quest, in particular, and of the *Dialogue* as a whole, have challenged the historicity of the encounter. However, the largely favourable presentation of Trypho who, despite his obstinate or obtuse refusal to be moved by Justin's arguments, and despite

Justin's regular attacks against him and against the Jews as a people, remains courteous and smiling to the end, carries a note of authenticity. While the *Dialogue* is considerably nearer to a monologue, and the weakness of Trypho's own contributions have prompted the charge that he is little more than a 'straw man' for Justin's argument, he has as a character rather more flesh and blood.[3] Moreover, it is hard to attribute the references to the Bar Kochba revolt to mere literary effect, although their role within the theological argument is undeniable. Justin, too, undoubtedly has good knowledge of Jewish practice and exegesis, in particular of issues that would have been important in Jewish–Christian debate. There is, then, little reason to deny that Justin engaged in such a debate with many a Jew – Trypho himself, probably with good reason, suspects that he had done so on several occasions in the past (50.1) – or that Ephesus would provide a convincing location for such an encounter.

It remains true that the *Dialogue* is far from a careful record of a single, or rather two-day, debate. Neither is Justin simply using the benefit of hindsight to present what he would have liked to have said, and to conveniently muzzle his opponent. The 'dialogue' form has a long pedigree with recognisable literary conventions and devices, and must envisage an audience for whom such a style would be familiar and persuasive.[4] Moreover, the arguments reflect more than the accumulated experience of debate with Jews. Later church tradition remembered Justin as the refuter of heresy, and Justin's defence of the consistency of God through both the old and new dispensations betrays a concern with gnosticism and in particular with Marcionism. We may suspect that he is using old arguments against Marcion in this new but theologically related setting, and that their application would not be lost on all his readers.[5]

Inevitably this raises the question of intended readership. While Justin is obviously writing as a convinced Christian, and moderates none of his polemic or argument for his Jewish interlocutor, the relation between image and reality in his presentation of Judaism would carry a different significance according to whether his readership was Jewish, or Christian, or educated pagan. A purely pagan readership seems least likely, although it has been claimed in the light both of the name of Marcus Pompeius to whom the book is dedicated (141.6) and of the literary form with its echoes of Socratic dialogue which would appeal to an educated audience.[6] The argument that educated pagans must be in view because of the primary philosophical interests of the opening chapters is contradicted by the presentation of the Jew, Trypho, as himself adopting a starting-point within philosophy. To carry any conviction such a presentation must have seemed plausible, and, if so, a Jewish audience with similar interests can hardly be excluded. Both the Jewish partner in the *Dialogue* and a number of differences from the *Apologies*, for example the assumption of the authority of the scriptures and the absence of any developed teaching about the Logos in the former, in contrast to the denial of a special place for the Jews in the latter, show that the concern with Judaism is more than a cloak for an exposition of the rationality of the Christian philosophy.[7]

In favour of an internal Christian readership is the reasonable scepticism that very many Christian writings were read by anyone except the Christians themselves, or that their authors had any other real expectations. Internal concerns, too, surely motivate the full discussion of the range of attitudes towards Christians who maintain the observance of the Jewish Law (47), the discussion of Christian millenarianism (80), and the arguments which seem to be directed against Marcionism (35.5; 56.16).[8] As we shall see, Marcion's divorce between the Father revealed by Jesus Christ and the God of the Jewish scriptures, and his rejection of those scriptures, necessitated a searching assessment by the Christians of their claim to be the heirs and true fulfilment of the promises to the Jews. Polemic first as a sect within Judaism and then with Judaism as 'other' had always been a means of differentiation and of formation of self-identity; the attraction of Marcionism demanded a far more precise argument and a much clearer defence of the Christian veneration yet non-observance of the Jewish Law. This defence went hand in hand with anti-Jewish polemic, for only by discrediting Jewish claims to understand and follow the Law could the radically contrary Christian stance be justified. The following century Tertullian apparently reused, with minimal alterations, material from his earlier writing *Against the Jews* in his sustained attack *Against Marcion*.[9] Similarly, Justin also may be reusing material from earlier polemic, which has borne fruit here in his interpretation of the status of the old covenant and of God's intention within it.

Yet to the extent that the *Dialogue* reflects genuine Christian–Jewish argument and seeks to counter actual Jewish objections and exegesis, it seems unlikely that it has only a Christian audience in mind. We may add to this the urgency with which Justin carries out his task; this is no mere justification of a position already held but betrays a deep awareness that only a little time remains for the Jews to choose the way of salvation. Justin must wrestle with his apologetic task in order to 'be innocent on the day of judgement' (38.2); however hopeless he may feel the Jews' position to be, he cannot rule out that still more may join those 'who are being saved' (64.3), and his closing plea is for them to 'expend every effort in this great contest for their own salvation' (142.2). That they do not take heed, but fail to be convinced by all his powers of persuasion, is only further evidence of the realism of the account.

Despite this realism we may well ask how seriously Justin anticipated that Jews would work their way through his long treatise, or whether he was not rather both establishing his claim to innocence of any responsibility for their disbelief, and contributing fuel to a continuing debate conducted by others. A similar question can of course be asked of the apologetic literature, and, as there too, choosing the second alternative does not simply bring us back to the 'internal Christian solution'. Whether at first or second hand, the Jews are a real audience and so too must their representatives be; they cannot simply be the projection of the 'dark side' or the 'negative' of Christian struggles to establish a secure identity.

A further solution to the question of readership is that the intended audience are a 'bridge group', perhaps gentiles strongly attracted by Judaism, on the verge of becoming proselytes, yet who now provide fertile ground for Christian proselytising.[10] Such people would demand a serious rebuttal of the Jewish claim to be the faithful interpreters of the scriptures, and the question of circumcision, a repeated feature in Justin's argument, might provide both the key to their failure to take the step of fully converting to Judaism and at the same time a source of continual uncertainty regarding the validity of Christianity. They would not feel themselves implicated in Justin's harsh and unconciliatory attacks against the Jews past and present, while the repeated charges against the incompetence of the Jewish teachers and the warnings against undue dependence on them might be most effective with those who were still open to persuasion. In addition, specific references to such potential proselytes have been found at various points in the *Dialogue*, for example in Justin's proclamation to Trypho and 'those who wish to become proselytes' (23.3), in his urging that only a short time remains for their conversion (proselytism: προσήλυσις) (28.2), and in his warning against deceiving those who listen to them (32.5).[11] This might suggest that Trypho's companions are seen as serious enquirers about Judaism and as the 'hidden' audience of the debate. They represent the market for which both Jews and Christians were in competition, and, in the time-honoured way of all propaganda, Justin is establishing both his 'product's' superiority in every respect and the obsolescence of his competitors' alternative.

This solution combines the positive arguments in favour of both a Jewish and a pagan audience while seeking to give a historically specific context for the appeal. Yet this is perhaps its weakness, for, in order to be targeted, this group – usually labelled the 'God-fearers' – must have a clear profile both to outsiders and to themselves. That this was in fact the case remains one of the unproven hypotheses of scholarship;[12] certainly there is nothing in Justin's *Dialogue* to substantiate it – while this may be ascribed to good tactics, he knows no half-way group and has but limited interest in proselytes.[13] Although the old man whom he meets by the shore and who leads him to Christianity points first to the prophets before speaking of Christ, Justin does nothing to suggest that such a path could be followed by those who were drawn first to Judaism. Moreover, the presentation of Trypho's companions is not fully favourable; they greet his opening remarks with rude laughter for which Trypho has to apologise (8.3; 9.2), and any hope that they might be open to persuasion in the light of the dissatisfaction one of them feels with answers given by the Jewish teachers (94.4) is dispelled by the vehemence of their objections which Justin likens to the behaviour of a crowd in a theatre (122.4). To the end Justin's appeal is to 'you', the Jews, and the final choice to be made is between

Jesus Christ and not the *Jewish* teachers but '*your* teachers' (142.2).

It remains true that many of Justin's arguments would make good sense in a missionary context.[14] Parallels have often been drawn between Justin and Luke–Acts and these parallels include the argument from fulfilment of prophecy. One setting for this argument in Acts is Paul's debate with Jews within the synagogue where God-fearers are often presented as in the audience and as particularly receptive (Acts 13.16–43). The *Dialogue* could be seen as adopting a similar setting.[15] Tertullian identifies the Jewish disputant of his *Adv. Iud.* as a proselyte (*Adv. Iud.* I.1), while Celsus, the second-century opponent of Christianity, had read the now lost *Dialogue of Jason and Papiscus* (*C. Cels.* IV.52). This does not mean that we can move first from the literary setting to the original historical setting, and then to the ultimate audience of the final literary work – a set of relationships which is by no means clear even in Luke–Acts. It does sharpen the question how far Jewish–Christian competition, explicit or not, for converts was a significant factor in the first two centuries.[16]

This is probably as far as we can go at this point on the question of the intended audience of the *Dialogue*. The discussion has shown that it is dangerous to posit too exclusive alternatives. Internal Christian concerns have shaped Justin's sources as well as his present argument; a tradition of missionary concern which included those who might equally be attracted by Judaism can also not be excluded; sympathetic pagans might be swayed by some of the arguments. However, the *Dialogue* is what it purports to be, a contribution to debate with the Jews, but a contribution which is only equivocally successful in taking seriously the other side's views and which prefers to work with a combination of realism and projection.

As we shall see, this assessment of purpose is largely confirmed by the presentation of Judaism. Clearly, since the *Dialogue* is both considerably longer than the other texts discussed here and, unlike them, is explicitly concerned with Judaism, we cannot explore at length the nature of Justin's argument with Judaism nor his use of the scriptures, both of which have been fully analysed elsewhere.[17] Rather more pertinent is the accuracy of his knowledge of Jewish practice and rabbinic exegesis,[18] although this too can only form the background to our concern with his presentation of Judaism. On this most studies are agreed that, although Justin on occasion does attribute to the Jews both specific exegesis that cannot be confirmed from Jewish sources, and some exegesis or views which seem inherently unlikely, the extent of his accurate knowledge of rabbinic exegesis, and, equally important, the numerous parallels between his own and Jewish interpretation suggest considerable contact between Christians and Jews. Justin's dependence on Jews probably extended from interpretation of the scriptures to the text of those scriptures itself. It is possible that for his knowledge of the Septuagint he often had recourse to Jewish copies – hence his accusations that their teachers had altered the text as originally translated, particularly where it differed from that given in his other (testimony) sources (*Dial.* 68.7 etc.).[19] This too implies he had access to the synagogues where he acknowledges that copies of the scriptures were to be found (72.3).

Naturally, such contact is not admitted by the *Dialogue* itself. True, we find Justin the Christian in debate with Trypho the Jew, but there is no suggestion that Justin is learning or could learn from Trypho. The relationship can only be the other way round, and, although Trypho remains at the end both as courteous and as unconvinced as he was at the beginning of this two-day marathon, at various points he admits the persuasiveness of Jusin's exegesis and the inadequacies of the explanations of the Jewish teachers (60.3; 63.1; 94.4), including some improbable concessions, such as that the Messiah would suffer (89.2).[20] Christianity's continued dependence on Judaism, particularly for the understanding of the scriptures they now claimed for their own, was none the less real but could never be admitted.[21] How far the reverse was true, that some on the Jewish side found aspects of Christian teaching or exegesis persuasive while remaining unconvinced by the total package, is a tantalising question but one that is outside our brief for the moment.[22]

Trypho the Jew

The debate is both between two individuals, Justin and Trypho (with the latter's friends in the background), and between two groups, Christianity and Judaism. The 'I' and 'you' of the initial encounter (3) soon becomes 'we' and 'you [pl.]' (10.1). Yet this is no debate between church and synagogue, and neither Justin nor Trypho are authoritative figures representing their respective religions. Eusebius considered Trypho 'one of the leading Hebrews of the day' (*H.E.* IV.18.6), and is often supposed to have identified him with the famous Rabbi Tarphon; that Justin intended such (or that it is historical) is unlikely, for he is more concerned to uncover Trypho's dependence on the Jewish teachers.[23] More probably, Eusebius himself created a suitably impressive opponent for Justin by building on Trypho's description of himself as a Hebrew (3) and on the group of friends/disciples who accompany him.

As often noted, Trypho is something of a hybrid figure; he introduces himself as a 'Hebrew of the circumcision' and as a fugitive from the recent war in Palestine (1.3). Yet he has had a philosophical training and it is from this standpoint that he approaches Justin (1.2); indeed, it is Justin who reprovingly points him to 'your own law-giver and the prophets from whom you can gain more than from philosophy' (1.3). The modern reader will add to this picture Trypho's obvious dependence on the Septuagint, his ignorance of Hebrew, and his inability to explain the name 'Israel' (125.1), but it is unlikely that Justin's readers would have seen anything contradictory or improbable in that, for they were in no better a position. It has been suggested that Trypho thus deliberately combines the worlds of Palestinian and Hellenistic Judaism,[24] but this reflects a modern perspective which senses a separation or tension between the two.

The question must be approached on two levels: although the use of 'Hebrew' for a Jew does become more frequent in pagan writers in the second century,[25] the presentation of Trypho as a 'Hebrew from the circumcision' reflects a Christian definition. The reference to the Bar Kochba revolt and the depiction of Trypho as a fugitive anticipate the importance of both the war and the subsequent exclusion of the Jews from Jerusalem in Justin's future argument – Trypho helps embody what for Justin is one of the purposes of circumcision, to mark out the Jews for the punishment meted out through those events (16.2). Even though most Christian encounters and disputes must have been with contemporary Jews of the Diaspora, it is the Jews of the scriptures and of Judaea who are their 'normative' literary opponents, something which is an essential feature of Christian theological perception of Jewish identity.

The background of Justin's actual Jewish opponent(s), whether we think of Trypho as largely drawn from life, or of Justin bringing together the experience of a number of such debates, represents the second level. As we have already seen, despite all the errors, there are a remarkable number of agreements between views attributed by Justin to his opponents and scriptural interpretation known from rabbinic sources, and also between Justin's own exegesis and Palestinian Jewish sources; by contrast, despite his Logos theology, Justin's knowledge of the diaspora Jew Philo remains disputed.[26] One explanation of this 'Palestinian bias' could be that Justin was born in Samaria and that his conversion, initial Christian experience, and even early controversies with Jews conceivably may have taken place within Palestine or Syria.[27] The alternatives would be either to emphasise Justin's dependence on earlier sources or traditions, or to use the *Dialogue* as evidence for the presence in the Greek Diaspora of interpretations of scripture which have only survived in rabbinic, Hebrew or Aramaic, sources. There is obviously truth in each of these perspectives, and at this point we cannot seek greater precision. The same question arises on two further issues: in ch. 47 Justin treats with considerable sensitivity and as a living current concern the position of Christians who continue to follow the Jewish Law, while throughout he presents the Jews as thoroughly dependent on their teachers. In each case we shall need to ask how far this reflects the situation of Christianity or of Judaism outside Palestine.

As often noted, the whole debate between Justin and Trypho is conducted with calm reasonableness and courtesy, particularly, one feels, on the part of Trypho who must put up with Justin's harsh outbursts against the Jews without replying in kind (e.g. 28.1). Only occasionally does he react with anger and never does he share in the rude laughter of his companions. This is often taken as evidence of both the realism of the account and the possibilities of open debate between Jews and Christians in the middle of the second century. While the modern reader, who perhaps finds Justin's exegesis somewhat stretched, feels a certain sympathy with Trypho's scepticism, there is enough to indicate that we are meant to come away with a sense of Jewish obduracy. Justin repeatedly accuses him of being fond of strife (64.2), of withdrawing agreements already reached (68.2), of contradicting before he has heard the full argument (115.3). Indeed, Justin's efforts to keep a logical order to his treatment and arguments are continually hampered by Trypho posing inappropriate questions (36.2; 45.1; 50.2), although we may doubt whether without them the *Dialogue* would be considerably more clearly structured![28]

Yet Trypho's questions and objections do not simply establish his obstinacy. On the one hand, he offers no sustained counter-argument, thus allowing Justin to conduct what is at times virtually a monologue, which Harnack called 'the monologue of the victor'.[29] On the other, the extent of his concessions serves the interests of Justin more than those of our historical knowledge. Not only does he fail to criticise Justin's execrable philology (103.5; 113.2) and offer no decisive objections to Justin's charges of Jewish falsification of the scriptures (73.5), but he shows himself persuaded by Justin's demonstration that one who is called both God and Lord, and yet who is not to be identified with the Creator of all, appears in the scriptures (60.3; 63.1); he accepts too the suffering of the Messiah, particularly as prophesied by Isaiah 53 (89.1–2; 90.1), even though this is contradicted by the conception of a victorious Messiah which he holds elsewhere.[30] Admittedly Philo also adopts a 'philology' which betrays his ignorance of Hebrew, and goes a long way in identifying the subject of many Old Testament theophanies with the Logos whom he can call 'a second god'.[31] Against a background of diaspora Judaism Trypho may seem a less implausible figure than he does against rabbinic or Palestinian Judaism, but the decisive background is surely Justin's apologetic. Old Testament evidence for the suffering of the Messiah was both the essential key to early Christian proof from prophecy and apparently the most novel element. Justin needs Trypho's support both to establish the Christian claim and to underline the Jewish obduracy that none the less failed to recognise in the crucified Jesus the suffering Messiah. Perhaps too he needs Trypho's support against other enemies; if Marcion demanded a 'Jewish' literal reading of the Old Testament and on this basis 'proved' the inferiority of the Jewish God, Trypho the Jew approves Justin's literal or non-allegorical exegesis which establishes that 'there is no God above the maker of the universe' (56.16).[32]

Both as individual opponent and as representative of the Jews, Trypho defies any simple characterisation. The ambiguities in his presentation are the result of the number of roles he fills, superimposed perhaps on a historical reality. Certainly he is more than a straw man whose only task is to present a foil for Justin's own arguments. He is both Justin's opponent who will demonstrate the obduracy of the Jews and his ally in furthering the argument and in defeating other unnamed foes. He reflects too the ambiguities of Justin's own understanding of the Jews. Rightly understood, Judaism is the only true philosophy (1.3; 7.1); Justin could not have had the same sort of dialogue with a Greek philosopher as he has with Trypho, for Judaism and Greek philosophy do not stand on a par as 'preparations for the Gospel'. Justin's philosophical journey in the opening chapters is a journey which leads nowhere until he is introduced to those who are older than 'all these supposed philosophers', the prophets (7.1). His guide, the old man whom he met by the sea-shore, points him only to the prophets; it is the task of all that follows to show that the prophets when rightly understood lead to Christ. Trypho represents both the possessor or heir of the true philosophy, and its misappropriation or misinterpretation; hence he cannot simply be cast in the negative shadow of Christian self-identification and separation. Justin also still hopes for the salvation of some Jews (28.2; 32.2; 64.2–3; 120.2), but his hope is tempered by a deep pessimism and conviction of Jewish obduracy, a pessimism which at this stage is rooted more in experience than in theological necessity. It is this realism rather than any lack of hope on Justin's part which leaves Trypho unconvinced at the end, in contrast to later 'Adversus Iudaeos' writings which often end with the miraculous submission and conversion of the Jewish opponent.

The Conflict between Judaism and Christianity

a) *Circumcision and the Law*

Despite all the difficulties in discerning a clear structure in the *Dialogue*, three issues dominate the debate: the status and observance of the Law, Christology, and the identity of the people of God. Trypho's position is clear from the start – to please God Justin must 'first be circumcised and then observe, as laid down, sabbath, festivals, and new moons of God, and, in short, do all that is written in the Law' (8.4); Christian speculation about Christ is folly and self-deception, and soon becomes blasphemy when recognised as claiming for him the status of God (38.1). Justin is no less explicit: 'the one who fails to acknowledge Christ fails to acknowledge the counsel of God, and the one who insults and hates him clearly equally hates and insults he who sent him. And if anyone does not believe in him, he does not believe the messages of the prophets who proclaimed and preached him to all' (136.3).

Despite the dominance of the christological theme, particularly from Justin's perspective,[33] the issues introduced by Trypho provide the sharpest and most searching debate. In the passage just quoted, Trypho appeals to circumcision, sabbath, festivals and new moons, those aspects of Judaism which were most easily observed in the Diaspora. Although not explicitly prescribed in the Law, the observance of the new moon as mark of the new month was significant in the Diaspora;[34] its inclusion here when it plays no further role in the debate points to the authenticity of the catalogue in the mouth of a Jewish objector. Justin may, perhaps, already have Isaiah 1.11–16 in mind, a passage which clearly colours his counter-argument: 'What to me is the mass of your sacrifices [cf. *Dial.* 13.1]?... if you offer a flour offering [cf. 13.1, σεμίδαλις] it would be in vain... Your new moons and sabbaths and great day I cannot endure. Fasting [cf. 15, νηστεία] and giving up work [cf. 23.3, ἀργεῖν] and your new moons and your feasts [cf. 43.1] my soul hates. Wash yourselves and become clean [quoted at 18.2].' Justin had already used this passage in the *Apology* (37.5–8), combining it there with Isaiah 58.6–7, which he quotes more fully at this point in the *Dialogue* (*Dial.* 15). Yet if he had wanted to pattern his opponent's description of the essentials of Judaism on a polemical refutation he already had to hand,[35] he surely would have shaped it more closely to his needs, and would have included sacrifice, which is important for him (23.3; 43.1) but suits his exegetical appeal to scripture rather better than Trypho's actual situation. Trypho himself acknowledges the realities of the Diaspora and of Jewish life after the loss of the Temple more realistically: he affirms that although the whole Law cannot be observed – no longer can the Passover lamb, the goats for the Day of Atonement or other sacrifices be offered – some things are possible: 'Keeping the sabbath, being circumcised, observing the months, and washing after touching anything forbidden by Moses or after sexual relations' (46.2).[36] The list is notably similar to Philo's minimal definition of Jewish identity in the diaspora setting of Alexandria.[37]

An even clearer note of authenticity is sounded in Trypho's objection: 'although you claim to be pious and consider yourselves different from other people, you do not separate yourselves from them at all neither do you distinguish your way of life from that of the gentiles' (10.3). This is no charge of Christian lawlessness, for Trypho has already dismissed pagan slanders against Christians and has declared the demands of the Gospel to be all but impossible (10.2).[38] It is instead a declaration of the Jewish understanding of the purpose of the Law and its observance – he specifically names feasts, sabbath and circumcision – an understanding that was bound to be put into effect in daily life. Pagan objections to Judaism complain about their antisocial behaviour, and all the evidence of Jewish participation in civic life cannot destroy the reality of separation in daily rhythm that observance of sabbath and calendar will have created.[39] Justin's immediate response is to deal first with the Law and its intention; only then does he come to the purpose of Jewish separation, which for him is the function of circumcision and which is focused in Jerusalem and Palestine (16.2, see below). Trypho's fundamental objection about social separation, which reflects genuine diaspora concerns, is never fully met, and is therefore all the more authentic.

A further concern of Trypho's, but one that is in fact introduced by Justin himself, is eating food sacrificed to idols. The theme of idolatry is an important one for Justin: idolatry is the hallmark of the pagans, and it is from idolatry that they as former pagans have turned (11.4; 69.4; 130.4). Rejection of idolatry may already have been a theme in Jewish propaganda,[40] but Justin turns it back against the Jews as he accuses them of the very same sin: throughout their history they continued to practise idolatry, not only in making the golden calf, a key incident for

Justin as for later writers,[41] but also in the time of Elijah and beyond. Christians are those who have turned away from idolatry and now face death rather than return to it (34.8; 46.6–7; 130.4). 'Who are the idolaters?' must be a living question in the propaganda war where Christians have taken over the self-recommendation of the Jews, and a central tenet of their appeal to the pagans. Trypho's searching objection that surely many 'who say they believe in Jesus and are called Christians do eat meat which had been sacrificed to idols and say there is no harm in it' (35.1) is therefore the more dangerous and must be vehemently denied by Justin.[42] The refutation of heresy – for Justin attributes such laxity to gnostic groups (35.2–6) – is thus inseparable from the maintenance of Christian credibility against the traditional 'virtues' of Judaism. For the same reason the charge of Jewish idolatry and the appeal to the golden calf incident does not only serve to demonstrate Jewish disobedience from the beginning as it does in later authors; it is an integral part of Jewish–Christian competition.

It was not just the propaganda competition which fired the debate about idolatry, but also persecution. Christian endurance to death is the most telling proof of their rejection of idolatry (34.8; 35.7–8). At the same time Justin denies that Christians avoid circumcision and sabbath observance out of fear of the consequences – as again their readiness to die demonstrates (18.3). Perhaps we hear echoes here of Jewish charges against Christians who were seen as in this way evading any response both to Hadrian's prohibition of circumcision, and to the other restrictions which followed the Bar Kochba revolt, as too they avoided showing any common cause with the Jews in that revolt.[43] There was a real argument here, as Trypho himself acknowledges by his puzzlement at the apparent incongruity between their endurance and their failure to observe the Law (19.1).

Elsewhere Justin accuses the Jews of failing 'to confess him as Christ out of fear of persecution by the authorities' (39.6; 44.1). He knows very well the reality of their sufferings as a result of the Bar Kochba revolt; for him, however, this does not constitute proof of their faithfulness to the Law but rather of the opposite – their just deserts for their disobedience, and the fulfilment of prophecy. Christians, in contrast, suffer when they have committed no such crime: in the words of Micah 4.6 they are those 'who are afflicted and cast down' and to whom is promised vindication (109; 110.5). Justin acknowledges here that he is appropriating for the Christians a prophecy which the Jews claimed for their own suffering (110.6), and not just appropriating it but holding them responsible for Christian 'affliction'. Once again he betrays the sharpness of the competition behind his own confident interpretation.

Yet if Christians avoided the suffering of the Jews, so did Jews escape that meted out to Christians. In his thorough discussion of the observance of the Jewish Law by Christians (47), Justin distinguishes carefully between Christians who are persuaded to keep the Jewish Law while maintaining their Christian confession, and those who give up their earlier faith and take up such Law observance (47.4). The note of public testimony in his description of this last group as 'denying that he is the Christ' perhaps suggests they were thus escaping persecution and claiming the protection of Jewish privileges. It may be, however, that such a formal denial was a prerequisite of acceptance (or reacceptance) into the Jewish community.[44]

In all this we detect a vigorous debate or claim and counter-claim between Jews and Christians, not only in private but also in their presentation of themselves to an interested public. For Trypho, a separation marked by observance of circumcision, sabbath and festivals is the proud hallmark of the Jews. In the midst of the pagan society of the Graeco-Roman city, where the reality of 'idolatry' was never out of sight, they were uncompromising in their rejection of any suspicion of acknowledging those gods. Their readiness to suffer, perhaps only spasmodically demanded in the Diaspora but vividly exemplified in the Jewish revolt under Bar Kochba and in the context of the prohibition of circumcision and probably of other observances, is proof of their faithfulness to the Law. To all this Christians have surrendered any claim. Justin throws back at them the testimony of suffering, either dismissing or reinterpreting any Jewish experience, while appealing to Christian suffering as the authenticating witness of their own response both to Jewish Law and to idolatry.

Like a veil over the sharpness of debate hangs Justin's theological interpretation of the Law and of the Christian attitude to it. Here we hear only Justin's voice and not the Jewish response, but Justin chooses his arguments with care and behind them we may see the views he is countering. On the one hand circumcision, sabbath observance, fasting, and even unleavened bread – his own addition to the earlier list – are symbols of a true spiritual reality which Christians do observe. There is a second circumcision (12.3; 19.3; 113.6f.; 114.4) which the Christians enjoy, just as they too observe a continual sabbath, and not one limited to a single day (12.3); there is a true fast, a true observance of the rejection of old leaven, and a true bathing not of the body but of the soul (12.3; 14.1–4; 15.1–6). God accepts from Christians the sacrifices which please him (29.1). Justin is not simply saying here, as would be most effective against Marcion, 'we Christians do accept and observe the Law, but in its true meaning'; instead he says, 'you have a circumcision, and so do we; ours is second in number, and so annuls any need for the first, and is a circumcision of the heart and not of the flesh alone' (cf. 114.4). This rhetoric which retains the authority of these fundamentals while redefining their content is the language of active competition.[45]

This is not the whole of Justin's understanding of the Law, and particularly of the provisions for circumcision, sabbath and sacrifices.[46] In a significant passage he declares, 'we have not fixed our hope through Moses or through the Law, otherwise we would be the same as you' (11.1).[47] The Law is also the mark of differentiation between Christians and Jews; given to the latter on Mount Horeb, it was temporary and properly belonged to the Jews alone. Yet the Law had its purpose, a negative one as a response to their unbelief and hard-heartedness (18.2; 23.2; 46.5), but one which at the same time had a positive side in leading them to penitence and obedience (30.1). This argument is undoubtedly a response to the Marcionite challenge, for Justin uses it to refute any suggestion that God acted inconsistently or that more than one god was involved in the different demands made at different times (23.1; 92). Yet Justin gives it particular potency in direct response to Jewish assertions.

It is against the background of the Jewish interpretation that his understanding of circumcision appears most effective. Circumcision was indeed given as a *sign* (σημεῖον) from the time of Abraham – as Genesis 17.11 asserts, a verse which Justin quotes, carefully omitting the dependent genitive 'of the covenant' (23.4). It was a 'sign whose purpose was that that you might be separated from all the other nations including us' (16.2), words echoing Trypho's earlier demand for separation. Yet the purpose of such separation was 'that you alone might suffer what you now justly suffer, ... for it is by nothing else than by your physical circumcision that you can be recognised among other people' (16.2–3). This was why circumcision was ordained for the Jews alone (19.2) – here Justin ignores his assertion elsewhere that other nations did practise circumcision without any benefit (28.4) – for God knew in advance that 'your people would become deserving to be ejected from Jerusalem, and for none of them to be permitted to enter there' (92.2).[48] That whoever is not circumcised on the eighth day 'is to be destroyed from this people' (Gen. 17.14) is not the proof text for circumcision as the *sine qua non* of receiving benefits from God, as Trypho claims (10.3), but ensures that none will escape the foreordained punishment (23.4).[49] Thus the 'sign' becomes something negative, to be contrasted with 'a work of righteousness' (23.4–5), it is something 'given' which God does not desire (28.4), and separation becomes a sign not of favour and election but of predetermined punishment. A clever example of this reversal of symbols comes in 120.2, where Justin takes the promise to Abraham that his descendants would be as numerous as the sand of the sea-shore and refers it to the innumerable mass of the Jews who have rejected the word of God and failed to join the remnant 'in the portion of Christ'; like the sand they are 'sterile and fruitless'.

This rhetoric of reversal of the formative symbols of the opposition group, particularly by a breakaway sect, is a familiar and sociologically recognised means of differentiation and self-justification. As such it does not demand the actual presence of the opponent, since its main function is an internal one. Yet in the present case the focus on circumcision and the repeated concern with the consequences of the Bar Kochba revolt show that the argument with Judaism is a very live one.

Of all the characteristics of Judaism which Justin both recognises and relativises, circumcision is the most important. He repeatedly returns to it, even when the question of the Law is no longer his central concern. In part this comes to him from his Christian heritage, for the necessity of male circumcision was a living and divisive issue in the earliest stages of Christianity. Thus his appeal to Genesis 15.6, where Abraham's faith in God is counted for righteousness, echoes that of Paul (Rom. 4.1–12); but, whereas for Paul, who also picks out the use of 'sign' from Genesis 17, the circumcision which follows is a sign of that faith, for Justin it is a sign for the future, for judgement of the Jews who fail to believe (23.4; 92.1–3).[50]

Undoubtedly, circumcision posed a particular problem to Justin because, unlike the commandments pertaining to sabbath and sacrifices, it antedated Moses, going back to Abraham; this meant it fell outside his general argument about the purposes of the Law given under Moses. Yet the sheer range of arguments which Justin marshals against circumcision, some of them new in the history of the debate, suggests that the issue was an urgent contemporary one determined by more than logical argument.[51] It may not be chance that Justin's admission that Jesus was circumcised, alluded to in 67.5, is nowhere explicitly reported. He is also only too aware that his own lack of circumcision will not dispose Trypho (and others?) to pay him much attention (28.2).

As we have seen, this dominating concern has been interpreted as reflecting the competition between Jews and Christians for the 'God-fearers' who, attracted by Judaism but hesitant to convert and be circumcised, provided fertile ground for the missionary endeavours of the Christians.[52] Christianity's surrender of circumcision would be both attractive to them and, as the final hurdle they balked at, a possible flaw. Justin's surprising and novel appeal to female experience as evidence of the irrelevance of circumcision for piety, namely that women are equally able to be righteous and pleasing to God but are physically unsuited for circumcision (23.5), might be particularly pertinent if, as often claimed, a sizeable number of God-fearers or proselytes, and of those from this group who became Christians, were women.[53] In a similar vein he cites not just the patriarchs who were righteous but did not observe the Law, but also 'Sarah, the wife of Abraham, and Rebecca, the wife of Isaac, and Rachel, the wife of Jacob, and Leah, and the other similar women up to the mother of Moses' (46.3): these too, being uncircumcised, pre-empted appeals to Abraham's circumcision.

Chapter 23, where a number of these arguments are developed, centres on the appeal to 'you, Trypho, and those who wish to become proselytes' (23.3). It includes the arguments from nature which does not observe the Law, and from the late introduction of the Law in the history of the righteous – even Enoch was not circumcised – arguments which belong comfortably in a missionary context.[54] Similar arguments in Jewish sources appear to reflect 'proselyte' concerns, and may sometimes counter Christian claims.[55] In such a setting we may also be justified in hearing faint echoes of pagan criticism of Judaism. While advocating a continual 'sabbathising' (σαββατίζειν), Justin mocks them for thinking that piety lies in 'doing nothing' (ἀργεῖν) for a single day; while the verb is used in Jewish sources (2 Macc. 5.25), it also recalls Seneca's derogatory attitude to the sabbath as idleness (*vacare*).[56] Similarly, Tacitus also had interpreted circumcision as a desire 'to be known by their difference', a condemnation allied to the notorious Jewish 'hatred of the human race'.[57]

We have already seen that it is difficult to limit Justin's readership to the 'God-fearers'; yet that the issue is a live one does seem likely. The situation was no longer that of the days of Paul, when the relationship between emerging Christianity and Judaism was still being worked through; Christianity was now predominantly gentile and the suggestion that converts should first be circumcised would not in most circles be heard at all (47). We should therefore see the competing (missionary) appeals of the two religions, and Christianity's claim to represent the true meaning of the prophets, to be the true Israel, as inspiring the debate. It was a debate whose other voice may sometimes be heard in rabbinic literature and whose logic was less self-evident than Justin assumes.[58]

Recent circumstances helped focus on circumcision. Hadrian's ban on circumcision may have fired the revolt under Bar Kochba and certainly continued after it.[59] Admittedly, support for the revolt seems to have been largely local and apparently did not come from the Diaspora. Yet we have already suggested that the non-involvement of Christians was a source of grievance, perhaps particularly among fugitives from Palestine. It is in this role that Trypho is cast, although with little credibility, and the debate between the two is carried out against the background of a discussion by Trypho's friends 'concerning the war that had taken place in Judaea' (9.3).

The war is a recurring theme throughout the *Dialogue*. On one level it is the goal of the Jewish history of unbelief; when circumcision set the Jews apart for suffering it was a suffering not only now fulfilled in the desolation of their land and cities, and in the prohibition of any Jewish entry into Jerusalem, but one foreseen from the very beginning by God (16.2; 92.2); even the survival of a few has divine and prophetically foretold purpose 'for the sake of the gentiles' (21.1–2); the giving of the Temple not only kept the people from idolatry (22.11) but also ensured that, as the only permitted place for sacrifice, once it was destroyed after Christ's passion, all sacrifices, in particular Passover and Atonement, would cease (40.2; cf. 46.2).[60] Jerusalem has suffered war because of the sins of the people, but will no longer suffer this in the eschatological age when inhabited by the nations who answer the call (24.2–3: Isa. 2.5–6). That their land is now laid waste and they are for the first time leaderless confirms the prophecy of Genesis 49.8–12 that the Jews would not lack a ruler until the coming of the promised Messiah (52.4); it is also the consequence of their refusal to heed Christ's promise of the 'sign of Jonah', whose preaching saved the city of the attentive Ninevites from destruction – and even with this evidence they do not repent (108.1–3). Justin knows that they interpret their suffering as a fulfilment of prophecy (Micah 4.6), but in truth this only applies to the Christians and not to the guilty Jews (110.5–6). They have brought upon themselves the judgement of destruction foretold by the prophets – Isaiah 5.18–25 and 16.1 (133; 114.5).[61]

Although this last theme was to become a common one in Christian polemic, Justin's distinctive use of the failure and consequences of the revolt points to its immediacy for both him and his audience. Whether or not explicitly, he enters into what must have been a searching debate about the possibilities of sacrifice and forgiveness without the Temple by asserting that the destruction was God's predetermined goal in limiting sacrifice to Jerusalem and of so ensuring its cessation.[62] Yet his most barbed attack is that circumcision was intended to effect the separation of the Jews for their present punishment. It has been suggested that Justin believed, whether or not with good grounds, that the Romans examined all comers for circumcision in order to effectively exclude all Jews from Jerusalem.[63] While this would give an added twist to his argument it is not really necessary (and historically seems rather unlikely). The revolt already was integrally associated with circumcision, through Hadrian's prohibition of the practice; Justin wholeheartedly agrees but turns it from faithful martyrdom to a concealed and deeply ironical divine purpose – fighting to the end for circumcision the Jews bring upon themselves the end which was God's centuries-old purpose for circumcision.

The Bar Kochba revolt was far more significant than our limited sources betray, not only in its extent and consequences,[64] but also in its immediate impact on Jewish and Christian self-defence and polemic, particularly in the public arena. Of course, Trypho would have had other responses which Justin does not allow us to hear;[65] even here he stubbornly – as Justin presents it – ignores his opponent's explanation of circumcision and insists that, even after the loss of Jerusalem, obedience to God's Law is possible, through circumcision and sabbath, new moons and ritual bathing (46.2–4).

We may hear one more echo of Trypho's (or Judaism's) response to the new situation in 117.1. Here Justin quotes Malachi 1.10–12 to prove that God rejects the sacrifices offered by the Jews and their priests but accepts the Christian sacrifice, particularly in the eucharist. 'Yet', he admits, 'even now in your contentiousness you say that God does not accept the sacrifices in Jerusalem from those called the Israelites who were *then* living there; but he has said the prayers through the men of that race who were *then* in the Diaspora are accepted and calls their prayers sacrifices.' The tenses used and the word 'then (τότε)' make the time reference of this Jewish exegesis difficult to interpret, but the 'even now (μέχρι νῦν)' suggests that this was a Jewish response to the destruction of the Temple and the cessation of sacrifice, but one that may already have been made before that by Jews cut off by distance from the Temple: they still had a divinely acknowledged form of sacrifice, prayer.[66]

In the debate over circumcision and the Law we sense the urgency of these issues, not just as they come from an earlier theological tradition, nor as demanded by the threat of Marcion's wholesale dismissal of the Old Testament. They lie at the heart of Christian perceptions of themselves and of Judaism, but also of Jewish perceptions of themselves and of Christianity. That means they belong both to polemic and to self-presentation in the wider world. Theologically, Justin struggles to establish the purpose of the Law, its symbolic function and historically curtailed role, but his arguments betray the reality and the persuasiveness of the Jewish maintenance of the Law. Between the lines we can see that the Judaism he encounters is not what he would have it be. Behind Trypho too we hear the echoes of a counter-presentation which makes him more substantial than the 'straw man'. We cannot yet say that this is 'the monologue of the victor'.[67]

b) *Christology and the Scriptures*

Although Justin's christological argument occupies such a central place in his attempt to persuade Trypho, it is for our purposes rather less important. As evidence of his knowledge of Jewish tradition it has attracted particular attention because he not only, like his predecessors, seeks to prove that Jesus is the Messiah who fulfils the prophecies of the past, but also uses the theophanies of the Old Testament to establish the pre-existence and divinity of Christ.[68] In both arguments he refers to the alternative exegesis of the Jews or else has Trypho present such an alternative. Not all of this 'Jewish' exegesis can be authenticated, and some seems unlikely, but enough does have parallels to lead to the conviction that Justin did have immediate knowledge of post-biblical Judaism.[69] Indeed, his setting of the exegesis in a polemical context may accurately reflect the origin of Jewish interpretations which now survive independently of this context. For example, the historicising interpretation of the royal psalms, applying them in most cases to Hezekiah, may have developed as a reaction against their messianic interpretation by Christians or others (33.1: Ps. 110.4; 85.1: Ps. 24.10).[70]

　　To establish the pre-existence of Christ, Justin appeals both to the theophany traditions of the Old Testament (56: Gen. 18; 75.1: Ex. 23.21), and to those places where the words 'Lord' and 'God' are so used as to allow the interpretation that more than one figure is involved (56.12: Gen. 19.23–25: 'And the Lord rained down on Sodom brimstone and fire from the Lord out of heaven'). Justin has to counter both Trypho's initial objection that those 'angels' who appeared to Abraham were indeed angels (56.5), and also the views held by Jews who accepted the existence of a second 'power' but denied its separation in any way from God (128.2–3). Both his choice of passages and his reference to this theology of an 'indivisible and inseparable power' can be paralleled by rabbinic polemics against those who believed in 'two powers in heaven'. Although the rabbinic sources never explicitly identify the adherents of this 'heresy', Justin reveals both the part played by gentile Christians like himself in the argument, and that it was not only Christians who were involved in such speculations.[71]

However, while Justin may help us to detect and yet not to overestimate hidden Christians behind the debates of rabbinic Judaism,[72] it is Justin's presentation of Jewish attitudes to scripture which is most important for us. Justin knows that the debate must be carried out on the basis of the scriptures accepted by the Jews (56.16; 68.2); he avoids as far as possible appealing to Jesus's words, unlike later writers 'Against the Jews' who make good use of Jesus's own attacks against his contemporaries in the Gospels. It is the scriptures which both unite and yet divide Jews and Christians for Justin: the words written on phylacteries are, after all, words 'which we consider in every way holy' (46.5). The simple proof from prophecy, which requires only exegetical skill on the one hand and the insight to recognise its truth on the other, is proving inadequate. The conflict over the right interpretation is becoming a conflict over the right to interpret, even a conflict over the right to possess the scriptures.

In the *Apology* Justin acknowledges that the scriptures belong to the Jews. Setting great store by the effectiveness of the proof from prophecy for his pagan readership,[73] he appeals to 'the prophets of God among the Jews' (*Apol.* 31.1). Adopting the legend of the translation of the Law first found in the second-century BCE *Letter of Aristeas,* Justin extends it to include the prophets as well:[74] the words of these prophets, written down in their own Hebrew tongue and arranged by themselves, were preserved by the kings of the Jews until the king of Egypt, Ptolemy, pro-

cured both the books and their translation with the co-opera-
tion of King Herod (*sic*) (*Apol.* 31.2–4). Thus these books have a
doubly authenticated line of transmission, being preserved both
by the Egyptians in Ptolemy's library, and by the Jews throughout the world. The only problem is that the Jews who read the
books fail to understand them, while Christians recognise in them
the fulfilment of prophecy at the coming of Christ (31.5, 7–8).
In this way Justin both preserves the aura of antiquity of the
prophecies to which he appeals, and evades any accusation that
the Christians had invented or corrupted them in their own
interests. That the Jews possessed their own sacred writings would
be well known, whether or not anyone would bother to check
the copy in the great library of Alexandria.

In debate with Trypho Justin adopts a rather more aggressive
approach. Trypho must heed him because his arguments are
not crafted by human skill but are those spoken by David, Isaiah,
Zachariah and Moses; Trypho will recognise them, 'for they are
contained in your scriptures'. 'Rather', Justin immediately cor-
rects himself, 'not yours but ours, for we believe them, while
when you read you do not understand the sense in them' (*Dial.*
29.2). Yet he knows that the 'holy and prophetic scriptures' are
found among 'you', the Jews (32.2; cf. 87.4, 'your prophets'),
that they are read each day by the Jews (55.3), who claim to
know the very letters of the scriptures (70.5), and that copies
are to be found in the Jewish synagogues (72.3).

Justin knows no other version of the scriptures than the Greek
translation, and assumes that it is this which the Jews will also be
using, thus confirming the diaspora setting. Yet it is here that
his troubles begin: the Jews (or their teachers), he concludes,
have been tampering with their own Greek scriptures. They read
'young woman' (νεᾶνις) instead of 'virgin' (παρθένος) in the
important 'messianic' verse, Isaiah 7.14 (43.7; 67.1 (Trypho);
84.3), and give other alternative readings in crucial passages
(120.4–5: Gen. 49.10; 124.2–3: Ps. 81(82).7; 131.1: Deut. 32.8;
137.3: Isa. 3.9–10). They refuse to accept the authority of
Ptolemy's translation and seek to offer their own (71.1),[75] and
they even delete entire passages (68.7; 71.1–73.4; 84.4). This latter, which Trypho finds surprising but does not dispute (73.5),
is for Justin a more heinous crime than even the making of the
golden calf or the killing of the prophets (73.5–6); this means it

is part of their determined and destructive opposition to both Christ and his disciples.

Justin knows the Greek version of the scriptures which the Jews used, probably not just from debates but from actually having had the opportunity to study them. While some of his difficulties seem to arise from the fact that this version apparently was a 'Hebraising' version compared with the Septuagintal texts which have come down to us, rather more go back to the discrepancies between the Christian collection(s) of Testimonies from which he drew and the copies of the whole Bible, or of continuous biblical text, for knowledge of which he was perhaps dependent on Jewish sources.[76] Like subsequent Christian exegetes, he was highly vulnerable to the Jewish charge of inaccurate knowledge and limited skill in the interpretation of the scriptures.[77] The battle could not simply be won by counter-charges of blindness, hard-heartedness and lack of the divine grace to understand, important though these are (32.5; 34.1; 53.2; 55.3 etc.). The charge of falsification takes the offensive at the most vulnerable point, but in regularly agreeing only to rely on those scriptures and on the text acknowledged by the Jews (73.6; 120.5; 124.4; 131.1), Justin admits the vulnerability as well as the unacknowledged continuing Christian dependence on what in practice really were Jewish scriptures. This is why too he brings no such charges against the Jews in the *Apology* – where they would probably backfire against the Christians – but instead implies their faithful transmission of the prophetic words.

Justin, of course, has the advantage in choosing which passages to cite, and Trypho gets only a few opportunities to challenge him on his selectivity (27.1; 'Why do you selectively say the things you want from the prophetic words, but not mention those which clearly command sabbath observance [Isa. 58.13–14]?'). Yet when it comes to interpreting these passages Justin has to contend with contrary Jewish understanding. Here, as we have seen, the voices we hear are largely authentic, and we need not examine them or differentiate between the reliable and less so. The overall impression is that the Jews are also interpreting their scriptures, and that they often have alternatives to the Christian exegesis which cannot simply be ignored. Although Justin often simply refers to 'your', the Jewish, exegesis, he knows that it ultimately derives from the Jewish teachers or exegetes.[78]

Image and Reality

Certainly it is they too who bear the ultimate responsibility both for the tampering with the text 'whenever it conflicts with their foolish and conceited opinion', and for the obstinate refusal to accept the messianic nature of the prophecies to which Justin appeals (68.7–9; 71). It is their attention to detail and their readiness to light upon the slightest inconsistency or error which forces Justin to the thoroughness of his own exposition (115.3–6).[79] At the same time they occupy themselves with interpreting mere details of scripture of no significance while evading the important, namely that which can be interpreted christologically by Justin (112.4). The teachers are not only interpreters of scripture, but it is as such that the ultimate conflict is between them and Christ; the crucial decision is between listening to them and listening to Christ – as presented by Justin (94.4; 112.5; 140.2; 142.2).

Justin is evidently simplifying a very complex situation in Jewish and Christian competing use of the scriptures. First, the Christians were, albeit unwillingly, still very dependent on the Jews for knowledge of and access to the scriptural text. Thus, on the one hand, Justin reflects the disadvantages of Christian dependence on inherited collections of scriptural texts, whether or not we think of fixed 'Testimony Books', which had sometimes already been 'redacted' in the interest of Christians; on the other, the role of the Septuagint was changing as the Christians claimed it for themselves as authoritative while a corresponding tendency among the Jews moved towards a Greek text which was closer to the Massoretic text.[80]

Secondly, Christian understanding of the scriptures continued to draw from Jewish exegesis – not all of Justin's 'Jewish' exegesis can be taken from earlier '(Jewish-)Christian' tradition – while also developing only those, or new, patterns which met its eventual needs. At the same time, Christian exegesis continued to be met by an alternative Jewish exegesis of the same passages, an exegesis which sometimes may itself have been developed in opposition to the former.

Yet, thirdly, the predominant Christian interests in scripture were not always the same as those of the Jews, even while they shared overlapping attitudes and approaches. This was not simply a matter of Law (Jewish) against prophets (Christian), although there are elements of that contrast, and Justin is moving towards a presentation in these terms. So he urges his hearers to despise the teachings 'of those who exalt themselves and want to be called Rabbi' and to pay their attention to 'the prophetic words' even to the point of sharing the fate of the prophets; otherwise 'you cannot receive any benefit at all from the prophetic [words]' (112.5) – although the archetypal 'blessed prophet' in this passage is Moses![81] Similarly, the related contrast between 'literal' (?legalistic) Jewish and 'spiritual' (?prophetic) Christian understanding of scripture, common in later Christian polemic, is only just developing in Justin. He criticises their 'historical' exegesis of the 'messianic' prophecies and psalms (see above) and their anthropomorphisms (114.3), and he also condemns the Jewish teachers who permit polygamy by appealing to the patriarchs' marriages, failing to understand the more divine intention which made these symbols and not norms (134; 141.4).[82] Although these contrasts were to become fixed models in later writers,[83] a more varied picture of exegetical concerns on the Jewish side is betrayed by Trypho's interest in Christian millenarianism (80), by the long discussion on the interpretation of the theophanies, by the need to tackle apparent inconsistencies in scripture (65.1), and by the lively debate as to whether the universalistic passages of Isaiah point to proselytes or to the Christians (122).[84] Trypho finds Justin's exegesis 'contrived ... and blasphemous' (79.1), while Justin says the Jews deceive themselves by the 'equivocal terms' (ὁμονύμαι λέξεις). Both clearly agree that scripture is a riddle, demanding interpretation; both debate changes of names, the Jews those of Abraham and Sarah, the Christians that of Joshua (113.2)![85] It is evident that the Jews have not conceded the victory to the Christians and left them with either the text or the prophets while turning to the ever finer understanding of the Law. Christians and Jews are engaged in a contest (ἀγών) (68.2; 78.10): a contest about and a contest for the scriptures.

c) *Christ versus the Teachers*

For Justin, the ultimate contest, however, is between allegiance to the teachers and allegiance to Christ (142.2). Both Jewish erroneous exegesis and their spurious editing of the text of the scriptures itself are the work of the teachers who thus blind the ordinary people to the true understanding of God's message; for their part the people are in thrall to the teachers and to their tradition (9.1; 38.1–2; 48.2). Yet their activity has a darker side than mere intellectual antagonism. Falsification of the text is more heinous than that most heinous of Jewish crimes, the making of the golden calf, and is thus parallel to the murder of the prophets and of Jesus himself (73.5–6). Their hostility to Christ and to the Christians also takes a more direct and personal form. They are responsible for the slanders against both Jesus and Christians which are to be heard throughout the world (117.3).[86] They instruct the people to avoid any conversation or debate with Christians (38.1), and are even responsible for the scorning of the Son of God after the synagogue prayer (137.2). The most natural impression is that they are the driving force behind all the opposition to Christianity and that the people are largely passive under their rule.[87]

Such an impression fits well with the traditional picture in earlier scholarship of post-70 CE Judaism as dominated by the rabbis, who took stringent measures to exclude Christians from the synagogue community and who largely moulded the future shape of Judaism. Justin's attack against their love of the title 'rabbi' would reflect the formal use of this title after 70 (112.5), although he is, of course, quoting Matthew 23.7 here, while his emphasis on them as 'teachers' would accurately represent the dominant ethos of their leadership. In particular, his description of them as 'Pharisee teachers' (137.2; cf. 102.5; 103.1) would, according to this view, betray the historical link between the rabbis and the pre-70 sect of 'Pharisees', a historical link which few church Fathers acknowledge. Although many do see a spiritual link which permits the use of Jesus's words against the 'scribes and Pharisees' against their Jewish contemporaries, generally they seem to think of the Pharisees as no longer extant.[88]

The scorning of Jesus 'after the prayer' belongs to a series of passages, discussed below, which claim that the Jews curse both Christ and Christians, passages which have usually been referred to the *Birkath ha-minim*, the blessing directed against 'heretics', according to tradition introduced under Gamaliel II (*bBer.* 28b–29a), and sometimes seen as explicitly if not exclusively designed to exclude Christians from the synagogue.[89] This (137.2) is both the most explicit such reference, locating the scorning 'after the prayer', and the only one to place responsibility on the 'Pharisee teachers'. Their responsibility for the rumours against Christ and Christians (117.3) is then naturally linked with the charge that the Jews (in this case not the teachers in particular) have sent out specifically appointed ('ordained') men from Jerusalem warning against the appearance of 'the impious sect of the Christians'; they claim that the source of this sect was a 'certain Jesus of Galilee, a deceiver (πλάνος), whom we crucified but whose body his disciples stole in order to claim his resurrection' (17.1; 108.2). Justin also complains that despite his miracles Jesus's contemporaries rejected him as a 'worker of magic and deceiver of the people' (μάγος καὶ λαοπλάνος) (69.7). Whether or not on good historical grounds, later Jewish sources also lay this as the fundamental charge against Jesus (*bSan.* 43a), and its currency outside Palestine in the second century is confirmed by its repetition by the Jew quoted by Celsus.[90]

The instructions not to discuss with Christians, which Trypho affirms (38.1) and Justin repeats (112.4), also have echoes in rabbinic sources: *tHull.* 2.20–2 warns against any social (NB) intercourse with 'heretics' (*minim*), while later tradition (*bAbZ.* 17a and 27b) recounted salutary examples of those who risked too close contact with notorious heretics, often taken to be Christians.[91]

Yet these surprising parallels with rabbinic sources force us to ask whether the Judaism of Ephesus and the rest of the Diaspora was already dominated by the Rabbis by the middle of the second century. Rabbinic sources themselves betray limited interest in the Diaspora while suggesting that real control even of Palestine took a considerable time to establish; surviving evidence of diaspora Judaism, on the other hand, albeit largely archaeological, shows little evidence of rabbinic control in this period.[92] Justin's evidence is itself more ambiguous than at first appears when read in the light of the rabbinic material, and he may be attributing to the teachers a variety of measures which he has drawn from various sources. For example, that the messengers are sent from Jerusalem (17.1), and that the teachers are there associated with the high priests, hardly fits the post-70 CE situation; it may even be an elaboration of Acts 28.21.

In 137.2 Justin actually accuses them of 'scorning the King of Israel', language which does not fit surviving versions of the

Birkath ha-minim: 'And for apostates let there be no hope; and may the insolent kingdom be uprooted quickly, in our days. And may the *nosrim* and the *minim* perish quickly; and may they be erased from the Book of Life; and may they not be inscribed with the righteous.' Moreover, he specifically attributes this measure to the local leadership – 'as your synagogue chiefs (ἀρχισυνάγωγοι) teach' – supplementing this by his personal interpretation as 'obedience to the Pharisee teachers'. We probably should not seek too precise a reference for these measures: that local communities would have taken measures against disruption by the Christians on their own initiative is highly probable, and local authorities are probably indicated by 'the rulers [of the people]' to whom are attributed various countermeasures in 73.5 (by Trypho), 82.3 (influenced by Isa. 1.23), and perhaps in 39.6.[93]

There is, then, no simple identification between known 'rabbinic' measures against Christians and those which Justin describes, nor between the rabbis and his 'teachers'. The model of the pervasively responsible teachers seems to be one he has imposed, either from his experience of Palestinian Judaism or because of the dominance of teaching within his own understanding of Christianity and its relationship with Judaism. Perhaps, too, as a teacher, Justin had debated with other Jewish teachers and perhaps, too, as we have seen, learned from them. We cannot assume that the Judaism of Ephesus was necessarily under the thumb of the teachers nor that the conflict with Christianity was on every level a matter of teaching. In fact there is much to suggest that it was not.

d) *Jewish–Christian Hostility*

In puzzling contrast to Trypho's sustained moderate and courteous demeanour are not only Justin's regular harsh attacks against his Jewish interlocutors, and against the Jews generally, but even more his repeated charges of extreme Jewish hostility against the Christians. Most simply he claims that they hate Christians (39.1), but their hatred takes active form. They curse or anathematise in their synagogues those who believe in Jesus (καταράω: 16.14; 93.4; 95.4; 96.2; 108.3; 133.2; καταθεματίζω: 47.4; βλασφημέω: 35.8), and even curse Jesus himself (95.4;

133.6).[94] Whenever they have the possibility or power they go so far as to kill the believers (95.4; 122.2; 133.6), although their present political subservience has deprived them of this power and it is left to the gentiles to put into effect their cursing by putting to death those who make a Christian confession (16.4; 96.2). In this the Jews are only acting in continuity with their killing of Jesus, for which they fail to repent (133.6), and even with the killing of the prophets before him (16.4).

A number of theological themes have inspired Justin.[95] First and foremost, the theme of the killing of the righteous prophets, and pre-eminently of the righteous one, as the hallmark of Jewish unbelief and disobedience, is one which the Christians took over from Jewish tradition (cf. Wis. 2.12–20 etc.; Matt. 23.34–35; Acts 7.52).[96] Whilst in its Jewish form it formed the background for an explanation of present suffering and for an appeal to repentance, in Christian hands it both established Jesus as the one sent by God in the line of the prophets, and justified an uncompromising condemnation of the Jews. A significant corollary of this framework for understanding the death of Jesus is that Roman participation in it is largely ignored.

Secondly, Justin knows, and explicitly contrasts with their 'ceaseless *cursing* of him and those who belong to him', Jesus's injunction that Christians should love those who hate them and 'bless those who *curse* them' (133.6: Luke 6.28; cf. 96.3, quoting Luke 6.35–36).[97] A rhetoric of contrast reinforces the characterising of each party.

Thirdly, Justin tackles with considerable care the Deuteronomic injunction that crucifixion brings or implies a *curse* (from God) (Deut. 21.23).[98] This for Trypho is a far greater obstacle than the mere assertion of a suffering Messiah, and he introduces the problem three times before Justin finally takes it up (32.1; 89.2; 90.1). In answer, Justin, like Paul in Galatians 3.10–13 but possibly independently,[99] appeals to Deuteronomy 27.26, the curse on all – which he takes to include gentiles as well as Jews – who do not obey the whole Law, and presents Christ as the one who took upon himself the curse which lay upon all humankind (95). He goes beyond Paul by introducing the story of the brazen serpent from Numbers 21.8–9 – a story which has the added advantage of presenting God as apparently commanding Moses to act (i.e. to make an image) in contradiction to the

Law he had already ordained: when the people gazed at the
serpent Moses lifted up they were freed from the bites of the
serpents plaguing them. This serpent, evoking the serpent which
was cursed by God in Genesis 3 and which was the source of
death, was not itself the means of salvation but was a type of
Christ, who brought deliverance from the 'bites of the serpent',
as predicted in Isaiah 27.1 (91.4; 94.1–5; 111–12). Only when he
has established this is Justin able to tackle Deuteronomy 21.23:
the Jewish endeavour both to curse Christians and to demonstrate that he was crucified as 'cursed and an enemy of God' (cf.
93.4) is an obscene response to what Christ did in accordance
with God's will, and itself fulfils the words of Deuteronomy 21.23
– the curse on the one who hangs upon the cross is the curse the
Jews seek to put into effect (95.2–96.2).

These biblical models have helped shape Justin's presentation and explain why he so often accuses the Jews of *cursing*
Christ and Christians. The latter should not be taken too formally; he can also speak of them reviling or despising (137.2),
rejecting and dishonouring (16.4), blaspheming (35.8; 122.2;
126.1), profaning (120.4 from Mal. 1.11). Neither have biblical
models created the accusations. The variety of language and the
pervasiveness of the theme in different contexts breathes an atmosphere of immediacy and of brooding hostility. It is both a
general hostility and one which takes quite specific and even
official forms – in the synagogues (16.4), after the prayer,
following the direction of the rulers of the synagogue (137.2).
The general, at times, may be nothing more than the continuing refusal of the Jews to believe, which for Justin constituted a
form of blasphemy, coming as it did from those to whom the
prophets had spoken (35.8; 126.1). That the specific included
the *Birkath ha-minim* discussed above can be neither proven nor
excluded, for Justin's language is too inexact to make a clear
contribution to the disputed history of that prayer.[100] It is probable that, either on a regular basis or in specific circumstances,
there might be liturgical expression of the exclusion of those
following particular (deviant) beliefs or practices as a means of
maintaining the purity of the community.[101] Such expressions
both would be the forerunners of the *Birkath ha-minim*, and,
especially in the Diaspora, would have continued after its formulation. Those who had been attracted to Christianity but

returned to Judaism (47.4) might be required to declare their renunciation of past beliefs. There was also the public debate between Christians and Jews to which outsiders could listen; sympathisers who had heard Christian preaching might take their questions back to the synagogue; on these occasions too Jews would have vehemently denied the Christian use of the scriptures or the possibility that the crucified Jesus could be the promised Messiah. Again missionary competition would sharpen the accusations on both sides.

Most specific among the charges of Jewish hostility are those claiming that the Jews seek to put Christians to death.[102] These fit into a theological framework which holds the Jews responsible for the murder of the righteous one, of the righteous prophets before and of his followers after; a tradition which, as we have seen, has Jewish roots. Moreover, Justin has to modify the charge by admitting that they want or seek to kill those who believe (110.5; 122.2), that they would do it when and if they had the power (16.4; 95.4; 133.6), but that in the present circumstances of powerlessness it is in fact the gentiles who actually condemn Christians to death (96.2; cf. 131.2). Although he attributes to proselytes a particularly virulent hostility, which could appear to be a genuine reflection of the diaspora situation,[103] here too he can only accord them the desire to kill, and is rather more concerned to demonstrate that they do not fulfil the universalist prophecies of the scriptures (122.2). In the *Apology* Justin also accuses the Jews of hatred and of killing Christians when-ever they can, but for proof he appeals only to his readers' imagination and to Bar Kochba's reprisals against Jewish Christians (*Apol.* 31.6; 36.3). In accordance with the general theme of that work he there prefers to attribute persecution to the work of the demons (*Apol.* 57.1; cf. *Dial.* 131.2).[104]

Justin is clearly convinced of Jewish hatred of Christians; he is of course equally convinced that Christians do not respond with hatred but with a dominically enjoined goodwill and prayer, although this does nothing to soften his polemic. He may also believe that Jews were behind at least some of the denunciations or other moves which led to the persecution of Christians. That the mutual conflict between the two groups sometimes led to moves against Christians is of course possible, but he signally

fails to prove that the Jews were the main force behind the persecution of Christians in the second century.[105]

The Language of Competition and Take-over

Right at the beginning of the debate with Trypho, Justin sets out
his ultimate understanding of the relationship between Christians and Jews: 'For we are the Israelite, the true and spiritual
one, race of Judah, and of Jacob and Isaac and Abraham' (11.5).
With this Justin marks a climax in the growing claim by Christians to take over the rights and privileges of the Jewish people.
Before him Christians claimed to be the heirs of the new
covenant, to be the children of Abraham and recipients of the
promises, but it is Justin who first speaks of Christians as 'Israel'.[106]
'As therefore your whole race, from that one Jacob, who was
surnamed Israel, were called Jacob and Israel, so we, from Christ
who begat us for God, are called and are Jacob and Israel and
Judah and Joseph and David, and true children of God' (123.9).
To the Christians belong the other titles of Israel: they are the
true high-priestly race (116.3), to them belongs the term 'people' (λαός), a term usually kept for the people of God (110.4),
even 'a holy people', not 'citizen assembly (δῆμος) or barbaric
tribe' or (foreign) 'nation' (119.3); they will receive the inheritance in the holy city (26.1), a promise Justin takes literally; the
gifts that earlier beonged to the Jews have been transferred to
the Christians, in particular prophecy (82.1). This concentra-
tion on the church as Israel means that Justin does not join the
movement among his contemporaries in calling Christians 'the
third race', which would obscure the claim to be taking the place
of Israel as the people of God's election; he does, however, speak
about them as 'another people' or 'race' (119.3; 138.2). The
dialectic is well expressed when he says, 'There are two seeds of
Judah and two races, as there are two houses of Jacob, one born
of blood and flesh, the other of faith and the spirit' (135.6).

The discontinuity between the two people is all the sharper
because the 'new people' who have sprung up are characteristically drawn from the gentiles (119.3–5). 'You', the Jews,
are set over against 'we', who are Christians and are those who
have turned from paganism (122.5; 130.4).[107] Justin knows that

some Jews would be saved, but they are a very few (136.1), and he is rather more conscious of the negative side, that the words of hope do not apply to the vast majority of the Jewish race but only to a few, just to the patriarchs and prophets and any others who are pleasing to God (120.2; 130.2). Only rarely does Justin seem to see a twofold procession into the church, from the Jews and from the gentiles, once as prefigured in the ass and its foal on which Jesus rode into Jerusalem (53.4), and once in the two sisters, the weak-eyed Leah and Rachel, synagogue and church (and not synagogue and gentiles!), for both of whom Jacob/ Christ served (134.3–6). Justin no doubt knew of Jews within the Church, both in the past and still in the present (cf. 47), although their numbers were small. Yet for him the gentile experience was both historically and theologically the norm. There is no sense of gentiles being grafted into the Jewish stock, but of a new creation, into which a few Jews might find their way, but as individuals and as exceptions. Joining 'the other people' would be as disruptive for them as it would for pagans – something that by Justin's time was very clearly socially true.

This take-over bid is totally uncompromising and, not surprisingly, is met with anger by Trypho and his companions (124.1). They should not think that they alone are Israel, Justin retorts (123.6), although in practice he hardly seems to accord them any right to this name any more. Trypho responds in stunned surprise, while his companions react to Justin's interpretation of Isaiah 42.6–7, particularly 'the light to the gentiles', with all the rowdiness of a theatre crowd (123.7; 122.4). Yet they have their own counter-attack: the scriptural promises of the enlightenment of the gentiles are fulfilled in the coming of proselytes to Judaism (122.1, 4). Justin cannot simply dismiss this argument by slandering the behaviour of the proselytes; by condemning their intense hostility towards Christians he only admits their loyalty to Judaism. Instead he must disprove their exegesis, which he does by arguing that since proselytes are fully integrated into the Jewish people, they are bound by the same Law and covenant and so do not meet the requirement demanded by God's promise of a new covenant (122.1–123.2). There is no common ground between proselytes to Judaism and Christians; the former are circumcised and belong to the Jewish people, Christians are not circumcised and so are rightly called in their own right a people and a nation (123.1).

The lively character of the debate points to the immediacy of the issue for Justin and the church. Justin is taking the very scriptural passages and the technical terminology with which the Jews spoke of gentile conversion and applying them to the Christians; such a procedure need not only be explained in sociological terms as part of the process of establishing self-identity by comandeering key symbols of the erstwhile parent, but also as signalling one of the most hotly fought-over spoils of war. In the implicit, if not explicit, missionary situation of existence in the Graeco-Roman city, where Judaism and Christianity from an apparently common base were adopting different strategies towards the approach of potential sympathisers,[108] legitimacy was as important for those outsiders as for those within.

Another weapon in this struggle is the claim to be God-fearing (θεοσεβεῖς). Justin, like others of his contemporaries, claims this epithet for the Christians in conscious opposition to the Jewish claim.[109] When pagans turn from idolatry to Christ they are turning to the true fear of God, they become those who fear God (30.3; 52.4; 53.6): Christianity is 'fear of God' (θεοσέβεια), Christians are the God-fearers (91.3; 110.2, 4). We do not need to turn to Jewish sources to see that this belongs to the language of competition. Trypho himself protests that Christians do not behave in any way as those who fear God (οἱ φοβούμενοι τὸν θεόν) – as evidenced by their failure to keep the Law (10.3–4); Justin, for his part, declares that their history of disobedience and idolatry shows that the Jews have not the slightest sense of the fear of God (θεοσεβεῖν, 46.6). They consider themselves to be but they are not either lovers of God or understanding; 'we' are proven to be both more understanding and more God-fearing (118.3); God promised to Abraham 'a nation of like faith, and God-fearing and righteous, but it is not you' (119.6).

Justin is, then, offering his hearers a sharp 'either/or' decision; there is no possibility of any position which tries to keep both options open. He shows his sensitivity to this issue in facing Trypho's question concerning Christians who maintain some observance of the Jewish Law (47). Here he must decide how far compromise can go, and his careful consideration reflects not only theological nicety but also the immediacy of the issue. In fact, Justin takes what even on his own admission is a moderate view. He allows that some converts from Judaism may wish to continue their observance of the Jewish Law; this is a sign of weakness but, so long as such people neither impose their convictions on nor refuse fellowship to other Christians, Justin would treat them as fellow-believers. Surprisingly, he even extends such openness, although somewhat more hesitantly, to gentile Christians who have been seduced to observance of the Jewish Law. Those he excludes from salvation are, first, Christians who not only want themselves to observe the Law but also seek to impose their convictions on others and who refuse fellowship to non-observant Christians; secondly, those who give up their Christian faith and take on Jewish observance; and, lastly, of course the Jewish people who never turn to faith, particularly those who participate in the cursing of Christians.

Given Justin's uncompromising view of the Law, in particular of circumcision and its purpose, his concessions here are surprising; the presence of circumcised gentile Christians in a church which is defined in contradistinction to the Jews and their proselytes by their not being circumcised (123.1) can surely only be allowed by Justin on pressing practical grounds. His sensitivity – in sharp contrast to that of Ignatius[110] – may be coloured by his Palestinian experience where we might expect to find this sort of situation; but his concern suggests the issue was not a merely theoretical one either for Justin in the Ephesian situation or for his readers in Rome. He may be seeking to keep 'within the fold' any gentile Christians who had adopted observance of the Law and who now found themselves spurned by other less conciliatory Christians, and who therefore could easily be won into separatist Jewish-Christian groups or even be increasingly attracted by Judaism itself. Justin's accusation that Trypho himself wanted to persuade him to adopt some observance of the Law (47.1), although belonging to the rhetoric of the debate, may suggest that Jews might still endeavour to win over any Christians who seemed interested in the validity of the Law. We are again in a 'missionary' situation.

Justin's maintenance of the Church as drawn characteristically from the gentiles leads the way to another suggestion by Trypho. 'You gentiles who hold the name Christians' may acknowledge him as Lord and Christ and God, but 'we who are

servants of the God who made him' have no need to confess or
worship him (64.1). The suggestion has a surprisingly modern
ring, but Justin's response is uncompromisingly adamant. He
accuses Trypho personally of being shallow and argumentative,
and only from his own fear of God's judgement does he hesitate
to exclude the possibility that any individual Jew might be saved.
Yet such as are can only be saved through Jesus Christ and as
'part of his portion' (64.2–3). The only exception Justin is
prepared to make to this is those in the past who did what is
universally, by nature and eternally, pleasing to God, which
itself is enjoined in the Law; they will share the salvation of the
righteous patriarchs of old, but this too is a salvation 'through
this Christ' (45.2–3).

Of particular importance among the righteous of old is Jacob,
and Justin even introduces him into this Old Testament quotation (45:2–4 drawing on Ezek. 14.20) . 'Jacob' appears as frequently as Abraham in the *Dialogue*, and it is his name (which is
also Israel) that Justin claims for the Christians (123.9). In so
doing he may be deliberately forestalling Jewish objections to
Christian appeals to Abraham, which pointed out that the
chosen people was descended only from the line through Jacob
(125.5).[111] The other side of this claim was of course the reinterpretation of the whole of Jewish history since Abraham.

Image and Reality

There can be no doubt that Justin was encountering a Judaism
of which he, in spite of himself, allows us regular glimpses, but
which was very different from the image he projects through
his refutation of it. This Judaism, which we shall call 'Trypho's
Judaism', can be both paralleled and complemented by our
other diaspora sources, although the surviving evidence for Jews
in Ephesus is disappointingly meagre.[112] However, we may
assume the community was not dissimilar to others of the
Ionian coastal area. Both Josephus (*Ant.* XVI.27–65) and Philo
(*Leg.* 315) record rescripts protecting their rights, while,
perhaps a little later than Justin, they included among their
number both a 'Chief doctor' and a priest who was also a
Roman citizen.[113]

Contrary to Christian interpretation of the loss of the Temple as establishing the decisive terminal point, Trypho's Judaism affirms the obligation of continuing obedience to the Law of God, particularly in the observance of circumcision, sabbath and festivals; they also observe certain laws of purity and practise ritual bathing. They understand their worship in the Diaspora as a sacrifice acceptable to God fulfilling scriptural promises, and Justin can assume that they would agree that effective prayer requires weeping and tears, and reverent prostration (90.5). They possess copies of the scriptures in the synagogue, at least in Greek translation, and these are regularly read, studied and exegeted. The importance of such study in contemporary Judaism is implicitly betrayed by Justin's interpretation of the house (οἶκος) built by the sons of the prophets gathered round Elisha (2 Kings 6.6) in 'synagogal' terms: they intended 'to declare and study the law and injunctions of God there' (86.6). We have already met the use of 'house' of a synagogue at Kyme,[114] while the importance of the scriptures is attested in a variety of ways. Synagogues, although later than Justin, have niches for the scrolls, while at Elaia, not far from Ephesus, one Pancharios was honoured with the epithet 'lover of the commandment' (φιλέντολος).[115] Distant from the *Dialogue* in place but not in time, Trypho's and Justin's concern about Jesus as subject to the curse of Deuteronomy may acquire a different complexion in the light of appeals to 'the curses (written in Deuteronomy)' threatened against grave despoilers in Phrygia.[116]

In Trypho's Judaism the older Greek translation is being brought closer to the Hebrew text through new translations, and they are developing new patterns of exegesis particularly of prophetic passages; the failure of the two revolts may also have prompted a general curtailment of messianic expectation and alternative exegeses. Both developments are well attested and were not only motivated by a reaction against Christian use.[117] The translations/revisions of Aquila and Theodotion are to be dated to the second century; according to tradition, the latter came from Ephesus while the former, a proselyte, was born in Pontus even if that was not the location of his activity.[118] Yet messianic expectation is by no means dead: Trypho has a lively interest in the subject and also in other eschatological themes, particularly regarding an interim, earthly kingdom. Scriptural experts or teachers play an important role in Jewish life, but they were not the only influential figures within the community – Justin also refers to rulers and 'rulers of the synagogue'. The former term is an obvious and well-attested one; the latter may sometimes have been a less 'liturgical' and 'official' one than Justin's own concerns suggest.[119] However, 'the synagogue' may be becoming increasingly the defining centre of Jewish life, and the term, at least in Christian eyes, is becoming characteristic of the Jewish community; although Justin can use it of the Christian gathering – they are in one soul, one 'synagogue' (gathering) and one *ecclesia* (church) (63.5)[120] – he not only refers to Jewish synagogues as the characteristic place of scriptural study, of prayer and of cursing Christians (16.4; 47.4; 72.3; 96.2), but also uses 'your synagogue' (sing.) in parallel to 'your people' and in contrast to 'the gentiles' and 'the church' (53.4; 134.3). His interpretation of Psalm 21(22).17, which puts the blame on the 'synagogue of the wicked' for Christ's death, presupposes the familiarity of the term for the Jewish community (104.1).

Although the Bar Kochba revolt had little immediate impact on the Diaspora, it probably prompted a wave of refugees, and certainly, like the First Revolt, encouraged some reflection on the meaning of the consequent suffering.[121] The key part played by circumcision during the revolt and its aftermath helped focus attention on this as the hallmark of God's people and perhaps sharpened bitterness against the Christians who not only stood aloof but turned the defeat to their theological advantage. However, Justin betrays no knowledge of any prohibition of circumcision: perhaps this does not suit his theological argument, or perhaps its prohibition after the revolt was focused in Judaea.

In contrast to the perceptions of piety in the Graeco-Roman world, the Jews were claiming to be properly 'God-fearing'; this was not just a matter of self-defence but was part of a self-advertisement within the city in which they lived, as is confirmed by its epigraphic use.[122] Whether or not engaged in active missionary activity, they could hardly avoid a 'public face'. Consequently they did attract both proselytes and sympathisers; however, the distinction between the two is clear. It is only the proselytes who are fully members of the people of Israel, and both their privileges and their place as prophesied by scripture are warmly defended. Whether this was always how *they* perceived it may be less certain!

Synagogues probably also took measures against Christians on a local basis if necessary, although there is no certain evidence of a concerted or centralised counter-attack – nor is such likely. Perhaps in the setting of synagogue services or of Torah study, the Christian claim to fulfil the scriptures was denied and Jesus himself was labelled a deceiver, a charge we also find in later Jewish sources; Christians along with other dissident groups may have been liturgically excluded from the promises of God through the words of the synagogue prayer. Harsh action was taken against Jews who adopted Christianity, and any who turned (or returned) to the Jewish community from Christianity were required to publicly repudiate their former faith. However, we need not assume that this was as regular, or loomed as large in people's consciousness, as it does for Justin!

The Jews appeared sufficiently unsympathetic to the Christian position to lay themselves open to the accusation of collabaration in the persecution of the latter, and it is not impossible that they may have traded on their privileged position when any public disturbance involved both groups. Yet equally common must have been the total disinterest and contemptuous mockery exhibited by some of Trypho's companions. Others, again like Trypho and others of his group, were willing to enter into debate; although Justin is correspondingly contemptuous of the questions and arguments they bring, these could not be ignored. Unfortunately the *Dialogue* affords us only a blurred glimpse of them, but we have noted the focus on observance of the Law, on the problems posed to Jewish monotheism by Christian views of Jesus, and on the proper interpretation of scripture. They may also have argued that the Christian appeal to the argument from prophecy absolved the Jews of all responsibility for the death of Jesus, 'for it had to happen', a position Justin seeks to forestall (141.1) and one which is also found in Melito.[123]

We may add to this picture a few more details which Justin lets us see in passing. We may leave aside his references to Passover, including the details of the presentation of the lamb for roasting (40.1–3), to the goats used in the Day of Atonement ritual (40.4–5), to the observance of the Feast of Unleavened Bread

(14.3), and to the scarlet thread in their fringes, together with the use of phylacteries (46.5); in each of these cases his starting-point is scripture, although it is possible that he shows knowledge of rabbinic interpretation or of characteristic Samaritan practice.[124]

In a passing reference Justin acknowledges the existence of Jewish exorcism. Part of his argument for the resurrection and exaltation of Jesus as Lord and Son of God is the efficacy of exorcism in Jesus's name. By contrast, any Jewish attempt to exorcise in the name of one of their kings, patriarchs or prophets is doomed to failure, although an appeal to the God of the patriarchs probably would be effective. However, he notes, most Jewish exorcists prefer the use of pagan-style charms and amulets (85.2–3). There is ample evidence that Jews were famed as magicians and exorcists, and that their skills were considered highly effective, so that pagan practitioners even made use of the name of the powerful Jewish deity.[125] Again, the appeal to Deuteronomy in the grave curses reflects this type of attitude to scripture, while there is evidence of Jewish 'magic' at Ephesus, itself famous for such practices (Acts 19.17–20).[126] Exorcism clearly played a significant 'missionary' role as well as an apologetic role (*Apol.* 2; 6) – and therefore also a competitive role (Acts 19.13–17); the recital of the effective deity's qualifications (*Dial.* 30.3; 76.6) could also serve as a teaching instrument.[127]

Even more allusive is the catalogue of Jewish sects which Justin cites in defence of the existence of those who claim the name Christian but whose teaching disqualifies their claim. 'So too one would not recognise as Jews the Sadducees, or similar heresies of the Genistai and Meristai and Galileans and Hellenians and Pharisees [and] Baptists' (80.4). Justin offers this apologetically, as if treading on sensitive ground; yet he also considers these as contemporary groups and not drawn from the records of the past. The identities of these sects have been much debated, although several are hardly self-designations.[128] The Sadducees are usually assumed to have disappeared after the loss of the Temple in 70 CE, while the Pharisees, strangely occupying the penultimate place, are often considered the pre-70 forebears of the far from sectarian rabbis. Although the total number seven is probably formulaic, it might be better to take the last two terms together, producing a 'separatist' group practising multiple baptism or washing, such as seems to have continued in Palestine even after 70.[129] 'Meristai' is probably derived from the Greek root 'to divide' (μερίζειν) – whether they divided the divinity or were themself divisive/separated – and 'Genistai' may derive from a Greek translation (γένος) of the Hebrew *min*. These two would then reflect generalised designations for separatist or heretical groups, which undoubtedly did continue to exist in the second century and which included Jewish Christians![130] The remaining terms are even more enigmatic, although as likely as any other is the suggestion that 'Galileans' could indicate Jewish Christians and 'Hellenians' those adopting Greek practices or views of some kind. As evidence of a continuing diversity within Judaism, at least in Christian eyes, the list is important, but its tradition-history and elucidation remain problematic.

Very different from these glimpses of a lively and self-confident Judaism is the picture which Justin projects through his polemic and exegesis, the picture which he wants his readers to have ever before their eyes as they encounter the reality. Justin's Judaism is characterised by its past history as drawn from and by the scriptures, particularly from the castigations of the prophets. The use of the prophets for this purpose in Christian polemic follows a well-mapped path. The prophetic proclamation of judgement was made from within, as part of an appeal to repentance and as a prelude to the promises of redemption and hope; in Christian hands it became a judgement from outside, a proof of refusal to repent and evidence of exclusion from the promises which were now the possession of the Christians, and thus it also became a means of self-justification.[131]

Justin's part in this scheme, extensively repeated, is easily sketched. The Jews are fundamentally hard-hearted towards all that God asks and promises; they are idolaters, and they are murderers of the righteous. The Law was given to control their leaning towards idolatry, exemplified above all in the incident of the golden calf but an enduring characteristic even after (19.5; 20.4; 132.1 etc.): frequency of repetition alone serves to justify a charge which could be maintained only on biblical and not on contemporary evidence. Thus it is Christians who have turned from idolatry, not converts to Judaism, who are joining an inherently idolatrous people (46.6–7). Moreover, they ('you') murdered the prophets, just as in due course they murdered the righteous one and continue to seek to murder those who believe (93.4). Jewish history is thus marked by a simple and consistent pattern determined by these formative events; their present attempts to corrupt the scriptures are defined by ('more terrible than') the making of the golden calf, and their refusal to believe in Jesus by their sacrifice to Baal (73.6; 136.3: 'Although *you* did not sacrifice to Baal .... you did not accept Christ'). Just as the recital of a saving history forms and maintains the identity of those who confess their part in it, the identity of the Jews is established by the repeated recital of their history of unbelief: 'So you *always* ... at that time sacrificing to the calf, and *always* appearing ungrateful and murdering the righteous and puffed up on account of race' (102.6); this recurring 'always' (ἀεί) makes the specific into the timeless (so also 27.2; 93.4; 131.4). Brought together, the traditional recital of God's saving acts for the people becomes a celebration not of faith but of faithlessness (131.3–133.1): 'And when these and all such wonderful and amazing things were done for you and witnessed ... you were condemned by the prophets ... and you dared such things against Christ. God knowing beforehand that you would do these things gave this *curse* against you through Isaiah the prophet: [Isa. 3.9–15; 5.18–25]'. As in the history of God's saving acts so also in the history of ungrateful response, the prophetic witness lifts out of the mundane the determinative and establishes its normative character.

A whole range of terms serves to define the Jews; most characteristic is their 'hardness of heart' (σκληροκάρδια). With Justin this becomes the most comprehensive term for the Jews.[132] The term itself is not widespread in the Greek Old Testament (noun: Deut. 10.16; Jer. 4.4; Sir. 16.10; adj.: Prov. 17.20; Ezek. 3.7; Sir. 16.9), while its single occurrence in the New Testament is when Jesus declares that the Law regarding divorce was given to them on account of their 'hardness of heart' (Mark 10.5 = Matt. 19.8). Although he does not quote this passage, Justin may have been strongly influenced by it: for him that hardness of heart was the first of all the grounds for the giving of the Law (18.2; 27.2; 46.5; 67.4, 10), or at least of certain of its injunctions (44.2; 45.3), and, in particular, those regarding offerings and sacrifices (43.1; 67.8 – an understanding with which Trypho agrees).[133] Yet his

Old Testament texts allowed him to see this as a fundamental characteristic which encompasses the whole of their history (16.1 (Deut. 10.16); 27.4 (Ezek. 3.7); 39.1; 114.4; 123.4). Their present failure to accept the witness of the scriptures to Jesus has the same source (53.2; 68.1; 137.1), and, if they continue to curse and even try to kill those who do believe, punishment will be exacted from them as from those who are 'unrighteous, sinners and altogether hard of heart and foolish' (95.4; cf. 46.7).

Although the first two terms of this catalogue, ἄδικοι and ἁμαρτωλοί, can be used generally as appropriate, the Jews (also 19.5; 14.2; 141.2) share them in particular with the evil power (78.10) and with heretics (35.5); 'foolish' (ἀσύνετοι) comes to Justin from Jeremiah 4.22 and so can be reserved for the Jews and their teachers (20.4; 27.4; 32.5; 92.6; 119.2; 134.1). Also reserved for the Jews, but not on obvious biblical grounds or from earlier tradition, is 'ungrateful' (ἀχάριστοι) (19.5; 27.2; 102.6; 131.4). Other terms, however, are shared with heretics: 'lawless' (ἄνομοι) (16.5; 123.3; heretics: 35.5, 6), 'impious' (ἀσεβεῖς) (92.4; heretics: 35.5; 80.3), 'atheist' (ἄθεοι) (92.4; 120.2; heretics: 35.4–6; 80.3; 82.3). Since the last term was used against Christians by Jews as well as by pagans (17.1; 108.2), it clearly belongs to the interchange of slander and accusation. Trypho's uncompromising reply to Justin's initial account of his conversion leaves us in no doubt that Jews would have also accused Christians of being lawless as well as blasphemous (8.3–4). The use of the same terms to characterise both Jews and heretics is probably more the result of disqualifying both in contrast to Christian self-legitimation than a conscious step in the process of equating Jews with heretics in a 'medicine chest of all heresies' (Epiphanius) and, much later, in legislation. That the terms could become standard and formative in defamation of the Jews is also true, but in Justin they are still part of a reciprocal war of name-calling.[134]

The same ambivalence is true of terms held in common with the evil power. There is in Justin, more implicitly than explicitly, the beginning of what has been called the 'demonisation' of the Jews.[135] The persecution of Christians is not only the work of the Jews, either directly or through pagan agency, but is also to be attributed to the demons and the army of the devil, 'through the service which is offered to them by you' (131.2; for demonic responsibility without explicit Jewish help see 18.3). A similar accusation underlies the charge that the Jewish response to God's saving acts 'extends even to sacrificing your own children to demons and in addition to all this attempting such things against Jesus' (133.1; cf. 73.6). However, the *Dialogue* does not develop this theme as far as some of Justin's near contemporaries were to do.

Thus Justin's Judaism is a near-monolithic entity of unbelief. For all his Logos doctrine, far more prominent in the *Apologies* than in the *Dialogue*, which gives non-Jewish history also a role in the 'preparation of the Gospel', the Jews occupy a special place. They alone are or possess potentially the true philosophy, a potential never fulfilled by them; they alone are culpable for that failure. Trypho's Judaism is something very different: a viable religious alternative, pursuing its own piety in obedience to God's Law. Both are still visible, something that was not to last long in the 'Adversus Iudaeos' literature.

Notes

[1] Major accounts of this literature may be found in A. Williams 1935; Wilde 1949; Schreckenberg 1990.

[2] For the classic acceptance of Eusebius's information see Zahn 1885–6; for considerable scepticism see M. Hoffmann 1966; Hyldahl 1966; van Winden 1971, all of whom emphasise the literary nature of the *Dialogue*.

[3] See Trakatellis 1986 and below, pp. 109–13.

[4] On the dialogue form see M. Hoffmann 1966; Voss 1970.

[5] See Stylianopoulos 1975: 20–32, and below, pp. 105–6. Prigent 1964 presents a detailed argument that much of the *Dialogue* is drawn from Justin's *Refutation*, whose order he then seeks to reconstruct from the disorder of the former. He has failed to persuade many, although Justin's use of earlier material, including perhaps of testimony sources, seems likely.

[6] So Voss 1970: 35–8, who does recognise that the *Dialogue* may have had its origin in genuine debates, but that it now is shaped by the literary Socratic tradition; he suggests that it may be countering Jewish missionary propaganda. For a critique of the 'pagan' argument see Stylianopoulos 1975: 169–95.

[7] As argued for example by Hyldahl 1966: 294. For the differences see Purves 1889: 97–100.

[8] See Cosgrove 1982 for a Christian audience.

[9] So Tränkle 1964, who argues convincingly for the authenticity of the *Adv. Iud.* and for its priority; see pp. 264–5.

[10] For this and what follows see Donahue 1973.

[11] So Zahn 1885–6: 57; Nilson 1977; and ctr. Sylianopoulos 1975: 174–89.

[12] See further Lieu 1994a.

[13] See, however, 122.2 where he emphasises the zeal of proselytes against Christians and 32.5 which accuses Trypho/the Jews of deceiving not only themselves but those who listen to them.

[14] For this and what follows see Skarsaune 1987: 256–9.

[15] Thus Skarsaune accepts that Trypho's companions may be seen as would-be proselytes.

[16] See further below, pp. 120–1, 137–8.

[17] See Barnard 1964; Prigent 1964; Shotwell 1965; Skarsaune 1987; Stylianopoulos 1975.

[18] See the classic study of Goldfahn 1883; also Harnack 1913; Higgins 1967; Hirshman 1992–3; Hruby 1973; Shotwell 1965; Sigal 1978–9.

[19] See Skarsaune 1987: 43–6, and below, pp. 127–8.

[20] See Higgins 1967.

[21] Compare Origen's and Jerome's ambivalence towards the Jewish teachers from whom they learnt so much.

[22] The question is inseparable from that of the origins of gnosticism. See also Segal 1977.

[23] See Hyldahl 1956 for arguments against the identification. Zahn 1885–6 accepted that the identification was intended and assumed Eusebius drew it from the supposedly lost introduction to the *Dialogue*.

[24] Goodenough 1923: 93–5.

[25] Arazy 1977; Tomson 1986: 128.

[26] Shotwell 1965: 93–115.

[27] Skarsaune 1987: 246.

[28] As suggested by M. Hoffmann 1966: 28, cited with approval by Skarsaune 1987: 165.

[29] Harnack 1913: 92.

[30] See Higgins 1967. It has been much debated whether there was a Jewish messianic interpretation of Isa. 53 (including propitiatory suffering) which has been censored out by anti-Christian polemic, but the internal inconsistency in Trypho's views as well as Justin's manifest apologetic concern makes it hazardous to rely on the *Dialogue* as evidence.

[31] See Williamson 1989: 103–44.

[32] So Skarsaune 1987: 210.

[33] Christology is the main topic of 31–118 (Skarsaune suggests 48–118).

[34] See Thornton 1989; Lüderitz 1983: 70. 1.16–17; 71. 1.24 (= *IBerenike* 18, 17).

[35] As argued by Skarsaune 1987: 168.

[36] Justin anticipates this reference to bathing in 14.1 where he speaks of them building for themselves wells which are broken and useless. He is quoting Jer. 2.13 here so we may hesitate to appeal to him for diaspora practice, but see E. P. Sanders 1992: 223 and the frequent proximity of synagogues to water sources. However, Hirshman 1992–3: 379 notes the omission of study of Torah.

[37] See Mendelson 1988: 51–75 who finds circumcision, sabbath, festivals, especially the Day of Atonement, dietary laws and rejection of intermarriage as central foci of Philo's understanding of orthopraxy.

[38] Ctr. Origen in *C. Cels.* VI.27 who holds the Jews responsible for pagan slanders against Christians, a charge accepted by some scholars; see Henrichs

1970: 22–4. This is different from Jewish charges against Jesus according to Justin, below, p. 131.

[39] See Rajak 1985a: 252.

[40] *Jos. & Asen.* 8.5; 10.12–13; *Syb. Or.* IV.27–30; cf. 1 Thess. 1.9; 1 Peter 4.3; Aristides, *Apol.* 15.5 (Syr.).

[41] See Smolar and Aberbach 1970.

[42] On the history of prohibitions stemming from the Apostolic Decree of which this is part see Simon 1970.

[43] This suggests that the ill-feeling against Christians at that time may not have been limited to the Jewish Christians whom Justin himself says were persecuted by Bar Kochba for failing to acknowledge him as Messiah (*Apol.* 31.6).

[44] On treatment of apostates in Judaism see E. Bammel 1987.

[45] See Vos 1990 on 'persuasive definition', giving 'a new conceptual meaning to a familiar word without substantially changing its emotive meaning' (pp. 45–6). Justin is the first to speak of a *second* circumcision.

[46] On Justin's understanding of the Law and on what follows see Stylianopoulos 1975 who, however, asserts that Justin separates the parts of the Law which are predictive from those which had a historical purpose. As what follows shows, this introduces a clearer structure than Justin himself adopts.

[47] Is this a response to the Marcionite charge that in retaining the Old Testament they were the same?

[48] Although at 92.2 Justin at first includes the laws relating to sacrifice in this general purpose, he then narrows it to circumcision by repeating the assertion that it is only circumcision which distinguishes the Jews from others.

[49] See Stylianopoulos 1975: 137 for Justin's 'biting irony' in this use of a text Trypho has introduced; also Skarsaune 1987: 172.

[50] See Stylianopoulos 1975: 117–19.

[51] He appeals to the righteous before Abraham who were not circumcised (27.5); to God's creation of man as uncircumcised (29.3); to the other peoples who also practised circumcision, thus denying its distinctiveness for the Jews (! 28.4); to the experience of God's favour without circumcision (29.1); and even to the fact that women cannot be circumcised but are equally able to do what is pleasing to God (23.5).

[52] See above pp. 106–8; so Donahue 1973: 105–38, who sees this group as the intended audience of the *Dialogue*.

[53] The importance of women among God-fearers and proselytes is often asserted but difficult to prove; Acts certainly mentions a number of such women who became Christians; see Bremmer 1989. On Justin's argument see Lieu 1994b.

[54] See Skarsaune 1987: 324–6; Lieu 1994b: 366.

[55] See *Pes. Rabb.* 23.4; *Gen. Rabb.* 46; Lieu 1994b: 362–4.

[56] Seneca, *De superstit.* apud Augustine, *De civ. Dei* II.11 (Stern 1974–84: I.431); however, note Ignatius's negative use of σαββατίζειν, pp. 33–4 above.

[57] Tacitus, *Hist.* V.5.2 (Stern 1974–84: II.19): circumcidere genitalia instituerunt, ut diversitate noscuntur.

[58] See n. 55 and Friedländer 1878: 96–9; Williams 1930: 85 n. notes that in *Gen. Rabb.* it is denied that Enoch was always righteous (ctr. Justin, *Dial.* 43.2).

[59] See Isaac and Oppenheimer 1985: 44–9; circumcision is given as the provocation in *Hist. Aug. Hadr.* XIV.6.

[60] This of course happened after the first revolt in 70, but Justin treats the two as a unity; see also *Apol.* 32.1–4.

[61] Skarsaune 1987: 183 overinterprets 114.5 'Surely there is not a desert where the Mount of Sion is?' (Isa.16.1), where the grammatical form implies a negative answer, as a subtle reference to the fact that now gentile Christians inhabit the city.

[62] On Justin's initiative here and the relative rarity of the theme after him see Stylianopoulos 1975: 120–1.

[63] Stylianopoulos 1975: 138–41, who also notes that this interpretation of the destruction is largely ignored by later church tradition, recurring only in Tertullian and Irenaeus who depend on Justin.

[64] See Isaac and Oppenheimer 1985.

[65] On Jewish response to the Bar Kochba revolt and loss of Jerusalem see Simon 1986: 3–5; Bokser 1983.

[66] So the words attributed to Eleazar after the destruction; see Simon 1986: 13; Goldfahn 1873: 199; van Unnik 1983a: 99–100 argues that Justin is referring to the time of the prophet.

[67] Harnack 1913: 92.

[68] See Kominiak 1948.

[69] See above pp. 108–9 and n. 18.

[70] So Goldfahn 1873: 106, 152; Hruby 1973.

[71] Segal 1977: 13, 118–19, 221–5.

[72] See also the argument by Smolar and Aberbach 1970 that the development of rabbinic interpretation of the golden calf episode was directed against Christian anti-Jewish use of the incident.

[73] See pp. 178–80.

[74] M. Müller 1989: 104–10.

[75] Barnard 1964: 400 sees a reference to Theodotion here.

[76] Convincingly argued by Skarsaune 1987: esp. 43–6. On the Hebraising tendency see P. Katz 1957. Kraft 1978 emphasises the variety of text forms in non-Christian Judaism.

[77] See Horbury 1992: 79, 84–5.

[78] Jews generally: 20.3; 32.4; 33.1; 34.1; 43.8; 64.5; 68.7; 77.2; 85.1; 97.4; 110.6; 112.1; 113.2; 122.1; teachers: 43.8; 62.2; 68.7–9; 83.2; 110.1; 112.2–4; 117.4; 118.3; 120.5; exegetes: 36.2; sophists: 129.2.

[79] In 115.6 he stresses their attention to 'accuracy' (ἀκριβές), a term familiar from Josephus's description of the Pharisees.

[80] On both these movements see P. Katz 1957; Hengel 1992. On Christian–Jewish contact, Treu 1973.

[81] Moses is considered a prophet in both Jewish and Christian exegesis.

[82] Lowy 1958 argues that monogamy was the norm but that rabbinic exegesis often assumes polygamy, possibly in disputes with sectarian exegesis.

[83] See for example Origen, *C. Cels.* V.60 and Horbury 1992: 97.

[84] On the importance of this issue and its significance for the question of readership see pp. 106–8, 137–8.

[85] On scripture as a riddle see Barton 1986: 186–7.

[86] This contradicts Trypho's dismissal of charges of immorality against Christians (10.2). In 117.3 the teachers are joined with the high priests, perhaps because Justin is using a tradition which held the latter responsible for the diffusion of rumours from their centre in Jerusalem before 70 CE.

[87] So Harnack 1913: 57.

[88] Irenaeus, *Adv. haer.* IV.12.1 exceptionally talks about the spurious Law 'which even to this day is called the Pharisaical', but most writers do not treat the Pharisees as in any way literally extant and some (Eusebius, *In Isa.* I.81; II.36) assert that they belong only to the past.

[89] The literature on this is now extensive; see especially Kimelmann 1981; Horbury 1982; S. Katz 1984: 48–53. See further below pp. 131–2, 134–5.

[90] Origen, *C. Cels.* I.28; II.48. See further J. Maier 1978: 219–29, 249–52; Stanton 1992a: 237–43.

[91] On *tHull.* 2.20–2 see Alexander 1992: 15–16; on the stories in *bAbZ.* see J. Maier 1978: 144–60, 182–92.

[92] See Rajak 1992; Goodman 1994b: 208–9.

[93] It is not clear whether this refers to persecution by Jewish or Roman authorities.

[94] See further references below.

[95] On what follows see Lieu 1996.

[96] On what follows see Skarsaune 1987: 277–80, 288–95.

[97] The quotations are not exact but the use of καταρᾶν from Luke 6.28 is important. That Christians pray for the Jews is repeated in more general terms at 35.8.

[98] For an analysis of this whole section see van Unnik 1979; Skarsaune 1987: 216–20; Lieu 1995a.

[99] So van Unnik 1979: 496–7.

[100] See above, pp. 130–2 and n. 89.

[101] See L. A. Hoffmann 1981.

[102] See Hare 1967: 66–79; Lieu 1996.

[103] So Harnack 1913: 81.

[104] In *Apol.* 63.11 the demons prompted the Jews to put Jesus to death, a theme absent from the *Dialogue*. See further Lieu 1996 and Root 1984.

[105] See further pp. 91–4.

[106] Except perhaps in Gal. 6.16. On the theme see Richardson 1969.

[107] See also 46.6–7; 69.4; 110.3; 116.1; 119.5.

[108] For a summary of this see Segal 1987, and for caution about Jewish missionary activity Goodman 1994a.

[109] See pp. 84–5 and Lieu 1995b: 497–501.

[110] See pp. 31–3.

[111] See Skarsaune 1987: 346–7.

[112] Horsley 1992: 125–6.

[113] Julius the 'Chief doctor': *CIJ* II. 745; M.Ar. Moussius: *CIJ* II. 746. See Robert 1960: 381–4; Trebilco 1991: [index].

[114] *CIJ* II.738 (built by Tation); see above, p. 89.

[115] *CIJ* I. 190, although this may reflect later developments.

[116] On these see Trebilco 1991: 60–74; Waelkens 1986: 171–4; Strubbe 1994. *CIJ* II.760 from Acmonia specifically threatens 'the curses (ἀραί) which are written in Deuteronomy'.

[117] See above, p. 128 and n. 80. Treu 1973 emphasises that changes to the Greek translations were motivated by the independent desire to improve on earlier ones.

[118] Schürer 1973–87: III. 493–504. However, the use of the LXX in third-century grave curses, if these are Jewish, shows it continued to be used by diaspora Jewish communities; see Strubbe 1994: 87–9.

[119] In Philo, *Leg.* 315 the rescript of G. Norbanus Flaccus to the Jewish community of Ephesus is addressed to 'the rulers'; on 'rulers of the synagogue' see Rajak and Noy 1994. *IEph* IV.1251 from Ephesus mentions 'the rulers of the synagogue and the elders'.

[120] A. Williams 1930:132 thinks this refers to the unity of believers as individuals, as members of the Jewish race, and as members of the Christian church.

[121] See above n. 65.

[122] See Lieu 1995b.

[123] See p. 213, but it is possible that this was equally an inner Christian problem.

[124] See Sigal 1978–9; Barnard 1964.

[125] For a study of Jewish amulets and magic bowls, Naveh and Shaked 1985.

[126] See Horsley 1992: 125 for a magical gemstone from Ephesus inscribed with Exod. 3.14; Kraabel 1968: 56–9.

[127] See S. Davies 1980: 25–8 on the place of exorcism in the apocryphal Acts.

[128] See Simon 1957; Black 1958–9; Sigal 1978–9: 83–5.

[129] Hegesippus (in Eusebius, *H.E.* IV.22.7) includes the Hemerobaptists in his list of 'opinions among the Israelites'. The root 'prsh' means 'to separate' and the term is used occasionally in rabbinic literature of separatist groups.

[130] See above pp. 124–5, on 'two powers' and Segal 1977.

[131] See Ruether 1974: 124–31, 228–32.

[132] The term itself is little used before him: on the biblical usage see below; in the Apostolic Fathers and apologists it otherwise comes only in a citation in *Barnabas* 9.5 and in *Hermas, Vis.* III.7.6. Stephen uses the related 'stiff-necked' (Acts 7.51 cf. Exod. 33.3, 5 etc.); the underlying conception is rather more widespread.

[133] Skarsaune 1987: 314–20.

[134] See Davids 1973: 181–5.

[135] On this in Justin see Root 1984.

5

THE APOLOGISTS

The appearance of the first *Apologies* during the reign of Hadrian marks a new step, not only in the development of Christian literature but also in Christian self-awareness. Ostensibly directed not to the church for inward consumption but to the wider society, or even to those in authority over it, the conventions and norms of that society shape their language and argument. Justin Martyr's debt to Greek philosophy on the one hand, and his contribution to future Christian thought on the other, is but the best example of this.[1] On the surface, then, the 'Apologies' signal a crucial move in the thought and evolution of the church both away from the domination of the legacy of her origins within Judaism, and towards her independent activity on the public stage. Yet this is only half the story, for it is at precisely the same time that we find the development of another literary form, the polemic against the Jews. Both, of course, have their precedents already in the New Testament, but only as themes embedded within other literary contexts; now they emerge as independent literary genres.

Under Hadrian we meet the first apologist, Quadratus (Eusebius, *H.E.* IV.3.1–2), and also the first sustained anti-Jewish polemic, although not in Asia Minor, the *Epistle of Barnabas*.[2] Indeed, according to the later apocryphal *Letter from James to Quadratus*, which survives only in Armenian and Syriac, Quadratus himself was famed both for his commitment to the truth of the Gospel and for his exertions 'against both Jews and Gentiles'.[3] If, as has been argued, the *Letter* does represent independent Jewish-Christian tradition, Quadratus may have been chosen as the recipient for this pseudonymous harsh polemic against Jewish unbelief and hostility not only because he was traditionally directly linked with the apostolic age but also because of a tradition of his polemics against the Jews; this would

155

then complement his apologetic writing to which Eusebius refers.[4] Quadratus's *Apology* has not survived; the hypothesis that it is to be found in the *Epistle to Diognetus* – Eusebius's quotation from the former (see below) neatly fitting into the lacuna between *Diog.* VII.6 and 7 – although highly attractive for our purposes because of the strong anti-Jewish tone of that *Epistle*, has little else to commend it, and the *Epistle to Diognetus* probably belongs to the end of the second century.[5] As it is, the few lines of Quadratus's *Apology* quoted by Eusebius which speak of the survival even 'until our own time' of some of the recipients of Jesus's healing powers (*H.E.* IV.3.2) tell us little about the gist of the whole: that demonstration could be directed against a number of other claimants to, less enduring, healing powers, whether Jewish, pagan or gnostic.[6]

These two new styles of argument continue throughout the century, with a number of leading thinkers writing on both fronts – Justin with his two *Apologies* together with the *Dialogue against Trypho*, and two figures who are for us little more than names on the pages of Eusebius, Apollinarius of Hierapolis and Miltiades, both of whom wrote *Apologies* as well as separate works *To the Greeks* and *To the Jews* (Eusebius, *H.E.* IV.27.1; V.17.5). These writers share more than their common literary goals. In all probability Quadratus came from Asia Minor, traditionally from Magnesia,[7] whether or not he is to be identified with the Quadratus who belonged to the immediately post-apostolic age and who was famed, along with the daughters of Philip, for his prophetic gifts (Eusebius, *H.E.* III.37.1; V.17.3).[8] Apollinarius and Miltiades also came from Asia Minor, while Justin's encounter with the Jew Trypho took place there, in Ephesus. To them we should add Melito of Sardis, whose *Apology* survives mainly only in fragments quoted by Eusebius, and who, while not writing explicitly against the Jews, conducts a vigorous polemic against them in his *On the Pascha*. We see here evidence not only of the creative and lively nature of Christianity in Asia Minor, but also of the broader social, intellectual and literary context in which it had to claim its ground.

The reasons, both internal and external, which prompted the emergence of the 'Apologies' have been extensively discussed. At the risk of creating an unbalanced picture of the rhetorical role of the Jews within them, we shall here focus on the narrower issue of their Judaic context, guided by the obvious question whether there is any relationship between the synchronous development of apologetic and of anti-Jewish literature. No doubt it was inevitable that the most creative intellects of Christianity would find themselves forced to face all the various concerns that beset her, without there necessarily being any inherent relationship between their apologetic and anti-Jewish writings or those against 'heretics'[9] – Apollinarius also wrote against the Montanists, Miltiades against the Montanists and against the Valentinians, and Justin against Marcion and against 'all heresies' generally. Thus far their writings can be seen as but reflections of the four fronts against which Christianity in this period felt the need to defend herself – the state, the philosophers, the Jews and the heretics – provoking responses to each of them.[10] However much these were already issues in the New Testament period, the form they now took was new; new too was the Christians' readiness to take the initiative in direct response. Yet, if we focus here on apologetic, none of those involved in these encounters was charting new waters. If Christianity was to explain itself to society, it was to a society of which the Jews were a part, often as a visible and distinctive group, a society, too, which was well aware of Jewish peculiarities and which saw many of these reflected in the Christian groups. Not surprisingly, the Jews had already set a precedent in apologetic – in defence against pagan detractors and in claiming superiority when measured by the nobler values of their time. There could not, then, fail to be a link between Christian apologetic and a polemic which countered any rival Jewish claims.

For literary evidence of such prior Jewish apologetic we have to look for the most part outside Asia Minor, and, for its origins, perhaps to as far back as the second century BCE.[11] In the first century CE, among his voluminous works Philo wrote an *Apology on behalf of the Jews*, while Josephus's defence of Judaism popularly known as *Against Apion* is more properly an apology, and possibly originally bore a more appropriate title.[12] Leaving aside the question of intended or actual audience, 'apologetic' arguments can also be found in a range of other Hellenistic Jewish writings, the majority of which survived only in Christian hands. At the heart of many of these arguments lies the claim to antiquity – that Abraham or Moses preceded the founding figures of other cultures or institutions and were themselves the source of all that was of value in knowledge or in philosophy. Yet, in making this claim for themselves, the Jews were not only reflecting the values of their age, such as its respect for antiquity, but were also using the same techniques and arguments as their competitors in the debate.[13]

Although we have no apologetic writings which can be securely traced to the Jewish diaspora communities of Asia Minor, that they were immune to the apologetic debate seems unlikely. Certainly they engaged in their own forms of apologetic exercise. Much of our knowledge of these communities in the late Republic and early Empire may be traced to this apologetic concern. The collection of decrees and documents in Books XIV and XVI of Josephus's *Antiquities* witnesses to their struggle to secure and establish their rights; apart from the vexed question of their civic status, Jewish rights to observance of the sabbath, to separate food supplies, to meeting together and to collecting taxes, as well as freedom from requirements to attend court proceedings on the sabbath, had all been regularly infringed and had been made the subject of appeals to provincial or central Roman authorities.[14] The role of literary apologetic in winning a positive response can only occasionally be glimpsed, but a decree by the people of Pergamum reveals the power of the argument from antiquity: '... remembering too that also in the time of Abraham, who was the father of all the Hebrews, our ancestors were their friends, even as we find in the public records' (*Ant.* XIV.10.22 [255]). When the city of Apameia minted coins showing Noah, his wife and the ark, they too may have been making 'some sort of "official" acknowledgment of a traditional mythological bond of some antiquity between them' in response to Jewish apologetic.[15]

Despite the absence of any documents after the reign of Augustus, it is improbable that there was no further need of any apologetic at all by these Jewish communities;[16] certainly the collection and preservation of the responses favourable to the Jews, however and wherever effected, suggests their continuing usefulness in future stress. The degree to which many Jewish communities were integrated within the social and political life of the cities by the third century witnesses to the overall success of their efforts.[17] Moreover, these Jewish communities would continue to value the patronage of influential pagans such as Julia Severa, who provided for the building of a synagogue at Acmonia in the time of Nero, and perhaps even the Emperor Lucius Verus, to whom the Jews of Sardis apparently dedicated a statue with a Hebrew inscription.[18]

Even where the Christian church contained few born Jews it necessarily entered a situation where this was a significant part of the background. Just as the Jewish communities of Asia Minor had preserved rescripts in their favour, so too did the Christian communities of the same area, perhaps consciously following their precedent. Most notable are the rescript of Hadrian to Minucius Fundanus, governor of Asia in *c.*124–5 CE, (Eusebius, *H.E.* IV.9.1–3),[19] and a further one ostensibly from Antoninus Pius to the *koinon* of Asia (*H.E.* IV.13.1–7), which, although spurious in its present form, may contain a historical nucleus.[20] Like Josephus and his sources before him, Justin, who concludes his *Apology* by quoting the former rescript (*Apol.* 68), clearly recognises the apologetic value of recalling such evidences of earlier imperial protection; so too does Melito, who, in his *Apology* to Marcus Aurelius, appeals both to these and to a number of other imperial rebukes 'frequently to many' (Eusebius, *H.E.* IV. 26.10). Melito's confidence in the existence of these, and the Christian preservation and 'creative editing' of the imperial edicts, points to an established pattern of apologetic activity.[21]

Yet the Christian debt to their Jewish predecessors went beyond such judicious hoarding. They also followed them closely in their apologetic arguments, in the desire to demonstrate the greater antiquity of Moses over against his Greek 'imitators' (Justin, *Apol.* 44.8; see also Tatian, *Ad Graec.* 36.1), in the 'exposure' of the folly of Greek worship of idols, and in the presentation of Christianity in predominantly ethical terms.[22] Although the second-century apologists of Asia Minor never explicitly cite earlier Jewish writers,[23] their debt to earlier, and perhaps to contemporary, Jewish apologetic is unmistakable, even while we recall that both were only effective because they were participating in a more ecumenical 'literary discussion that had a long history and continued to flourish in their own day'.[24]

The obverse of this unmistakable continuity and indebtedness was that the Christians had to differentiate themselves over against the Jews. This was not only a matter of the internal need for self-definition, but an apologetic and missionary necessity as well. In general terms it would be easy to suppose that the Christians had to distance themselves from the negative perceptions of the Jews commonly conveyed by collections of the pagan literary sources. Yet, as we have seen, in practice it may have been the relative success and integration of the Jewish communities which most demanded a Christian response, whether it be their attraction of adherents with various degrees of interest and commitment, their ability to have become well established in city life, participating without necessarily syncretising, and in individual cases gaining citizenship, wealth or other signs of status, or even their contributions to the public life of the city (as in the case of the controverted 'former Judaeans' of Smyrna), and their enjoyment of the patronage of high-placed citizens.[25]

The contemporaneous appearance of both apologetic and anti-Jewish literature in the reign of Hadrian reflects that emperor's religious policies in general and his attitude towards Jews and Christians in particular. His reign seems to have brought a period of calm to the Christians and perhaps led to the hope of better relationships with secular authorities. His relations with the Jews would appear crucial for the Christian position, whether it be the early, apparently conciliatory, period following the upheavals under Trajan, when some may even have anticipated the possibility of the rebuilding of the Temple, or the events leading up to the Bar Kochba revolt and the subsequent (or continuing) proscription of circumcision and perhaps of certain Jewish observances.[26] How Jewish communities in Asia Minor were affected by the events in Palestine we cannot be certain, although an influx of refugees during or after the revolt seems likely – Trypho in Justin's *Dialogue* being paradigmatic. That they, and their Christian neighbours, knew nothing about the revolt seems impossible. Besides providing the backcloth to his *Dialogue* which is probably set in Ephesus, in his *Apology* Justin, although then in Rome, reports Bar Kochba's persecution of Jewish Christians and repeatedly draws attention to the Roman capture and devastation of Jerusalem and Judaea (*Apol.* 31.5; 32.3, 6; 47.1).

The situation at the beginning of Hadrian's reign which to some suggested the sought-for revival of the Jewish fortunes and cult would present a double threat to the Christians, the threat to their own self-understanding as God's new people and the danger that Christian converts might now find themselves attracted to a vindicated and protected Judaism;[27] it would also demand that the Christians, as they 'entered the market-place', clearly differentiated themselves and identified their own claims. In the later years, even if the revolt in Palestine under Bar Kochba and the restrictions that followed it had few direct repercussions in the diaspora communities of Asia Minor, the ancient world recognised the cohesion of the Jews wherever they were to be found; this would only provide the Christians with further reason to distance themselves. The focus on circumcision and the claim by Christian writers that this was given to the Jews in order to distinguish them *for punishment* (Justin, *Dial.* 16.2; Tertullian, *Adv. Iud.* 3)[28] is evidently not just an internal development from Paul's theological debates about circumcision; it is an adoption of the perception of circumcision in the public sphere, whether we think of its association with the 'calumnies' accompanying the exaction of the 'Jewish tax' under Domitian – Suetonius, *Domit.* 12.2 describes the physical exposure and examination of a defaulter – or its proscription which may have prompted and which was perpetuated after the revolt under Hadrian.[29]

In the event it seems that Hadrian maintained a policy which was largely favourable to the Christians and that they suffered nothing, even if they also gained nothing, as a consequence of the Bar Kochba revolt. Later in the century, Marcus Aurelius is reputed to have described the Jews as 'stinking and rebellious', words which, if authentic, were sufficiently well known to have survived to be repeated two centuries later by Ammianus Marcellinus (*Hist.* XXII.5.5); again it would be in Christian interests – whether addressing the emperor directly, or public opinion, or, as seems likely, both – to distance themselves from this people.[30]

The wider context for this is the popular perception which must have assumed some relationship between Judaism and Christianity even when few members of the church were born Jews. This is hardly surprising; for all the Christian writers' emphases on the separation between the two, Judaism and Christianity must have appeared remarkably similar when set against the backdrop of city life. True, the Christians opened their message to all, as they were at such great pains to emphasise, but

they developed new patterns of exclusiveness which often must
have seemed far more threatening to the stability of society than
the Jewish form. Jews may well only marry among themselves,
but the behaviour of a Christian convert, particularly a woman,
towards the pagan spouse might lead to the break-up of the
marriage (Justin, *II Apol.* 2). Nor was it obvious that the Christians had jettisoned the less desirable aspects of Judaism.
Although Tacitus already knows the Christians as a distinct
group, his association of them with Judaea and his contemptuous description of them recalls his earlier diatribe about
the Jews.[31] Suetonius speaks of the Jews expelled from Rome
under Claudius 'impulsore Chresto' (*Claud.* 25.4); the confusion among scholars as to whether there is a reference to
Christ(ians) reflects not only the middle of the first century
when Christians were little more than (a) group(s) within Jewish communities, but perhaps equally Suetonius's own confusion. The sources regarding the punishment of Flavia Domitilla
during the reign of Domitian are not agreed as to whether it
was Jewish or Christian sympathies which brought her down-
fall – and modern scholarship shares that disagreement.[32] From
Asia Minor itself, Lucian, who knows and mocks Christianity,
describes Proteus Peregrinus during his 'Christian' phase in
remarkably Jewish-sounding terms, while Epictetus, who was born
in Asia Minor, talks of baptism as the mark of becoming Jewish, apparently identifying Judaism and Christianity.[33] Each of
these authors comes from about the time of the first Apologies, signalling both the growing awareness of Christianity
among the literary élite and their residual association of it with
Judaism.

It may have been in response to the Christian apologetic that
Celsus acknowledges both Christian origins in Judaism and their
rejection of those origins – but sees nothing commendable in
either; for him Judaism can at least boast the advantage of antiquity, which the Christians have deliberately forsaken (Origen,
C. Cels. II.1, 4; V. 25, 33). However, modern scholarship's occasional difficulty in deciding whether a surviving document, inscription or remains are Jewish or Christian, although sometimes
owing to the incomplete state of preservation, often mirrors the
continuing possibilities of confusion for the contemporary, casual
or contemptuous observer. The relationship between Christian-

ity and Judaism was quite differently perceived by Christians (and by groups within them), by Jews, by the general populace, which included both Jews and Christians as well as their neighbours or even families, and by the state which saw no grounds for extending to the Christians the privileges long accorded to the Jews. It was the difference of perceptions by these different constituencies which demanded apologetics.

So who might have been expected to read these works –which is not the same as deciding who did read them? The question is one which has been extensively discussed regarding Jewish apologetic;[34] there, however, only a few of the surviving writings seem to have been framed explicitly as an Apology to a given audience. The earliest Christian Apologies are explicitly addressed to the reigning emperor, and broadly would have followed contemporary practice if they had been intended either for presentation 'personally' during an imperial visit to the area, or for sending to Rome.[35] Miltiades' *Apology to the Worldly Rulers* (Eusebius, *H.E.* V.17.5) perhaps signals a turn to the, in immediate terms more influential, regional or provincial authorities, if such are intended by the epithet; [36] the ecumenical title of the same author's *To the Greeks*, however, evinces the development of a literary type.[37] Yet, from the start, publication implied the hope that by appealing for imperial protection they would persuade the reading public, Jew and gentile, not to engage in persecution or harassment of the Christians. A recurring theme throughout the literature of the period is that persecution comes from the unjustified activity of 'evil men stirring up trouble against us', hoping to take the opportunity to 'plunder those who have done nothing wrong' (Quadratus and Melito in Eusebius, *H.E.* IV.3.1; V.26.5). Given the social circumstances already outlined and the continuing possibilities of local violence, such motivations could equally have inspired the earliest Apologies, although these, as we have seen, belong to times of peace and not of stress. If Celsus is responding to Justin's *Apology*, then the latter had found if not persuaded its intended reader![38] Yet, whatever the intention of their authors, it would not be surprising if the primary readership comprised Christians seeking to give (or gain) a rational account of their faith.

The intended or actual audience of the 'Dialogues with' or 'Books against the Jews' has been equally controversial. Justin's

Dialogue prohibits excluding a Jewish audience on the supposed grounds that by the second century contacts between Jews and Christians were too limited to allow any real communication.[39] On the other hand, and particularly as the genre develops, their final literary form hardly restricts the audience. In so far as these writings were for public consumption they could also have reached interested pagans, and it may be that their arguments and use of scripture would be more likely to persuade such an audience than the Jews themselves.[40] Moreover, with perhaps greatest success, internally they would have both met the need for self-definition and provided the raw material for public debate. In practice this may bring the audiences of the two genres in close proximity to each other and prohibit too sharp a dichotomy between the impulses behind them, although we should not underestimate the considerable differences in style and argument, evident already in Justin's writings.[41] Thus Miltiades', unfortunately lost, *To the Jews* and *To the Greeks* faced one front even while facing two. Yet, as we have seen more than once, the 'market-place' in which Christianity found itself in city life was not a carefully segregated one. The public which was ever a potential source of harassment and persecution, at least from the Christian perception, included Jews as well as pagans; the audience which might now see Christianity as an offshoot of Judaism, now as a renegade member, included pagans as well as Jews. Apology and differentiation were a public necessity and a public activity.

Aristides

a) *The Races among Humankind*

The *Apology* of Aristides illustrates particularly well this twofold concern for differentiation and for self-presentation, and allows us to explore the different ways it could be developed. Admittedly the *Apology* is more commonly associated with Athens than with Asia Minor:[42] according to the prescript the author styled himself, 'Aristides the Philosopher of Athens', while Eusebius's *Chronicle* placed Aristides' address immediately following Hadrian's initiation at Eleusis and munificence to Athens.[43] Against this, however, it could be argued that the identifying epithet might indicate absence from that city, while the *Chronicle* immediately follows with the request by Serenius Gran[ian]us, proconsul of Asia Minor, regarding the Christians, and Hadrian's reply to his successor, Minucius Fundanus.[44] Neither the *Apology* itself nor Eusebius in his *Church History* provide a location, although Eusebius, who makes no claim to having seen a copy, does loosely associate Aristides with Quadratus; the latter, we are told, probably with a higher degree of certainty, also addressed the Emperor Hadrian (*H.E.* IV.3.1), and he is more commonly associated with Asia Minor.[45]

Further complicating the issue, contrary to the evidence already cited and to its own title, the Syriac version addresses the *Apology* to Antoninus Pius, Hadrian's successor. Rendel Harris, who first published the Syriac text, suggested, on rather slender grounds, that Aristides presented his *Apology* to Antoninus Pius during an unrecorded visit to Asia Minor, perhaps at Smyrna.[46] Internal evidence contributes little to a final decision either between Athens and Asia Minor or regarding date: there are some links with Asia Minor traditions, while the condemnation of homosexuality in the Syriac version (17.2), which may seem to us inappropriate in an address to Hadrian, has to contend against the weight of other evidence associating the apologist with that emperor.[47] With this caution, and from necessity, given the failure of Quadratus's *Apology* to survive beyond a brief paragraph,[48] we may turn to Aristides' suggestive argument.

The uncertainties regarding its original dedication are only the beginning of the larger problems which arise from the survival of the *Apology* in a Syriac version, while a Greek text exists only as an incorporated part of the eighth-century *Life of Barlaam and Josaphat.*[49] Inevitably, this new setting has led to substantial modifications of the Greek, whereas the Syriac, although often seen as a largely faithful translation, undoubtedly has also undergone some editing; any reconstruction must be eclectic, and must also recognise the reasons, often dogmatic, which have led to the different redactions.

There are only passing references to any 'calumnies' against the Christians which might demand a defence (17.4, 6 Syr.; 17.1 Gk.); instead, seizing the initiative, Aristides affirms the incomparable nature of the Creator God and exposes the folly of all forms of worship which suppose God has form, limits, or needs. The argument is not a new one, having both Stoic and Jewish precedents;[50] through Aristides' pen its goal is that the Christian understanding of God alone has the fullest grasp of truth. He demonstrates this by dividing humankind according to their perception of the divine (2) into 'races' (γένος), the last of which are the Christians. According to the Greek text there are three such 'races' in the world: those who worship a number of so-called gods, the Jews and the Christians. The first of these is itself subdivided into three further races: the Chaldaeans, whose archetypal error is deification of the elements (3–7); the Greeks, whose gods act scandalously and with 'human' passions (8–11); and the Egyptians, whose incomparable impiety extends to the worship of irrational creatures as well as of the incestuous Isis (12).

By contrast, the Syriac, largely followed by the Armenian, speaks initially of four races, 'the barbarians and the Greeks, the Jews and the Christians': the barbarians occupy the place the Chaldaeans take in the Greek, while the tirade against the Egyptians is appended to the denunciation of the Greeks.[51] Both divisions have had their advocates: the untidiness of the Syriac may speak in favour of its originality, although we may wonder at an inconsistency which derives the barbarians from Cronos and Rhea (2.3) and yet attributes the introduction of these gods to the Greeks (9.2).[52] More noteworthy is the fourfold division which by its phrasing links the barbarians and the Greeks together on the one hand and the Jews and Christians on the other. This alignment of the Jews and Christians accords with the Syriac version's generally more conciliatory attitude to Judaism, usually seen as more authentic than the hostility of the Greek with its echoes of later polemic.[53] However, the antithesis to the barbarians who are coupled with the Greeks might seem particularly perverse, since in the eyes of many of Aristides' contemporaries it was Jews and non-Greek Christians who were barbarians:[54] 'barbarism' was the antithesis of the Roman ideal of '*humanitas*' and was readily laid as a charge against anything which rejected or undermined the values of the city and Empire.[55] Cicero derides Judaism as a 'barbarian superstition' (*Pro Flacco* 28.67), while Josephus knows those who denounced the Jews as barbarians who had made no useful contribution to civilisation (*C. Apion.*

II.148); in turn Celsus extends the reproof to the Christians (*C. Cels.* I.2). Christian writers such as Justin (*Apol.* 5.4; 7.3) and later Melito (Eusebius, *H.E.* IV.26.7), however, acknowledge their 'barbarian' origin, whereas others turn it to effect by reminding the Greeks of their debt to barbarian culture (Tatian, *Oratio* 1.1).[56]

Yet there is an ambivalence found already in Jewish responses to the wider culture; in the Maccabean context the 'barbarians' are those who oppose the Jewish religion (2 Macc. 2.21; 4.25; 10.4), while Philo can contrast the ordered system of Jewish Law with the Greek and barbarian world (*Vita Mos.* 2.17–18), despite his acceptance elsewhere of a simple division of the world into 'Greek and barbarian' (e.g. *De spec. leg.* I.211, 'men, women, Greeks, barbarians, those on the mainland and those assigned islands'; II.44; 65). Similarly, Christians might reject being labelled 'barbarian', as does Justin himself (*Dial.* 119.4), in consciousness of their own new identity, a conviction with its roots in Colossians 3.11, 'not Greek and Jew, circumcision and uncircumcision, barbarian, Scythian …'. In such a context the division 'barbarian and Greek, Jew and Christian' does not sound entirely out of place.

The tripartite division of the Greek, however, can claim a number of close if not interdependent parallels. The *Kerygma Petri* also urges appropriate worship of God, the unseen and all-seeing creator of everything, not 'according to the Greeks' nor 'according to the Jews', for 'what belongs to the Greeks and the Jews is old, but you, Christians, [are] those who worship him in a new way and third kind' (τρίτῳ γένει: Clem. *Strom.* VI.5.41) – although γένος here is placed in opposition to 'what belongs to' the Greeks and Jews and seems to suggest more a 'type' than a 'race'. In the later *Epistle to Diognetus* Christianity is 'a new race and way of life' which neither acknowledges those considered gods by the Greeks nor observes the superstition of the Jews (*Diog.* 1). The close similarities of context extend, as we shall see, to detail and language, and suggest at the least a common tradition. However, these should not be overemphasised; only in Aristides' *Apology* is there a clear sense of 'race' as a subdivision of humankind, with genealogy and extended characteristics, while in the, at first sight parallel, tripartite division of the Greek version the Greeks form only a subdivision within the first race, 'the worshippers of the so-called gods'.[57]

It is true that the idea of Christians as a third race does become more standard, as we shall see from Tertullian, but the theme continues to allow for considerable variety in application. In a gnostic reinterpretation of the apologetic tradition, the *Tripartite Tractate* determines the essential types of humankind to be the spiritual, the psychic and the material races, although earlier, in terminology not so distant from that of Aristides, the writer speaks of 'those who were wise among the Greeks and barbarians' and 'what has come from the race of the Hebrews', among whom only the righteous point to the coming Saviour (*N.H.* I.5.109.24–112.35; 118.14–119.35).[58] Given such variety, and although neither version as we have it may represent directly the original, the Syriac division into four should not be too easily dismissed.

In claiming to be 'a race' the Christians betrayed a significant sense of self-identity, perhaps developed in an Asia Minor setting: Melito's *Apology* laments the persecution that has hit 'the race of those who fear God' (Eusebius, *H.E.* IV.26.5); the same epithet is also used of Christians in *M. Poly.* 3.2, while in 14.1 and 17.1 they are 'the race of the righteous'.[59] The pejorative use of the term on the mouths of opponents to imply alienation from and a threat to the state may have demanded a response: Suetonius had already described Christians as 'a race (*genus*) of men holding a *new* and mischievous superstition' (*Nero.* 16.2), while Tertullian rejects the slur 'the third [perhaps, least significant] race' (*tertium genus*) (*Ad nat.* I.8; *Scorp.* 10). While some Christian writers avoid the concept, frequently its apologetic potential is developed: Aristides says Christians are indeed a race who are blessed more than any other people (17.5).[60]

Yet internal factors were of greater influence. The shaping of that sense of being a distinct race in a setting of opposition and persecution had its roots in Jewish experience, particularly within the Maccabean context, and carried with it the self-conscious contrast with and superiority to all the other nations. This response to the threat of religious suppression and of 'pagan' religiosity was one which the Christians either imitated or inherited.[61] In apologetic literature the designation serves a similar function, again already in a Jewish setting: the *Sibylline Oracles* speak of the Jewish people as 'the race of the most righteous' or of 'the pious' (III, ll. 219; 573), and make the same contrast as does Aristides with those who with empty deceit worship human creations of gold or some other material. It may even be that the Jews spoke of themselves as a 'third race' in this setting.[62] Thus Aristides and other Christian apologists were both adopting and even acknowledging the Jewish claim to be a distinct race, and at the same time pre-empting it by denying their claim to superiority or finality.

b) *The Jewish Race and their Religion*

The divergence between the Syriac and Greek versions in their account of the Jews is particularly marked, but in this case the latter is tendentious and clearly betrays its secondary character. The Greek version (14) speaks of the origin of the Jews with Abraham, Isaac and Jacob, of their sojourn in Egypt and of their deliverance thence by God's 'mighty hand and uplifted arm' through Moses their lawgiver. Despite the many wonders and signs they proved unfeeling and ungrateful, worshipping the gods of the nations, killing the prophets and righteous men sent to them, and finally handing over to Pilate for death on a cross 'the Son of God'. So they were destroyed by their own lawlessness. Yet 'even now they worship the only omnipotent God', but not 'according to knowledge' (cf. Rom. 10.2) for they deny the Christ as Son of God; thus they are no different from the 'gentiles' (ἔθνη), since, although they appear to come close to the truth, they are in fact far from it. In this account the Jews are identified entirely in terms of their rejection of Jesus, reaching back into their earlier history, in a neat digest of standard Christian indictment.

The tenor of the Syriac is very different and maintains better the argument of the *Apology*. Here the Jews reckon the origin of their 'race' from Abraham, a claim Jewish apologetic writings were also at pains to emphasise, and which was acknowledged by their pagan contemporaries.[63] The descent continues with Isaac, Jacob and his twelve sons who moved from Syria to Egypt; there they were called 'the race of the Hebrews' by 'their lawgiver', but later were named 'Jews' (2.5) – a contrast which echoes the tendency in other literature of this period for 'Hebrews' to be used of the 'romantic past'.[64]

The Syriac version's account of the Jews' understanding of God and of their common life could even be drawn from Jewish sources (14):[65] thus they believe that there is one God, maker of all and omnipotent, and that no other god is to be worshipped. In worshipping God in this way, and not his creation, 'they are closer to the truth than all peoples' – a superiority the Greek has denied! They imitate God in their love for other people, manifested in their compassion for the poor, their ransoming of captives, and their burial of the dead. These and similar practices they have received from their 'forefathers of old', an assertion which is here an occasion not for criticism, as is the appeal to 'traditions from the elders' in Christian anti-Jewish polemic, but for approval, acknowledging the value of antiquity and tradition in apologetic debate.

However, the account continues:

> although in their own belief they think they worship God, in the manner of their actions it is the angels and not God himself whom they worship, for they observe Sabbath and new moon, the feast of unleavened bread and the great fast [or perhaps 'the great day'],[66] the fast and circumcision and the purity of foods. For all this, they do not observe these things perfectly.

Here, too, Aristides belongs to a wider tradition of the characterisation of Jewish belief. Colossians 2.16, 18 (23) warns against being judged in matters of '**food** and drink, or participation in a feast or **new moon** or **sabbath**' or regarding '**the worship of angels**' (cf. also Gal. 4.9–10). Even closer is the exhortation in the *Kerygma Petri* not to worship like the Jews, 'for they alone, thinking that they know God, without proper knowledge **serve angels** and archangels, month and moon,[67] and if the moon does not appear they do not celebrate the so-called first **sabbath**,[68] neither do they celebrate the **new moon** nor the **feast of unleavened bread**, nor the feast nor **the great day**' (Clem. Alex., *Strom.* VI.5.41). Perhaps also related is the much harsher polemic against the Jews in the *Epistle to Diognetus*: this too warns against 'worshipping according to the Jews' who, although they rightly take God to be one and lord of all, worship him wrongly, in this case by supposing that God is in need of the offerings they make (3). The Jews are further condemned for their timidity regarding **foods**, their superstition concerning the **sabbath**, their pride in **circumcision**, and their dissimulation concerning the **fast** and **new moon**. Moreover, they study stars and moon in order to observe months and days (4). Both the *Kerygma Petri* and *Diognetus* introduce this criticism of Jewish worship following a polemic against 'the Greeks', who have no true understanding of God.

Despite the parallels between these texts, we should not think of literary dependence so much as of a fairly fixed tradition of polemic.[69] It is a tradition which may have been influenced by the language of Isaiah 1.13–14 (LXX), 'your **new moons** and **sabbaths** and **great day** I cannot endure; the **fast** and idleness, and your new moons and your **feasts** my soul hates', a passage also quoted by Justin, *Apol.* 37.5.[70] In this case the different uses of the tradition are equally important. *Diognetus* betrays its place in the development of polemic through the use of pejorative terms like 'timidity' and 'superstition', and through its detailed critique of sabbath, circumcision and calendar observance; in contrast to this, Aristides sees Jewish observances as evidence of the worship of angels and does not speak, as does the *Keryma Petri*, of the worship of the moon itself. His tone is noticeably more moderate, particularly in its wider context.

Neither the use of a tradition, nor the variations on it, can establish either ignorance of or acquaintance with contemporary Jewish practice. Yet the facets of Judaism on which these authors focus are those familiar to the pagan observer – circumcision, sabbath, food and fasting – characteristics which attracted both repulsion and imitation. These issues too played a significant role in Christian separation from Judaism, but in these apologetic texts (except for *Diognetus*) it is not as theological principles but as identifying religious marks thay they are attacked. Even if being drawn from tradition, as characteristics familiar to pagans and to Christians they may still reflect contemporary awareness, particularly when combined with the possible dependence on Jewish apologetic in the earlier clauses of Aristides' description. Thus a distinctive note is sounded when Aristides goes beyond the *Kerygma Petri* in referring to the question of foods and to fasting, which were acknowledged marks of the Jews; Colossians and later *Diognetus* do note 'food' as an issue, but only Aristides defines it as a matter of 'purity'. This possibility of real awareness makes 'the worship of angels' the more contentious: is it merely a deduction from – or rather an interpretation of – the study of the moon to fix the calendar, which itself seems historically probable?[71] Or did the Jews of Asia Minor – for here we have the added 'support' of Colossians – worship angels?

Here epigraphical evidence may offer some support:[72] angels appear in a number of inscriptions from western Asia Minor, and while some are clearly pagan, whether or not under Jewish influence, some at least must be Jewish; so, one dedication could be made 'To the great and most high and heavenly god and his holy angels and his venerable house of prayer (προσευχή)'.[73] Later literary evidence confirms the role of angels in Jewish or Christian ('judaising') groups within the area, although finding there already a fertile source for such ideas, allowing the suggestion that 'Angels, who linked men with the gods in all three religious systems, helped to bind together the diverse strands of pagan, Jewish, and Christian belief in later Roman Anatolia.'[74] It would not be surprising if such beliefs could both make their own contribution to Christian thought and become the occasion of scornful disparagement.

c) *Jews and Christians*

That, at least according to the Syriac presentation, there is a particular relationship between the Jews and Christians is already suggested by their pairing within the fourfold division of human races. The 'genealogy' of the Christians, while maintaining the implicit sympathy towards Judaism, gives only ambiguous support to explicating this.[75] The Christians are a fourth race with their own genealogy derived from Jesus Christ (so also the Greek, 15): no greater antiquity is claimed and descent from Abraham is left without argument to the Jews. It is not clear whether we should see a contrast between the origin of the Jewish *race* (*gns*) in Abraham, and that of the Christian *religion* (*dhlth'*) in Jesus Christ, since as the text stands the barbarians trace both race and religion to Cronus and the other 'ur-gods'.[76]

This genealogy is amplified in almost credal language, abandoning the symmetry of the thumbnail sketches of the three earlier races: so first, 'it is said God took and put on flesh from a Hebrew[77] virgin and so the son of God dwelt in the daughter of men'. Then an appeal to the 'Gospel' supports what follows: Jesus was thus born from the tribe (not 'race') of the Hebrews – the name first received by the Jews according to the previous paragraph; a reference to his twelve disciples suffices to authenticate his incarnate activity (*mdbrnwth'*), before 'he was pierced through (*dqr*) by the Jews', died and was buried.[78] The confession ('they say') continues with his resurrection after three days, his ascent into heaven, and the world-wide mission of the twelve disciples; this finally returns to the name 'Christians' being given to those who now accept the proclamation, and so to a reaffirmation of the 'four races of humankind'. Here Jewish responsibility for the crucifixion does not become an occasion for their condemnation.[79]

The initial account of the Christian race similarly pays no attention to their Jewish competitors and yet betrays its thorough grounding in their values and apologetic: it is 'their law (*nmws*) and manner of life' that mark the Christians out, the Syriac, here and throughout the section, providing a better guide to Aristides' argument than the Greek (15.12).[80] Indeed, in similar words to those already used of the Jews, they too are credited with coming closer to the truth (and precise knowledge) than other peoples.[81] They too worship but one God, creator of all, and none other besides him – the Greek characteristically adds a more distinctively Christian note by supplementing with 'through the only begotten Son and holy spirit';[82] they follow the commandments received from him,[83] while holding on to the belief in the resurrection of the dead and in the life of the age to come. These commandments belong to the common Jewish and Christian heritage:[84] prohibition of adultery, of false witness, of keeping a deposit and of envy, honour of parents; Christians are marked by their goodwill towards their enemies, by their egalitarian attitudes towards slaves who become Christians (in the Syriac only), and by their chastity in and outside marriage.

The account of Christian 'law and manner of life' is, especially in the Syriac, much fuller than that of the Jewish, but in esssence it does not go far beyond the latter's compassion for the poor, redemption of captives and burial of the dead: Christians too bury their poor, supply the needs of and if possible ransom those imprisoned for the name of their Messiah; they even fast for the charitable purpose of meeting the wants of the poor and they rejoice over the death of the just as also over the birth of a child, rejoicing too at the premature death and departure without sin of the latter, while they weep over those who fall into sin and die. The communal nature of this benevolence is perhaps more noticeable, with an emphasis on their recognition of even the slave or stranger as 'brother' 'in God', and in that it is the poor, the imprisoned, or those *from their number* who die whose needs they meet; but perhaps in the ancient world this group-reference would be taken for granted for the Jews also, for Tacitus acknowledges their readiness in compassion, and immediately follows with their fierce hatred against all others (*Hist.* V.5.1). Similarly, although only the Christians are said not to worship foreign gods or idols in human likeness, nor to eat food sacrificed to idols,[85] such sentiments equally reflect Christianity's Jewish heritage.

The authority for the Christians' behaviour, and the place where Aristides' account may be authenticated, is 'their scriptures' which the king is repeatedly invited to examine (15.3; 16.3, 5; 17.1).[86] Since he appears to distinguish them from the 'Gospel', where the king can find the account of Jesus authenticated (2.7),[87] these other writings must include the Jewish scriptures; Aristides gives no hint of this, and in his earlier account he had not credited the Jews with any writings. When he acknowledges there are 'more difficult things' both said and done in them (17.1), he betrays, however, the difficulties in the Christian claim to the 'Old Testament' which did not only contain the ethical values he has advertised!

There is in Aristides' predominantly ethical presentation of Christianity little that would not be at home in a Jewish Apology. The style of description, most of the virtues listed and the combination with the expectation of future reward or judgement could easily be paralleled, for example, in Ps. Phocylides, *Sentences*, or in the *Sibylline Oracles, Book II*, which probably belongs to Asia Minor (?Phrygia). *IV Sib.* closes by urging penitence to avoid the wrath of God, the abandonment of their crimes, and the seeking of forgiveness for past sins by bathing in rivers and by prayer (ll. 162–70); in similar vein Aristides, forgetting both barbarians and Jews, and speaking of only *Greek* debauchery and opposition, gives the assurance of forgiveness to one who converts and confesses past sins committed through ignorance, but promises a terrible judgement to come to all others (17.4–7).[88]

For the reader, Christianity as presented by Aristides is marked by a distinctively Jewish ethos, which is only confirmed by the fundamental contrast between the Christians whose prayers uphold the world, and 'all the other peoples who are deceived and deceive, wallowing before the elements of the world' (16.6),[89] a contrast from which the Jews are surely excluded. Yet this collapsing into a bipartite schema, integral to the kerygmatic climax of the *Apology*, inevitably leaves the Jews no certain place in the scheme of things, for good or ill. In telling contrast to the *Kerygma Petri*, which does offer repentance to 'someone of Israel' (Clem. Alex., *Strom.* VI.5.43), Aristides' offer is to the Greeks, his audience, and their only hope in the face of the judgement coming upon the human race (*gns*) is Jesus Christ.

Aristides will allow no doubt as to the blessedness of the Christian race (17.5);[90] it is through their prayers that the world is sustained (16.6), a familiar apologetic theme (cf. *Diog.* 6.7); the truth and vigour of Christian life and teaching will brook no competition for anyone who cares to look into them (16.3–5); despite being the fourth 'race', they are in truth a *new* people in which there is a union with the divine (16.4).[91]

d) *Aristides and Judaism*

Aristides' ambivalence towards the Jews invites a similar ambiguity regarding any relationship he may have had with the Judaism of his day. On the one hand there is the overall Jewish tone throughout the *Apology* – according to Harris, 'a remarkable continuity with Jewish ethics' – which led Geffcken to suggest that it belonged more in a Jewish-Hellenistic than in a distinctively Christian camp.[92] Indeed, it has even been possible to argue that the *Apology* was a Jewish polemic against pagan polytheism from the time of Hadrian, clumsily interpolated in the fourth century in favour of a fourth race, the Christians.[93] A more nuanced explanation is preferable. A predominantly ethical presentation of Jewish values has deep roots, and different flowerings in both Palestinian and Hellenistic Judaism.[94] In the former we find the development of 'Noachide commands' incumbent upon gentiles and sometimes interpreted as the requirements for sympathisers to Judaism: Jub. 2.20–27, an early witness to that development, demands justice and modesty, acknowledgement of God as creator and honour of parents, love of neighbour and avoidance of sexual sin; it also requires abstention from blood and so from animal flesh, a concern Aristides ignores. In some Hellenistic Jewish literature, including Ps. Phocylides, *Sentences,* and some of the Sibylline literature, this ethical distillation of Judaism is offered without apparent discrimination between Jew or gentile, and sometimes without even reference to distinctive Jewish cultic tenets like circumcision or sabbath; Ps. Phocylides, unlike Aristides, even avoids issues relating to idolatry.[95] That the goal of such literature was 'the promotion of God-fearing and conversion' is disputed,[96] and perhaps not critical for our purposes. Such traditions evidently were absorbed into the Christian tradition, as we see already in *Did.* 1–4; the 'Apostolic Decree' of Acts 15.20, 29, with which Aristides has some contacts, particularly in the Western text form with its omission of the reference to 'what is strangled' and inclusion of the negative Golden Rule,[97] claims the authority of the regular reading of Moses in the synagogues of the Diaspora. Aristides too has had access to Jewish apologetic material, perhaps directly since he betrays a minimum of 'Christianisation', and he has used it surprisingly even-handedly in the interests of both Jews and Christians.

Whether behind this we should see the Jews and Christians maintaining tolerably friendly relations, with the church 'if not any longer under the wing of the synagogue, [having] apparently no objection to taking the synagogue occasionally under its own wing',[98] is another question. The description of the Greeks and barbarians has a certain antiquarian air about it, betraying more of an interest in 'the history of religions' than in description of any contemporary reality of which both author and readers had experience. So too, although Geffcken may have overstated the case in saying he knows little more about the Jews than Tacitus, *Hist.* V.5,[99] Aristides' account of Judaism suggests a dependence on tradition and written sources, leaving us uncertain how far he could appeal to his

Jewish neighbours, how far his 'friendliness' is genuine, perhaps claiming the benefits of Jewish security and good-standing, or, rather, how far it derives from a sense of their irrelevance for his immediate situation. If, in spite of himself, he shows how for some Judaism and Christianity could present a common front against the pagan world, he also shows how for some Judaism might have no inalienable place either within the world they inhabited or within that they opposed.

Justin Martyr

a) *Defeated Judaeans*

However, common front or implicit elimination were not the only alternatives, and for Justin Martyr the picture is far more complex. Although his *Apology* to Antoninus Pius was written in Rome, the major themes of his thought had their earliest formation in Asia Minor, and the differences in argument from his *Dialogue* – which we shall not discuss here – reflect not time and location but genre and audience. Yet common to both is the need to appeal to Jewish sources at the same time as effecting a distancing from Judaism in the presentation of Christianity.

The language of 'race' does not provide Justin with a way of understanding the Christians' place in the world. In a simple division of humankind there are but the Greeks on the one hand and the barbarians on the other, although the latter are almost exclusively represented by the Jews (*Apol.* 46.3). Thus far the Christians also claim a barbarian origin, for it was among the barbarians that 'the Word himself took the form of and became man and was called Jesus Christ' (5.4; 7.3). Yet, through the presence of the Word, in which the whole human race has a share (46.2), 'Christians [before Christ]' may be found 'both among the Greeks – Socrates and Heraclitus and others similar – and among the barbarians – Abraham, and Ananias and Azarias and Misael, and Elijah, and many others' (46.3).

Beyond this, Abraham plays no significant role in the *Apology*;[100] any disputed claims to him as 'father' are passed over in silence, and instead the Jews' descent is traced to their 'forefather' Judah, 'from whom they have come to be called the Jews'

(32.3, 14). This descent, although less common than that from Abraham or Moses, is known to pagan sources,[101] but Justin uses it with particular effect, ignoring entirely the importance he had laid in the *Dialogue* on the Christians' claim to Judah.[102]

Through Judah ('Ιούδας) the Jews are tied firmly to the land of Judaea ('Ιουδαία), not only the place of Jesus's birth and crucifixion 'by the Jews' (= *Judaeans*: 'Ιουδαῖοι) (13.3; 34.2), but recently subjugated by the Romans, as Justin is careful to emphasise (32.3–6). This is 'the land of the Jews' (ἡ γῆ 'Ιουδαίων), devastated by the Romans in fulfilment of prophecy, particularly in the aftermath of 'the revolt of the Jews' (ἡ 'Ιουδαίων ἀπόστασις) under Bar Cocheba (31.6; 47; 53.3, 9). This heavily ethnic and geograpical definition of 'the Jews', again absent from the *Dialogue*,[103] contrasts sharply with Cassius Dio's comments: 'For the land has been named Judaea and they themselves Jews. I do not know from where this title began to be applied to them, but it refers also to all other people who are zealous for their laws, even if of another race' (*Hist. Rom.* XXXVII.17.1);[104] it may also have particular apologetic force when set against Tacitus's assertion that Judaea was the origin of the 'pernicious [Christian] superstition' (*Ann.* XV.44).[105]

Christians do not belong to the same 'genealogy': few from among the Jews or Samaritans – the mention of whom reinforces the localised and non-Greek character of the Jews also – have become Christians, and those that have are 'less true' than gentile believers (53.3–10).[106] In the *Apology* Justin looks for no conversion from the Jews but only for their final recognition of their shame at the eschatological revelation (52.10).[107] This distancing, whose obverse, positive counterpart is the idea of 'Christians before Christ' among Greeks and 'barbarians' (above), is underlined by the repeated stress on Jewish hostility to Christ and to Christians. By choosing, perhaps from necessity, as his best example of this hostility the fearsome tortures applied to Christians by 'the leader of the revolt of the Jews during the recent Jewish ('Ιουδαϊκός) war', Justin effects a sharp disassociation which decisively aligns the Christians with the Romans.

b) *Jewish Prophecy and Misunderstanding*

Yet the argument needs be made so emphatically precisely

because the Christian claims rely so heavily on their Jewish roots. Jesus is of the seed of Jacob, the father of Judah, and so at once both independent of the latter and yet descended from and identified by the prophecies to him (32.12–14 (Num. 24.17)).[108] An appeal to the fulfilment of Jewish prophecy constitutes the core of the *Apology* (31–52).[109] For Justin scripture offers a 'rational' and convincing argument for the truth of Christianity against those who so readily bring forward 'myths' about the 'supposed' sons of Zeus (53.1); the argument from prophecy does not work by 'faith' so much as by persuasion and proof, indeed it is summoned in order to refute charges of the blind faith of the Christians.[110] Justin assumes that the validity of fulfilment can be verified by the Romans themselves, either from the records of Cyrenius's census ('who was your first governor in Judaea'), or from Pilate's later report (34.2; 35.10; 48.3), while the devastation and appropriation of the land at their own hands remains as a living witness (47; 53.9). Although Justin affirms the value of the oracles of the Sibyl or of Hystaspes, their primary contribution is as pagan and philosophical support for the final conflagration of the world (20.1 (?= *IV Sib.* 172–8); 44.12); it was primarily through the prophets of the Jews that the word of God was active before Christ spoke, all pagan similarities being either the crude imitation of demons or the simplistic misunderstanding of the Greek philosophers, pre-eminently Plato (44.7; 54.1–4).[111]

The Jews are pre-eminently those to whom and through whom the word of God or the prophetic spirit has spoken in the past. Any other features we might expect to be noticed are ignored: hence in his defence of Christian ethics there are no Jewish or scriptural allusions, neither, in unmistakable contrast to the *Dialogue*, is there any discussion of the Jewish Law.[112] Sabbath, synagogue, and other characteristics of Jewish worship play no role: Christian worship and the foundational death and resurrection of Jesus are dated by reference not to the sabbath but to 'the day of Saturn' (ἡ κρονική) (67). Moses is not the first lawgiver nor the founder of Jewish worship as he is so often in pagan perception and Jewish apology, and as in the *Dialogue*, but only the first prophet (32.1; 33.6; 44.1 etc.).[113] As prophet, however, he is 'older than all writers' (54.5) and so precedes all his pagan competitors, not least Plato who borrowed from him the doctrine of creation (44.8; 59.1–60.11). The argument, strange to our ears, was not a new one, and in principle would have struck Justin's readers as highly plausible.[114] Yet it was one which seemed more likely to favour the Jews than the Christians. Thus Justin agrees that the Jews are those who continue to possess and to read the scriptures in which the prophecies were written. The story of their translation into Greek, which, as the text stands at present, Justin mistakenly attributes to the help given Ptolemy by the Jewish King Herod (31.1–5), plays a crucial role here: it authenticates Justin's arguments based on the Greek text and allows an appeal both to Jewish possession of these scriptures and to their availability in the great library of Alexandria. Not surprisingly, Justin makes no claims here that the Jews had falsified these scriptures, claims which, ironically, in the *Dialogue* are buttressed by the Ptolemy legend.[115]

Yet the Jews who possess the books of the prophets are at the same time those who do not understand what they read (36.3; 49.5). '*All* the Jews teach even now' that it was God who spoke to Moses in the burning bush, not recognising that it was God's own son and messenger (63); thus they fail to see what *gentile* Christians, with no prior insights or preparation, perceive, namely that the scriptures point to the life and person of Jesus Christ. It was but as an extension of this failure to understand, and with no better reason, that the Jews first crucified Jesus (35.6; 38.7) and now treat Christians as their enemies, even killing and punishing them 'whenever they have the power' (31.5; 36.3). Justin's only example of this is Bar Kochba's torture of Christians who would not surrender their confession of Jesus as Messiah (31.6), an example which immediately follows his account of the translation of the scriptures into Greek: it would, as we have seen, have been a particularly potent example, giving the Christians all the credit. Nothing suggests that Justin had other evidence he could have cited, and elsewhere he acknowledges that the primary source of persecution is the Romans themselves (45.5–6).[116]

c) *The Hostility of the Demons*

The malevolent activity of 'the demons' provides a consistent backcloth to Justin's whole argument in the *Apology*. Identified with idols and false deities (9), it is they who are responsible for all myths (21; 54.1), for apparent pagan 'imitations' of Christianity (23.3; 66.4), and for the heresies which beset the church (26; 58.1). More ominously, they are the source of all hostility to the word of God, from the persecution of Socrates in the past (5.1, 3) to the sentence of death directed against those who read the writings of Hystaspes, the Sibyl or the prophets (44.12) The false accusations against and the irrational persecution of Christians are equally the work of 'the evil demons' (10.6; 57.1). It is a sinister step when the Jews are brought into this scheme: again, in a context exposing their false exegesis and misunderstanding of the scriptures, the Logos, having become human, suffered all that the demons ensured he would endure 'through the senseless Jews' (63.10).[117]

d) *Justin's Apology and Judaism*

Justin's *Dialogue with Trypho* pre-empts any need to discuss his knowledge of or contact with Judaism; his awareness of Jewish exegesis and Jewish worship is beyond doubt. Yet his presentation of Judaism and of Jewish–Christian relations takes a very different form in the *Apology*. The givenness of the relationship is no less important in the apologetic context than it is in direct debate. Christianity is not self-authenticating but relies on the argument from (Jewish) prophecy, and only on these grounds can it gain a credible place in the competition for antiquity and originality. The Jews are thus identified by their inalienable place within this competition, a place which was already recognised in public debate. The need to defend Christian intepretation against Jewish 'misunderstanding' implies a recognition that in that public debate the Jews would appear to have the advantage – after all, as Justin acknowledges, it is they who 'possess' the prophecies. At the same time the Jews had equally to be identified by their disqualification from continuing in the competition; this was a disqualification which was easier to establish on political grounds – by identifying them in terms of Judaea, the revolt, and the Roman subjugation of and exclusion of the Jews from their own land (47.6) – than through theological argument. While continuity may mark the relationship between the Christians and the prophecies possessed by the Jews, radical discontinuity or even opposition had to mark that between Jews and Christians.

The Apologists of Asia Minor

a) *Melito and the 'Barbarians'*

Melito presented his *Apology* to the Emperor Marcus Aurelius under quite specific circumstances:[118]

> For that which has never before happened, the race of the God-fearers is now being persecuted, afflicted with new decrees throughout Asia (Eusebius, *H.E.* IV.26.5).

This allegation of **new decrees throughout Asia** marks a new stage in the context for an Apology; it implies something more formal than an intensified swell of regular hostility in the wake of a recent series of natural disasters, for which Christians were so often held responsible. Melito diplomatically expresses his doubts whether they could really have originated in the express command of the Emperor (IV.26.6), and he may have been right: certainly, any official action or injunction involved has left no lasting trace on our sources.[119]

The fragments of the *Apology* quoted by Eusebius (*H.E.* IV.26.5–11) offer only a little help in guessing the main thrust of Melito's argument, but that little is pregnant with potential. Addressed to the 'philosopher Emperor', Christianity is **our philosophy** (ἡ καθ' ἡμᾶς φιλοσοφία);[120] indeed, it is **the philosophy of the Empire** with which Marcus Aurelius is entrusted:

> For our philosophy first flourished among barbarians, but having come to flower among your peoples at the time of the great reign of Augustus your ancestor, it became particularly for your Empire an auspicious benefit. Since then the might of the Romans has increased to be great and lustrous; and of this you have become the prayed-for successor, and will be, along with the boy, as you protect the philosophy of the Empire which was nursed with and shared a beginning with Augustus (IV.26.7).

In a striking alignment of 'church and state', as the Empire has flourished so has Christianity, or rather the reverse – as Christianity has flourished, so has the Empire increased in strength and blessing, suffering no harm or set-back (IV.26.8): the argument, similar to that of Aristides that the beautiful things in the world abound because of them and that the earth is established through the prayer of Christians,[121] neatly reverses the popular blaming of all disasters on the Christians.[122] No word is spoken of divine protection, but the message is clear – if Christianity should cease to flourish, no one will be answerable for the consequences to the Empire but the Emperor himself, who would have so failed to maintain the enlightened policy of all but the best-forgotten of his predecessors. The sole exceptions were Nero and Domitian, wrongly persuaded by the slanders of evil men to comply with false accusations against Christians (IV.26.9); yet they only serve to establish a simple rule: only bad and corrupt emperors persecute – thus Melito played his part in creating a 'historical tradition' which has at least persuaded many after him. They were rightly rebuked 'in writing' by the present Emperor's 'pious fathers'; it is here that Melito appeals specifically to the letters of Hadrian and Antoninus Pius which ruled out any change of policy towards the Christians, adopting, as we have seen, an apologetic device initiated by Jewish communities before him.[123]

Of Christianity's Jewish roots there is only a passing mention. While, with a little stretching of the imagination, Christianity **flowered** among the peoples of the Empire **at the time of Augustus**, under whom Jesus was born, but did not work (Luke 2.4), Melito acknowledges it **first flourished among barbarians**. In this cursory acknowledgement of the Jewish origin of both Jesus and the Christian movement, Melito is deliberately downplaying the contemporaneity of the springing up (among barbarians) and the first flowering (among your peoples at the time of Augustus). However, in his *On the Pascha* he unequivocally celebrates the presence of Jesus in the past history of the Jews;[124] so here in claiming 'barbarian' Judaism as the fertile soil for Christianity he may also be pre-empting any damaging comparisons between Christianity's novelty and the antiquity of Judaism .[125] Yet, just as for Justin

novelty should need no defence because truth is to be valued
above even tradition (Justin, *Apol.* 2.1), it is more important for
Melito that the freshness and vitality of Christianity share in the
freshness and vitality of the Empire. The same could not be said
of the Jews: for all their acceptance within the life of the city and
perhaps their contribution to its prosperity, they are barbarians;
barbarians here is not a religious term as in Aristides nor a cultural one as in Justin,[126] but a political one – Melito has just used
it of those 'barbarian enemies' whom one might justly punish,
although even then not with the ferocity now being levelled
against the Christians (*H.E.* IV.26.6). Neither could the Jews,
for all their antiquity and local prosperity, tie their well-being to
that of the Empire since Augustus, nor appeal to the general
support of Hadrian in the recent past.

Yet, if such echoes of an undercurrent of polemic against the
Jews are to be heard, they are only echoes, amplified by the polemic of the *On the Pascha* and by the imaginative reconstruction
of the impact on the beleaguered Christians of a well-established
flourishing Jewish community, (anachronistically) presupposed
by the magnificent and centrally placed synagogue of Sardis.[127]
Melito has even been supposed to be making some sort of counter-thrust, provoked by the visit of the co-emperor Lucius Verus
to Sardis in 166 when he may have received among other hon-
ours that of a statue bearing his name in Hebrew dedicated by
the Jewish community, although the address to a single emperor
implies a date after Verus's death in 169.[128] It is more than imagination which is at work when the 'shameless sycophants and
lovers of other men's goods', whom Melito blames for taking
advantage of the 'new decrees' (Eusebius, *H.E.* IV.26.5), are identified by some scholars as the Jews;[129] for this then poses as a
covert (but spurious) justification for Melito's virulence in the
Peri Pascha – one that has no support in the text. While we may
agree that whatever the state of the Jewish community of Sardis
in the late second century, it must surely have had some impact
on Melito and his church, it may not have been envy but a desire
to distance themselves from those 'barbarians' whom Marcus
Aurelius had derided as 'stinking and rebellious' which motivated Melito's *Apology*.[130]

b) *'Jews', Politics and Internal Enemies*

With the remaining apologists of Asia Minor we have neither their work surviving nor such abundant evidence of the Jewish communities which they encountered. We know only that both Apollinarius of Hierapolis and Miltiades wrote Apologies as well as works 'in answer to the Jews'.[131] Apollinarius apparently included in his Apology an account of the famous 'miracle' of a thunderstorm which saved a Roman legion fighting by the Danube, and attributed it to the prayers of the Christian soldiers (Eusebius, *H.E.* V.5.4), a demonstration which might further the argument of loyalty to the state, as well as of the power of miracle. Hierapolis had a strong Jewish community with its own archives and the means to handle, at least theoretically, the sizeable fines imposed on those who disturbed the graves of its members.[132] A certain Publius Aelius Glykon makes provision for the decoration of his family grave on the Feast of Unleavened Bread by the Guild of Purple-dyers and at Pentecost by the Guild of Carpet-weavers (*CIJ* II.777): however these Guilds be interpreted, the inscription testifies at the same time both to the maintenance of Jewish festivals and to a degree of integration into civic structures.[133]

We might reasonably expect such a community to have been reflected in Apollinarius's writing: R. M. Grant attempts such a reconstruction for Apollinarius's apologetic and his work against the Jews; he argues for an original close relationship between the Christian and Jewish communities evidenced by that earlier Hierapolitan, Papias, with his use of Jewish apocalyptic traditions, and by Ignatius's failure to write to or mention the city 'perhaps because its Christianity was closer to Judaism than he liked'.[134] Papias's 'apocalyptic enthusiasm, close to Judaism, cannot have encouraged him to admire the Roman state or church [*sic*]'; Grant suggests that Apollinarius, perhaps in response to Marcus Aurelius's derogatory remarks about the Jews,[135] may have had political and not just theological provocation for an argument *To the Jews*, which would cohere with his apologetic intentions. However, while it is true, as we have seen, that a distancing from Judaism could go hand in hand with an affirmation of loyalty to the state, this need not have signalled a reversal in existing relationships: adoption of Jewish traditions, as by Papias, is not evidence for an affinity with Judaism, as Justin, himself a millenarianist, demonstrates.

Similar uncertainty surrounds Miltiades, of whom we know even less. Like Melito, Miltiades apparently presented his defence of Christianity as an apology for his 'philosophy', but the address to 'the cosmic rulers' suggests a degree of literary artifice (Eusebius, *H.E.* V.17.5); perhaps intended were the provincial authorities rather than the Emperor himself, although whether the epithet hinted at the 'earthly' limitation of their real power over the Christians is less sure.[136] Like Apollinarius and perhaps Melito,[137] Miltiades was an opponent of Montanism, although the future montanist, Tertullian's favourable assessment of him as 'ecclesiarum sophista' (*Adv. Val.* 5) may suggest that it was the excesses of ecstatic behaviour – 'that a prophet should not speak in ecstasy' (Eusebius, *H.E.* V.17.1) – rather than the movement as a whole which he opposed. Polemic against Montanism, which through its apocalypticism appears to have been more confrontational against the state, might well have demanded clear internal differentiation as well as public apologetic; that it would also require a distancing from anything Jewish is less certain. Despite the many attempts to argue the reverse, there is little to suggest that either in practice or in external perception, by 'catholic' Christians or by public authorities, Montanism was in any sense Jewish.[138]

It has been suggested that in their double front against Greeks and against Jews, and in Miltiades' local address for his Apology, these two writers provided a model for Tertullian, and even that Tertullian's *Against the Jews* may owe much to the work of these predecessors.[139] The suggestion is hardly capable of proof, and it would be hazardous to adopt the reverse procedure and to deduce the main themes and style of Apollinarius's or Miltiades' arguments towards the Jews from Tertullian's own polemics. Yet the loss of their writings is the more tantalising, not least because Tertullian is somewhat harsher against the Jews and more uncompromising about the finality of Christianity in the *Apology* than when writing 'Against the Jews': is this ambivalence to be traced to his circumstances or is it a heritage from his earlier sources?[140] The question demonstrates the intricate interplay between genre, context and tradition.

c) *Piety and the Fear of God*

A common theme in the Apologies is the defence of the Christians as pious (εὐσεβής) or, more importantly, as God-fearing (θεοσεβής).[141] According to the title of the Syriac version, Aristides' *Apology* concerned 'the fear of God' (*dhlth 'lh*): although Eusebius describes Aristides as 'faithful and devoted to our piety' (εὐσέβεια: *H.E.* IV.1.3), the Syriac probably represents a Greek original θεοσέβεια (fear of God).[142] Quadratus's *Apology*, according to the same passage of Eusebius, was also 'concerning our fear of God (θεοσέβεια)', while 'concerning piety' may have been the title of Apollinarius's work.[143] Melito too was prompted by the persecutions hitting 'the race of the *God-fearers*', an epithet he shares with the *Martyrdom of Polycarp* (3.2).[144] Piety (εὐσέβεια), is an important term in Greek sources, both literary and epigraphical; while it could encompass respect due to family and state, it signalled particularly the reverence due to the gods, and plays a significant role in inscriptions of the imperial cult in Asia Minor.[145] It is not surprising that the claim to piety should become a central concern in apologetic, against the all-too-frequent charges of *im*piety and disloyalty to the gods of city and state. Thus 4 Maccabees asserts the Jews' pre-eminent claim to piety by giving a focal emphasis on how 'pious reason' should be the master of the emotions (4 Macc. 1.1; 6.31; 17.1, 3 etc.), something demonstrated by the readiness of each of the martyrs to die 'for the sake of piety'. The related but rarer 'fear of God' (θεοσέβεια) seems to have become increasingly favoured by Jews and Christians as a more appropriate equivalent, because it could point to worship of the one God; again both literary as well as epigraphic sources testify to this to the extent that in the latter its presence is almost an indication of Jewish (or, later, Christian) provenance.[146] Once again, in 4 Maccabees fear of God lies at the heart of the martyrs' suffering and of their triumph (7.6, 22; 15.28; 16.11).[147]

Not surprisingly, Christian apologetic joins in this competition for the title 'pious' or 'God-fearing', unashamedly claiming it even in the titles of their appeals. The text of Aristides'

Apology gives only ambiguous justification for the claim, referring once to 'their fear' (*dhlthhwn*) of the Christians as opposed to 'the race' of the Jews (*Apol.* 2.5, 6).[148] Justin, however, combines 'piety' with 'philosophy' in a calculated appeal to the ideal of the philosopher-ruler: those who are pious and philosophers will honour and love the truth alone (*Apol.* 2.1–2; 3.2; 12.5).[149] The rhetoric may well have been learnt from Jewish precedent or developed in the same context. Although an explicit denial of Jewish claims to the same epithets is not evident in the apologetic literature, it is elsewhere, as we have seen in Justin's *Dialogue*,[150] and, outside Asia Minor, in the *Epistle to Diognetus* (3.1, 3; 4.5, 6; 6.4). Yet an implicit denial, especially where the Jews are labelled as 'barbarians', must have been hard to ignore.

Image and Reality

Only in general terms is there an overall consistency in the image of Judaism in the apologists. Such consistency as there is, is founded in the dilemma explored earlier: Judaism represented the heritage of Christianity, its means of access to the claims to antiquity which played such a crucial role in the competition for validity and authority in the contemporary world. At the same time Judaism represented an (but not the only) obstacle to Christianity's credibility in that competition. In different ways the image is one that affirms the antiquity but disqualifies the Jews from the competition. The affirmation of antiquity was one already made by Jewish apologetic and accepted by some pagan writers. The disqualification, however, takes two forms. One is political – the identification of the Jews as 'barbarians', the evocation of their rebellious tendencies and their defeat at Roman hands; this may seem superficially persuasive, although it ignores the contemporary reality in Asia Minor where diaspora Jewish communities were far from identified through their Judaean links. The other is unashamedly an image: when Justin asserts that the Jews misunderstand the prophecies they possess he is not saying that they themselves find difficulty in reaching a persuasive interpretation; their misunderstanding is apparent to the Christians alone. Similarly, when Aristides says the Jews in fact worship angels, he acknowledges that this is neither their understanding nor their intention, which are the worship of God; it is an insight presumably available to the Christians alone.[151]

Behind this imposed schema lie the Jewish communities which were, in different ways, one part of the apologetic context, not least by engaging in their own apologetic, perhaps including the claim that they and their adherents were 'God-fearers'. Yet beyond this and the picture already sketched, some further aspects of their life inevitably shine through. The anchoring of the claim to antiquity in the scriptures was itself already part of Jewish apologetic: Josephus derides any claim to veracity by Greek historians in comparison with the care with which Jewish records were kept, and appeals not only to the continuous history covered by the scriptures but also to prophetic inspiration as the ultimate guarantee of their consistency and authenticity (*C. Apion.* I.5–8 [23–43]).[152] Justin's argument suggests that this was known and that the 'possession' of the scriptures by the Jews continued to have this authority.

We should add that what had been recognised officially was the Jewish communities' rights to live according to their 'ancestral laws' (πατρίοι νόμοι) or customs (Josephus, *Ant.* XIV. 10.12, 17, 21, 25 [227, 235, 245, 263–4]; XVI.6.2, 4, 6 [163, 167, 171] etc.); in their apologetic literature it was equally these for which they had been persecuted and suffered (2 Macc. 6.1; 7.2, 24, 37; 4 Macc. 4.2; 5.33; 9.1; 16.16 etc.). This was a conjunction which the Christians could not emulate, but whose significance would have been hard to avoid.

The importance of the reading of the scriptures and of their interpretation 'in the synagogue' needs no further demonstration, but Justin's extensive appeal to the fulfilment of prophecy in an apologetic context suggests a further, less expected function. Again, Josephus also assumes that readers will find it credible that Alexander the Great was himself persuaded by a prophecy from Daniel which found its fulfilment in his own conquests, and on that basis permitted the Jews to follow their own laws (*Ant.* XI.8.5 [336–8]). It may be an exaggeration when Justin refers to the prohibition on pain of death of reading the books of the prophets as well as the Sibylline writings and those of Hystaspes (*Apol.* 44.12), but the continued writing and rewriting of Sibylline Oracles shows that prophetic writings widely carried a numinous attraction; their appropriation by the Jews (and by other peoples) indicates the apologetic and intellectual benefits possession of prophecies from antiquity could offer.[153] The argument about their fulfilment would have been taken very seriously, if not in the imperial chancery then at least on a popular level – especially if it could be shown that recent events detrimental to their rival interpreters were themselves predicted, namely the destruction of Judaea and Jerusalem, and that the Christian side had scored at least some points. By contrast, it may accord with public perception that Judaism is not characterised in the apologetic context primarily by its adherence to its scriptures as Law.

The relationship between public perception, 'image' and actual practice is more intricate when we come to Aristides' 'thumbnail sketch' of Jewish worship. On the one hand his catalogue belongs to a tradition he shares with the *Kerygma Petri*, with *Diognetus*, and perhaps already with Colossians and Galatians; moreover, his claim for the Jewish worship of angels is, as we have seen, a confessedly Christian interpretation. On the other hand, the catalogue matches well popular perceptions of Judaism, which, although distorted and partial, had some roots in actual practice. Observation of sabbath, new moon,[154] fasting, circumcision and purity of foods needs no special comment; the keeping of Unleavened Bread, which must include if not indicate Passover, and perhaps of the Day of Atonement, needs only be added to other evidence of Jewish calendar in the Diaspora.[155] Even the charge of worshipping angels may, as we have seen, have some grounding in local practice, while not suggesting patterns of 'marginal vs. official' Judaism or of the value-laden 'syncretism'.[156] Equally, the virtues of Judaism that Aristides extols, although inevitably not of the sort to find epigraphic confirmation beyond the common concern for burial and the rights of those buried, fit without difficulty in the world of the ancient city.

Behind the polemics we glimpse a Judaism which made sense within the religious context of the time. The picture painted is inevitably distorted and deficient, but it explains the need for the Christian apologetic argument far better than the legalistic Judaism of modern perception or the misanthropic and mutinous Judaism of ancient – and some more recent – constructs. The apologetic arguments against the Jews were not exercises in theoretical self-justification, but were addressed to living needs.

Notes

[1] On Justin and philosophy see among others, Hyldahl 1966; Joly 1973.

[2] On this see Carleton Paget 1994.

[3] §2; van den Broek 1988, with the translation on pp. 57–8.

[4] For Quadratus as 'discipulus apostolorum' see Eusebius, *Chron.* CCXXVI. Van den Broek 1988 argues for the letter as representing independent Jewish-Christian traditions in its account of the bishops of Jerusalem; however, it should be noted that Eusebius's reference to Quadratus (and Aristides who is referred to at the end of the Armenian version of the *Letter*) is almost directly followed by his discussion of the bishops of Jerusalem (*H.E.* IV. 3–5).

[5] For the argument see Andriessen 1947, who also accepts Jerome's identification of the two (or three) Quadratuses and already appeals to the apocryphal letter from James. See also Otto 1872: 338 for the suggestion as already proposed by Domerus in 1845.

[6] See Grant 1988: 36.

[7] Otto 1882: 336–7.

[8] This is generally seen as more likely than his association with Athens, which seems to have arisen from his juxtaposition with Aristides and has even led to his, chronologically unlikely, identification with the later bishop of that city (Eusebius, *H.E.* IV.23.3) in Jerome, *De vir. illus.* 19. On the problem see Bardy 1949. However, Barnard 1964a and Grant 1988: 35–6 accept his association with Athens and Hadrian's visit there; see also below.

[9] On the suggested impact of Montanism on apologetic and perhaps anti-Jewish polemic see below, p. 186, and n. 138.

[10] So Osborn 1973: 1 who speaks of the fronts from which Christianity was under attack.

[11] See Schürer 1973–87: III. 609–16; Collins 1983. For the possibility that 4 Macc. comes from Asia Minor see van Henten 1994: 68 and above, p. 81.

[12] See Schürer 1973–87: III. 609–10, 866–8; I. 54–5.

[13] See Droge 1989: 1–48.

[14] On this and what follows see Rajak 1985b; on the petitions included see Schoedel 1989.

[15] Seager and Kraabel 1983: 181; see also Trebilco 1991: 86–99, who argues that the Jews had drawn on the traditional name of the city, Apameia Kibotos (= chest/ark), originally a reference to its commercial importance, and who also points to *I* and *II Sib.* which appeal to the flood narrative and Noah's preaching of repentance.

[16] See further pp. 6, 201.

[17] See Mitchell 1993: II. 35–6, and above, pp. 5–8.

[18] On the statue see Kraabel 1968: 205, 213; Seager and Kraabel 1983: 179, and for the question of its relevance to the acquisition by the Jews of Sardis of their magnificent basilica synagogue pp. 202–3 below.

[19] Also preserved appended to Justin's *Apology* 68; the Latin does not survive. See Guyot and Klein 1993: I.45, 325–6, and, for discussion, Hengel 1984–5: 163–9.

[20] This is also found following Justin's *Apologies* in Cod. Parisinus Graec. 45 (see Marcovich 1994: 161–4).

[21] See Freudenberger 1967 who suggests the adoption of a Jewish precedent in such a collection of documents; Guyot and Klein 1993: I. 430 speak of 'christliche Fälscherkreise' interpolating and collecting imperial letters prior to Melito.

[22] For these themes in Jewish apologetic see Collins 1983; see also below, pp. 173–5, on the *Apology of Aristides.*

[23] As do Theophilus of Antioch and Clement of Alexandria, see Droge 1989: 8.

[24] Droge 1989: 11.

[25] See pp. 88–90.

[26] On this see Speigl 1970: 88–95; Hengel 1984–5, esp. p. 161 on the significance for Christian apologetics. On Hadrian and the Jews see also Herr 1972.

[27] Many scholars have seen a similar situation behind the *Epistle of Barnabas*; see Lowy 1960; Carleton Paget 1994: 9–30 assesses the evidence and prefers a Nervanic date.

[28] Tertullian may be dependent on Asia Minor sources, see below, pp. 186–7.

[29] See further pp. 121–3.

[30] Grant 1988: 81, 86–7 supposes that he was referring to the Jews who supported the revolt of Avidius Cassius which did take hold in Palestine of which the latter was governor, although this hardly indicates deliberate Jewish participation; that there had been local, otherwise unrecorded, disturbances, is not impossible; see Millar 1993: 117. Birley 1966: 263–4 decides that the story is apocryphal and thinks it likely that Marcus Aurelius engaged in philosophical discussion with Jewish teachers and that he is the 'Antoninus' of Talmudic sources. For the textual variants see Stern 1974–84: II.506. E. Gabba, 'L'*Apologia* di Melitone di Sardi', *Critica Storica* 1 (1962) 469–82, reported in Drobner 1982: no. 29, gives this as the provocation for Melito's *Apology.*

[31] Tacitus, *Ann.* XV.44; *Hist.* V.4–5; see Grant 1988: 31–2, 204–5; Lieu 1994c: 111.

[32] Cass. Dio, *Hist.* LXVII.14.1f.; Suetonius, *Domit.* 15.1; Eusebius, *H.E.* III.18.4; see P. Lampe 1989: 166–72.

[33] Lucian, *Peregr.* 11; Epictetus, *Disc.* II.9.19; see Lieu 1994c: 112–13.

[34] Most notably by V. Tcherikover; see the brief discussion by Collins 1983: 1–10; Goodman 1994a: 65–6, 78–81.

[35] See Kinzig 1990; Schoedel 1989 who sees them as 'apologetically grounded petitions' (p. 78).

[36] See Barnes 1971: 102–4 and below, p. 186.

[37] So Kinzig 1990.

[38] See Droge 1989: 76–81.

[39] On this and the whole debate see pp. 106–9.

[40] On the debate about audience see the discussion about Tertullian's *Adv. Iud.* in Fredouille 1972: 267–70; Tränkle 1964: LXVIII – LXXIV.

[41] See pp. 177–81.

[42] So without discussion Grant 1988: 35–6. Links with the *Kerygma Petri* (see below) have suggested an Alexandrian origin, but this has no support in any of the early references.

[43] *Chron.* CCXXVI. The dedication in the Armenian and the *title* in the Syriac version of the *Apology* give an address to Hadrian (but see below); the epithet 'of Athens' is found in the dedication of both versions.

[44] Yet Minucius Fundanus's proconsulship is probably to be dated prior to Hadrian's initiation, on which see Cassius Dio, *Hist. Rom.* LXIX.11.1.

[45] However, see above n. 8; Eusebius says he has a copy of Quadratus's *Apology* but merely states that Aristides' writing 'is preserved by many'.

[46] Harris 1891 and for the suggestion as to a setting at Smyrna, pp. 16–17. Geffcken 1907: 30, who follows the Syriac in its address to Antoninus, accepts Quadratus's association with Hadrian and Athens and suggests that this led Eusebius wrongly to assign Aristides to the same occasion. Seeberg 1893: 246, 296 accepted the association with Antoninus but left the question of location open while rejecting Smyrna on the (unconvincing) grounds that the author shows no direct knowledge of Judaism.

[47] The full name 'Marcianus Aristides' in the Syriac address to Antoninus may speak in its favour; see Geffcken 1907: 29 who argues for the early development of two recensions. Grant 1988: 36–9 suggests two stages in the redaction of the *Apology*, a first form, largely following the Greek, belonging to the time of Hadrian, and a second edition, lying behind the Syriac, under Antoninus Pius. While this solves the problem of the address and the inapplicability of the highlighting of Greek homosexuality when Hadrian had not long met his favourite Antoninus, it ignores the signs of more developed doctrine in the Greek. Grant also ignores that the 'relatively favourable picture of the Jews' which he finds in the Hadrianic Apology is found only in the Syriac.

[48] See p. 156.

[49] On this see Robinson in Harris 1891. There is also Armenian evidence for the early part of the *Apology*. References here are to the text and chapter and verse divisions of Goodspeed 1914, and to Harris 1891 for the Syriac, with reference also to Geffcken 1907.

[50] See Geffcken 1907: 34–41.

[51] The Armenian is missing here.

[52] = Harris 1891: (3)/*g* ll. 8–9; (11)/*y*'ll. 13–14.

[53] See Seeberg 1893: 169–71; the fourfold pattern is also accepted by Richardson 1969: 207–10.

[54] On this and what follows see Speyer and Opelt 1992: 835–51. On these grounds Robinson in Harris 1891: 90 and O'Ceallaigh 1958 reject the division adopted by the Syriac.

[55] See Gordon 1990: 236–8.

[56] See Droge 1989: 197 and below, pp. 182–4.

[57] In *Ker. Petri* 'Greeks' may indicate 'pagans' since to them is ascribed the worship of creatures which was a standard charge against the Egyptians – see the Syriac of Aristides!: so Nautin 1974: 99–100.

[58] The blaming of heresies among the Jews on different readings of the scriptures, and the appeal to the prophets in this text (111.30–113.34), also echo both apologetic and anti-Jewish writings.

[59] On what follows see Lieu 1995b and above, pp. 83–5.

[60] In the Syriac only; see further below, p. 195 n. 91.

[61] See above, pp. 83–4.

[62] So Baeck 1935, suggesting dependence on Hosea 6.2; Karpp 1954: 1124–5 suggests an original contrast between Jews, Greeks and Egyptians. Compare also the *Tripartite Tractate* quoted above, where the Hebrews are third after the Greeks and the barbarians.

[63] Cf. the decree of the people of Pergamum cited above, p. 158.

[64] In the Syriac the 'genealogy' of each race is given at the initial division (Harris 1891: (3)/*g*), before the detailed discussion of their views of the divine, whereas the Greek, which only retains it for the Jews and the Christians, puts it at the start of the relevant sections (so Goodspeed 1914,who gives a Latin translation). The failure of the Syriac to mention their rescue from Egypt 'by their lawgiver' (in the Greek and implied by the Armenian) suggests even this version is corrupt. See Arazy 1977: 135–7 for the 'sentimental' use of 'Hebrews' for the heroes of the past in Hellenistic Jewish literature.

[65] See Marmorstein 1919: 75–7 who cites rabbinic parallels, and Geffcken 1907: 83, who rightly compares Josephus, *C. Apion.* II.211 (cf. also 190–2); see also below, pp. 175–6. For the text see Harris 1891: (22)/*kb*–(23)/*kg*.

[66] Seeburg 1893: 393 suggests reading 'the great day' here which would involve the confusion of only one letter and avoids the repetition of 'fast' and the obscurity of 'the great fast'. In this case the words translated 'the feast of unleavened bread and the great [day]' together may refer to Passover and Unleavened Bread. On 'the great day' in this context see p. 72 and, more importantly, the parallel in *Ker. Petri* below. However, a reference to 'the (great) fast' could point to the Day of Atonement: see Justin, *Dial.* 40.4 and Skarsaune 1987: 179.

[67] The 'personification' of month (μήν) is odd and has prompted the suggestion of a 'rapprochement' with the Phrygian God Men: Simon 1971: 127–8.

[68] Nautin 1974: 105 suggests 'the sabbath which they say is of first importance', although this is not a natural way of taking the Greek. On this passage see also Stanton 1992b: 95–7.

[69] So Paulsen 1977 already for Colossians.

[70] Cf. p. 114.

[71] See Thornton 1989.

[72] On this and what follows see Sheppard 1980–1.

[73] Sheppard 1980–1: p. 94, no. 11 (?early third century); Sheppard argues that this is still pagan, albeit under Jewish influence, but this is overcautious; see Mitchell 1993: II. 36; Hengel 1990: 37.

[74] Mitchell 1993: II. 46.

[75] For the Syriac see Harris 1891: (3)/*g*–(4)/*h*. See above n. 64 for the different structure in the Greek which prefixes the genealogy to the description of the Christians in §15.

[76] So Siker 1991: 152–3, contrasting the *physical* descent of the Jews from Abraham with the *spiritual* descent from Jesus of the Christians; but he does not note that both terms appear in the Syriac account of the barbarians. However, since the Armenian only refers to 'race' at that point, the Syriac may be corrupt. Neither term is used of the Greeks. The Greek version does not make same the distinction.

[77] So also the Armenian; the Greek says 'holy' and omits the later reference to Jesus's Hebrew origins, just as it made no reference to the name 'Hebrews' in the account of the Jews. Seeberg 1893: 68 points to the same phrasing in a fragment of Aristides' (?) *Epistle to all Philosophers*, whose authenticity he defends.

[78] The last two verbs are omitted by the Armenian and may represent a redactional addition in the Syriac. Harris 1891: 14 translates with an over-technical 'crucified by the Jews' (cf. Goodspeed 1914: 5: Lat 'crucifixus est'), and suggests this may have belonged to the creed known to Aristides, drawing par-

allels from Justin – and we might add Melito – strengthening the Asia Minor connection.

[79] Contrast the Greek version, above, p. 169.

[80] Harris 1891: (25)/*kh*. The Greek speaks of 'the way of truth' leading to the 'eternal kingdom promised by Christ in the life to come'.

[81] 15.3 = Harris 1891: (23)/*kg* ll.10–11; for the Jews see 14.2 = Harris 1891: (22)/*kb* ll. 19–20; however, before the summary of their misguided worship, the Syriac did say that the Jews stray from 'accurate knowledge' (14.4). The Greek, which had no equivalent to the former affirmation of the Jews, says of the Christians 'they beyond all the nations of the earth have found the truth'.

[82] See also nn. 77, 80, 83.

[83] Greek: 'of the Lord Jesus Christ'.

[84] Cf. below, pp. 174–6 and nn. 94–95.

[85] Only in the Syriac, 15.7, 5 = Harris 1891: (24)/*kd* ll. 8–9; (23)/*kg* ll. 20–3. The avoidance of idols and of their offerings frame a negative form of the Golden Rule (alone in the Greek), recalling the Western text of Acts 15.20, 29.

[86] = Harris 1891: (23)/*kg* ll. 8–9; (26)/*kw* ll. 6–7, 11–15; (27)/*kz* ll. 1–4; the Greek here is much briefer, but it does appeal to 'the scriptures of the Christians' (Goodspeed 1914: 21, n. 10).

[87] 2.7 = Harris 1891: (4)/*d* ll. 1–4; the Syriac is obscure, while the Greek explicitly refers to the 'holy writing called *evangelic*' (15.1) which Geffcken 1907: 84 accepts as reflecting the original.

[88] = Harris 1891: (27)/*kz*–(28)/*kh*; this is not represented in the Greek, perhaps because of its new literary setting in *Barlaam and Josaphat*.

[89] = Harris 1891: (26)/*kw*; the last clause is omitted by the Greek; 'peoples' = ἔθνη/ '*mm*'.

[90] = Harris 1891: (27)/*kz* ll. 20–1.

[91] 16.3–6 = Harris 1891: (26)/*kw* ll. 3–22; for the last claim see ll. 10–11 where 'people' is '*m*', perhaps representing a Greek λαός.

[92] Harris 1891: 13; Geffcken 1907: XL; Seeberg 1893: 170, 'Es ist ein tastender Versuch, auch über dieses Volk etwas zu sagen.'

[93] O'Ceallaigh 1958.

[94] See Collins 1983: 137–74.

[95] See Collins 1983: 143–8; the prohibition of blood and food sacrificed to idols in *Sent.* l.31 is usually considered a Christian interpolation.

[96] Segal 1990: 200; Collins 1983: 167–8 is more nuanced, while Goodman 1994a: 112–14 on the Noachide laws and 65–6, 78–81 on the Hellenistic literature is much more dismissive.

[97] See above n. 85 and note this 'Rule' both in Tobit 4.15 and in *Did.* 1.2; the relation of the decree to the Noachide commands is not directly relevant here.

[98] Harris 1891: 13.

[99] Geffcken 1907: 82; so also Seeerg 1893: 296.

[100] He otherwise appears only at 63.7, 11, 17 in a quotation of Exod. 3.6, 15.

[101] Pompeius Trogus, *Hist. phil.* I.5 (= Stern 1974–84: I. 137); Plutarch, *De Iside et Osiride* 31 (= Stern 1974–84: I. 259).

[102] *Dial.* 11.3, 5; 123.5, 9; 135.6–136.1.

[103] Besides the association with Jesus (*Dial.* 30.3; 78.4), Judaea is only mentioned as the original home of Trypho (9.3), while 'Jews', which is far less frequent because of the direct address, can have a religious meaning in 'the synagogues' or 'heresies of the Jews' (72.3; 80.4; cf. also 77.3; 103.3.5).

[104] On the mainly non-geographical use of 'Jews' in epigraphical and other sources see Solin 1983: 647–9.

[105] See above p. 162 and n. 31.

[106] Contrast the position taken in the *Dialogue*: see pp. 136–7.

[107] Ctr. p. 106.

[108] Following the appeal to Gen. 49.10 at the beginning of ch. 32.

[109] This is not sufficiently taken account of by Hyldahl 1966: 263–7, who argues that Justin separates the political and juridicial 'church-state' question from the theological 'Jews-Christians' question. Cf. Shotwell 1965: 30–1 for the greater importance of proof-texting in the *Apology* than in the *Dialogue*.

[110] So Joly 1973: 88–9.

[111] See Droge 1989: 53, 58–9.

[112] νόμος is never used of the Jewish Law (*Apol.*15.5; 39.1; 40.8; II *Apol.* 2.4; 5.2); on the *Dialogue* see pp. 113–19.

[113] The *Dialogue* does know Moses as prophet (97.1) but usually associates the Law with Moses; see pp. 117–20. On Moses as prophet see also Athenagoras, *Suppl.* 9.1.

[114] See Droge 1989: 59–65.

[115] On this important theme in the *Dialogue* see pp. 125–7. See Skarsaune 1990: 216–17 on Justin's different uses of the Aristeas legend.

[116] On the question of Jewish involvement in persecution see pp. 91–2, 135–6.

[117] For this in the *Dialogue* see *Dial.* 131.2 and p. 135.

[118] I am assuming that the Syriac *Apology* preserved under Melito's name does not stem from Asia Minor; see Zuntz 1952: 195–6; Millar 1993: 477–8. It fits well in a second-third century context in its concern about the emperor cult but says nothing about the Jews; however, Joseph, Elijah and Cuteba are *Hebrews* worshipped as gods by the nations.

[119] See Frend 1965: 268–70, who suggests they may have been part of a general action against new cults; Birley 1966: 279, 328–9 suggests decrees permitting the use of criminals to meet a shortage of gladiators, although these were directed to the Gallic provinces, see Barnes 1968: 578–9.

[120] See also Justin's emphasis on 'piety and philosophy' as uniting Christian and imperial interests, *Apol.* 2.1; 3.2; 12.5; Holfelder 1977; this combination is not found in the *Dialogue*.

[121] Aristides, *Apol.* 16.1, 6 (Syr. only) = Harris 1891: (25)/*kh* ll. 17–18; (26)/ *kw* ll. 17–18.

[122] Eg. Tertullian, *Apol.* 40.

[123] See pp. 158–9.

[124] See p. 212.

[125] See Schneemelcher 1975, Kraabel 1971.

[126] See pp. 166–7, 177.

[127] See further pp. 203–4: the synagogue is now dated to the third century and later.

[128] And before the elevation of Commodus as emperor in 177, against Kraabel 1968: 213 and Hansen 1969: 98–9, who suggest it was presented to Verus. Frend 1965: 295, n. 3 suggests 176 when Marcus Aurelius visited Asia Minor.

[129] Among others, by van der Waal 1979: 145; see p. 207.

[130] In 175: see above p. 161 and n. 30.

[131] That is if we accept the text at Eusebius, *H.E.* IV. 27 which credits Apollinarius with two books against the Jews. However, there is both manuscriptal evidence and the negative testimony of Jerome in favour of its omission and it may be that the attribution has come in through assimilation to the writings of Miltiades listed at *H.E.* V.17.5, although the wording is not identical.

[132] *CIJ* II. 776–80; *CIJ* II. 779 speaks of 'the most holy treasury and the most holy *gerousia*'.

[133] See Trebilco 1991: 178.

[134] Grant 1988: 86–7.

[135] See n. 130 on Melito.

[136] So Grant 1988: 91 who suggests an echo of 1 Cor. 2.6–8 (where κοσμικούς is not used), although this seems an odd line to take in an Apology.

[137] Melito wrote on prophecy (Eusebius, *H.E.* IV.26.2).

[138] M. Sordi 1962 relates the Apologies of Apollinarius, Melito, Miltiades and Athenagoras to Montanism, which she sees as characterised by a 'nostalgie giudaizzanti ed antiromane'.

[139] So Barnes 1971: 102–4, who denies the influence of Justin's *Dialogue* on Tertullian. Tränkle 1964: LXVIII – LXXIV also suggests that Tertullian follows the footsteps of the Greek apologists with their double front but accepts dependence on Justin.

[140] See Fredouille 1972: 267–70, who attributes it to the fact that Jews were the intended audience of the *Adv. Iud.*

[141] On this and what follows see Lieu 1995b.

[142] So the Syriac translation at 1 Tim. 2.10. Seeberg 1893: 264–5 argues for θεοσέβεια on the grounds that borrowing from Aristides explains its use in *Diognetus*. A title does not survive in the Greek text; see above, pp. 164–5.

[143] Photius, *Cod.* 14 refers to (a) work/s 'concerning truth and concerning piety', on which see G. Salmon 1877: 132.

[144] See pp. 83–4.

[145] See Friesen 1993: 39–40; 146–50.

[146] Robert 1964: 44.

[147] See also *III Sib.* l. 573; *IV Sib.* ll. 135–6; Lieu 1995b: 494.

[148] See above, p. 172 and n. 76; = Harris 1891: (3)/*g*, ll. 14, 20; elswhere Aristides' vocabulary for Christian worship or doctrine is markedly non-technical (16.3, 4, 7).

[149] See above, n. 120.

[150] Eg. *Dial.* 92.3; 110.2; 118.3; see p. 138.

[151] See Hurtado 1988: 33–4.

[152] See Barton 1986: 59–60.

[153] See Potter 1990: 109; Schürer 1973–86: 618–54.

[154] See p. 114.

[155] See *CIJ* II. 777 cited above, p. 185.

[156] This framework is that used by A. Williams 1909 and Simon 1971.

6

MELITO OF SARDIS:
THE *PERI PASCHA*

That chance – combined of course with meticulous scholarship – is so often the mother of startling new insights is nowhere more clearly demonstrated than in the case of Jews and Christians in Sardis. M. Simon's *Verus Israel* (1986), first published in 1948, lists neither the city nor its now famous second-century Christian writer, Melito, in the index; the bibliography dealing with relations between Jews and Christians in this city of proverbial past greatness now grows by the year. This is not of merely local significance; the rewriting of the history of Judaism in Sardis has meant the rewriting of the history of diaspora Judaism, at least in Asia Minor.[1] The Christians too must find a new place in this redrawn picture. The case of Melito and Judaism at Sardis cannot be simply transferred to every other situation about which we know little more than echoes, but it must set question marks against confident assumptions and presuppositions. Here, then, we may properly start not with the literature and its images, but with the recently re-imaged/re-imagined reality.

Returning to Sardis, the history of its Jewish community has often been drawn, traced back by many to 'the exiles of Jerusalem in Sepharad' in Obadiah 20 – Sardis bears that Aramaic name in a bilingual inscription found there.[2] Whether or not the earliest Jewish population was of direct Judaean origin, they would probably have been dominated soon by the families from Mesopotamia settled in Phrygia and Lydia by Antiochus III (223–187 BCE), apparently as reliable pockets of loyalty (Josephus, *Ant.* XII.3.4 [147–53]). It is natural to suppose that such an origin would have secured for them certain rights within the cities in which they were settled, as Josephus himself claims, but the question whether, and, if so, when, the Jews held citizenship in Sardis and the other cities remains a vexed one.[3]

Among the various documents affirming Jewish rights that Josephus preserves from the Roman period, several refer to the Jewish community in Sardis (*Ant.* XIV.10.17 [235]; XIV.10.24 [259–61]; XVI.6.6 [171]). They offer glimpses both into the concerns and priorities of the community, and, in spite of Josephus's intention, into the harassment or obstacles they could meet on their way.[4] At the heart of both lay the Jews' long-held right to 'assembly (σύνοδος) according to their ancestral laws', including possession of 'a place (τόπος) of their own' for this purpose: we should not ignore the text and call this place yet a 'synagogue', for in the first decree the focal activities carried out here seem more concerned with the governance of their communal life, including cases of civil dispute. The second decree, this time a resolution by the people of Sardis provoked by apparent infringement of Jewish rights, requires in addition provision of a place 'to build and dwell', where, coming together on the stated days, 'they might fulfil their traditional prayers and sacrifices'. On one reading, 'sacrifices' (θυσίαι) represents the Jewish non-sacrificial 'synagogue' worship or a pagan misunderstanding of the same. It is not impossible, however, that, far from the Temple in Jerusalem, Jews of Sardis did on occasion offer sacrifice, whether at Passover, or as gentile converts or 'God-fearers'.[5] None the less, by the end of the first century BCE they still recognised at least the symbolic significance of Jerusalem in the far from symbolic way of collecting and sending regular contributions there (*Ant.* XVI.6.6 [171]). Moreover, their dietary idiosyncrasies, which so often in the literary sources invite only mockery, had been taken sufficiently seriously for the market officials to be instructed to ensure their supply – perhaps a reference in particular to red meat. Any who were Roman citizens were undoubtedly included in the exemption from military service, which they found incompatible with their religious life (*Ant.* XIV.10.13, 18 [230, 236–7]).[6] It is tempting to supplement these details with others from the decrees relating to neighbouring cities, as perhaps Josephus intends his readers to do: the 'stated days' on which the Jews of Sardis win the right to meet together (*Ant.* XIV.10.24 [261]) are surely the sabbaths whose unimpeded observance is granted, in adjoining decrees, to their neighbours at Ephesus and Halicarnassus (*Ant.* XIV.10.23 [258]; 10.25 [263–4]). Yet as important as the underlying coherence is the lack of uniformity of detail and of language: the Jews of Halicarnassus acquired the right to construct not 'a place' but 'houses of prayer' (προσευχή) by the sea.

Neither is the picture one of uninterrupted enjoyment of privileges; in instructing 'the magistrates, council and people of Sardis' (XIV.10.17 [235]; XVI.6.6 [171]), the Roman authorities were responding to repeated appeals by the Jews who found their past rights curtailed, while the decree of the people of Sardis themselves was prompted by the prior complaints of the Jews and the latters' citation of the decisions of the Roman Senate in their favour (XIV.10.24 [260]). We catch glimpses of the regular erosion of rights which, perhaps, could only be restored when the support of an influential patron had been won to plead before 'the council and people' or to gain access to the Roman governor; such restoration in turn may only have exacerbated tensions by being imposed from above. Yet, at the same time, the detailed specificity of provision bears equal witness both to the expectations of the community and to the recognition accorded them by those in authority.

There follows a silence of some two hundred years when we know little of the fortunes of the Jewish community, although they too must have suffered the consequences of the disastrous earthquake of 17 CE. Beyond this, it has often been assumed that they found increasing acceptance under the more stable conditions of the Empire;[7] this may be too sanguine an interpretation of the sources when we consider the indirect testimony of the antipathy to the Jews manifested in Ephesus in Acts 19, and the potential resentment any failure to participate in the flourishing imperial cult might provoke.[8]

It is the long-drawn-out programme of rebuilding following the destruction wrought by the earthquake which eventually brings the Jewish community back into our sight again.[9] Sardis had suffered particularly badly and received considerable tax exemptions (Tacitus, *Ann.* II.47) which prompted an extensive and ambitious programme involving reutilising areas which for long had not been under construction. A large bath–gymnasium complex occupied a significant place among the new public buildings; this was fronted at the east end by a large palaestra, to the north and south of which were planned two chambers apparently providing facilities for exercise or changing. The process, however, was a slow one and continued for as long as two centuries, and desire for magnificence probably outstripped practical possibility and financial resources; at some stage the still incomplete southern chamber was blocked off from the gymnasium complex to form a basilica whose length ran from west to east. An apse was created at the west end, perhaps to meet its initial use for judicial purposes by the city, although this is no more than a guess. In time, however, the basilica was apparently made over to the Jewish community, and, during the years which followed, the community proved themselves able substantially to refurbish their new centre, individuals providing mosaics, wall-cladding and other donations, and recording the fact for posterity – and for our edification. Clearly datable to the fourth century are further decoration and modification, including the creation of an atrium at the east end by the erection of a cross wall which incorporated a, or more probably two, Torah shrine(s) to the side(s) of the main door.[10] In the following years of upheaval in the Empire the 'synagogue' continued to provide for and to reflect the needs of the community; despite the 'triumph' of Christianity, the Sardis synagogue did not suffer the fate of many of its fellows, of adoption as a Christian church. With further repairs in the sixth and early seventh centuries it remained in Jewish hands until sharing in the destruction of the city of Sardis in 616 CE.

The Jewish community was a well-established and recognised group within city life, and the possession of this strategically placed synagogue would ensure their continued visible public presence and status. Already the transfer of the basilica into their hands acknowledged their status and their wealth, and perhaps their size, for by modern standards the basilica could accommodate an estimated one thousand people. Confirming this external recognition, they themselves affirmed their commitment to the city in which they lived. A number record themselves as 'citizens of Sardis', some had even served as councillors for the city – two of whom were goldsmiths; a fragmentary Hebrew inscription has been read as bearing the name 'Verus', perhaps honouring the emperor who visited the city in 166 CE. At one stage it was suggested that he may even have been instrumental in permitting the transfer of the building to the Jews, but the inscription has been reinstalled in a third-century wall and its earlier location is unknown.[11]

Yet the question of the date of the hand-over remains both crucial and contested. A relatively early transfer, early in the third century if not at the end of the second century, would give weight to a picture of nearly uninterrupted and growing confidence on the part of the Jewish community, and could contrast sharply with the supposedly struggling Christian community, facing unprecedented persecution about the same time.[12] The dating of the uncontested remodelling to serve the needs of the synagogue and of the donation by Jewish benefactors of the mosaics counsels caution; the *reconstructed* synagogue which so awes the modern visitor belongs to the fourth century, and an alternative scenario would see the building's secession to the Jewish community more in terms of the economic instability of the late third century and of that community's ability to respond to possibilities for corporate benefaction.[13]

It would be hazardous, then, to assume that the apparently self-confident participation in the life of the city witnessed by the synagogue inscriptions was already a mark of the Jewish community in the second century.[14] However, it is still valuable to allow those material remains to project an image of the community they record. Although that image cannot explain Melito's counter-image, as had been supposed when they were assumed to be contemporaneous, setting the two beside each other helps explore the uncertain relationship between image and reality.

Judaism in Sardis: the Synagogue

Perhaps the strongest components in that image are the confident maintenance of the distinguishing marks of corporate Jewish identity together with signs of a high degree of integration within the life of the city: it was to a synagogue and its distinctive requirements that the Jews of this city continued to display and commit their wealth, and it was also there that they identified themselves as 'citizens of Sardis'.[15] Eight are 'councillors', while some hold other offices. While their affluence and participation may reflect the conditions of the third century, they clearly had not been won at the cost of assimilation to their pagan surroundings.[16] Indeed, this has been a major element in the reconsideration of the nature of diaspora Judaism to which the Sardis synagogue has contributed so much. That Judaism can no longer be looked at and judged through a lens crafted by rabbinic Judaism, itself perhaps more an image projected by the literature than a true reflection of life even in Palestine. The distinction between adaption to their home environment, which is both inevitable and easily illustrated, and an assimilation which implies the surrender of distinctive patterns of belief or life and the adoption of other incompatible ones, is an important one, even if the line between the two may sometimes be a narrow one and be viewed differently from different perspectives. Seen through the remains of the Sardis synagogue, the Jews of the third, and perhaps already of the second, century in this city of Asia Minor had neither shut themselves off from all physical or intellectual contact with the life of the city, nor had they so identified with it that they had lost clear identity: it is this which forms the character of diaspora Judaism as Melito or his audience would have encountered it.

We may give content to this outline: within the synagogue, the Jews and any casual visitors, and here we may include if not Christians then perhaps some who later converted to Christianity, would encounter the symbols which both marked their distinct identity and created a place for that identity within the wider city. We may think of the frequent representations of menorahs both on the fabric of the building and on bowls and other vessels;[17] an incised lulab and shofar were close to the Torah shrine(s) built into the added east wall. The latter in themselves point to the importance of the Law – not a new concern but perhaps a developing one if the wall was a later addition to an earlier synagogue.[18] The enormous reading-table, perhaps replacing an earlier one, albeit at the opposite end of the synagogue to the Torah niche(s), tells the same story.

The great fountain in the atrium may have served for purification purposes, but it was also substantial enough to be included in an inscription listing the public fountains of the city, presumably demanding its accessibility for non-Jews.[19] A few formulaic fragments of Hebrew remain, but clearly Greek was the language of daily and, we must suppose, of religious use. Not only do donors declare themselves to be citizens and councillors of Sardis, they are also 'fearers of God', θεοσεβεῖς, most probably Jews claiming for themselves what loyal pagans frequently claimed with the word 'pious' (εὐσεβεῖς).[20] Pagan claims are again echoed as numerous donations are said to be in fulfilment of a vow; it is a Jewish piety which acknowledges that the wall-covering is given 'out of the gifts of Almighty God', but the influence of Greek philosophical ideas allows them also to speak of the divine 'providence'.[21] Some apparently pride themselves on belonging to the 'tribe of Leontios';[22] a conscious allusion to the lion of Judah seems probable, although it would be difficult to miss the 'coincidence' that the lion was the symbol of the city of Sardis itself, or to fail to note that two Lydian lions proudly stood on either side of the great reading-table and, unlike the reused eagles which supported it, were damaged but not defaced.[23] Yet the floor mosaic which would meet the eyes of the congregation as they faced towards the apse was of a great vine growing from a vase curiously similar to the crater in the forecourt, a mosaic which has nothing to distinguish it from any pagan decoration elsewhere.

Beyond this we catch few glimpses of synagogue life. The synagogue is notoriously empty of anything else which might speak of the varied activities that took place there – the lamps and bowls incised with menorahs give no hint of any distinctive use, and any other furnishings or furniture have long since gone. The apse, although probably not built by the Jews, provided the only surviving seating, presumably for the elders and other leading figures of the community. However, synagogue officials are not recorded, although one inscription found in a shop records a 'Jacob the elder'; in this community, in contrast to some others in the Diaspora, people preferred to be identified by their civic rather than by their communal role.[24] At a later date this may have changed: an inscription from the fifth century (?) records Samoe, who is both a priest and also a 'teacher of wisdom' (σοφοδιδασκάλος); his role in the Diaspora as a priest is far from certain, but Samoe was presumably also the local equivalent of a rabbi, although on what authority and grounds we can hardly say.[25] His office confirms that the reading and teaching of the Law were an intrinsic part of all that took place there, but the semi-technical term may be evidence of the influence of developments in rabbinic Judaism on the Diaspora in the fifth century. In that context, the apparent replacement of an earlier inscription by his may signal a deliberate counter-claim to the 'secular' influence of the donors who proudly recorded themselves as councillors, in turn confirming the secure place they had previously held in the synagogue.[26]

Christianity in Sardis: Melito

In the magnificence of the synagogue the Jews were reflecting the social and economic conditions of a later century.[27] How far had the seeds for this already been sown in the sixties and seventies of the second century, when Melito, writing and preaching for the Christians of Sardis, was earning for himself Tertullian's critical estimate of his 'elegant and declamatory style, [despite which] many held him to be a prophet' (Jerome, *De vir. illus.* 24)? The history of the Christian church there before his time is largely forgotten, so that an origin in 'the synagogue', and/or as part of Pauline missionary activity,[28] or through the unrecorded work of other evangelists, must remain a matter of conjecture. The church in Sardis is one of those addressed by the prophet of the Apocalypse (Rev. 3.1–6), but the charges against it – that despite its appearance of life it is dead, and that all but a few have 'polluted their garments' – are particularly general and allow few conclusions as to the nature of the threat perceived by the author.[29] Not addressed by Ignatius, it is only with Melito that the church comes back into view.

The bulk of Melito's writings have been lost, and survive only as a list of titles collected by Eusebius (*H.E.* IV.26.2); their number and scope probably reflect both the skill of their author and the range of issues confronting the church at the time, apparently including the teaching of Marcion and the Montanist movement, although scholarly attempts to deduce specific concerns from the sometimes textually corrupt titles seem doomed to disagreement and failure.[30] In his *Apology* to Marcus Aurelius Melito complains of 'new decrees' against the Christians; since the novelty of persecution is an essential part of Melito's apologetic scheme, this offers little proof that the church had up till then (*c.*169–77) experienced few troubles.[31] It is possible, but perhaps unlikely, that the Christians of Sardis escaped entirely the persecutions that hit Smyrna and Philadelphia in the time of Polycarp, or those which led to the deaths of Thraseas and of Sagaris (Eusebius, *H.E.* V.24.2–6), and perhaps of others of whom we now know nothing.

Equally, Eusebius's account tells us nothing about the make-up of the Sardis church or about its relations with Judaism: a number of scholars have suggested that the informers whose punishment Melito urges in his *Apology* may have been Jews,[32] but this too is empty conjecture fuelled by the virulence of the *Peri Pascha* to which we are coming, and by the image of an already powerful Jewish community, soon to be, if not already, in possession of their strategically placed synagogue. Scholars have been too quick to project a counter-image of a small and struggling Christian community; Melito's own rhetorical skills could betray an established educational and social background not at all inferior to that of his Jewish contemporaries.[33]

More intriguing is the journey Melito made as the first recorded pilgrim 'to the east as far as the place where it was proclaimed and performed'; here he 'learnt accurately the books of the Old Testament', and, as well as listing them, made extracts, presumably proof texts, for his correspondent, Onesimus (Eusebius, *H.E.* IV.26.14). Yet it is what this report leaves unsaid which raises as many questions as what it records. Why did he need to travel to Palestine for this purpose? Was it because relations with the local Jewish community were so bad that he could not even ascertain from them the number and proper order of the books – which Onesimus had requested?[34] Or was he aware that Christians of Asia Minor were using a wider range of books than their Jewish neighbours, but also that those Jews were not as reliable an authority as the Jews of Palestine?[35] Or were his intended informants not the Jews but the Christians of Syria, whose voice he would take more seriously than those Jewish neighbours?[36] The list he proceeds to give would allow each of these possibilities: in content it largely conforms with what is widely agreed to be the 'Jewish canon' by this period, with the notable exception of Esther;[37] the order, however, follows more closely that of the Greek translation which in time was to become the 'Christian Old Testament'.

Whether or not the problem and his journey reflect the necessities forced on him by scriptural debate with the Jews of the region, Melito's language refers only to 'the ancient books', 'the old testament' (another first), and 'the place where it was preached and done', all reflecting a world defined by the Christian Gospel. A short excerpt which may come from the 'extracts from the law and the prophets concerning the saviour' which Melito composed after his visit (*H.E.* IV.26.13) confirms this picture: here the events and people of the past do not point to a fulfilment in Christ but rather he was 'among the prophets a prophet ... with Isaac bound ... with Moses a captain'.[38] This position, confirmed by other fragments and by the text to which we are coming, belongs not to a pattern of argument and demonstration but to a totalising universe which has absorbed the past. It may, then, not be so surprising that, unlike his contemporaries, Apollinarius and Miltiades, who shared his concerns with Montanism and with Marcion, Melito wrote no tractate of real or implied debate with the Jews – at least according to Eusebius.

However, first among the books Eusebius lists – it seems not from firsthand knowledge – stand 'two concerning the Pascha', the term used for the Jewish Passover and also for the Christian festival which 'replaced' it. From Eusebius's brief statement that it was occasioned by a local dispute arising from the coincidence of the (?anniversary of the) martyrdom of Sagaris and the Paschal season (*H.E.* IV.26.3), it would be natural to assume that Melito's prime concern was the defence of Quartodeciman practice of which he was thirty years later to be remembered as a leading advocate.[39] Instead – and illustrating the hazards of our dependence on Eusebius's fragmentary and often second-hand evidence for the early history of the church – Melito's work proves to be a homily whose advocacy has rather earned the words: 'his indignation against the Jews for their blind ingratitude prompts him to a bitter and violent invective against them, which gives the homily a place in the *adversus Judaeos* literature, although it is passionate and denunciatory rather than argumentative'.[40] These words by the first editor of the newly discovered homily in 1940 have been repeatedly echoed in the decades which followed and have led naturally into the growing bibliography with which we started this chapter.

Judaism in the Peri Pascha

a) *Context and Argument*[41]

The discovery of the synagogue at Sardis has forced its modern interpreters to position the *Peri Pascha* on a stage where Judaism could hardly be ignored; yet if we are to find the members of that synagogue on its pages, it will only be by an imaginative entering into the rhetoric, its silences as well as its words, its structure as well as its polemic. For this is not an Apology nor a demonstration but a 'homily',[42] preached to the Christian congregation gathered for the celebration of the saving death of Christ. The exact course of that celebration is lost to us, but its focus for Melito and his flock as Quartodecimans would have been the 14th of the Jewish month of Nisan – or, according to the Jewish reckoning by which the day commenced at sunset, 14 to 15 Nisan. At the heart of their observance was the Paschal fast which was broken by the celebration of the eucharist. The precise timing of the fast and its ending was – as it still is for modern scholars[43] – a matter of dispute between the churches (Eusebius, *H.E.* V.24.8–17), but it is in this setting that we may picture Melito delivering his passionate and rhetorical homily.

Indeed, the rhetoric gains added impact in the setting we may create for it: if the Christians were gathering in the darkness of evening or night, Melito's extended and graphic description of 'the darkness that could be grasped' in which the death which could not be grasped sought out and grasped the first-born of Egypt (§23, l. 145) would be all the more real. Christians who were well aware that their fast coincided with the festivities of the Jewish Passover meal would find themselves caught up into the events of the Passion as Melito thundered – ostensibly to Jesus's contemporaries:

> You were celebrating,
> He was starving;
> You were drinking wine and eating bread,
> He vinegar and gall;
> You were bright of face,
> He downcast;
> You were rejoicing,
> He was oppressed;

You were singing,[44]
He was being judged; ... (§80, ll. 566–75)

Yet as a homily, delivered in a 'liturgical' context, it shares with worship in general that it does not only make real for those who share in it that which they hold by faith, it also offers them an understanding of meanings hidden to human eyes. This too is Melito's express purpose – he will declare 'the mystery of the Pascha' (§§2; 11; 65, ll. 10, 65, 448).[45] Possession of the true meaning of the mystery is indispensable for salvation and so determines those who are within, those who are without: Egypt was struck not just because she did not participate in the Pascha but because she was 'not initiated into the mystery' (§16, ll. 97–8). It is the Christians as they listen and participate who are the initiates, perhaps contrary to any outward perception.

The heart of the mystery for Melito is the Pascha, the Passover deliverance of Israel from Egypt, which has a twofold significance – temporal in that which was written in the law, timeless in Christ, 'the Pascha of our salvation' (§69, l. 479). This duality, which runs throughout the homily, is expressed even in the structure of the whole, and again serves to create two separate and contrasting worlds.

The first part commences with a prologue, a 'masterpiece of early Christian preaching',[46] which develops the theme in a series on antitheses.

So is it new and old,
Eternal and temporal,
Mortal and immortal,...
Old according to the law,
New according to the word,
Temporal according to the [type],
Eternal on account of grace (§§2–3, ll. 7–14)

And the law became word
And the old new,
  proceeding from Zion and Jerusalem,
And the command grace ...
And the man God. (§7, ll. 41–5, 48)

Yet that last line sounds already an important note which is equally indispensable to the whole: for Melito all the acts of God can be predicated of Christ; it is to him that the doxologies, such as that which closes the prologue (§10, ll. 63–4), are addressed, and it is he who will define the meaning of both old and new.

The main body of the first part of the *Peri Pascha* starts by paraphrasing the institution of the Passover as commanded by Moses (§§11–15, ll. 65–91); it then leads into a lengthy, vivid and dramatic description of the final plague, the slaying of the first-born of Egypt by 'the angel of righteousness' (§§16–30, ll. 92–198). The first-born desperately struggle against the relentless grasp of silent death who stalks in the palpable darkness; the land is covered with the unburied dead; Pharaoh is clothed with grief-stricken Egypt; distraught parents act out a grotesque dance of death. Yet in the midst of this scene of terror and desolation 'Israel was protected by the slaughter of the lamb ... and the death of the lamb proved a wall for the people' (§30, ll. 196–8). This itself is a mystery and points to what has yet to be disclosed: what was it that stayed the hand of the angel –

The slaughter of the lamb
Or the life of the Lord?
The death of the lamb
Or the type of the Lord? (§32, ll. 203–6)

It is indeed as **type** that the power of the mystery is to be understood. All communication works by parable, all artifacts depend on a prior plan or model. The model is necessary but its only purpose is to point to, or to embody, the reality which it serves. Once this reality is completed, the model surrenders its value, its time is over. As with the mundane, so too with the heavenly: the Gospel is the reality of which the Law was the parable or comparison, 'the people' the model for the church; 'that which had its value in the past, now is made valueless by the appearance of the truly valuable' (§43, ll. 278–9). This reversal of values is proclaimed in a rising crescendo of antitheses between the sacrifice, Temple and Jerusalem of old, and the new, which reaches its climax in the outpouring of God's grace in all corners of the world –

And there dwells the almighty God,
Through Jesus Christ to whom be glory for ever. Amen. (§45, ll. 298–300)

The natural break which occurs here (§45), and which may signal the division between what Eusebius describes as Melito's two books 'Concerning the Pascha',[47] allows a new step in a direction whose basic presuppositions and goal are, however, harmonious with the first 'book'. Now attention turns from the model to the essential structure of the reality. The link is forged more securely by the question and answer; 'What is the Pascha (πάσχα)?': the name comes from that which took place – from the suffering that took place comes 'to suffer (πάσχειν: *paschein*)' (§46, ll. 303–5). This spurious etymology which traces the transliterated form of the Aramaic '*pesach*/passover' to the Greek verb 'to suffer' would only – and evidently did – appear cogent to Greek-speaking Christians.[48] Melito was not the first to make the connection, and neither would he be the last. For him it points not only to the suffering of Christ but also to the human situation of suffering into which Christ entered. He reaches back to the story of the creation of humankind, of the disobedience in Eden, and of the consequent casting out 'into this world as into a prison of the condemned' (§§47–8, ll. 311–29). The human inheritance of mortality, dishonour, slavery and death was compounded by the tyranny of sin whose most vivid consequences are the murderous turning of father against son, brother against brother, friend against friend, and even – an unceasing source of horror even in the midst of the privations of siege warfare – the slaughter by a starving mother of her own child. The graphic language is not merely overblown rhetoric; Josephus's account of the dire straits of the siege in Jerusalem reaches a similar climax of horror (*B.J.* VI.3.4 [201]), and we may wonder whether Melito was well aware of the resonances.[49]

This universal setting of enslavement by sin and imprisonment by death is the occasion for the 'fulfilment of the mystery of the Pascha in the body of the Lord' (§56, ll. 396–7); but already throughout the history of 'the people' (of Israel) his sufferings were foreshadowed, in Abel, Isaac and Joseph, and in Moses, David and the prophets, both when they were rejected and when they spoke of him (§§59–65, ll. 415–50). Yet now another important step can be taken[50] – these do not merely point to Jesus as their fulfilment; he himself was suffering in them then, and has now come to earth, and brought about a new 'Exodus' deliverance from slavery and death (§§66–71, ll. 451–504).

At this point style and direction change dramatically:

This man has been murdered!
And where was he murdered? – In the heart of Jerusalem.[51]
By whom? – By Israel.[52]
Why? – Because he healed their lame ... (§72, ll. 505–8)

Turning to Israel, a crescendo of charges accuses her directly of baseless ingratitude:

You dishonoured the one who honoured you ...
You killed the one who gave you life. (§73, ll. 520, 524)

In a dramatic turn of *dramatis personae*, 'Israel' is made to justify her defiance of the law:

Yes, I killed the Lord. Why? Because he had to die! (§74, ll. 528–9)[53]

Had to die obviously voices a Christian perspective: because scripture foretold it. Yet, Israel is told, this gives no grounds for justification, still less grounds for evading responsibility. His suffering, his dishonouring, his condemnation and crucifixion should have been at the hands of others, of those who did not belong to the people for whom he had performed so many miracles – of a foreign, uncircumcised people (§76, ll. 537–44); at the hands, we might say, of the Romans who feature in Melito's account of the Passion only as those who admire Jesus (§92, ll. 672–7). The denunciation intensifies as Israel is accused, again in graphic and rhetorical detail, of plotting and preparing, of scourging and crowning him with thorns, of binding his hands 'which formed you from the earth' and offering gall to that mouth 'which offered you life', of killing 'your Lord on the great feast' (§79, ll. 553–65).[54]

Here, as we have already seen, with vivid contrast Israel's Paschal celebrations are set against Jesus's suffering, made the more unspeakable because the one on whom they inflicted such sufferings is their Lord, the one who formed them, honoured them and called them 'Israel', the one who shaped all creation, who called the patriarchs and led Israel from Egypt and throughout her history – this is the one whom **you killed**! (§§81–5, ll. 582–624).

The litany of lawsuit, plea, accusatory question, judgement-threat and appeal to witnesses 'from all the families of the nations' continues with unabated vigour. Finally, Melito's Christology and castigation meet:

> The one who suspended the earth is suspended,
> The one who fixed the heavens is fixed firm,
> The one who fastened the universe is fastened to the tree,
> The master is insulted,
> God is murdered,
> The King of Israel is killed by an Israelite right hand. (§96, ll. 711–16)

Even here neither indignation nor rhetoric are satisfied; even the created order responded to the suffering of the Lord (§98, ll. 725–9). Yet Israel's disregard has earned her the disregard of the Lord. The anguish she did not feel over his death she has been made to feel over her own fate. She who dashed him to the ground now lies herself dashed to the ground; but – and here we echo both the beginning of the section and lead into the triumphant epilogue –

> You lie dead
> But he is raised from the dead
> And has ascended to the heights of heaven. (§100, ll. 745–57)

Israel now is forgotten as the risen Christ declares his saving work and invites 'all the families of humankind' to find forgiveness for their sins. Christ's self-proclamation is echoed by the acclamation of the preacher celebrating him from creation to salvation to exaltation to the right hand of the Father, and so to a triumphant doxological climax (§105, ll. 792–803).

Occupying rather more than a quarter of the whole,[55] the length and vehemence of Melito's tirade directed personally against Israel stand out with stark bluntness even in the midst of all his highly wrought rhetoric. Small wonder that it has earned both heated condemnation and anxious apologetic.[56] Yet there is more to Melito's response to Israel than the charge of deicide, and it is from his decision to start with the reading of 'the Hebrew Exodus' that we too must begin before we can move to his other starting-point, the Christian community in Sardis and the never-absent Jews.

b) *Israel, the People*

However, even if we assume them to be never absent, Melito nowhere mentions 'the Jews' – it is with **Israel** and with **the people** (λαός) that he deals. As the latter they are first and foremost the people to whom came God's saving deliverance; the people who received both their being and their name from God, or rather from **the Lord**, who for Melito is Jesus Christ. Yet this does not remove them from contemporary reality into the pages of scripture; 'people' (λαός) continued to be the distinctive self-designation of the Jews even in the Diaspora, and could be seen as such on many an epitaph, no doubt also in Sardis itself.[57] Whether or not in explicit confrontation with them, Melito does not deny them the epithet, nor, as did some of his Christian contemporaries (*Ep. Barn.* 13.1, 3, 5), does he claim it for the Christians as the real or new people of God.[58] Instead, he simply empties it of present value – 'the people were made void when the church arose' (§43, l. 276).

By contrast, in the second 'book', throughout the long invective against Israel, the term 'people' largely disappears,[59] only reappearing in the last stanza which introduces the declaration of Israel's final defeat. There, in an emphatic position at the beginning of each clause, it is repeated sonorously four times as the failure of **the people** to tremble is contrasted with the trembling of the earth, to fear with the fear of the heavens, to tear their clothes with the tearing (of the Temple veil) by the angel, to lament with the thundering of the Lord from heaven (§98, ll. 725–9). Throughout this second 'book' it is, instead, **Israel** who is addressed, and addressed personally as **you**. This creates both a continuity and a contrast with the first half (book) where 'Israel' is used of the people who are protected and preserved from the touch of death. Israel does not belong to the language of type or model; unlike 'the people' (or Jerusalem or the Temple: §§44–5, ll. 280–300), Israel is not made void or emptied of value with the appearance of something new. Even with the appearance of the fulfilment she remains, now as ungrateful and lawless Israel whose sick the Lord healed; it is as

King of Israel that Jesus died, **by an Israelite right hand** (quoted above). It is at this point (§96, l. 716) that **the people** and **Israel** come in parallel again; 'the people's' failure to tremble or fear (just quoted) was Israel's failure; her failure then has been recompensed since by her fear of her enemies, her lamenting over the loss of her first-born, her tearing of her clothes over her own dead. Only now do we hear a faintly ominous echo: although Israel is not identified with Egypt we cannot help but remember Egypt's lamenting over the death of her own first-born, themselves dashed to the ground.[60] The final note comes as no surprise: **you lie dead**.

Replacement of the 'people' and Israel's culpable rejection of her Lord are not brought together as effect and cause. Replacement already belongs to the nature of the Pascha as type or model, and, indeed, to Melito's whole interpretation of scripture in these terms. Within this scheme there is an inevitable tension between continuity and discontinuity, or between analogy and antithesis. The old had value in that it contained the hidden model of the new; so the new must be understood in categories provided by the old – Passover, lamb, blood. Yet, with the appearance of the fulfilment, the model has lost all intrinsic value. Moreover, the fulfilment brings with it new categories, no longer law but word, no longer type but grace, no longer people but church. Seen from the other end, since it was already the Lord who was present, not only in the death of the lamb but also in the rejection and suffering of Abel, Isaac, Joseph or Moses, these have, perhaps, an abiding value, albeit a hidden one.

We see here a positive evaluation of the Old Testament scriptures which would have provided an effective defence against Marcion, and his dismissal of them may arguably be in view. On the other hand, such a scheme leaves no room for any continuing significance of 'the people' or of their Passover celebrations. This illustrates well how often a polemic against Marcion is tied to a polemic against Judaism, but equally how there is no single pattern in which this is effected.

The replacement theology is not just an integral part of the first 'book' but also forms its concluding climax (§§44–5, ll. 280–300). Not only is the once-valuable blood of the lamb now empty because of the spirit of the Lord, but the Temple below is now valueless on account of the Christ above, the Jerusalem below on account of the Jerusalem above. The themes may be inspired by the New Testament (Gal. 4.26), but they are probably equally inspired by the destruction of Jerusalem and the exclusion of Jews from the city, most recently after the Bar Kochba revolt (as in Justin, *Dial.* 40);[61] they may even implicitly deny the Passover hope attributed already to R. Akiba which looks forward to the renewed celebration in a rebuilt Jerusalem (*mPes.* 10.6). This paragraph ends by contrasting the 'narrow inheritance' and 'little plot' with the broad sphere of grace and with God's dwelling in all corners of the earth 'through Christ Jesus': Melito acknowledges only 'biblical' Israel and the confined land he had visited, ignoring contemporary diaspora (i.e. Sardis) Judaism; perhaps, like Justin,[62] he deliberately defies any claim by that Judaism to fulfil the universalist prophecies. The contrast throughout this conclusion between 'then: ποτε', when all these things had honour, and the repeated 'but now (νῦν δε) [they are] without honour' reinforces this conscious defiance.

c) *The Implied Defendant: 'O Israel'*

However, the preacher addresses his reproaches not to a people who are already replaced but to an Israel who deserves to die (§90, l. 663). This means that the violence of his polemic is not shaped by a salvation-history perspective, nor by an interpretation of scripture which adopts and objectifies the prophetic denunciations. There is, as we have seen, continuity with the past: Israel remains the nation created and rescued by the Lord, the theme of the first part of the homily. Yet this is no longer the primary focus of attention. Most naturally, of course, it should be the contemporaries of Jesus, still 'Israel', who provide that focus, but it is not limited to them alone. In this section the direct second-person address, **you** or **O Israel**, creates an implied hearer, or better an 'implied defendant', to be distinguished from the implied (Christian) audience of the *Peri Pascha* who are included in the contrastive **we**. Repeated hints bring this implied 'defendant' out from the past to be identified with an Israel today who shares the same failure and same responsibility as those of Jesus's time. Israel's imagined defiant reply that she killed the Lord because he had to die earns the rebuke 'you

have been deceived' (§74, l. 530) and leads later to the charge
'you have not cleared yourself before the master' (§77, l. 546) –
in both cases the perfect tense points to the persistence of their
failure.[63]

Similarly, retribution is not threatened in a future judgement
but is an already-experienced reality: the main section of the
second book ends with the solemn statement that, as Israel once
failed to lament for the Lord, so now she has lamented for her
first-born dead; as she dashed the Lord to the ground, so too
she has been dashed to the ground, showing no pity she has
found no pity (§99, ll. 730–44).[64] Given the character and genre
of the *Peri Pascha* it is not surprising that Melito fails to make any
explicit reference to the destruction of Jerusalem under Titus
seen as a judgement for the death of Jesus, or to point to his
prophecies of the event, as do other authors.[65] Yet we should
perhaps hear an allusion both to the words of Jesus and to scripture – **dashed to the ground** echoes Luke 19.44 and behind it
Psalm 137(LXX 136).9. Earlier, when 'the people' failed to rend
their clothes, the angel rent (his) (§98, l. 727), a clear allusion
to the rending of the Temple veil seen as presaging its end and
the Lord's abandonment of his people.[66] Now the charge is
repeated, '*you* did not tear your clothes when the Lord was hung',
but this time with its consequence, 'so you have **rent** your clothes
over your slain' (§99, l. 737–8): abandonment is no theological
judgement but the bloody reality of the costly defeats of the two
Jewish revolts. As we have seen, both the hints that Melito
alludes to Josephus's account of the first revolt, and his focus on
the annulment of the Temple and its system,[67] confirm that his
hearers will be persuaded not merely by the force of his rhetoric
but by its confirmation in their own knowledge and experience.
It is not merely a biblical Israel whom he addresses but a contemporary Israel defined by the disastrous consequences of both
the first revolt and perhaps the more recent one under Bar
Kochba. So his earlier judgement, 'for that it was necessary that
you die' (§90, l. 663), now finds its answer – 'You lie dead!' (§99,
l. 745).

d) '*Israel*' *and the Jews of Sardis*

The dead cannot hear, and behind the 'implied defendant' so

sentenced are the living. We have already caught echoes of their presence: their celebration of the Passover, with rejoicing and eating of bread and drinking of wine, with singing, music and even with dancing,[68] as well as with the typical reclining at table (§79–80, ll. 565–81), prompted Melito to contrast their festivities with Jesus's suffering and leads him to charge Israel with having **killed your Lord on the great feast** (l. 565) – here, following Johannine chronology, a reference to Passover.[69] In 'historical' terms the Passover meal, which, in contrast to other days, was eaten later in the evening, could not coincide with Jesus's time on the cross, and this has led some to identify 'the great feast' with the Feast of Unleavened Bread.[70] Yet such historical considerations are of less significance to Melito than the symbolism of Passover when 'the people rejoices, Israel is sealed' (§16, ll. 95–6), and the pointed contrast as the Christians of Sardis fasted and then gathered to hear the homily while their Jewish contemporaries were celebrating – particularly if those celebrations were the source of envious comparisons.[71]

The **Israel** Melito addresses never openly appears as the Jews of Sardis; yet those who listened in that setting could hardly have avoided making the connection.[72] As in all worship, but that of Passover and Pascha in particular, the past becomes part of the present, and they would have identified themselves as the 'implied confessors', sharing the first person 'he ransomed *us* from the world's service ... he delivered *us* from slavery to liberty' (§§67, 68, ll. 461, 473). The **you** addressed with such dramatic urgency equally could not be confined to the past, particularly if the Christian audience were aware how closely their own confession echoed the Passover affirmations of the Jewish celebration. But those Passover celebrations are declared a parody of the truth and no witness to the Jews' inheritance in the Exodus deliverance. In the opening words:

The scripture of the Hebrew Exodus has been read
And the words of the mystery have been plainly stated (§1, ll. 1–2)

Melito acknowledges that the book of Exodus is **Hebrew** – something of an antiquarianism – admitting that the book, at least in origin, did not belong to the Christians, although avoiding assigning it explicitly to the (contemporary) Jews. However, it is only for Christians that **the words of the mystery have been plainly stated.**[73]

As **people** too the Jews of Sardis have no value; the self-conscious claim to God's special election is worthless. As **Israel** they also share in the judgement which overtook their fellows in 'the land where it was proclaimed and done' (Eusebius, *H.E.* IV.26.13–14). If they claim, perhaps in their worship, in their names, or in the decoration of their synagogue, to be the recipients of God's past guidance, all the more grounds for casting against them the charge of ingratitude.

We may doubt whether any Jew of Sardis ever heard the charge; we may wonder too whether any Christian carried what he or she had learnt into an open debate. The play on the word 'Pascha' would be more likely to convince a Christian than a Jew, and Israel's defence that she killed the Lord because he had to die would be more likely to be heard on Christian lips, either in rhetorical imagination or in objection to a deterministic use of the scriptures, than from a Jewish mouth. Yet however much or little the argument of the homily found its way into direct debate, it belongs none the less to the confrontation between 'church and synagogue' in Sardis. It creates for its Christian hearers an interpretation of the Jewish community; it confronts the latter's celebrations and religious confidence with the denial of their existence as God's people, and affirms that their claim to the Exodus deliverance is but to a fading shadow.

Judaism and Christian Preaching in the Peri Pascha

Yet if Melito never openly addresses the Jews of Sardis, what traces have they left in his preaching? There are some hints that Melito's language owes more than might be expected to Jewish interpretation and celebration, and that this betrays rather more interaction between Jewish and Christian groups than the distancing of his polemic projects.

a) *The 'Hebrew Exodus'*

We have already seen that when Melito starts his address by look-

ing back to what has already taken place in the worship, the
reading of the 'scripture of the Hebrew Exodus', there is an
acknowledgement of the antiquity of that book. That **Exodus** is
the biblical book of that name and not a general reference to
'the Exodus events' or 'the Exodus deliverance' is clear: Melito
does not use the word 'Exodus' elsewhere for the event, neither
is the departure from Egypt the most significant part of it for
him. The epithet **Hebrew** is more ambiguous, and the interpretation followed here has not always been agreed. A natural alternative would be that it refers to the language in which the book
was written: we might have to picture the Christians first hearing the scriptures read in Hebrew, a language few, if any, would
understand, and then being provided with a translation or
('targumic') interpretation in Greek, the **plainly stated** of the
second line. Only then would Melito deliver his homiletic interpretation, the sole part of the proceedings preserved for us.[74]

It might seem unlikely that the Christians would follow such a
procedure unless their Jewish neighbours also used Hebrew, at
least for reading from Torah. The practical problem, moreover,
of providing readers could be met by (or would demand) something like the second column of Origen's hexapla, where the
Greek transliteration of the Hebrew would provide at least the
key to the vocalisation of the Hebrew text.[75] Despite this, the
evidence militates against such an intriguing scenario. There is
little to suggest the knowledge and regular use of Hebrew in
diaspora Judaism; the Jews of Sardis recorded themselves and
their donations in Greek, while the small handful of Hebrew
inscriptions or grafitti probably confirms their ignorance rather
than their knowledge of the language. We would have to assume
that for the central 'religious' act of the reading of the Law,
particularly at Passover time, these Greek-speaking Jews retained
the 'sacred tongue'.[76] Yet Jewish sources suggest that, at least at
this period, Hebrew was a rarity in the Diaspora, and make provision for ignorance of it even within the Land of Israel. This is
even more clearly the case with the Christians: the Septuagint is
the Bible of the expanding Christian church, even in their
polemic with Jews, and the few Christians who wanted to learn
Hebrew did so in Palestine with the help of Jewish rabbis.[77]
Despite his journey to Palestine to collect the list and order of
the Old Testament, Melito's Bible seems to be the Septuagint,

both in the text that he quotes and in his probable use of the Wisdom of Solomon.[78] Melito's 'neutral' antiquarian use of 'Hebrew' is repeated when he describes Jerusalem as the 'Hebrew' city as well as 'the city of the law' and 'the city of the prophets' (§94, ll. 695–7).[79] We cannot decide whether behind the neutrality lies any dependence by the Christians on their Jewish neighbours for the text they read.

b) *The Passover Haggadah*

However, in a very real sense Melito was meeting a similar need in relation to the scriptural text and the past as that felt by the Jewish community. With the loss of the Jerusalem cult in 70 CE, and perhaps already before that in the diaspora situation, alternative ways of offering the direct experience of their religious faith had to be developed, and the Passover, both because of its centrality and because it was a home and family celebration, would be a focus for such developments. Here the requirement not simply to read the scriptures but to expound them in the context of the Passover meal offered an ideal opportunity for 'the present and past [to] illuminate each other, enabling the participants to relate more fully to the exodus experience and to see it as paradigmatic of their own situation'[80] – words equally applicable to Melito's own enterprise of leading present participants to enter into the Paschal reality effected by Jesus and even into the Exodus experience which pointed to it:

> He ransomed us from the service of the world
> as from the land of Egypt,
> And freed us from the slavery of the devil
> as from the hand of Pharaoh. (§67, ll. 461–4)

However mediated, Melito's 're-reading' of the Exodus text, particularly in the 'second book' from §45, shows numerous links with the Jewish Passover Haggadah and with the brief account in the Mishnah (*mPes.* 10), both in specific details and in structure.[81] Some of the parallels are thematic: Stuart Hall has shown how the requirement to start with the disgrace and end with the glory (*mPes.* 10.4) is matched by the movement of the second book which opens with the 'disgrace' of the disobedience in the

Garden of Eden and the oppression under sin; it moves through
the redemption 'as from the land of Egypt' and ends with the
glory of the risen Christ who proclaims 'I lead you to the heights
of the heavens' as once the people were 'led to ... the land flow-
ing with milk and honey' (Deut. 26.9).[82]

According to *mPes.* 10.5, attributed to R. Gamaliel, three
essential aspects of the Passover meal must be interpreted, the
lamb, the bitter herbs, and the unleavened bread: Melito
acknowledges the command laid on them (**you**) to 'eat
unleavened bread with bitter flavours' (Exod. 12.8) and gives
these his own interpretation, no longer the bitterness experienced at the hands of the Egyptians but:

> Bitter for *you* the feast of unleavened bread...
> Bitter for you the false witnesses you set up,
> Bitter for you the ropes you prepared,
> Bitter for you the scourges you plaited...
> Bitter for you the hands you bloodied.[83] (§93, ll. 678–91)

However, the symbols are torn asunder as he claims for Christians (**us**) the redemption won through the Paschal lamb:

> This is he who rescued *us* from slavery to freedom,
> from darkness to light,
> from death to life,
> from tyranny to an eternal kingship. (§68, ll. 473–6)

This carefully balanced stanza[84] has regularly been noted for
its close parallel to the words of the Passover Haggadah and to
mPes. 10.5, prompting the suggestion that it betrays knowledge
of them and their development:

> Therefore we are obliged to thank, praise ... him who did for our
> fathers and for us[85] all these wonders...
> He brought us out from slavery to freedom,
> from sorrow to joy,
> from grieving to festivity,
> from darkness to a great light,
> from servitude to redemption.[86]

However, liturgical language is notoriously fluid, and a number of variations of the formulae are found, with the Mishnah of the Jerusalem Talmud giving only the first line.[87] Moreover, the general contrast scheme of redemption can be found in various forms elsewhere, and is not restricted to a Paschal context. In a prayer for Asenath's conversion, Joseph addresses God as the one who 'called [all] from the darkness to the light, and from the error to the truth, and from the death to the life' (*Jos. & Asen.* 8.10),[88] and a number of parallels are to be found in Christian literature.[89] Thus Melito's wording, although in a Paschal setting, cannot simply be given a place in a neat development of the text as if already reached before the end of the second century and in use in Asia Minor Jewish communities. Instead, we see something of the complex process by which liturgical formulation is achieved, and of the interaction between liturgical language and other genres. It was a process, as we shall continue to demonstrate, in which not only internal dialogue but also interaction between Jewish and Christian claims to 'own' and interpret the same foundational texts played a significant role. Thus the denial in the Passover Haggadah that redemption was through an angel, although not datable to the time of Melito,[90] may be a response to suggestions that it was the act of an intermediary whether by Christian (*Peri Pascha* §17, l. 105) or by Jewish (Wisd. 18.15) interpreters.[91]

A further debate about Melito's use (and counter-use) of Passover traditions is provoked by the long recital of the saving acts they had experienced and which, so ungratefully, they failed to value (§§83–90, ll. 608–60):

> It was he who chose you and guided you
> from Adam to Noah,
> from Noah to Abraham,
> from Abraham to Isaac…
> It was he who guided you to Egypt
> and guarded you there and nurtured you.
> It was he who lightened your way with a pillar…
> It was he who came to you
> healing your suffering ones…
> Ungrateful Israel, come and enter judgement with me
> for your ingratitude…

Later, post-Talmudic, forms of the Passover Haggadah include a recital of thanksgiving for each stage of God's redemptive acts: 'If he had... it would be enough for us' (*dayyenu*).[92] However, Melito has not simply taken and reversed this song of praise as might at first appear. Anticipations of his reproaches are already to be found in the Jewish tradition, embryonically in the prophets, Amos 2.6–10, etc., and more fully in 5 Ezra 1.13–24, *if* this text has a Jewish substratum, and in Tg. Ps. Jonathan to Deuteronomy 1.1. The relation between such reproaches and the *dayyenu* is disputed, and again a fluid and dynamic interaction between liturgical and other genres is more convincing than a simple linear development. Melito alone cannot supply the missing link, providing the Paschal context, an early date, and the point of transition of the reproach counter-form into the Christian tradition;[93] but he does belong within this fluidity and interaction which also encompasses both Christian and Jewish traditions.

We have already seen that Melito's appeal to Genesis 22 reflects a similar scenario.[94] In the *Peri Pascha* Isaac joins Abel, Jacob, Joseph, Moses, the prophets and the Paschal lamb as models in whom the reality was already present: in each case it is that Isaac was **bound** which provides the point of comparison: 'If you want to see the mystery of the Lord, look at ... Isaac who was similarly bound (συμποδιζόμενον) ...' (§59, ll. 415–24; cf. §69, ll. 480–8; Frag. 15, l. 21). The analogy is more fully explored in the surviving fragments which may conceivably come from Melito's *Extracts*.[95] Here, the ram (κριός) which actually was slaughtered provides a more potent symbol, allowing a certain elision with the sheep (πρόβατον) of Isaiah 53.7, led 'to the slaughter' (εἰς σφαγήν) (Frag. 9, ll. 2–5). Yet, as positive 'model', Isaac too was 'bound like a ram' (Frag. 9, ll. 15, 23),[96] although a new twist is added when the Lord '[was] bound, released ... and ransomed us', even as 'Isaac was released from his bonds' and ransomed by the ram (Frag. 10).

The emphasis on being **bound**, which we have also found in the *Martyrdom of Polycarp*, is particularly notable. Although it is an inevitable element in Jesus's arrest and trial (Mark 15.1; John 18.12: δέω), the theme clearly has been generated not by that but by the story of Isaac who was bound by the feet (Gen. 22. 9, συμποδίζω: so *Peri Pascha* §59, l. 417; Frag. 9, ll. 15,[23; Frag. 11, l. 6]).[97] This element of the Isaac narrative was also emphasised in developing Jewish interpretation, drawing on the use of the same verb to describe Isaac's bonds and the distinctive bonds of the Tamid, the daily offering in the Temple (*mTam.* 4.1), עקד (*'aqad*); from this arose the use of the term 'Aqedah for the whole event and for its interpretation as in some sense atoning. Melito's development of the theme can only presuppose existing Jewish exegesis, even though the stages in this are difficult to date with precision.[98]

For Melito, Isaac's silence and his unhesitating compliance as, carrying the wood, he was led by his father to be slain, establish him as a model of Christ's own offering. Yet the emphasis is on 'model'. Ultimately, 'Christ suffered, Isaac did not suffer' (Frag. 9, l. 9). Although this contrast does not come in the *Peri Pascha*, we may still recognise in this fragment Melito's pointed use of πάσχειν, 'to suffer', by which he refers to Jesus's death. In retrospect, in the light of Jewish interpretation of Isaac's 'self-offering' as sacrificial and as atoning, this sounds very much like a polemical denial of such exegesis, highlighting its weakest point, Isaac's failure to be sacrificed. Indeed, Melito goes further: Isaac was 'redeemed' by the ram, which itself prefigures Christ. Christians do not just possess the reality; even the 'model' subordinates the Isaac on whom the Jews rely to the one who was offered in his place.

The rabbinic and targumic traditions which most contribute to such a Jewish interpretation are notoriously difficult to date.[99] Adding to this the difficulty of drawing conclusions from Palestinian evidence for diaspora thought – although Wilken usefully points to the presence of the scene in the art of Dura Europos as well as at Beth Alpha[100] – we cannot be sure in what form Melito's contemporaries may have known the 'doctrine'. The most convincing interpretation would see Jewish and Christian ideas developing in interaction, something they were to continue to do, with Christian counter-exegesis itself prompting new interpretative strategies.[101]

In Jewish tradition the 'Aqedah is associated both with Passover and with New Year, with some dispute as to which is most original, although arguments for an early association with Passover seem most convincing.[102] If Melito had developed the contrastive use of Isaac more fully in the *Peri Pascha*, we might find here a further element in the polemic, a denial that Isaac's self-offering had anything to do with the true Pascha/ *paschein*. The original setting of the Fragments is unknown, and, while the use of πάσχειν (Frag. 9, ll. 9–10) is not enough to prove a Passover context, they indicate the wider importance of the theme for Melito and, perhaps, for his contemporaries.[103]

Less convincing is the suggestion that further evidence of Melito's place in Jewish-Christian interaction is to be found in his description of Jesus as the '*one who comes* from heaven to the earth on account of the one who suffers' (§66, l. 451) and again as 'the *one who comes* to you, who heals your sufferers' (§86, ll. 625–6), in each case '*aphikomenos*: ἀφικόμενος'. The Passover prescriptions in *mPes.* 10.8 include the obscure words 'After the Pascha they must not [?dismiss/ adjourn [with]] the *aphiqoman* (אפיקומן)', apparently a transliteration of a Greek term. The meaning of this prescription has been long debated, in rabbinic as well as modern times; most probably it refers to some banqueting custom or perhaps to revelry (cf. Greek, ἐπὶκωμον), while the traditional interpretation refers it to the dessert (*tPes.* 10.11: nuts, dates or parched grain).[104] Some, however, have claimed an underlying reference to expectation of the Messiah as 'the one to come' (ἀφικόμενος) at Passover, symbolised by the separation of a piece of unleavened bread.[105] Melito's distinctive application of the epithet to Jesus has been hailed as evidence of this messianic interpretation as already current in Asia Minor in the second century and therefore arguably as the original derivation of the term. Yet here supporting evidence from the Jewish side is lacking, and Talmudic discussion gives no clear hint of a messianic significance. Apart from Melito's characteristic solemnity, there is nothing to isolate this particular formula as peculiarly significant.[106]

This range of echoes and polemics does not mean that Melito is merely imitating the themes of the Jewish Passover Haggadah. For him the central theme is that of the sacrifice of the lamb and the suffering of Jesus; in the Jewish tradition it is the deliverance at the Red Sea.[107] Yet neither does this mean that Melito has simply parted company with the Jewish tradition: a new interpretation of a normative and foundational event is itself an inherently competitive or polemical act, the more so when done deliberately. That it is self-conscious and deliberate seems inevitable, and it is hard not to imagine that Melito's exposition of the true

mystery of the Pascha both owed something to and coloured Christian–Jewish encounters in Sardis. It is of course true that the Passover Haggadah as we know it belonged to the family celebration
and not to the communal gathering at which it is easier to envisage interested observers. Moreover, it is inherently likely that the
Christian celebration of the Pascha would have demanded a
developing interpretation long before the time of Melito; he would
not have needed to go with a blank slate to the synagogue to look
for ideas – and he may not have wanted to, since it was to Palestine that he went to ascertain the books of the old covenant. Certainly we cannot recreate the Passover liturgy or language of the
Jews of Sardis in any detail from that of Melito. Yet they surely did
share many of the elements we have sketched, rendering Melito's
interpretation particularly forceful and challenging to Jewish self-
identity – at least in Christian eyes.

Polemic and Context: Motivation in Melito's Argument with Israel

It would be wrong to project from the strength of Melito's
polemic the strength of the Jewish community at the time, as
has frequently happened.[108] It is only scholarly imagination which
makes Melito's major motivation the Jewish community of Sardis,
vibrant, self-confident and influential, while the Christians strug-
gled with poverty of numbers, poor self-image and insecurity.
Yet recognition of the interweaving elements which contributed
to the passion of the *Peri Pascha* should not make us simply
remove the 'synagogue' from the map altogether.

a) *'On the holy Pascha': the Theoretical Engagement*

That Melito's exposition does gain some of its immediacy or
specificity from his own setting alongside the Jewish community
in Sardis may be confirmed from another homily, *On the holy
Pascha*, sometimes assigned a near-contemporary date and geographical origin. In the manuscript tradition this Paschal homily is variously attributed to Chrysostom or to Hippolytus, while
a recent edition dates it to the fourth or fifth century, although
dependent on a work of Hippolytus;[109] however, the parallels in

style and method with Melito's homily have prompted a vigorous argument for locating it in second-century Asia Minor.[110] Yet if this dating could be sustained, and the doctrinal sophistication and the familiarity with a range of New Testament texts must raise doubts, the concurrent reflective abstraction and lack of urgency would be equally remarkable.

This homily also describes the Pascha as a mystery and as a type which was fulfilled through Christ. It makes a similar use of opposites ('out of passion impassibility', 1.2), but, in contrast to Melito, develops the use of typology so as to stress that what belonged to the Law was only a shadow (2.1). This leads to an explicit discussion as to 'what is the Law and what is the need of the Law?' and why it was introduced after the Passover (5). The answer uses a mixture of images – the Law was a reflection of the life of heaven and a restriction on sin, a guide for piety, a bridle for the stiff-necked and a messenger of Christ. Most characteristic is the detailed typological development of the prescriptions relating to the celebration of the Passover in Exodus 12.1–15, 43–49, with, we should note, its Quartodeciman association of the crucifixion of Jesus with the slaughter of the Paschal lamb (23). Starting from the first month points to the beginning of creation, following 'a secretly recounted saying of the Hebrews' (17.2); taking the lamb on the tenth day points to the Decalogue as the highest dogma of the Law, and keeping it until the fourteenth signifies the gap between the Law and the Gospel (20, Exod. 12.3, 6); the command not to break any bone of the Passover victim points to the resurrection with the body. Direct address to the Jewish people remains in the background, despite the occasional 'O Israel' (22; 25; 50), with its echoes of Melito. Although the homily sees in the killing of the victims 'by the whole congregation of Israel' (Exod. 12.6) a reference to 'unbelieving Israel who became guilty of his precious blood, that of old by murdering, that up to now not believing' (24), the point is not developed and leads to only limited reproach. The blood on the lintel of the two doorposts points to the 'two peoples' and recalls that Jesus was sent to Israel first (Exod. 12.7; 25), but later the two thieves crucified alongside Jesus are signs not only of the 'two peoples' but also of the two reasonings of the soul, one penitent and one not (54.1).

Judaism here has no immediacy: the prescription of Exodus 12.44, that the slave, once circumcised, may eat of the Passover, symbolises that the one who was enslaved in sins shall be circumcised in heart, leave slavery and eat with freedom (40) – there is no apologetic here about circumcision. That the Passover is to be shared by the freed and the proselyte is fulfilled in that all are free in Christ – 'you are no longer slave, no longer Jew, but free; for we have all been made free in Christ' (42, cf. Gal. 3.28, 'neither Jew nor Greek, slave nor free'); the wording indicates an audience who still were 'Greek' and for whom 'Jew' was little more than a metaphor. Another contrast with Melito is that for this author Egypt is identified with idolatry, from which the Passover brings deliverance (10, 12); the absence of this identification in Melito is notable, for it is a common one in interpretations of the Exodus deliverance,[111] and would have been highly appropriate to the Sardis situation as to any Graeco-Roman city. We may see here a confirmation by silence that Melito looks more to the Jewish community than to other aspects of city life. The more developed Christology, detailed typology and weaker correlation with the Jewish Passover Haggadah in structure and detail may point to the later date of this homily, but they also serve to highlight the immediacy of Melito's own work.[112]

b) *Melito's Theological Heritage*

Contrast with this Paschal homily shows that it is not merely the Paschal setting nor even the specifically Quartodeciman provenance which determines Melito's sustained and dominating anti-Jewish stance. Yet there is enough in common to remind us that Melito neither worked in a social and theological vacuum, nor was a single-issue thinker. With him, as with the whole development of anti-Jewish polemic, a number of forces come together, and the interplay of these personal, social and theological factors has helped produce the vehemence of his attack.[113] For example, the sheer impact of that vehemence owes much to his rhetorical style with its use of dramatic repetition, of antithesis, parallelism or crescendo; rhetorical questions, exclamation, and long sequences of statements or phrases with the same beginning heighten the force and engage the reader. Although some of these forms suggest Semitic stylistic influence, Melito probably belongs to the contemporary rhetorical traditions of the Second Sophistic characteristic of Asiatic writers of his time, perhaps even having been formally trained within it. His readers (or first hearers) no doubt would have been more familiar with the style and have found it less overblown than many modern readers.

Among theological factors, we need to include the threat posed by the teaching of Marcion. His attempt to isolate the past activity of God in the history of the people of Israel and through their scriptures by positing a second, lower God provides a recurring undercurrent through our second-century writers. As we have seen, Melito meets the challenge by presenting the provisions of the Old Testament as a type or model for the reality to come, but also by involving Christ in creation and in the past suffering of the people.[114] Yet, if an awareness of the Marcionite challenge to the Christian use of the Old Testament has added warmth to his defence of it as model, it can hardly account for the vehemence of his accusation against Israel of ingratitude; the most effective weapon against Marcionism was to accuse the Jews not of ingratitude but of blindness and, perhaps wilful, misunderstanding of the true import of the scriptures.

Melito's christological heritage can also hardly be ignored. If he has earned the epithet of the 'poet of deicide' it is because his attribution of the acts of God to Christ enables him to say of the crucifixion of Jesus, 'God is murdered!', and to accuse 'Israel' of killing the very one who created the heavens and formed them as his people. It is in the tirade addressed to Israel that this identification of the activity of Christ with that of God is most fully developed;[115] his horror at Israel's ingratitude is the greater because the one whom she put to death and the one who gave her life are the same. Here rhetorical extravagance, conviction of the unity of God's work – effective if not designed in opposition to Marcion – and a theological tradition combine with the passion of his polemic. It is difficult to assign priority to any of these factors, for example to suggest that opposition to Marcion has moulded his Christology, or that Christology has created the anti-Jewish polemic. Instead they have nurtured each other. Melito's Christology is drawn from the tradition in which he stands: he shares what has variously been called a modalism,

christocentric monotheism,[116] or monarchianism[117] with other
Christian writers from the area, and it is confirmed by fragments
of his other writings which bear no trace of anti-Marcionite or
anti-Jewish concern; yet it is at its most stark when faced with the
rejection and death of Jesus at Jewish hands. Anti-Jewish polemic
has sharpened theological statement, but the reverse is equally
true.[118]

Melito was a Quartodeciman, and although there is no ex–
plicit apologetic within the *Peri Pascha* in favour of this practice
or some particular form of it, we are bound to ask how it has
coloured his attitude to the Jews. In timing their own celebration according to the Jewish Passover, Christians may well have
been practically dependent on their Jewish neighbours for determining the date, perhaps even following the Jewish dating when
that was wrong (so Epiphanius, *Pan.* 70.10.2, 6). It has been argued that this in turn could have invited the charge of open
theological dependence or of judaising: apparent proximity
could necessitate vigorous demonstration of actual distance, and
this would still be true even if the idea that the fast was 'for the
Jews' (*Syr. didasc.* 21; Epiphanius, *Pan.* 70.11,3) was an early and
general part of Quartodeciman practice – although there is no
hint of this in Melito. The violence of Melito's polemic might be
just such a distancing, implicitly making void any accusation of
judaising.[119]

In fact again the situation is likely to have been rather more
complex than this. Although the limited scope of evidence for
early Quartodeciman practice prohibits confident conclusions,
there is no suggestion that in the second-century controversies
the charge of judaising was ever raised, neither does anti-Jewish
polemic reach quite the same peak in other Quartodeciman
writers as in Melito.[120] Melito was writing first of all for a home
audience, and while there may have been debates within the
Quartodeciman tradition, such as that at Laodicaea which according to Eusebius provided the occasion for Melito's homily,
the defence of the tradition was directed in the main towards
Rome. No doubt the eventual introduction of the Sunday Easter
observance had the advantage of severing the links with Judaism,
but this is the wisdom of hindsight, while the debate at the time
centred more on precedence and tradition and on the unity of
the church.

Yet the Passover/Paschal celebrations do seem to have provoked both a historical and a literary hostility between Jews and Christians. The events behind and the final literary form of the *Martyrdom of Polycarp* bear eloquent testimony to this, as too perhaps does the coincidence of the anniversary of the martyrdom of Sagaris at the Paschal season which was the occasion for the dispute at Laodicaea. Lohse's argument that the Quartodeciman Easter involved not only an earnest expectation of the Lord's return but also a fast for the Jews is perhaps thrown into question by the absence of these themes in the *Peri Pascha*,[121] but, both by its choice of date and by the probable prominence of the theme of the fulfilment of the Exodus and Passover story, it could hardly have avoided at least an implicit confrontation with the Jewish Passover. In the face of a strong Jewish presence, Quartodeciman practice would have a lively apologetic rationale.

In Jewish history the Passover had often been the occasion of warm nationalistic and religious feeling when passions ran high.[122] For diaspora Jews it was a time which 'simplifies social relationships, emphasises mythic history and sets up an atmosphere in which the culture's central values may be examined'.[123] Christians claimed the same mythic history but denied those central values, asserting for themselves new values and a new understanding of the past. To that extent Quartodeciman practice belonged to the confrontation between church and synagogue, and had its home in a context where that confrontation was a living concern.[124] Whether such theological opposition was also expressed in public hostility remains unknown, and cannot justify a return to the position that the Jews of Sardis responded by denouncing Christians or joining in popular attacks against them;[125] the only violence we have evidence for remains the literary violence of Melito's polemic.

Important too is Melito's scriptural tradition; he does not quote the New Testament as scripture but he knows the Matthaean tradition of the demand for the Temple tax (Matt. 17.24: §86, ll. 632–3), and the Johannine story of the raising of Lazarus (John 11: §78, ll. 551–2), as well as more general Gospel echoes.[126] However, he also has close links with traditions found in the *Gospel of Peter*, in particular in the development of anti-Jewish tendencies within the Passion account.[127] As in the *Gospel of Peter* (1), unlike Pilate who washed his hands, they failed to clear themselves before their King (§§77; 92, ll. 546, 676); Herod is not simply involved (as in Luke) but takes a leading role and they have followed him (§93, l. 686; cf. *G. Peter* 1–2); it is the Jews who mock, judge and crucify Jesus, so that the Romans are almost written out of the story (§§75–6, ll. 532–45), and it is as 'King of Israel' that Jesus is crucified (§96, l. 716; cf. *G. Peter* 11 and contrast 'King of the Jews' in the New Testament Gospels). Like the *Gospel of Peter* but also like John, Melito knows the tradition that Jesus was nailed to the cross (§93, l. 680; *G. Peter* 21; John 20.25, 27), and dates the crucifixion to the Passover (implied in *G. Peter* 7). We might also compare the disciples who fasted, mourned and wept until the sabbath, and so presumably did not eat a Passover meal (*G. Peter* 27), with the proposed setting of Melito's homily following the Quartodeciman fast while the Jews ate, and also with the picture of Jesus who hungered, was afflicted and downcast (§80, ll. 566–81). The background and place of origin of the *Gospel of Peter* and its traditions are disputed,[128] and there are also significant differences – Melito never uses the word 'Jews', and also makes no mention of Joseph of Arimathaea or of Jewish consternation at the death of Jesus and the accompanying miracles. The tendency to focus all blame for the death of Jesus on the Jews is already part (but not the whole) of his 'scriptural' heritage, but he has chosen from that heritage those aspects which serve to sharpen the blame still further, and has developed those themes (for example, 'the King of Israel') which contribute to his own theological scheme.

Image and Reality in Melito

For Melito it is Israel – the image – which is ever present, making it possible for some modern readers to assert that contemporary reality is nowhere in view.[129] In contrast, the discovery of a 'contemporary' reality as all too visible has persuaded others of its ever-pervasive presence behind Melito's image, creating a new 'image' of Melito's reality: powerful synagogue, struggling church, a battle for possession of the past and for identity. Both views are too simple, and we have traced the different threads and the different layers which belong to the vivid tapestry of his *Peri Pascha*. Yet, if Melito is the heir he is also the source of many different threads; the very nature of his writing is, as liturgy, an exercise in image-building; with what immediate success we cannot say. Judaism hardly 'lay dead', but Melito would be remembered by subsequent generations and his homily translated far beyond the situation and the tradition which originally inspired it.

Notes

[1] Kraabel 1968 etc. led the way here; see Seager and Kraabel 1983: 178–86.

[2] See Hemer 1986: 134–6, but Schürer 1973–87: III. 20–1 cautions against reliance on the parallel without further evidence of Jewish presence at this early date.

[3] Schürer 1973–87: III. 129–30. In the decree of the people of Sardis in Josephus, *Ant.* XIV.10.24 (259), the description of 'the Jews living in our city' as 'citizens' is frequently assumed to be an interpolation.

[4] On the tension between Josephus's use of the decrees and the situation they reveal see Rajak 1985b.

[5] See Sanders 1992: 134; Bickermann 1980: 335; Cohen 1987: 166; on 'the place' see also Kraabel 1978: 17.

[6] This theme runs through from *Ant.* XIV.10.11 [223] to XIV.10.19 [240].

[7] So Trebilco 1991: 34–5, who sees the incident at Ephesus as evidence of rare sporadic trouble.

[8] See Rogers 1991: 10, 12 on Ephesus. Similarly Bonz 1990 argues that the emphasis on the imperial cult in the second century and inter-city rivalry over the status of *neokoros* would hardly favour Jewish prominence in the city. See also pp. 158–61 above.

[9] For what follows see Seager 1972; Kraabel 1978; Seager and Kraabel 1983; Botermann 1990; Goodman 1994b draws attention to how much of this reconstruction of events and purpose relies on scholarly imagination, and proposes a rather different reading of the evidence, which if not convincing does underline the dangers of over-confidence; cf. n. 24 below.

[10] Architectural needs seem to have dictated the building of two shrines, but whether only one, or both, were used for Torah scrolls is disputed; see Seager and Kraabel 1983: 170; Botermann 1990: 110.

[11] Seager and Kraabel 1983: 171.

[12] For this 'unprecedented' persecution see pp. 182–4 on Melito's *Apology*. On this reconstruction see Kraabel 1971 and the more nuanced 1992.

[13] So especially Bonz 1990, 1993; also Botermann 1990. Kraabel 1994: 75, n. 9 rejects Botermann 1990 on the weak grounds that the Jewish community's earlier history suggests it was already well established at the beginning of the Empire.

[14] As assumed by Kraabel 1971; Angerstorfer 1985: 205–20.

[15] See Kraabel 1968: 19; Seager and Kraabel 1983: 171.

[16] Ctr. Hemer 1986: 137.

[17] See the listing by Seager and Kraabel 1983: 175–6. A full excavation report edited by A. R. Seager et al., *The Synagogue and its Setting*, to be published by Harvard University Press, has long been promised.

[18] Seager in Seager and Kraabel 1983: 170 suggests that if the southern shrine was the only or primary Torah shrine, as indicated by the presence of fragmentary Hebrew inscriptions there alone, it would be at the corner closest to Jerusalem.

[19] On the water supply which belongs to a later period than our concern see Kraabel 1978: 21.

[20] So Robert 1964: 41–5; Lieu 1995b: 493, and above, pp. 187–8. However, it is impossible to prove whether they are Jews or 'sympathisers'.

[21] Seager and Kraabel 1983: 185–6.

[22] Eg. Robert 1964: no. 6, 'Aur. Olympios, of the tribe of Leontioi, with my wife and children, fulfilled a vow'. Robert (p. 46, n. 3) compares a later inscription from Side in Pamphylia: see Schürer 1973–87: III. 33.

[23] Hemer 1986: 258–9, n. 38; Robert 1964: 46–7; Kraabel 1978: 22–3. However, if these belong to the late fourth century they would post-date Constantine and could come from pagan sanctuaries closed in this period.

[24] Goodman 1994b: 217 draws attention to this failure to use distinctively Jewish terminology in his suggestion that the building could equally well have been built to house 'a cult of gentile, polytheist God-worshippers'.

[25] See Cohen 1981–2; Millar 1992: 101, 110–11.

[26] See Hanfmann and Bloom 1987, who note that his assertion of influence has been associated with the 'iconoclastic' defacement of animal figures in the mosaics and statuary.

[27] Whether the stability of the Severan era as those who favour a early date argue, or the instability of the late third century following the advocates of a later date.

[28] So Hansen 1969: 82–6.

[29] Hemer 1986: 149 suggests in the light of the dominance and probable influence of the Jewish community that 'the bulk of the church had found a *modus vivendi*, perhaps within the synagogue on Jewish terms'; but on the contrary it is noteworthy that there is no reference here to the 'synagogue of Satan' (ctr. 2.9; 3.9 of Smyrna and Philadelphia).

[30] See Hall 1979: xiii–xvii.

[31] See pp. 182–4.

[32] Hansen 1969: 94; van der Waal 1979: 145; Manis 1987: 398; above, p. 184.

[33] See Norris 1986 and especially M. Taylor 1995: 59–65.

[34] So Hall 1979: 66–7, n. 10.

[35] So Junod 1984: 111–12.

[36] So Beckwith 1985: 183–5.

[37] Lamentations may be included with Jeremiah; on the need for caution in speaking of a 'Jewish canon' see Barton 1986: 35–95.

[38] Fragment 15* in Hall 1979: 82–4; Hall (xxxvii–xxxviii) accepts its possible authenticity and notes (xvi) that other fragments with a similar exegesis have been attributed to the same source. See further below, pp. 225–6.

[39] By Polycrates of Ephesus in *H.E.* V.24.2–6. On Quartodeciman practice see pp. 232–3.

[40] Bonner 1940: 20.

[41] For the discovery of the manuscripts and the reconstruction of the text see Hall 1979: xvii–xxii; in what follows references are to Hall's edition by paragraph and line number.

[42] The exact genre of the *Peri Pascha* is disputed, and some scholars have described it as a Christian 'Haggadah' because of the parallels with the Jewish Passover Haggadah (see below, pp. 222–5). 'Homily' seems preferable although the relation between written text and oral delivery remains uncertain.

[43] The literature on the subject is vast; see the discussion by Hall 1984 and the extensive treatments by Lohse 1953.

[44] See van Unnik 1983b on whether Melito knew of dancing in the Jewish Passover and the possible link with Jesus's dance in the *Acts of John* 96–7.

[45] The phrase comes repeatedly in the first section but the word is not used after §65 which closes the first half of the homily (see below); it has been suggested that Melito's use of the term 'mystery' reflects the importance of pagan mystery cults, particularly of the Phrygian mother goddess, and even that, together with the description of him as 'eunuch' (*H.E.*V.24.5), it points to his past participation in this cult. However, the evidence can hardly establish this and the term 'mystery' was already used in Christian circles for the eucharist.

[46] Blank 1963: 43.

[47] See Hall 1979: xix–xxi, Hansen 1969: 68–9; however, Manis 1987: 391 rightly points out that §§1–45 only serves as an introductory paraphrase and discussion of hermeneutical principles which requires §§46–105 as its completion.

[48] And perhaps Jews, since Philo, *Quis rer. div.* 192–4, makes the same play as noted by Lohse 1953: 53.

[49] Schreckenberg 1990: 204 and Campenhausen 1970: 199 argue Melito was aware of Josephus's account.

[50] According to Hall 1979: xxiii the doxology at §65 closes this half of the second 'book', although a clearer break comes at §72 where the author turns to charge Israel directly for her ingratitude.

[51] See A. Harvey 1966, who argues that this reflects the time of Melito's visit when the traditional site of the crucifixion would be within the walls, in contrast to the general early tradition that Jesus was crucified outside the walls; however, a similar phrase is used in Josephus, *B.J.* I.4.6 [97] of Alexander Jannaeus's crucifixion of his opponents. As its use in §§93–4 shows, the reference is not of geographical significance so much as stressing the horror of this *in the midst* of Jerusalem.

[52] This line is supplied from the Coptic, Syriac and Latin epitome and has the advantage of providing three questions.

[53] So the Bodmer Papyrus. The Chester Beatty manuscript turns this into an accusation in the second person instead of a first-person claim.

[54] On this see below, p. 219.

[55] 243 out of 803 lines according to Hall 1979.

[56] See Werner 1966; Wilson 1986; Winslow 1982: 774 concludes that Melito was 'a misanthrope of the most bitter and spiteful kind'.

[57] See Robert 1960: 260–2.

[58] Except at the end of §68, ll. 477–8, where the language is determined by the quotation from Exod. 19.5–6 (1 Pet. 2.9) or by the Paschal tradition (see below, pp. 223–4); however, these lines do not come in the Bodmer Papyrus and may be a secondary addition.

[59] It is used at §57, l. 398 with the patriarchs and prophets, and at §61, l. 426 of those whom Moses addressed.

[60] 'Dashed to the ground': §26, l. 175; §99, ll. 743–4; first-born: §§26, 28, ll. 173, 185 etc.; §99, l. 736; lamenting; §29, l. 190; §99, ll. 735–6.

[61] See Kampling 1984: 182–3, who contrasts Augustine's (*Ps.* 63.9) metaphorical understanding of the Jews as dead.

[62] See p. 137.

[63] So Perler 1966: 179 ad §77 in accepting the reading proposed by Testuz 1960 at this point.

[64] The text in this section requires some conjectural reconstruction; the Chester Beatty papyrus is incomplete and the versions and the requirements of rhetorical structure suggest that the Bodmer papyrus also does not preserve the original text complete. See Hall 1979 ad loc. with apparatus.

[65] See for example Origen, *C. Cels.* IV.22 and Feischer 1964.

[66] See Bonner 1940: 41–5 for this interpretation in early Christianity.

[67] See above pp. 212, 216–17 and nn. 49, 61.

[68] See van Unnik 1983b.

[69] So Hall 1979: 43 and the majority of interpreters; see p. 72 on 'the great feast'.

[70] So Perler 1966: 181–3; this would agree with Synoptic chronology according to which Jesus's last meal with his disciples was a Passover.

[71] Hansen 1969: 154, 160 suggests this timing. On the attraction of Jewish celebrations for Christians see later, Chrysostom, *Adv. Iud.* I.1.5; 7.2.

[72] This is disputed by M. Taylor 1995: 73, but, while she rightly exposes the theological impulse in Melito's work, she underplays its emotive impact.

[73] On this interpretation see below, pp. 221–2.

[74] Lohse 1953: 75.

[75] On the purpose of this column and whether it provided only the key to vocalisation for those who knew Hebrew or enabled those without Hebrew to read the text see Emerton 1971.

[76] This is maintained as a strong possibility by Angerstorfer 1985: 37–46.

[77] So Origen and later Jerome.

[78] Most notably in the elaboration of Egypt's suffering (§§18–33, ll. 113–212, cf. Hall 1979: xl), although dependence on a common tradition of expansion of the Exodus narrative cannot be ruled out.

[79] This is missing from the Chester Beatty papyrus and so was not available to the early proponents of the 'Hebrew language' theory.

[80] Bokser 1984: 75; on the whole question see his discussion on pp. 67–75.

[81] On what follows see Hall 1971; Angerstorfer 1985.

[82] Hall 1971 finds a number of the themes of Deut. 26.5–9 within this section, transformed onto a universal plain; so, for example, humankind cast into the prison of the world and becoming prolific and of great age (§§48–9) recalls the people of Israel in bondage in Israel where they became a great nation.

[83] Kampling 1984: 88 notes the failure to quote Matt. 27.25 here.

[84] The extension into four sub-clauses is not paralleled in the surrounding verses, although there is a partial precedent at §49, ll. 335–41; see van Unnik 1983c.

[85] The Jerusalem Talmud reads only 'for us'.

[86] For this text of the Mishnah see Blackman 1952; Danby 1933.

[87] See the apparatus to Baneth 1968 ad loc.; Bokser 1984: 31, 120, n. 13.

[88] See Pines 1974.

[89] Hall 1971: 33 cites 1 Pet. 2.9; Col. 1.12–15; Acts 26.17–18; *1 Clem.* 59.2–3.

[90] See the strictures by Stemberger 1987 against reading the New Testament Last Supper accounts in the light of much later and unstable Passover Haggadah traditions.

[91] So Pines 1974.

[92] They appear in the *Siddur* of Saddiah Gaon but are not referred to in the Talmud or Midrashim: see *E.J.* ad loc.; Stemberger 1987.

[93] Werner 1966 and others after him have blamed Melito for the transformation of the *dayyenu* into the Improperia of the Catholic and Orthodox liturgies. Brocke 1977 rejects the *dayyenu* link but accepts the Jewish origin of the Improperia in Jewish self-reproach where, however, it is climaxed by a celebration of God's forgiving love. See further Flusser 1974, 1977.

[94] See pp. 77–9.

[95] See above, p. 208.

[96] Spiegel 1967: 85 refers to Tg. Jonathan to Lev. 22.27; 9.3 for Isaac, whom his father bound like a lamb.

[97] In the last two $\pi o\delta i\zeta\omega$ and $\dot{\epsilon}\mu\pi o\delta i\zeta\omega$ are used.

[98] So even the cautious P. Davies 1982: 656; on the whole issue see also Wilken 1976.

[99] See P. Davies 1979; 1982; Davies and Chilton 1978. For a positive account see Vermes 1973.

[100] 1976: 62.

[101] See P. Davies 1979 etc.; Spiegel 1967: 116–17 also brings in pagan influence in the idea of the atoning power of the human sacrifice of the first-born.

[102] Ctr. P. Davies 1979 etc. See Vermes 1976; Harl 1986: 471–2.

[103] Wilken 1976: 58, who suggests the extracts may come from another work 'On the Pascha'.

[104] See Bokser 1984: 65, 126 n. 62; Carmichael 1991: 50–3.

[105] Daube 1966, 1968; Carmichael 1991 has a full discussion of the debate with particular reference to Daube.

[106] Angerstorfer 1986: 64–73 decides that a reference cannot be excluded but recognises the considerable problems of demonstration, interpretation and dating. Melito uses the indicative of same verb elsewhere, not of Jesus (§§16; 18, ll. 97, 115).

[107] Bokser 1984: 26; the same is true of the homily discussed below, see Cantalamessa 1967: 440–1.

[108] As traced by M. Taylor 1995: 52–8; see above pp. 206–7 and nn. 32–33.

[109] Nautin 1951 (SC 27). In recent scholarship this is often abbreviated as *IP*, against *PP* for Melito's homily.

[110] Cantalamessa 1967, accepted by Daniélou 1969 and by several other scholars; it should be noted that Nautin does not accept the authenticity of Melito's *Peri Pascha.*

[111] See van Unnik 1983c and contrast Hansen 1969: 116–19, who argues that Egypt represents paganism and that Melito's use of 'mystery' language reflects an implicit polemic against the mysteries of the Phrygian mother goddess.

[112] Contrast Cantalamessa 1967: 49, who finds a similar balance between an anti-Marcionite stance and a reaction to a strong Jewish presence in the two

documents and uses it as evidence for the dating and provenance of *IP*. In fact the differences noted, together with the more explicitly developed high Christology of 46–7, may suggest a later date than that proposed by Cantalamessa.

113 On what follows see Wilson 1986b.

114 See above, pp. 212, 216.

115 Hübner 1989: 228–9 overstates the case in saying that Melito only uses theopaschite or modalist language in the attack against the Jews (see for example §104).

116 Hall 1979: 43.

117 Hübner 1989: 231.

118 Winslow 1982 argues that Melito's Christology is incidental rather than intentional and is driven by his polemic. Van der Waal 1979: 129–34 also notes parallels between Melito and the Roman creed and draws attention to the role of the confrontation with the synagogue in the development of doctrine and creed.

119 So Wilson 1986b: 96–7.

120 See Lohse 1953: 94–8; Grumel 1960 for anxiety about 'judaising' as a feature of the *later* Quartodeciman disputes.

121 Lohse 1953: 62–89; see the criticism by Hall 1979: xxiv–xxv.

122 *B.J.* II.1.3 [10]; IV.7.1. [402]; the crucifixion of Jesus.

123 Bokser 1984: 81.

124 See especially van der Waal 1979: 36–40, who argues that the development of the Easter Sunday practice took place in areas (first Jerusalem after 132 CE and then Rome) where the confrontation with the synagogue was less significant.

125 See above, pp. 184, 207 and n. 32; Kraabel 1992: 234 emphasises that, if Judaism was a theological problem for early Christianity, that does not mean the reverse was true; he notes that the survival of the synagogue and the later evidence of Jewish and Christian shops next door to one another points to better relations than Melito implies.

126 Bonner 1940: 39–41.

127 See Perler 1964.

128 An origin in Syria is usually argued, although on the basis of these parallels Perler suggests Asia Minor; see pp. 259–61.

129 E.g. M. Taylor 1995.

7

APOSTOLIC TRADITIONS

Polycarp and Papias

The variety of Christian life in Asia Minor in the second century, and of its literary production, has left but tantalising glimpses which warn us against sweeping generalisations. The early decades of the century are peopled by names, or epithets, whose importance probably outweighs by far our knowledge of them. Chief among these must be the 'Elders (Presbyters) of Asia Minor'; we meet them particularly through the testimony of Irenaeus, but when he appealed to them as guarantors of his own place in an unbroken line going back to the first Apostles and so to 'our Lord himself' (*Adv. haer.* II.22.5),[1] he was already creating through them an image of continuity and authoritative tradition which has defied any attempt to get back to an alternative account. Indeed, such is the priority of their function over their identity for him that only two names survive with any certainty, either included among them, or integrally linked with them: Papias of Hierapolis and Polycarp.

We have already explored the way that, in the world of the narrative, when Polycarp, 'that blessed and apostolic elder' (Irenaeus in Eusebius, *H.E.* V.20.7), went to martyrdom, the Jews assume a prominent place among the crowd who clam-oured for his death (*M. Poly.*12.2; 13.1; 17.2–18.1).[2] The ques-tion was bound to be asked, what during his life had earned this hostility? Later tradition answered by tracing competition in miraculous powers between Polycarp and the Jews back into the former's lifetime: in the fifth-century *Life* 28–9, Polycarp proves his superiority over the Jews, whose expertise in these matters is assumed, both by exorcising the servant of the magistrate and by quenching a devastating fire. The persuasive value of thaumaturgic one-upmanship would not be out of place in the religious propaganda of the second century;[3] however, casting the Jews in the role of the losers seems, surprisingly, to be a later literary theme, and the silence of earlier sources does little to encourage finding here an authentic note in Polycarp's circumstances.[4]

It is a different Polycarp whom we meet through the eyes and pen of Ignatius – this time, a young bishop who can be urged to be more committed than he is, and whose church must be encouraged to accord him full honour (Ignatius, *Poly.* 3.2; *Smyrn.* 8–9). Ignatius's letter to that church is the only one to refer to 'the Jews' and to hint at a Jewish presence among its members (*Smyrn.* 1.2; cf. 5.1),[5] but neither Jews nor Judaism belong to Polycarp's world, real or constructed, as witnessed by his own letter to the church at Philippi. While he notably starts this letter more democratically than Ignatius would favour, 'Polycarp and the elders with him' (Polycarp, *Philipp.* Pref.), he is even more dominated than his mentor by internal concerns. Although he appeals in parallel to 'the apostles who brought us the good news and the prophets who preached in advance the coming of our Lord' (*Philipp.* 6.3), the Jewish heritage of Christianity appears to be without conscious significance for him. When he speaks of 'ancient times' he refers only to the earliest faith of the Philippian Christians (1.2),[6] and he shows little regret about his admission that, although they are 'well trained in the sacred scriptures', he has no such advantage (12.1): these scriptures apparently are primarily the writings of the emerging 'New Testament', or chiefly known to him through them.[7] While his letter is rich in echoes of New Testament phrases, the Old Testament has made no direct impact on his thought. So too, in the world that he constructs, he remains within the broadly 'biblical' tradition of other early Christian writers; outsiders are 'gentiles' (Lat. 'gentes'), among whom, borrowing the words of 1 Peter 2.12, Christians are to live blamelessly (10.2), yet who will also be judged, marked as they are by ignorance of divine judgement. The characteristic of the gentiles is idolatry, yet it is not this which is a real threat for Christians so much as its 'equivalent', avarice (11.2). There is no other front against which Christians define themselves, and, in fact, little hint of any developed self-definition; unlike Ignatius, Polycarp nowhere uses 'Christians' or any other identifying term. Without a hint of polemic against, or of replacement of, any alternative pattern of cult or worship, he describes widows as 'an altar of God' (4.3).

Yet there is polemic within Polycarp's letter. In a sudden outburst he declares , 'For everyone who does not confess that Jesus Christ has come in flesh is an antichrist; and whoever does not confess the testimony of the cross is of the devil; whoever perverts the words of the Lord for his own desires and says that there is neither resurrection nor judgement, such is a first-born of Satan' (7.1). Looking backwards, the invective recalls that of the Johannine tradition (1 John 4.2; 2 John 7; 1 John 3.8; John 8.44), with which later tradition was to link Polycarp (Irenaeus in Eusebius, *H.E.* V.20.6). In its Johannine settings we can still trace the denunciation to its biblical and Jewish roots in an exegesis of the story of Cain, viewed as the offspring of Satan himself;[8] notoriously, the Fourth Gospel itself has turned the censure sharply against the Jews themselves. Of this background Polycarp shows no explicit knowledge; it was more probably a common tradition rather than the Gospel itself which he knew, and neither its Jewish roots, nor its ominous reapplication, have any place in his thought.

A generation later Irenaeus was to assert that Polycarp directed the charge **first-born of Satan** against the heretic Marcion (*Adv. haer.* III.3.4), and, following his lead, some have agreed that here at least, and perhaps elsewhere in his letter, Polycarp is attacking Marcion's doctrine.[9] If so, the softness of touch implies that he either failed to recognise the seriousness of the threat, or lacked the skill and resources to mount an effective counter-attack. As we shall see, later polemic against Marcion was forced to defend the unity of the God of Old and New Testaments by focusing all the theological ambiguities on the Jewish people. Polycarp shows no awareness either of the problem or of the strategy of response.

If Marcion does hide behind the **first-born of Satan**, there would be a strange irony: Jewish exegesis of the Cain and Abel story placed in the mouths of the brothers a quarrel over theodicy; for Cain God fails by acting according to rigid 'justice' or crass favouritism, while, in some accounts and similarly to Polycarp's opponents, neither resurrection nor judgement offers a convincing solution to the dilemma. It may have been

Marcion's challenge which provoked 'Cain's' complaints in such exegesis, eliciting a response from the Jewish side.[10] Could Polycarp, facing the same challenge, unknowingly have shared with the Jews recourse to this same exegetical tradition, one that already had, and would again, be turned against them?

The possibility would point to a world of interacting exegetical activity of which we have but a few echoes, some of which we have already explored. But here the echoes are perhaps too faint, and we do Polycarp more justice if we take seriously the anonymity of his polemic; his foes are defined only in negative terms, through the denial of the Christian affirmations which focus his world. It is a world on whose stage, as we have seen, neither Jews nor Jewish tradition take their place.

This is the more notable because Polycarp's earlier contemporary, Papias, and the other 'Elders' are frequently attributed Jewish tradition, albeit of a different sort. Jerome asserts that the shadowy 'John the Elder' of whom Papias speaks 'is said to have taught the Jewish tradition (*deuterosin*) of a millennium' (*De vir. illus.* 18); the label *Jewish* **tradition** is Jerome's own, as comparison with Eusebius shows, and, given his own and his contemporaries' use of *deuterosis* for the despised Jewish oral tradition,[11] it is derogatory rather than descriptive. This has not prevented more recent scholars from agreeing in labelling the teaching of the Elders reported by Irenaeus 'Jewish-Christian', whether assigned a Palestinian pre-70 or a later Asia Minor origin.[12] Obviously the catch-all term Jewish-Christian need not denote continuing close relationships with Jews;[13] Revelation, which belongs to a similar trajectory, has a marked ambivalence, and perhaps hostility, to the Jews (Rev. 2.9; 3.9), while the passages of vivid eschatological teaching ascribed to the Elders by Irenaeus remain silent on the question of their sources.

Papias himself, according to a late source, reported the death of John and his brother James at the hands of 'the Jews', while Barsabbas was given 'trial by poison' by the unspecified 'unbelievers';[14] even if genuine, such anecdotes related without their original context would tell us nothing about how, and how much, the Jews figured in his *Expositions*. In another famous passage Papias reported that Matthew composed the 'logia' in 'Hebrew dialect' (Eusebius, *H.E.* III.39.16); he means perhaps rhetorical style rather than language and again reveals little other than a tendency shared with other authors of the second century who only knew Jewish works in Greek to favour the term 'Hebrew'.[15]

If we were to allow the surviving remnants of these 'bridge-figures' to determine our picture of the full range of Christianity's concerns in Asia Minor in the first half of the second century, we would be forced to conclude that the Jewish presence in Smyrna, Hierapolis and Ephesus made little impact on or caused little concern to early Christian communities. There were pastoral needs enough arising within the churches' own life, while the preservation of teaching going back to the Lord himself and to the earliest disciples seems to have taken precedence over disputes concerning possession and interpretation of the Old Testament. Within this tradition it may have taken an impulse from outside to find Christian faith in danger of being undermined by its own Jewish heritage, and so to have to answer the question silently posed by contemporary Jews.

The Elders

Among the 'Elders', whose precise status, intra-relationships and authority Irenaeus gently blurs, stands one who may have responded to such an impulse. Irenaeus quotes him at length for his own purposes, because

> the Elder used to demonstrate the folly of those who, because of what befell those of old who disobeyed God, seek to introduce another Father by contrasting what the Lord came and did in his mercy to save those who accepted him (*Adv. haer.* IV.28.1).[16]

The charge refers to the rejection or denigration of the creator God which Irenaeus presents as characteristic of the 'gnostics' he is refuting, and which provides the focus of Book Four. At the same time his invocation of **the Elder** follows without a break his exhortation 'to obey the elders who are in the church', who represent both the unbroken tradition from the Apostles and the formal structures of the church, 'with the succession of the episcopate' (IV.26.2; 32.1).[17] As we have already suggested, Irenaeus shapes from this double use of 'elder' and 'tradition' a construct which successfully prevents us from recovering any alternative setting and identity.

Unlike most of Irenaeus's other anecdotal references to 'the *presbyter(s)*', his appeal here is part of an extended argument which commences in IV.27.1, 'As I heard from a certain Elder (*a quodam presbytero*)', and continues as far as 31.1(?2), 'By telling such things ... the Elder used to encourage us...', and perhaps even to 32.1, 'in this way was an elder [?], a disciple of the apostles (*senior apostolorum discipulus*) wont to argue'.[18] These chapters form a relatively coherent argument which traces instances of God's punishment or failure to punish as recorded in scripture, and tackles a number of issues or objections that these provoke, particularly as they address the justice of God. At various points the appeal to 'the Elder said' is repeated, at others indirect speech implies continuing quotation. Ever since Harnack's detailed discussion (1907), the chapters have been viewed as a sermon-homily or 'lecture' by the Elder, more or less faithfully reported by Irenaeus.[19] However, since Irenaeus describes his sources as oral ('the Elder said'), their written form must be his own work, even if drawn from notes made at the time of delivery, and so both incomplete and selective. Using these for his own purposes, he has undoubtedly combined them with his own observations so as to integrate them into his overall argument. For us now to separate out totally his own views from those of the Elder is nigh impossible: for a minimum we may judge the Elder by those sentences which are, either explicitly or implicitly by the use of indirect speech, attributed to him; on the other hand, clear inconsistencies and favourite Irenaean themes betray the latter's authorial hand. Between these two markers there must be considerable uncertainty.[20]

Even so, we catch something of a distinctive response to what were to become familiar problems. Thus Irenaeus and his 'guru' share a concern to defend the unity and consistency of God witnessed throughout the scriptures, as well as to reaffirm that the 'loving Father' or God of Christian faith will none the less judge those who wilfully turn against him (*Adv. haer.* IV.27.3: indirect speech). Yet Irenaeus distinguishes his own position when he sees it as no slur on the justice of God that he should punish the Egyptians, whose hearts he had himself hardened, in order to deliver his favoured people – for similarly, 'if the Jews had not become murderers of the Lord, which indeed lost them eternal life, and had not fallen into the abyss of wrath by killing the apostles and persecuting the church we could not have been saved' (28.3).[21] The Elder, by contrast, seems equally concerned that the people of the Old Testament should *not* be despised, but that the punishment recorded by scripture is sufficient for any wrong they did: 'We should not', he said, 'be proud nor censure those of old (*veteres*)', but rather fear lest *we* lose the forgiveness *we* have won; the punishment meted out to the worthies of old should lead all to a proper humility before God; Jesus's descent to Hades was to bring forgiveness to all those who had, in hope, put their faith in him; anyone who self-confidently despises them for their sins is doing no less than despise God's grace. Indeed, since they never condemned us neither should *we* condemn them but rather take the descriptions of their failings and punishment as a warning for ourselves (27.1–3).

This theme forms a sustained thread wherever the Elder is clearly the source: 'Scripture has sufficiently reproved him [David], *as the Elder said,* so that flesh nowhere may glory in the sight of God' (27.1). It appears again towards the final section of the argument in 31.1:[22]

> By describing such things about those of old the Elder used to encourage us and tell us, 'We ought not to rebuke those crimes for which scripture itself condemns the patriarchs and prophets ... but give thanks to God for them that at the coming of our Lord their sins have been forgiven'; he used to say that they too gave thanks and rejoiced in our salvation. 'As for those things scripture merely reports without condemnation, we have no right to be accusers'.

The **such things** which introduces this summary looks back to the preceding long defence of 'the people' (*populus*), which is itself introduced by the appeal 'as the Elder also used to say' (30.1). Here the argument is directed against those who found fault with them not only for stealing the goods of the Egyptians (at God's command), but also for then using their ill-gotten gains to furnish the Tabernacle for the worship of God.[23] The defence is simple and, even if elaborated by Irenaeus, belongs to the emerging ethos of the Elder: during their long years of slavery the people had more than earned what they took, while no Christian who continued to benefit from pagan society and the security brought by Rome had any grounds for feelings of superiority.[24] For the Elder the main goal was relatively simple: 'for this reason the Lord said, "Judge not that ye be not judged" [Matt. 7.1]' (*Adv. haer.* IV.30.3: indirect speech); this is a text Polycarp also used (*Philipp.* 2.3), although Irenaeus himself does not cite it elsewhere. Again, highlighting the differing perceptions, Irenaeus shows his own hand clearly when he proceeds to develop the typological significance of the whole Exodus events, appealing to John, the disciple of the Lord, who saw in the Apocalypse that the plagues visited upon the Egyptians would be experienced by all the nations of the earth (*Adv. haer.* IV.30.4).

The problem was not a new one; that God should instruct his people to steal from the Egyptians had (and has) long been a potential source of disparagement.[25] Signs of a Jewish apologetic can already be found in the pre-Christian period: Jubilees 48.18 says that the Israelites plundered the Egyptians 'in exchange for the servitude which they subjected them to by force', a defence echoed by Philo who stresses that avarice and covetousness played no part (*De vita Mosis* I.141); in later legend the Egyptian and Israelite claims for redress were acted out before Alexander the Great, perhaps reproducing Hellenistic Jewish defence against charges laid in popular 'anti-Jewish' polemic. If this were the case, then the Christian use of the accusation would be another example of adaption of pagan anti-Jewish sentiment.[26]

From the Christian camp, Tertullian was to tackle similar criticism of the Exodus accounts, now explicitly ascribed to Marcion (*Adv. Marc.* II.20.1–4; IV.24.5; V.13.6). For him the central issue is whether the God who prohibited stealing had revealed his inconsistency and amorality by instructing his people to steal; he departs from Irenaeus's defence, which he probably knew, by mentioning neither the Tabernacle nor the Christian appropriation and proper use of the goods they had gained from outsiders.[27] At the same time, Tertullian asserts that 'today the Hebrews have their own further answer to the Marcionites', namely that the amount they took was but a fraction of the compensation due their long slavery (II.20.3). That defence, as we have seen, considerably predated both Tertullian and Marcion; its continued presence in later Jewish writing (e.g. *bSan.* 91a;

Gen.R. 61.6) must make us ask how far contemporary Judaism found itself under threat from Marcion and his peers.[28] Yet there may be an important difference of emphasis: for the Jews their response was, at least in part, a matter of self-defence, for Tertullian it is a defence of God; in this the Elder may be as close to the Jews as he is to Tertullian.

The final allusion to the Elder (*senior*), if indeed the same person is in mind,[29] sums up what precedes as illustrating 'how in this way [he] used to debate about the two covenants [or testaments] showing both [to be] from one and the same God', and that there was no foundation to the arguments of those who attributed creation to 'angels or some power or some other God than ours' (*Adv. haer.* IV.32.1: indirect speech). Here the reference back (**in this way**) is to the intervening section since the previous summary quoted earlier (31.1); this comprises an exposition of Genesis 19.31–36, the story of the desperate remedy taken by Lot's two daughters when they realised that there was no other male to father children for them (Gen. 19.24–36). The two daughters, without physical lust, bear children through the one father, who alone can be the source of life-giving seed for them; the two daughters, fulfilling God's dispensation, are '*the two synagogues*' (31.1).[30]

The analogy is developed further and becomes more complex (31.2): the life-giving seed is the 'Spirit of the forgiveness of sins' poured out through Jesus, who as the Word of God is the father of the human race; at the same time, just as Lot's seed mingled with his own offspring, so the seed of the Father of all, the Spirit, 'united with flesh', enables '*the two synagogues*'[31] to produce children for God. Here, in the more developed allegory and in the incarnational language, we probably hear Irenaeus's voice, and the two synagogues, now more pointedly labelled the 'older and younger' (31.2),[32] must indicate Jewish Christians and gentile Christians. In yet a further allegorical development (31.3), Lot's wife, the enduring pillar of salt, is introduced as a type of the church, an image repeated a little later in Irenaeus's own exposition in IV.33.9, suggesting that by now Irenaeus has fully taken over the 'sermon'.[33]

Yet if the developed typological aspects betray Irenaeus's hand,[34] the Elder's different concerns can still be traced – his refusal to lay blame on Old Testament figures and his affirmation of the unity of past and present dispensations with which he concludes.[35] Lot's daughters, believing that only they and their father survive for the furtherance of the human race, merit no criticism. Moreover, if as equals they pointed to the **two covenants**, as **two synagogues** they surely represent the Jews and the Christians.

A similar concern with the relationship between the two 'synagogues' or now 'peoples' occupied (another?) 'one of the [Irenaeus's] predecessors' (V.17.4).[36] Again Irenaeus is defending the identity of the God revealed by Jesus with the Creator, in this case by showing that the sins forgiven by the former must have been committed against the one and the same God. Similarly, a tree (*lignum*) is both the source of our debt and the means of its remission. A prime illustration of this is offerred by Elisha, who saved the axe-head which was lost when hewing trees by throwing a 'tree' (*ligna/um*) into the water (2 Kings 6.6) – an analogy used in a more developed way by Justin, *Dial.* 86.6.[37] Continuing to explore the model, with its fulfilment in the tree/cross which shows the 'the height and length and breadth and depth', Irenaeus adds 'as one of our predecessors said, through the divine extending of hands gathering the two peoples (λαοί) together to the one God' (V.17.4). The exposition continues, whether or not on the same authority, that there were two hands because there were also the two peoples scattered to the corners of the world, the one head because God is one.[38] We meet here again an even-handedness and lack of polemic apparently characteristic of the Elders' attitude.

The identity of Irenaeus's Elders and other authorities remains a mystery, as too does their number and whether he cites them from oral or written sources. There is little point for us in trying to name figures when Irenaeus fails to do so, and surely would have done if it would have added weight to their authority. Instead it is their position within a chain of tradition going back to the Apostles which authenticates their teaching.[39] This gave Irenaeus the advantage of apparent antiquity in marshalling his own arguments against contemporary problems, although the effect is to blur the distinction between his sources and his own position. His own concern is with Marcion and with others like him who separated the Father or God of mercy proclaimed by

Jesus from the Creator of the Old Testament who is, at best, mercilessly just and thoroughly inconsistent.

That the Elder of *Adv. haer.* IV.27.1–32.1 had the same concern has been widely assumed; indeed, Harnack presented him not only as the first anti-Marcionite writer whose polemic survives but also as the earliest evidence for Marcion's *Antitheses*, which, so he argued, could be deduced from the Elder's 'synthesis'.[40] Certainly, it is important for him that 'their God and ours is one' (IV.27.2: indirect speech), while we have seen that the problem of the 'stealing' of the Egyptians' goods is shared with Tertullian's anti-Marcionite polemic; the affirmation that at his descent into Hades Jesus proclaimed the Gospel 'to them also' (IV.27.2: indirect speech) recalls Marcion's assertion to the contrary, at least as reported by his opponents, namely that the righteous of the Old Testament refused to believe in Jesus, whereas the wicked, such as Cain, were redeemed.[41]

Yet the Elder's response is different from that of later polemicists: where later anti-Marcionite writers, like Tertullian and even Irenaeus himself, were to focus their argument on defending the unity of God, even when this entailed (or particularly by) discrediting the Jews of the past, the Elder seems most concerned that 'they' were in danger of being despised by over-confident Christians. Those passages which are most certainly the Elder's warn repeatedly against going beyond scripture in condemning the sins of Old Testament worthies. A rigorist undertone, already noted by Harnack,[42] hints that those (Christians) who have already experienced forgiveness have less chance of futher remission than the people of the Old Testament, who, having experienced their just deserts, had the offer of forgiveness made to them in Hades (27.2). Thus the scriptural accounts serve not as an occasion for feelings of superiority but as a means of instruction, and are in some sense limited in time and extent, offering a 'type' for discerning Christians.

The defence that it is one and the same God who is at work serves here not so much the theological defence of the unity of God as to counter any supposition that there was no place for judgement in the 'Christian' God's activity: 'Their acts were written for our instruction, that we might know first that our God and theirs is one, who is not pleased by sins even when committed by the famous; next, that we should abstain from evil'

(IV.27.2: indirect speech). Since Marcion does not seem to have disparaged the Jewish people in this way,[43] it seems improbable that he is the primary target. Instead, those who did so deprecate **the people** or **those of old** may have been doing so in response to a heresy of a Marcionite type: a standard strategy in later polemicists against Marcion is to dwell at length on the Jews' consistent inability to rightly comprehend or to obey God; it was then a small step to an absolute denial of their present status as God's people. Given these consequences, we may justifiably wonder whether the Elder's more eirenic approach, together with his firm grasp of a continuity of sin and of grace, would have offered a more creative alternative. Yet it may not be necessary to appeal directly or indirectly to Marcion: both he and his opponents expressed existing tensions within Christian thought and self-definition; the Elder represents yet another voice in this debate. The question must be how far it was a debate carried out without reference to or regard for the Jews among their neighbours.

Obviously, there is nothing to suggest that the Elder was motivated by friendship for contemporary Jews; when he speaks of 'them and us' he means the people of the Old Testament and the Christians, whom he sees as typically gentile.[44] There is no hint that an alternative trajectory from 'them' to another contemporary people had been suggested to him, nor what his response would have been to such an alternative. The only indication may be in the identification of Lot's two daughters as the two 'synagogues', a model which carries little of the claimed superiority implicit in the alternative appeal to Rebekah's two sons, the two peoples (λαοί) of whom the greater would serve the lesser (Gen. 25.22–23).[45] Whereas the latter passage becomes a standard proof text in anti-Jewish argument (Rom. 9.12; *Ep. Barn.* 13.1–2; Irenaeus, *Adv. haer.* IV.21.2; Tertullian, *Adv. Iud.* I.3; Cyprian, *Test.* I.19),[46] later authors fail to follow the Elder and see the story of Lot and his daughters only as an occasion for moral admonition (Clement, *Paed.* II.81; Tertullian, *Monog.* 16.4; *Pud.* 6.10). If we cannot project Jews on to the Elder's stage, we do have to recognise their shadows, in the common exegetical arguments, and in a theological role which was to be largely ignored by later Christian image-makers.

Retelling the Story

'Apostolic tradition' did not only provide the buttress of authoritative exegetical argument against insidious novelties. An appeal to origins could also take the form of retelling the story of Jesus or of the first Apostles: this process did not come to an end with the first century, neither can the limits of the canon which were drawn later be treated as if they marked a dividing line in history, genre or authenticity from subsequent 'imitations'. The second and third centuries continued to witness 'Gospels', 'Acts' of Apostles, and 'Letters' purportedly sent by those same apostolic figures. Inevitably, in the earliest traditions surrounding Jesus and his immediate followers, encounters with the Jews would have played a major, if not the major, part. It is, as we have seen, widely assumed in New Testament scholarship that the early church's continuing and allegedly increasingly tense relations with the Jews of their own age further shaped the way those traditions were preserved, interpreted and retold. Thus, already in the New Testment Gospels Jewish responsibility for the death of Jesus is heightened and Roman responsibility correspondingly downplayed. The Sadducean or priestly aristocracy who wielded most power in Jesus's own day recede into the background and increasing obscurity, while the Pharisees assume the dominant role as Jesus's protagonists, a position which reflects the dominance of their successors, 'the rabbis', after 70 CE more than it does the real social situation of the Pharisees of Jesus's own day. We need not here subject this scenario to scrutiny, although to do so would expose a host of flaws and unsubstantiated assumptions; it is enough that in general terms it is a widely accepted picture and one which is often used as a basis for 'recovering' the actual nature of relations between the Christian and Jewish communities at the time and place of writing of the surviving documents. If this process is still happening at the very end of the first century, probably in Asia Minor, in John's Gospel, how far does it continue into the second, in the continued process of retelling and rewriting?

Here we face the initial problem that such literature, being for the most part either anonymous or pseudonymous, rarely betrays its place of origin. A useful starting-point, then, will be the *Acts of Paul*, a retelling of Paul's missionary activities; writing at the end of the second century, Tertullian refers to these *Acts* as the work of a 'presbyter in Asia', and, despite later scholarly debate about its 'orthodoxy', seems to see its main failing as its sanction of women's authority to teach and baptise (*De bapt.* 17). It had been written long enough before to have had time to circulate to Africa, and probably carried some of the authority of those circles of 'Elders' or 'Presbyters' who were the tradition-bearers of second-century Asia Minor.

The *Acts of Paul* stands in an ambiguous relationship to our canonical Acts, sharing some of the same traditions but betraying no explicit dependency. Paul works both in familiar territory (Antioch, Ephesus) as well as in 'new' locations (Smyrna), yet there is little attempt to retell 'canonical' events, even when they are presupposed. If the author knew Acts, then he has no embarrassment in supplementing it.[47] If indeed it was the author's intention to give 'a picture of Paul ... which would correspond to Church ideas in the second half of the 2nd century',[48] it is remarkable how far this 'picture' has changed socio-religious location. The Paul of the canonical Acts regularly starts his mission in the synagogue, even converts adherents, particularly women, and is persecuted by the Jews. The Paul of the *Acts of Paul* has little to do with the Jews, who rarely appear on the stage – perhaps only at Antioch where it seems they attempt to stone him, and later at Tyre where their role is unspecified but where Paul proceeds to perform a sucessful exorcism.[49] His conflict is primarily with the world of paganism – exemplified by the collapse of the temple of Apollo in Sidon, apparently in response to his prayer;[50] the names of those whom he encounters, whether followers, still including a number of well-placed women, or foes, are unmistakably Greek or Roman, to the extent that it is the Romans who protest at Nero's persecution of the Christians with the words 'these men are ours'.[51] The world in which Paul moves is the world of the household with its servants, of banquets, of rich women and leading citizens, of easy appeal to the governor or other authorities. Such a world, as our new picture of diaspora Judaism has taught us, need not be totally foreign to a Jewish context, and there undoubtedly are themes in the *Acts of Paul* which Christians would share with their Jewish neighbours;[52] there is a hint of such a background in the entirely non-polemical references to 'the Sabbath, as the Lord's day drew near', to 'the day of preparation', and to Pentecost.[53] Even so, for these *Acts* the Jews are largely invisible so that, at least in the present state of the text, Paul's own Jewish background is almost forgotten, and certainly does nothing to contribute to or to interrupt the flow of narrative.[54]

Paul's summary of his own, by canonical standards notably unPauline, preaching as he arrives in Italy confirms this picture:[55] Jesus was born after God had sent 'a spirit of power into the flesh, namely into Mary the *Galilean*'; 'he did great and wonderful works ... chose from the tribes twelve men', ... performed a catalogue of Synoptic-like miracles, and discoursed with his disciples in terms reminiscent both of the canonical and of non-canonical 'sayings' Gospels. All this comes as a climax after a 'salvation-history' summary of God's saving acts for '*Israel*', for 'as long as they kept the things of God he did not forsake them'; yet when he sent them the prophets to proclaim Christ, these 'suffered much and were slain by *the people*' who thus 'forfeited the eternal inheritance'.

Both the language and the theological outlook here are broadly similar to those of the apocryphal correspondence between Paul and the church at Corinth usually known as *3 Corinthians*, which is attested both independently and as part of the *Acts of Paul*.[56] In contrast to the general tone of the *Acts*, in *3 Corinthians* there is an explicit anti-heretical thrust: Paul writes in response to news of those who reject any appeal to the prophets, who claim that creation is the work of angels rather than of God, and who deny both the fleshly resurrection and Jesus's fleshly body, and hence his birth from Mary. Such concerns were probably more widespread than we might sup-pose, and although later developed by both Marcion and some gnostic systems, are as yet too general to be identified with either.[57] Paul's response is notable not only for its spirited defence of the obedient reception of the Holy Spirit by 'Mary the Galilean', but also for its understanding of the role and fate of the prophets: they were sent by the Creator God 'to the Jews first', to draw them from their sins; it was God's purpose to save 'the house of Israel', and so, inspired by 'a portion of the Spirit of Christ', they proclaimed the 'fear of God' (θεοσέβεια) (*3 Cor.* 3.9–10). Yet it was not the Jews but the unrighteous prince who desired himself to be

God who killed them; he it is whom Jesus was sent to conquer, and who continues to stir up heresy (3.15–21): it is, then, such false teachers, and not the Jews, who are 'children of wrath [who] have the accursed faith of the serpent' (3.19–20).[58] Here nothing is said about the response of the Jews to the prophets or to Jesus, nor about their ultimate fate; despite the polemical potential of the theme of the murder of the prophets,[59] and the Pauline tradition's attitude to the 'Law', '*Israel*' here simply belongs to the past.

The other contemporary apocryphal *Acts* add little more. Of these, perhaps the *Acts of Peter* has best claim to be of a similar date and also from Asia Minor, since it seems to have been known by the author of the *Acts of Paul*. Again the Jews belong to the past rather than to the world of the narrative: in Peter's preaching there is an echo of a development we find in the *Gospel of Peter* and elsewhere, when Caiaphas handed Jesus over not to Pilate but to the, presumably Jewish, 'cruel throng' (8);[60] so too, Simon Magus can say it was the Jews who destroyed Jesus, 'your god', and even 'stoned you [the disciples] who were chosen by him' (32, cf. Acts 14.19). That Paul's life is under threat is reinforced by memories of his frequent arguments with 'Jewish teachers', showing that 'Christ on whom your fathers laid hands ... abolished their sabbaths, fasts, festivals and circumcision' (1); however, there is little reproach in Peter's acknowledgement that 'neither the Jews nor we were worthy to be enlightened' (20). Yet all this comes as ancillary detail, and there is no sense of living concern or polemic with the Jews. Underneath everything, it is the devil who is to blame, who prompted Judas's betrayal, Herod's hardness of heart, and Caiaphas's surrender of Jesus.

'Jew' may have as much an ethnic as a religious significance; the archetypal opponent of the story, Simon Magus, is at one point described as 'a certain Jew' (6), probably a 'Judaean' since it was from Judaea that Peter had previously driven him (16–18, ctr. Acts 8.9–13, Samaria); similarly, Peter's climactic confrontation with Simon in Rome is advertised as 'two Jews discussing the address of God' (22)[61] – although this was, no doubt, how Christian disputes were seen by many of their pagan neighbours. Simon is rather depicted as a charlatan and magician who is filled with contempt at Jesus's Jewish or Judaean origins (14;

23); more fundamentally, he is again but an agent of the devil and does the 'works of his father' (16).[62]

Although it has sometimes been assumed that *1 Clement's* references to the deaths of Peter and Paul because of 'jealousy' (*1 Clem.* 5.4) refer to the machinations of the Jewish community in Rome,[63] these *Acts* know nothing of this, and the death of the two Apostles, in contrast to that of Jesus, is unequivocally at Roman hands. In a theme shared with the *Martyrdom of Polycarp* but without its polemic, Peter is promised a trial of faith on the coming sabbath – used as elsewhere competely neutrally[64] – before a crowd 'of the gentiles and of the Jews' (16); yet when the day dawns, the audience gathered in the forum are 'Romans', and those who come to take their seats are 'senators, prefects and officers' (23).[65]

The *Acts of John*, whose second-century origin in Asia Minor is now asserted less confidently than it used to be, hardly changes this picture. There is little of the 'anti-Jewish' concern of the Gospel attributed to John: it surfaces only once in a passing reference to Jesus's arrest by the 'lawless Jews under the law of the lawless serpent' (94) – a reference to the diabolic inspiration of their action against Jesus rather than of the Mosaic Law.[66] Again, the world in which John moves is the world of the wealthy household, of the theatre, and of the threat of paganism, and even more of the temptations of luxury and sexual desire. It is a world in which both Jews and Christian polemic against the Jews are absent.

This restraint is in marked contrast to the later apocryphal *Acts* of Apostles; in these the Apostles are more likely to encounter Jews and either to convert them or to suffer their hostility. In the later developments of the *Acts of John*, John successfully debates the scriptures with Jews, including a certain Philo, and triumphs by converting them; it is Jewish complaints to Domitian which lead to the persecution of Christians and the arrest of John himself.[67] Similarly, in the later *Acts of Peter and Paul*, the Jews conspire with Simon Magus, seek Nero's aid in banning Paul, and even try to provoke division between Peter and Paul;[68] moreover, a ninth-century retelling of the late *Acts of Andrew and Matthias in the City of Cannibals* makes the violent and bloodthirsty barbarians (?Scythians) of the title Jews.[69] Such examples could be multiplied in later *Acts* and martyrdoms of saints; in sharp contrast to the rarity of their appearance in the earlier accounts, the Jews now become the standard and vindictive enemy.[70]

This lack of interest in the Jews by the earlier apocryphal *Acts* is, in part, in accordance with their general lack of interest in scripture and in any history apart from that being recounted; it is this which, despite attempts to posit for them a very precise *Sitz im Leben*, undermines any reconstruction of their context.[71] It is possible to ascribe this to the *Acts*' primary interest in edification and in collecting current traditions for this purpose; but later experience would show that an edificatory interest, even one, as in the *Acts*, with a strong ascetic tone, could make good use of an opposition to 'the Jews' and all they represented.

Similarly, the *Acts* betray a powerful apologetic interest in the Apostles' superiority as miracle-workers, and particularly at exorcism, yet do not set this superiority over the Jews; again, other texts imply a competitive context for this motif, with the different religious groups, not least the Jews, vying for credibility on the basis of their miraculous powers, while denouncing those of the opposition as the ominous working of magic.[72] The claim that 'as far as miracle traditions and wondrous acts are concerned, the Christians appear to have won the religious competition with the Jews'[73] is, surprisingly, not exploited by the *Acts*. This is the more unexpected because at a number of points the *Acts* do echo traditions or concerns which in other writings are developed in this 'anti-Jewish' direction; similarly their foundational base traditions, in the Johannine and Pauline materials, would have seemed at the very least to have invited such a development. Their failure to do so, together with their depiction of an alternative lively narrative world, peopled by events, names and locations, some arguably familiar to author or audience, others clearly not so, witness to the fictional creativity of the period, images without a certain reality. If Christians adopted this 'creative Biblical [*i.e. New Testament*] exegesis' from the Hellenistic Jewish expansions of biblical narratives,[74] they have successfully hidden all traces of their Jewish inspiration, and their greatest debt is surely to the literary traditions and techniques of their age.

How far 'fictional creativity' is responsible for another continuation of the 'apostolic' genre, the Pastoral Epistles, is a matter of dispute. Yet, assuming these in their present form to be pseudonymous and post-Pauline, they too reflect a retelling of the story of Paul where the Jews have little place.[75] The Paul of these Epistles may have been once 'a blasphemer, a persecutor and proud' (1 Tim. 1.13), but there is nothing to suggest that all this had been part of 'his way of life in Judaism' as in the autobiographical Galatians 1.13, neither does his calling to be a 'teacher of the Gentiles' (1 Tim. 2.7; 2 Tim. 4.17) mark a radical change from his past or shape the major challenges of the future. It is remarkable that these letters give hardly any basis for determining either Paul's (real or fictitious) perception of Judaism or that of the author.

It is often assumed that the heretical teaching opposed by this author is or includes a 'judaising' tendency or a form of 'Jewish-Christianity',[76] but what is notable is how formulaic and oblique the language already is. The polemic focuses on 'human commands', disputes about purity or defilement or about the Law, and the desire to be 'teachers of the law' (Titus 1.14–16; 3.9; 1 Tim. 1.7); there is a danger of pernicious 'myths and genealogies', which are endless, silly or godless (1 Tim. 1.4; 4.7; Titus 3.9) – the universal language of denigration.[77] Only in Titus 1.14 do these tales become identified as 'Jewish', while the people who (probably) bear them are 'those of the circumcision', a Pauline epithet (Titus 1.10; cf. Gal. 2.12); but even here the pastor appeals not to scripture but 'to a certain prophet of their own', undoubtedly a pagan, to convict them (Titus 1.12). We may wonder whether the readers would have recognised as 'Jewish' the traits and terms modern scholars so confidently identify. If there is a real threat behind the conventional language, it can only be declared 'judaising' by an imaginative reconstruction of the total context.[78] For the text, Jews and Judaism, even as part of the inalienable 'image' of Paul and his theology, barely belong to the world of this author; without prejudging the authorship, the Pastorals do in this way share that world with Polycarp and 'the Elders'.[79]

A different 'retelling' and continuation of a 'New Testament' genre, one which could claim priority in this section, is the 'Gospel'. Here, the only possible text for inclusion must be the *Gospel of Peter*.[80] A reference by Serapion of Antioch, *c*.200 CE, reported by Eusebius (*H.E.* VI.12), secures it for the second century, and also gives a predisposition in favour of Syria. However, the themes it shares with Melito and, to a lesser degree, with Justin have led to it being claimed for Asia Minor.[81] Dominant among these common themes are the (probable) Passover dating of the death of Jesus (*Gospel of Peter* 5, 58), the focus of the blame for his death on the Jews who appear as the sole actors in his condemnation and crucifixion (1, 8–9, 21), which is as 'King of Israel' (7, 11),[82] and the heightened role of Herod in solidarity with them and in articulating the concerns of the Law (1–2, 5).

By contrast, Joseph of Arimathaea is not so much one of them but a 'friend of Pilate' (3, 23–4), while the latter absolves himself of any blame for the blood of the one he acknowledges as 'Son of God' (46). The guilt of the Jews is doubly reinforced, by themselves as they recognise 'the evil they had done to themselves' (25), and by the narrator's 'And they fulfilled everything and completed the sins upon their heads' (17). Although the author, displaying his ignorance, refers to particular groups – 'elders and priests' (25), 'scribes and Pharisees and elders' (28) – he also shares with the (?Ephesian) Fourth Gospel a generalised and alienating use of 'the Jews': it is 'fear on account of the Jews' which delays Mary Magdalene's attentions to the body of Jesus (50, 52) , and which even leads the witnesses of Jesus's resurrection to commit 'the greatest sin before God' and remain silent (48).

There are few indications as to how this increased hostility towards the Jews fitted into the wider interests of the *Gospel of Peter*, not least because we possess only a portion of the text, and no clues as to whether this hostility extended beyond the passion narrative.[83] It has been seen as merely a way of expressing the theological theme of divine necessity and scriptural fulfilment, or as the means for a summons to repentance;[84] neither explanation seems adequate when faced with the unsubtle elaboration of the Johannine tradition (John 19.31–33, 36), 'they ordered that his legs be not broken so that he might die in torments' (14). The strongest note, besides those inspired by the docetic Christology, is the apologetic one with its two-headed thrust. On the one hand, the resurrection becomes something attested by the soldiers, the centurion and the elders, even if fear of 'the people of the Jews' drives them to hide it; on the other, the Jews have worked for themselves their own judgement which will find its fulfilment in 'the judgement and end of Jerusalem' (25). Although there is no inclusive terminolgy for the faithful nor any reference to the gentiles, the former undoubtedly saw themselves as fully separate from 'the Jews'.[85] Yet there is little suggestion that contemporary polemics are the real inspiration: although there is a repeated emphasis on the proximity of the sabbath (5, 27, 34) and on *their* Feast of Unleavened Bread (5, 58), while the empty tomb is discovered on 'the Lord's day' (κυριακή), there is no attempt to turn this into a denunciation of the Jewish calendar or praxis.[86]

The meagreness of the fruits of this survey shows how unpredictable is the interaction between strong narrative tradition and contemporary context. A narrative may generate its own momentum towards intensification of characterisation, such as typifies the reworking in the *Gospel of Peter* of the canonical (-type) passion traditions, themelves apparently already on a trajectory of increasing hostility to the Jews; yet this signally fails to happen in the early apocryphal material associated with the Apostles where the potential of the negative role of the Jews in the canonical text is simply forgotten. In neither case is it possible to draw direct conclusions about the contemporary situation of either author or audience. When in the much later *Acts* the Jews do appear, this may again be more a matter of narrative dynamic and theological habit than of their actual importance for the later editors. We may suspect that contemporary Jewish communities, themselves also seeking patronage in the city, were of greater concern to the second-century audiences than to those of a post-Constantinian age, but beyond suspicion we cannot go.

Marcion: Key or Enigma?

Throughout our pursuit of 'the Jews' on the stage of second-century literature, one figure has repeatedly appeared in the background, although often lurking in the shadows: Marcion. We must now summon him to the fore for two reasons; first, Marcion himself has often been portrayed as a radical Paulinist,[87] who may properly feature in a chapter on 'apostolic traditions'.

Secondly, unquestionably he moulded the church's attitude to
the Jews in a way which was to be lasting; with Marcion the question of the Jews became an integral part of the question of God
and of the question of Christ.[88] The Christian response to
Marcion's disparagement of the God of the Old Testament as
put forward by Tertullian and others was to lay far heavier blame
on the Jews, for if God was one and Jesus was the promised Messiah there was no excuse for their failure to believe, while the
deficiencies of laws such as the *lex talionis* or the food regula-
tions reflected the need to impose a limitation on the people's
instinctive excesses. Yet, although his influence was strongest
after his arrival in Rome, Asia Minor was the scene of Marcion's
earliest activity, in his home town of Sinope and elsewhere,
and he was a catalyst for a number of Christian writers from
the area.[89]

Yet Marcion's own attitude to the Jews, of the present as also
of the past, as well as his position within the church's developing attitude towards them, particularly in Asia Minor, is fraught
with ambiguities. Since we know him only through the testimony
of his opponents, who fail to answer unequivocally our question
as to what were the decisive sources of inspiration for his heresy,
we do not have the means to examine the 'image and reality' of
Judaism in his thought. We can only deal with the polemicists'
'image' of Marcion's portrayal of and relationship with Judaism,
and reach back through that to try to catch some glimpse of his
own account.

a) *Ally or Enemy?*

In the eyes of his Christian opponents Marcion was, of course,
the enemy not of Judaism but of the Christian Gospel which saw
the revelation of God in Christ as the climax of God's revealing
activity in Israel's past history. Marcion's goal was the proclamation of the self-revelation in Christ of the eternal, totally 'other'
God, 'the Father'. Yet his distinction between this supreme
Father and the Creator God 'of the Jews' demanded a violent
attack against Jewish faith, history and practice. Not only was
that God responsible for the deprecated created order – hence
Marcion's docetic Christology and his asceticism, including the
rejection of marriage – but the records of his dealings in the

past showed him to be inconsistent in precept and purpose, prone to changeability and favouritism, liable to ignorance, swift to punish yet also to fail to punish where punishment was due, responsible for hardness of heart, for sin and for evil. He it was who told the Hebrews to rob the Egyptians, who laid down laws which he then either broke himself or encouraged them to break, who displayed both divine inconsistency, switching favour from Saul to David, and divine ignorance (Gen. 3.9, 11), and who imposed the merciless precept of an eye for an eye, or the meaningless demands of food and purity laws.[90]

Thus far, the Jews were caught up in the deficiencies of their God and could have no expectation of participation in the Christian vision of salvation. Marcion denied Abraham and the patriarchs a place in the Kingdom of God, eliminating them from Luke 13.28 (Irenaeus, *Adv. haer.* IV.8.1);[91] to underline the antipathy, while the wicked such as Cain did respond at Jesus's descent to Hades, Abel, Enoch, Noah and the other righteous, patriarchs and prophets, were left there 'because, he says, they acknowledged the God of the Jews' (Epiphanius, *Pan.* 42.4; cf. Irenaeus, *Adv. haer.* I.27.3).[92]

Inevitably this account could lead to a certain ambiguity; the prophetic indictment of Israel's refusal to respond (Isa. 1.3–4) could only refer to their disobedience towards the Creator God, contrary to the Christian 'discovery' of an anticipation of Christ himself (Tertullian, *Adv. Marc.* III.6.7–8). Yet, with an apparent inconsistency which Tertullian is quick to point out, Marcion did hold the Jews to blame for their persecution of the prophets, although in theory they were thus rejecting their own God and siding with the true God (IV.15.1–2; V.15.1–2).[93] Yet even this culpability does not seem to amount to much, certainly not to Harnack's judgement that according to Marcion the Jewish people were particularly evil, unfaithful and hard-hearted against their God.[94] Marcion may instead have held that 'if he [the Christ] had been their own they certainly would have recognized him and treated him with every religious devotion'; however, the apparent amelioration of their position is double-edged, for this offered them no real excuse when they (understandably) rejected him 'as a stranger and killed him as an opponent' (III.6.2).

Yet, in sharply isolating Jewish experience and worship of their God, Marcion did allow the Jews to retain their expectation of their (the Creator's) Messiah, the 'Iudaicus Christus' or 'Christus creatoris', who is yet to come and who will, perhaps, restore the people to the land (Tertullian, *Adv. Marc.* III.21.1; 24.1; IV.6.3). He also shared or adopted their exegesis by applying some of the so-called 'messianic prophecies' to past historical figures and events, earning himself the charge of 'championing the cause of the Jews' (Irenaeus, *Adv. haer.* IV.34.4); similarly, he restricted the fulfilment of particular universalist passages to the coming of proselytes and not to the joining of gentiles in the church (Isa. 16.4; 42.4: Tertullian, *Adv. Marc.* III.21.2).

By thus affirming the integrity of Jewish rejection of Jesus, and by adopting a 'Jewish' reading of the scriptures against the convoluted allegorisation or typology of Christian attempts to claim them, Marcion made possible Tertullian's picture of him as an ally of the Jews. Because he denied that Jesus Christ was the Messiah of Old Testament prediction, Marcion was 'forced to form an alliance with the Jewish error and construct for himself an argument from it' (*Adv. Marc.* III.6.2; cf. 23.1); in response, Tertullian addresses both the Jew and the heretic 'who has been guided by the Jew', demonstrating that there are two advents of the Messiah, the first in humility, the second in the majesty in which alone the Jews misguidedly still await him (III.7.1; cf. 16.3). In attacking Marcion's biblical exegesis Tertullian has to denounce the lies of the Jews (III.13.5), and only when he turns to denounce Marcion's docetism does he admit that the latter has now 'desisted from borrowing poison from the Jew, the asp, as they say, from the viper' (III.8.1). However, we should not be too quickly swayed by Tertullian's polemical attempt to link Marcion with the Jews; he also traces his ideas to the baleful influence of philosophy, even specifically of Epicurus (*Adv. Marc.* I.2.1; 13.3; 25.3; II.16.2–3 etc.), perhaps with some justification, although such a genealogy is standard among anti-heretical writers.[95]

If the work *Adversus Iudaeos* ascribed to Tertullian, or the relevant part of it, is authentic, we might claim further evidence of his perception that Marcion and the Jews represented an unholy alliance to be brought down with a common argument. The argument of the second part of the *Adv. Iud.* runs closely parallel to that of the second half of *Adv. Marc.* III, often to the extent of near verbal identity, particularly in *Adv. Iud.* 9 and *Adv. Marc.* III.12–14. Sometimes the same charges are laid against each antagonist, with only the necessary cosmetic adaptions: Marcion is addressed in the second person singular, the Jews in either the third or the second person plural,[96] but both can be urged to 'give back to the Gospel of truth' what the former 'coming later took away', what the latter 'do not wish to believe' (*Adv. Marc.* III.13.6; *Adv. Iud.* 9.10). Accusations imputed against the Jews through Marcion, are also laid directly at their own door.[97]

While the apparent dependence has led some to argue that the *Adv. Iud.* (9–14) is the work of a later imitator, H. Tränkle, in his edition of the work, feels that the technique is not unusual for Tertullian. Instead he suggests that Tertullian failed to complete his work against the Jews because it was only a 'shadow polemic' and lacked the urgency of a living conflict, that is, until it could be 'recycled' against Marcion.[98] Even so, Tertullian would not be recognising for the first time the (implicit) unnatural alliance between the Jews and Marcion: his polemic against the former drew as much on earlier literary sources as on direct experience of Jewish debate, and those earlier sources almost certainly included writers who had already fought on both fronts and perhaps made common cause out of them, perhaps Justin and Irenaeus, or the more shadowy Miltiades and Apollinarius.[99] Similarly, although Tertullian probably had access to Marcion's *Antitheses* for Books IV and V of his refutation, for the earlier books at least he drew in part on previous polemicists, including, once again, Irenaeus and Justin.[100] But this only sharpens the more urgent question: was Marcion 'the ally of the Jewish error' a figure Tertullian had drawn from Marcion's own words, from his own interpretation of Marcion's system and its implications, from the literary contingencies imposed by assimilating his earlier work, or from a reading of his predecessors who had already begun the process of attacking the one through the image of the other?

b) *Marcion and Judaism: Construct and Contemporaries*

To go behind the Christian polemic and discover the main impulses of Marcion's teaching is notoriously difficult. Yet how-

ever we balance the 'biblical theologian', 'gnostic thinker', or
'philosophically inspired thinker' in understanding Marcion's
rejection of the Creator,[101] the main contours of his disparagement of the 'God of the Jews' and of his radical exclusion of any
continuity between that God's activity and the Gospel, with all
their attendant ambiguities, stand out with vivid clarity. Inevitably, then, the Jews were for him defined primarily by their allegiance to their God, and to that extent defined also by the 'Old
Testament'. Yet his determination to excise from Christianity
any taint of Judaism shows that the latter also had some contemporary reality for him.

In this he was, perhaps, less innovatory. When he advocated
fasting on the sabbath so as 'to do nothing appropriate to the
God of the Jews' (Epiphanius, *Pan.* 42.3.3–4), Marcion was not
only demanding a palpable distancing, but was also entering an
existing debate which focused identity and separateness on this
symbol.[102] Other authors from Asia Minor expressed this sense
of structural self-identity by speaking of 'Judaism' and
'Christianism',[103] and Marcion seems to have followed suit.
Tertullian's summary of Marcion's message was that he 'set up a
great and total distinction as between justice and goodness, between law and Gospel, between Judaism and Christianity'
(… *quantam inter Iudaismum et Christianismum* : *Adv. Marc.* IV.6.3).
While the formulation may be Tertullian's own, he is clearly
borrowing the key terms from his opponent.[104] Neither **Judaism**
nor **Christianism** are found in Irenaeus or in Justin, two of
Tertullian's principal sources, and they appear together only in
Books IV and V of the *Adv. Marc.*, which were written at the final
stage of the work when Tertullian first had access to Marcion's
Antitheses.[105] Marcion apparently cited Luke 16.16 to establish
that with John the Baptist 'Judaism was to cease and Christianity
begin', a point at which Tertullian disagreed only that this came
about by 'some alien power' (IV.33.8); according to Marcion
they constituted two 'revelations' (*ostensiones*), the term Tertullian
reports him as reading at Galatians 4.24, the 'noble dignity of
Christianism' and the 'legal servitude of Judaism' (V.4.8).[106] No
doubt Tertullian has developed the use of **Iudaismus**, which
appears frequently on its own in Books IV and V, and also three
times in the earlier Books (I.20.3; III.6.10; 22.3), but we still hear
echoes of Marcion's own usage: at IV.11.1 Tertullian implies that

he is quoting Marcion that the tax-collector of Luke 5.27–39 was 'outside the law and unclean (*profanus*) to Judaism', while in V.2.1 he says that 'we *also* claim Galatians as the principal letter against Judaism' (V.2.1).[107] The extreme rarity of the terms in Tertullian's other writings supports the idea that he developed them, and perhaps even acquired them, from his encounter with Marcion's *Antitheses*, and that they therefore expressed the latter's conception of the two religions.[108]

According to Tertullian's account, Marcion was plainly anxious about the contamination of Christianity by 'Judaism'; his complaint (and, he thought, Paul's) was that Peter and the other Apostles were 'too close to Judaism' (*Adv. Marc.* V.3.1), and he charged the 'supporters of Judaism' with corrupting the Gospel of Luke (IV.4.4). So far it might be right to say that what Marcion was in practice most vehemently opposed to was 'judaising' (as defined by himself) rather than the Jews themselves.[109] Yet when it comes to his 'image' of Judaism, despite his affinities with Jewish arguments and his willingness to allow them to keep their eschatological hopes, he gives Judaism no continuing validity even apart from Christianity. If it had its validity in the past, it was still as a system of law bound to a deceiving God, and with the coming of John the Baptist it was to cease, perhaps to be effectively destroyed by Paul. The Jews who saw Marcion as a threat to be denounced and argued against were not deceived into reading an anti-Jewish polemic where there was none: certainly, they should not have observed the essentially 'pro-Jewish orientation' of his thought.[110] He allows them none of the virtues of their faith which are stressed in their own, or even in Christian, apologetic, and, although he does not join in the Christian competition for possession and the true interpretation of their scriptures, this does not make his assessment of them any the more positive. Neither was his theology of the Creator God *unintentionally* anti-Jewish.

The ambivalence in Marcion's position as anti-Jewish yet, in Tertullian's eyes, as 'ally of the Jews' led Harnack to suggest that Marcion originally may have been very close to Judaism, perhaps even coming from a proselyte family; like, but with even greater ferocity than, Paul before him – and for Harnack Marcion must be understood through his 'Paulinism' – on turning to Christianity he reacted against his heritage with the typical violence of a convert.[111] In similar fashion Hoffmann talks of the 'pro-Jewish orientation' of Marcion's theology and concludes that his 'error remains fundamentally a Jewish heresy'.[112] His explanation relies less on a psychological interpretation of Marcion himself, and looks more to his social and his theological context. The latter is provided already by the ambiguities of Paul's own theology, a 'vestigial Jewish Christianity'. The former is created by the situation of diaspora Judaism in Pontus in the aftermath of the two revolts: this Judaism was thoroughly Hellenised but was undergoing a conservative, rabbinic reaction typified by the literalism of the translation of the scriptures into Greek made by that other son of Sinope, the Jew Aquila; at the same time, the revolts, and ancillary disturbances in which the Jews of Sinope may have been involved, provoked a surge of anti-Jewish sentiment. Marcion is influenced both by the biblical literalism of an Aquila and by such anti-Jewish feelings, although his own rejection of the Old Testament cannot be labelled either anti-Jewish or antisemitic; his real concern was not with Jews but with judaisers within the church.[113]

Hoffmann's reconstruction of the Judaism of Pontus relies almost entirely on silence and supposition, while he certainly also pays too little attention to the philosophical dimension and sources of Marcion's system.[114] He is undoubtedly right to attempt to create for Marcion a social and theological context, but the philosophical and religious threads in that context are more complex than he allows. Yet it would be wrong to remove contemporary Judaism entirely from the broader context of Marcion's system and teaching.

The Jews may themselves have recognised in Marcion a serious antagonist against whom they were compelled to defend their own scriptures and history, sometimes providing ammunition for, if not making common cause with, the Christians. As we have seen already, Tertullian sets within a hypothetical disputation between Hebrews and Egyptians a claim that 'the Hebrews today affirm against the Marcionites' that what they 'plundered' at the Exodus was poor return for years of unpaid labour (*Adv. Marc.* II.20.3); Ephraem also suggests that 'the Jews themselves ... by the means of their true Scriptures have been able to overcome many teachings', although he hastens to add that in turn the Jews have been refuted by the church (*Against*

Marcion I, p. 53);[115] Justin is deeply sensitive to and shares Trypho's anxiety about any hint of another God than the Creator.[116] Rabbinic sources too on occasion seem to be countering attacks similar to those made by Marcion, and defend the unity of God, as well as providing explanations of incidents that might be misconstrued as evidence of ignorance or of inconsistency.[117] How far such defences were really against Marcion and his followers, how far merely evidence that he was not unique in his sensitivity to the ambiguities of the biblical narrative, must remain uncertain; we may be left with the rhetorical questions; 'is it at all likely that such a gigantic fight, for and against the Bible, should have left the Jews cold? Or could it remain unknown to them; a secret to those who visited the synagogues, and their spiritual leaders?'[118]

Marcion was not the first, neither would he be the last, to notice the ambiguities and the problems in the 'Old Testament' picture of God. Hoffmann may be right in supposing that some of Marcion's polemic against the Creator God could have been fuelled by pagan anti-Jewish arguments: Marmorstein, who argued most forcefully for the influence of the Marcionite threat on rabbinic internal apologetic, draws a vivid picture of pagan incredulity at the jealousy and wanton caprice of the supposedly morally and ethically superior God of the Jews: 'one can easily imagine the rhetors in the squares and the philosophers in the streets of Tiberias and Caesarea denouncing and blaspheming the God of the Jews for hardening the tender heart of kind old Pharaoh'.[119] If so, Marcion may have been equally aware of some of the Jewish counter-thrust: he knew Jewish exegesis of the 'messianic' and eschatological prophecies of the Old Testament, and, despite Tertullian's prohibition (*Adv. Marc.* I.10.3), perhaps did 'set up Abraham as older than the world', echoing the Jewish apologetic of Abraham's pre-existence but using it to limit the domain of the Creator God to the Jewish people.[120]

Probably even without the distortion of only knowing him through his opponents, Marcion's attitude to Judaism would remain something of an enigma, fraught with ambiguities. The image of Judaism is fundamentally negative, a religion founded on a flawed relationship with a flawed deity, religion and deity bound together in a theological ghetto of meaningless practice and idiosyncratic hopes. The relationship with the reality is twisted. The Jews of Sinope almost certainly did not live in a ghetto of any kind, but they may have expressed the sort of eschatological hopes and exegesis which Marcion allowed them. In denying the Jewish roots of Christianity, Marcion was in a sense according them the integrity they assumed, while answering what for many, pagan and Jew alike,[121] was the major offence of Christianity, its desertion of its ancient roots – by denying those roots. In introducing a new revelation from the unknown God in Jesus Christ he was tying his colours to the standard of the newness of Christianity which had long been a focal argument in the apologetic defence of Christianity.[122] In his exposé of the Creator God he was but picking up the strictures and taunts of both Christians and pagans before him. So far, his system could be seen as a response to an implicitly competitive situation where Christians had to hold their own alongside self-confident Jews and half-mocking pagans – who are, unfortunately, most hidden in all our reports of his theology. The paradox of Marcion is that he both represents and contradicts the church's attitude to Judaism before him, just as after him the church both violently contradicted and yet often came close to adopting his own attitude. After him image all but overwhelmed reality.

Notes

[1]   Greek text in Eusebius, *H.E.* III.23.3; here Irenaeus makes (some of) them contemporaries of 'John the disciple of the Lord'.

[2]   See pp. 59–70.

[3]   On competition in the miraculous see Achetemeier 1976 and pp. 92–3, 258.

[4]   Reinach 1885 suggests that the attribution of miraculous powers and the appeal to them as a last resort against a potentially devastating fire reflects authentic local traditions. There is, however, nothing to support Rokeah's (1982: 66) suggestion that Polycarp may have been 'one of the architects of this Christian policy of conversion' among the Jews.

[5]   See pp. 27, 43–4.

[6]   Presumably with reference to Paul's letter to them, cf. 11.3.

[7]   The reference to Psalm 4.4 which immediately follows at 12.1 is probably taken from Eph. 4.26.

[8]   See Lieu 1993: 467–72.

[9] R. Hoffmann 1984: 51–6. Hoffmann points also to the stress (?) on the identity of the God who raised Jesus with both the author of creation and the final judge in 2.1, and to the appeal to the prophets in 6.3 (so also Meinhold 1952: 1685–7). Harrison 1936: 266–84 argued that chs. 1–12 were written later than 13, after the emergence of Marcionitism.

[10] Levine 1971: 93f. sees an anti-Marcionite thrust in the targumic tradition.

[11] Millar 1992: 114–15; Lieu 1992: 85–6. Eusebius, *H.E.* III.39.7, 14 speaks instead of the παραδόσεις of John the Elder, without labelling them 'Jewish'.

[12] See especially Daniélou 1964: 46–8; and above p. 185, on Papias.

[13] Although Daniélou seems to imply this by speaking of toleration of the Jewish presence in Asia Minor permitting a more active Jewish messianism than elsewhere.

[14] So Philip of Side and possibly George Hamartolus; on the texts see Körtner 1983: 79–81; Kürzinger 1983: 118–19.

[15] So Kürzinger 1983: 20–3.

[16] Reading the singular 'presbyter' in conformity with the rest of this section, following the Armenian against the Latin 'presbyteri' (so Rousseau 1965: 756).

[17] Irenaeus deliberately and explicitly blurs the distinction between elders as 'tradition-bearers' and elders as within the continuous tradition of church office or the episcopate; this does not mean that all the 'Elders' were within the church structures of ministry, although some, like Polycarp, may have been.

[18] The different Latin terminology, 'senior' vs. 'presbyter', may represent a different underlying Greeek, but the significance of this is uncertain; however, Rousseau 1965: 796–7 reconstructs the Greek πρεσβύτερος.

[19] Harnack spoke of a 'Predigt' (1907), while Bousset, who with some caution broadly accepted his proposal, preferred a 'Vortrag' (1915). Rousseau 1965 includes the whole section (27.1–32.2) under the heading 'Enseignement du presbytre' but other analyses are more cautious; see the following discussion.

[20] Lightfoot 1891: 541–8 includes only IV.27.1–28.1; 30.1–31.1; 32.1 and even here brackets any material not included by the minimum definition just given.

[21] This seems to be Irenaeus's words since the section is introduced by a reference to the heretics 'of whom we have spoken'; however, Bousset 1915: 273 n. 2 sees that reference as an aside added by Irenaeus and preserves the rest for the Elder.

[22] This is the last appeal to the 'presbyter'; at 32.1 the different epithet, 'senior apostolorum discipulus', makes it uncertain whether the same authority is quoted, although the theme is the same; see n. 18 and p. 246.

[23] Only the opening sentence is explicitly assigned to the Elder but the re-emergence of reported speech in the middle of 31.3 for half a sentence appealing to Matt. 7:1–2 shows how precarious any clear reconstruction must be.

[24] See Clarke 1966 on the social status of Christians in the light of IV.30.1.

[25] See Childs 1974: 175–7.

[26] See Levi 1912; Marcus 1951: 519; Marmorstein 1950: 28.

[27] See Meijering 1977: 138–41, who refers to the adoption of this theme by Augustine, *Confess.* VII.9.15.

[28] For the argument that the defence against a Marcionite (-type) theology played an important role in the development of the Haggadah see Marmorstein 1929 and below pp. 268–9.

[29] See above, n. 22, and below, pp. 251–2.

[30] The introduction of 'the two synagogues' at 31.1 (Lat. 'duae filiae hoc est duae synagogae') is supported by a Greek fragment which reads only αἱ δύο συναγωγαί; the reference to the two daughters perhaps has been omitted by homoioteleuton. However, W. Harvey 1857: 252 rejects '[id] est duae synagogae' in the Latin as a gloss.

[31] The Latin adds 'id est duae congregationes' but this does not have the support of the Armenian and may be a translator's gloss (Rousseau 1965: 794).

[32] Lat. 'maior et minor' as the Vulgate of Gen. 19.31; the Greek probably read πρεσβυτέρα καὶ νεωτέρα with LXX.

[33] Against Bousset 1915: 272, who sees in 33.9 a cross-reference to the Elder's address in 31.3.

[34] Although at 28.1 the Elder does seem to have qualified the events of the Old Testament as 'typice et temporaliter et mediocrius', while in 30.1 which precedes this discussion he(?) encourages the search for 'a type' in the events.

[35] Loofs 1930: 101–13 recognises that most of the interpretation as we have it is Irenaean but feels he is able to argue back to the Elder's original intentions which he considers to be anti-Marcionite.

[36] Here the Greek survives as τις τῶν προβεβηκότων which the Latin renders as 'quidam de senioribus'; elsewhere the Latin can use 'senior' apparently as an equivalent of πρεσβύτερος (IV.27.2; 32.1) but Irenaeus's usage is not fixed enough to determine whether it is right in obscuring the distinctive phrase. Some scholars distinguish this tradent from the Elder of Book IV, and suggest he be identified with the author of the poems against the gnostic Marcus (I.15.6).

[37] See p. 141; Justin also finds a reference to baptism in the water.

[38] Daniélou 1964: 280 compares *Sib. Or.* I.372; VIII.302 for the cross gathering the two peoples as a Jewish-Christian theme, although there the reference is to 'measuring the whole world'. Tertullian makes a similar point in his exegesis of Eph. 2.11–20 in *Adv. Marc.* V.17.15 but without reference to the two hands and one head.

[39] The extant Latin text at *Adv. haer.* IV.27.1 implies that this Elder's link with the Apostles was indirect, although the later reference at 32.1 contradicts this. The contradiction may be resolved either by positing a mistranslation at 27.1 (Rousseau 1965: 729) or by taking 32.1 loosely (Harnack 1907:19).

[40] Harnack 1924: 316*–17*.

[41] Irenaeus, *Adv. haer.* I.27.3: they thought God was tempting them and did not respond to Jesus; Epiphanius, *Pan.* 42.4; see Harnack 1924: 294*–5*.

[42] 1907: 32–3.

[43] See p. 263; the Elder's rebuttal of any idea that this world was created not simply by another God but by some other power or by angels (IV.32.1) seems to go beyond Marcionite teaching.

[44] See *Adv. haer.* IV.30.3, 'cum essemus ethnici'.

[45] See above, n. 32, for allusion to the 'older and younger synagogue' in *Adv. haer.* IV.31.2, possibly in Irenaeus's expansion.

[46] See Simon 1986: 187–8 for the Christian use of the Genesis 25 text and for the possible rabbinic response.

[47] So Schneemelcher 1992: II. 232–3: in the absence of a modern standard edition, references are to this English translation. Rordorf 1988 concludes that there is no literary dependence although this involves an early date for the *Acts*

of Paul and a late one for the canonical Acts (both early second century); Bauckham 1993 argues the work was intended as a sequel to Acts.

[48] Schneemelcher 1992: II. 232.

[49] *PHeid.* 1–6 where the unspecified subjects of the verbs of stoning and expulsion are probably the Jews (Schmidt 1904: viii); *PHeid.* 40 where 'a crowd of Jews' is mentioned but the text is too damaged to allow any reconstruction of the course of events (Schneemelcher 1992: II. 250).

[50] *PHeid.* 37 (Schneemelcher 1992: II. 249–50).

[51] Schneemelcher 1992: II. 262.

[52] Bovon and Junod 1986: 162 stress the importance of alms and assistance in Judaism in contrast to an exclusively pagan context for the theme of patronage which has been found in the apocryphal *Acts*, for example by Stoops 1986.

[53] Schneemelcher 1992: II. 252, 258, 251; if the visit of Paul to Smyrna recounted in the *Life of Polycarp* 2 is drawn from the *Acts of Paul* (Bauckham 1993: 118, n. 30) we could add 'in the days of Unleavened Bread' and Paul's instruction of Christians into Passover and Pentecost.

[54] There is nothing to support the claim of Michaelis (quoted by Schneemelcher 1965: II. 333; not in 1992 edn.) that the description of Paul as 'a man small of stature, with a bald head and crooked legs, in a good state of body, with eyebrows meeting and nose somewhat hooked' is intended as 'the typical portrait of a Jew'; see Bauckham 1993: 139 for its Greek context. However, before his execution Paul prays 'in Hebrew' (Schneemelcher 1992: II. 262).

[55] Schneemelcher 1992: II. 259–60.

[56] Whether *3 Corinthians* was originally independent, as argued by Klijn 1963 and accepted by Schneemelcher 1992: II. 228–9, is immaterial for our purposes since if originally independent it would be prior, i.e. also second century and from Asia Minor.

[57] So Klijn 1963: 22–3.

[58] So they are implicitly 'children of the devil'; see above pp. 243–4 on John 8.44 and Polycarp, *Philipp.* 7.

[59] See pp. 133, 135 on Justin, and Lieu 1996.

[60] Schneemelcher 1992: II. 295. See below, pp. 260–1 on the *Gospel of Peter*.

[61] Lat.: 'conlocutio dei'; Vouaux 1922: 358 reconstructs προσηγορία and suggests the point is whether Jesus is to be addressed as God.

[62] See n. 58.

[63] See Fischer 1956: 30–1.

[64] The day of Christian meeting is 'the Lord's day' (30; *Berlin Coptic Papyrus* 8502, 128; Schneemelcher 1992: II. 285, 311).

[65] Vouaux 1922: 319, n. 7 notes that the author makes no distinction between Jews and gentiles, 'il n'y a plus pour lui que chrétiens d'une part, et non-chrétiens de l'autre'.

[66] See Junod and Kaestli 1983: 643–4, who note that this reference to the Jews is otherwise unparalleled in the *Acts of John* and may be further evidence of the more primitive character of this section.

[67] *Acts of John by Prochorus* 27; 32; Vat. 654 = Lipsius 1883–90: I. 379–80, 384, 477. Schneemelcher 1992: II. 430–1 dates these to the fifth century and later.

[68] Lipsius 1883–90, II. 297–9; an unholy alliance is established between 'the rulers of the synagogue of the Jews and the priests of the Greeks'!

⁶⁹ Lipsius 1883–90: II. 5; on the traditions in the *Acts of Andrew and Matthias* see Mueller 1993: 255–6.

⁷⁰ See Lipsius 1883–90 index; Parkes 1934: 121–50.

⁷¹ See Bovon and Kaestli 1986: 171.

⁷² See *Life of Polycarp* 28–9 and above, pp. 241–2; on the theme in the Apologies see above, p. 156.

⁷³ Achetemeier 1976: 156.

⁷⁴ So Bauckham 1993: 145.

⁷⁵ Rordorf 1988 argues that the Pastorals reflect parallel but independent circles of tradition to the *Acts of Paul*, thus placing the Pastorals in the second century and their location in Asia Minor; however, Bauckham 1993 argues persuasively that the *Acts* know 2 Tim. and Titus.

⁷⁶ U. B. Müller 1976.

⁷⁷ See p. 28 on this in Ignatius.

⁷⁸ E.g. Goulder 1994.

⁷⁹ Campenhausen 1951 argued for common authorship of the Pastorals and Polycarp, *Philipp*.

⁸⁰ On the *Gospel of Philip*, which is most probably to be located in Syria, see Sikers 1989.

⁸¹ See especially Perler 1964, and above, pp. 233–4.

⁸² Cf. Melito, *Peri Pascha* §96, l. 716 and ctr. 'King of the Jews' in the canonical Gospels.

⁸³ The fragments published by Lührmann 1981, 1993 are too fragmentary to add much; Wright 1985–6 suggests PEg 2 is part of the *Gospel of Peter*, but while it has a similar 'Johannine' anti-Jewish tenor, its terminology is different.

⁸⁴ See Dehandschutter 1989: 347–8; Denker 1975.

⁸⁵ Denker 1975: 79 suggests that the author sees Christians as a 'third race' although such terminology is not used.

⁸⁶ At 58 the author seems to consider the Sunday the last day of the Feast of Unleavened Bread. 28 seems to imply a Roman day with the sabbath beginning in the morning.

⁸⁷ Most notably by Harnack 1924; see also B. Aland 1973: 435.

⁸⁸ So Efroymson 1979: 105, 'Marcion's challenge or threat placed all the anti-Judaic themes in a new apologetic context, appending them to ideas of God and Christ in ways that came perilously close to permanence.'

⁸⁹ Traditionally for Polycarp (Irenaeus, *Adv. haer.* III.3.4, pp. 243–4) and conceivably for 'the Elder' (see pp. 251–2); Justin's polemic against Trypho draws on his earlier lost writing against Marcion (p. 104), while his presence is pervasive for Irenaeus. While each of these may be located in Rome, their common concern makes it improbable that anti-Marcionite polemic only took shape in Rome (ctr. Lindemann 1979: 391–2), although it remains possible that Marcion's teaching came to Asia Minor from Rome and need not prove he developed his system before going to Rome: Regul 1969: 188–95. However, it seems unlikely that his heresy already lies behind Ignatius's letters (ctr. R. Hoffmann 1982: 57–62).

⁹⁰ E.g. Tertullian, *Adv. Marc.* II.18–25.

⁹¹ Epiphanius, *Pan.* 42, Schol. 40 on Luke 13.28.

⁹² Cf. Origen, *C. Celsum* VI.53; see above, p. 251, on whether the Elder counters this. According to Irenaeus, Marcion attributed the righteous' failure to respond to their fear that they were again being tempted by their God.

[93] At 1 Thess. 2.15 Marcion emended the text to read 'their own prophets'.

[94] Harnack 1924a: 289*–90*; Harnack cites only *Adv. Marc.* V.15 ('und sonst!') and IV.26 where Marcion read Luke 11.19 as 'Beelzebub by whom your sons cast them out'.

[95] See Meijering 1977: 43, 75–7. The philosophical component in Marcion's thought should not be doubted, but probably belongs to the more generalised and eclectic philosophical views of the age.

[96] So *Adv. Marc.* III.12.1 'you say' ('inquis') = *Adv. Iud.* 9.1 'The Jews say' ('Iudaei dicunt'), although this is followed in 9.2 by 'notice ... inquire' (2p.s. 'spectes .... quaere') = *Adv. Marc.* III.12.2.

[97] *Adv.Marc.* III.13.5 (noted above) 'The Jews dare to lie' that the woman of the Immanuel prophecy is not a virgin; *Adv. Iud.* 9.8, 'you [pl.] dare to lie' ('Iudaei mentiri audent': 'mentiri audetis'). This is a common theme in polemic against the Jews; cf. Irenaeus, *Adv. haer.* III.21.1; Justin, *Dial.* 43.8 etc., pp. 126–7 above.

[98] Tränkle 1964: lxx–lxxiv; so also Barnes 1971: 53, 106–7. However, E. Evans 1972: xix–xx remains agnostic as to the authenticity of *Adv. Iud.* 9–14.

[99] For the former see Tränkle 1964: lxxiv–lxxv; for the latter Barnes 1971: 106–7. For these writers as sources for Tertullian's polemic against the Jews see above, pp. 186–7, and on Justin's reuse of his anti-Marcionite polemic in the *Dialogue*, pp. 104–6.

[100] See Barnes 1971: 127–8; 327 (from the 1985 postscript); E. Evans 1972: xx.

[101] Drijvers 1989: 84.

[102] See pp. 33–4, 71–4 on sabbath in Ignatius and in the *Martyrdom of Polycarp*. Rordorf 1966: 144 asks whether this influenced the development of fasting on the sabbath.

[103] See pp. 29–32 on Ignatius and pp. 85–6 on *M Poly.*

[104] It is notable that in *Adv. Marc.* Tertullian contrasts law with Gospel whereas in the *Adv. Iud.* he prefers the old vs. the new law.

[105] On the chronology and the dates of the *Adv. Marc.* see Barnes 1971: 327 (1985). 'Christianismus' comes only in these Books.

[106] Tertullian's words at IV.33.8, 'quasi non et nos ... agnoscamus' do suggest he is quoting Marcion here on the significance of Luke 16.16. At V.4.8 Tertullian is concerned to show that the allegory of Abraham's two wives, not excised from Gal. 4 by Marcion, demonstrates that both dispensations stem from the one God; his description of them may still come from Marcion. At V.6.10 Isa. 3.3 is interpreted of Paul, called 'out of Judaism for the building of Christianism'; here it is more difficult to know if there is an allusion to Marcion's words.

[107] Passages implying Marcion's use of the term are IV.4.4; V.3.1; uncertain are V.1.8; 3.5; 5.1; 17.9, all of which, with I.20.3, are about Paul.

[108] Outside the *Adv. Marc.* 'Christianismus' appears only once, in *Praes. haer.* 7.38. 'Iudaismus' is restricted to two references which may post-date Tertullian's encounter with Marcion's *Antitheses* (*De res. carn.* 50. 8; *Pud.* 17.; also Ps. Tert., *Adv. omn. haer.* 1; 3; 8) and, surprisingly, to one reference in the *Adversus Iudaeos*: in a discussion of Isa.7.14 and the meaning of 'Emmanuel', Tertullian appeals to 'believers from Judaism' who for 'God is with us' say 'Emmanuel'; the parallel in *Adv. Marc.* speaks of 'Christians, even Marcionites, among the Hebrews' (*Adv. Iud.* 9.26; *Adv. Marc.* III.12.2–3).

[109] Without my bracketed qualification, R. Hoffmann 1982: 233; cf. Wilson 1986a: 57.

[110] See below, pp. 268–9 and nn. 112, 118.

[111] Harnack 1924a: 330*; 1924b: 15–16.

[112] R. Hoffmann 1982: 227, 307.

[113] R. Hoffmann 1982: 4–8, 26–8, 231, 233; see also Wilson 1986a: 56.

[114] See May 1986; Drijvers 1987–8.

[115] C. Mitchell 1921: xxiv.

[116] *Dial.* 35.5–6; 56.16; pp. 112–13.

[117] Marmorstein 1929; Levine 1971: 93f.; see above, p. 248 and n. 26.

[118] Marmorstein 1929: 4; Marmorstein answers these questions by his analysis of the rabbinic sources.

[119] 1929: 25–6.

[120] So Meijering 1977: 35.

[121] See Origen, *C. Celsum.* II.1, 4; V.25, 33.

[122] See for example pp. 183–4.

8

THE JEWS IN THE WORLD OF THE CHRISTIANS

The Christian 'world' in second-century Asia Minor has two quite different referents. There was the wider political, social, cultural and religious world of which the early Christians were members; a world which was as yet in no sense Christian. Christians shared this world with their Jewish and pagan neighbours, unavoidably aware of them since often they were their family, their friends, their 'colleagues' and indeed their old selves. Then there was the social world or symbolic universe; the world of meaning and values which shaped their self-understanding and gave meaning to their experience, a world which was often at odds with the dominant social structures of the former world. This world too is peopled by Jews and by pagans, although now their relationship with them is very different.

We meet both these worlds through literature, and for the most part through Christian literature which offers only one window onto them. Even this literature is that which survives, only a portion of that which was written. If survival or loss is often a matter of accident – Melito's *Peri Pascha* has been rediscovered, Miltiades' *To the Earthly Rulers* has not – it is also sometimes a political act. Except for the accidents of fortune such as ensured the preservation of the library of Nag Hammadi, survival belongs to the victors: Marcion's *Antitheses* are lost, as too is anything written by Cerinthus, often labelled a representative of 'Jewish Christianity', or by Montanus and his followers who called their holy city 'Jerusalem'. By a certain irony, in order to hear their views we depend on their opponents who wanted to silence them.

The literature too is full of ambiguities. We may in the second century begin to leave behind the debates as to the

literary and therefore the social level of early Christian literature, yet questions of intended or actual audience remain.
Moreover, the social assumptions and attitudes of the Apologies, for example of Justin's appeal to all who want to be 'pious and philosophers', or of Melito's equation of the stability
of the Empire with the blossoming of Christianity,[1] are very
different from those of the apocryphal *Acts* of the Apostles. If
in the New Testament period the Paul of the Epistles is very
different from the Paul of Acts, and different again from the
Paul of the Pastoral Epistles or of the *Acts* which bear his name,
so, later, Polycarp changes guise through the eyes of Ignatius,
his own letter to the Philippians, the account of his martyrdom, or the later *Life*: yet each of these is a literary construct.

Each is also an argument, an exercise, as we have seen, in
rhetoric, seeking to persuade, to offer a convincing interpretation of the present, a perspective that others will adopt.
This means that most if not all early Christian writing was meant
to engage with people's lives; it was not the exclusive pastime
of the literary élite. Letters to the churches by Ignatius,
Polycarp, or the church at Smyrna (*M. Poly.*) were to be read
to all present; that too is the context envisaged by Melito's *Peri
Pascha*, and perhaps by pseudepigraphical Gospel or epistolary writings; the 'Elders' taught in some sort of community
and the apocryphal *Acts* probably also had a wide audience.
Only with the Apologies and with Justin's *Dialogue* can we be
slightly less certain of how they impinged on most early Christians' experience. We should not, then, construct too complete
a divorce between the world of literature and that of most people's daily lives.

Yet some distance between the two is inevitable. Literature,
especially ideological or doctrinal, tends to stress differentiation,
whereas social and religious experience tends to be more
untidy. This, as we have seen, is notably true of Asia Minor, where
archaeological and epigraphic evidence implies a far wider range
of common life and expression among pagans, Jews and Christians than the literary sources would at first suggest.[2] In sharp
contrast stands the image projected by *M. Poly.* of the 'customary' hostility of the Jews, siding with and outdoing the pagans in
opposition to Christian faithfulness, or by Justin in his uncompromising choice between 'your teachers' and 'our Christ'. We

should not too hastily project from the literature onto the stage of daily life, but neither should we assume that daily life belongs only to the first of the two worlds with which we started; it is also lived and understood in terms of the interpretative symbolic universe.

The formulae Christians, Jews and pagans shared on their tombs remind us that symbolic universes too may be shared or overlap.[3] In their veneration of angels or of 'God most high', members of each group were both sharing a common world-view and infusing it with their own distinctive outlook, giving it new and differentiated meanings which may not always be clear on the surviving monuments.[4]

Beyond this, Christians and Jews obviously also shared much in common, a subculture in the wider world, something betrayed, perhaps in spite of himself, by Aristides; at the same time they created out of what they held in common that which divided them. Scripture or, for Christians, the Old Testament is but the best example of this: in sharp opposition to their pagan contemporaries, they shared, often, as we have suggested for Justin, literally, the same text and the same exegetical principles, yet this became their most flexible weapon in denying each other's world. Indeed, each of our authors who adopts a rhetoric of differentiation, *M. Poly.*, Justin in his *Dialogue*, and Melito's *Peri Pascha*, betray both their common heritage and their continuing interaction with contemporary Jewish exegesis and interpretation.

Therefore, throughout these explorations we have continued to speak of 'image' and 'reality', while recognising that 'image' does not belong to the literary world alone, and 'reality' to the exernal; neither has it been possible to maintain a simple contrast between these, for each helps construct the other. So too, in exploring the components in this construction we shall not be *explaining* the Christian image of 'the Jew', as if it were the sum of all or any of these; even less shall we be *explaining* Christian anti-Judaism, as if it could be reduced to a phenomenon contingent upon a range of specific variables.[5] There has emerged from these studies no single 'image' and no single 'phenomenon', just as there is no single 'reality'. Yet there are recurring currents or themes to which we may return.

Scripture

Scripture, as we have already noted, was a major element in the subculture shared by Jews and Christians.[6] In the public sphere it belonged to the Jews: copies of the scriptures were to be found and heard in the synagogues; translated into Greek they were the subject of study and interpretation; they constituted the 'ancestral customs' which acted as a charter of rights for the Jewish communities, defining their practices, including worship, sabbath observance, and presumably circumcision, which were often given a protected status; they acted as an authoritative source of appeal in claims to antiquity and continuous record; they may also have had a numinous quality as a store of prophetic utterance or as powerful threat.[7] More fundamentally, the ways in which scripture or Torah determined their self-identity for the Jews are so multiform and well studied as to require only acknowledgement here: Trypho may stand as their spokesman.[8]

The Christians, as we have seen, were often dependent on the Jews for their texts, having to cope, as did Justin, with inconsistencies which arose through translation and frequently through interference from their interpretative use. Yet it is only in direct debate that this could lead to charges of corruption and falsification of the text; in the apologetic mode an appeal to unbroken continuity was more important. There, in the competition in the ancient world for antiquity, Christians had both to affirm that recorded in the scriptures and to deny its reference to their Jewish contemporaries. They had to justify their abandonment of the 'privileges' of sabbath observance and circumcision while retaining the probative force of prophecy, or even of the moral virtues that had become an apologetic truism.

In direct encounters their needs were different. Here competing exegesis moved to the centre, as perhaps it already had in earlier conflicts between groups within Judaism.[9] Possession of the scriptures, 'yours' or 'ours', now meant the exclusive right to interpret them, and to find in them the anticipation both of present convictions and of the opposing unbelief and disobedience. The image of the Jews is a function of these conflicting needs, and shifts accordingly: guarantors of antiquity and of a superior apprehension of the divine, blind readers of the text which points to Christ, preservers of the text or its falsifiers, perverted interpreters, and increasingly, those whose moral and religious failings are already written in and so can be read out of the prophetic rebukes of the past.

Yet there is so far little uniformity. For Ignatius the role of scripture in dividing Judaism from Christianity is poorly articulated, although prophecy has already been assigned a Christian identity; for Justin the argument is intricate, but the Old Testament is already a history of disobedience on the one hand, and of promise on the other, which shapes the contours of the present, for the Jews and the Christians respectively; for the Elder, however, unbelief and rejection do not yet belong indelibly only to the 'others'; for Melito scripture is more of a shadow or prototype in which Christ but not his killers are already to be found. Literalism and legalism are not yet the determinative marks of the image, although it is easy to see why they were to become so.

Christian Tradition

Already in the first century 'the Jews' are becoming the archetypal enemies of Christ and of Christians: as Jesus's death becomes paradigmatic for believers so too does the role of the Jews within it, as is well illustrated by 1 Thessalonians 2. 14–16. Here the image, 'the Jews' as those who killed Jesus, swiftly becomes fixed, recurring in formulaic or credal settings, as in Aristides' *Apology*, as well as in narrative, as in the *Gospel of Peter*, or in worship, as in the *Peri Pascha*. Continuing a process already found in the New Testament, the role of the Romans is submerged, while that of the Jews loses any element of contingency or specificity by being set within a continuous tradition of disobedience or of murder of the prophets. The *Martyrdom of Polycarp* owes much to the power of this image, although not to it alone, while Justin too sees Jewish persecution of Christians as more endemic and characteristic than Roman, even though the latter was the norm.[10] Yet in retrospect it was perhaps Melito, when he wrote Jesus's suffering into the total experience of the Old Testament, and when he cast not on some people restricted to a past narrative but on 'you' the awful responsibility of killing 'the Lord', who of our texts does most to shape an image which would not be forgotten. The 'demonisation of the other', typical of conflict between those who share a common heritage, assumes a new reality on a stage where God is chief protagonist.

Persecution and Martyrdom

It is not just that the Jews become associated with the suffering of Christians. Persecution and martyrdom become key elements in Christian self-understanding in the second century, providing a context where their distinctive identity could and had to be articulated. The 'stubborn' claim 'I am a Christian' signals the adoption of an encompassing world of meaning in which all alternative values are radically qualified. 'Christ-' compounds, the language of discipleship, the imagery of imitation, an ethos of separation from the rest of humankind, all develop naturally in this context.[11] It is not always easy to distinguish here between the real consequences of actual persecution and the creation of a mental world where persecution and conflict is the norm; hence the disparity between some scholarly estimates of the extent of actual persecution before 250 CE and its brooding presence in much Christian literature.[12]

Judaism has a double role in this process. It too went through a similar experience during the period, and developed its own imagery, language and literature in response; these have heavily influenced those of the Christians who continued to read, and eventually were to take over, the Maccabean literature: the third- or fourth-century manuscript which preserves a Coptic translation of Melito's *Peri Pascha* follows that with *The Martyrs of the Jews who lived under Antiochus the King*, namely 2 Maccabees 5.27–7.21.[13] Yet if Christian suffering was to have its testificatory value, Jewish suffering had to be disqualified. Indeed, it even becomes the 'negative' of Christian experience, a testimony to disobedience, to rejection by God, and to exclusion from the promises. This would have met other Christian needs; the dilemma of suffering and defeat, a recurring theme in biblical and Jewish thought, finds its theological resolution as punishment for the Jews, vindication for faithfulness for the Christians. Yet it seems that this was not worked out in isolation; we have caught echoes of debate, exchange of ideas and appeals to formative texts, perhaps a shared response to the values of the Graeco-Roman city.

Internal Conflict

That, despite evidence of such debate, the image of the 'other' is often shaped by internal conflict is on both the individual and the corporate plane a psychological truism which works at many levels. It would be possible, for example, and Marcion could act as a guide here, to see the Christian depiction of the Jews – as misinterpreting the true intentions of God's will and earning the Law as a control against unbridled lawlessness – as a projection of the Christians' own inner conflicts in the understanding of God and of human sin: 'the Jew whom they feared' of Harnack.[14] It is not then surprising when these Jews become targets of arguments directed against Marcion, or a means of discrediting him as their 'ally'. That the Christian refutation of Marcion was achieved only at the cost of a systematic denigration of the Jews, who became the scapegoats in justifying retention of the Old Testament, has been often enough pointed out,[15] although such recognition is a first and not a last step; alternative attempts to make theological sense of God's past activity, such as that represented by the Elder, witness to an as yet unfinished debate.

Yet there were other concerns, less obviously to do with the Jewish heritage or context of the early church. We have seen how in the *Martyrdom of Polycarp* the Jews become a cover for wrestling with Christian conflicts over the veneration of the martyrs. This, and the related problem of an undue enthusiasm for martyrdom, have often been associated with Montanism, against which *M. Poly.* may be waging a sustained polemic.[16] There is little to suggest that Montanism owed anything to specifically Jewish roots or contributed anything substantial to the image of Judaism in Christian counter-polemic; yet there may be an anticipation of how 'the Jews' could become a cover for a number of internal 'opponents' in the years to come.

Perhaps more pertinent was Quartodeciman practice and the controversies it generated. In a later period the charge of judaising or of following the Jews could be used to discredit opponents in the dating of Easter.[17] That the same was true in the second century is supposition; Quartodeciman practice may unite Melito and Polycarp, and Passover traditions may be important for both, but there is only silence to suggest that this demanded a self-defensive hostility against and a distancing from the Jews whom they mirrored.

Perhaps most notable has been the absence of a sustained conflict with Jewish Christians, so often seen as the real targets for Christian polemics against 'the Jews'.[18] Even Ignatius has largely failed to reveal their presence, while Justin, who does address their plight, does so remarkably eirenically.[19] This is not to deny the presence of those whom modern scholarship might so label; yet they are not inspiring anti-Jewish diatribe.

Defining Themselves

In all this we have seen how the image of the Jew belongs to the building of self-image, and how important this process is in the second century. While that self-image has structural as well as ideological dimensions, it is striking how little 'structure' there is in the image of the Jew in these texts. It has often been pointed out that already in Matthew's Gospel there is a careful distinction between 'their' synagogue and the church,[20] while the role of the Pharisees in both Matthew and John is held to reflect the organisation of Judaism at the end of the first century. There is little of this in the second century; for all his emphasis on meeting together, on doing nothing without the bishop, on structures, Ignatius does not see Judaism in similar 'group' terms, neither does he use of it the language of allegiance or belonging; certainly he speaks of systems and of their characeristic markers, sabbath and circumcision, but these are 'social' practices adopted by individuals, and he knows nothing of 'the synagogue'.[21] For the apologists the Jews are defined in terms of race, whether politically, culturally or religiously; as such they belong to the global stage of humankind on which Christianity is claiming its own place. Justin in his *Dialogue* does thinks of teachers and of synagogue rulers; he knows of synagogues as places of prayer where the scriptures are kept and presumably taught; yet he too does not think of opposing structures and membership, and 'church' (ἐκκλησία) is of little importance to him.[22] A scholarship which often has defined or interpreted Judaism in terms shaped by Christianity's own structural and ideological values must decide how far these texts refute such models, how far they suggest alternative, but perhaps equally false, ones.

Members of a Pagan World

Even while creating a self-identity which set it against the values of contemporary society, Christianity in the second century saw itself as 'belonging to the Gentile world in general and to the Roman empire in particular'.[23] Of course, this was for the most part no less true for the Jewish communities. Yet this is not how they appear through Christian eyes; only in the *Martyrdom of Polycarp* do the Jews make common cause with their pagan neighbours; elsewhere they are 'others', particularly as Christians increasingly identified themselves as drawn from a gentile past.[24]

We may then reasonably wonder how far Christians also adopted or carried over existing pagan attitudes to the Jews or their 'antisemitism'. This is a question which has been much debated,[25] and cannot be pursued in detail here. Yet we have seen how Ignatius, in focusing on circumcision and sabbath, reflects the perceptions of his pagan neighbours and, no doubt, of his own past, and how Justin makes play on the idleness of the sabbath, as well as on the Roman perception of circumcision in the aftermath of the Bar Kochba revolt. On an ideological level the animus that inspired pagan or Christian polemic was no doubt very different, yet to deny any connection is to divorce ideology from daily living. Pagan antisemitism, which also should not be universalised, is not the birthplace of, neither does it explain, the Christian manifestation; Melito, for example, owes little consciously to that aspect of his pagan upbringing, if indeed anti-Jewish rhetoric was as commonplace as collected sources too easily suggest. Yet if in shaping their own image the Christians were deliberately denying that imposed upon them by their pagan audience, in shaping the image of the Jews they could expect less resistance.

Competition

The image of a Judaism which Christianity has left behind has been repeatedly contradicted by the evidence of an implicit, only occasionally explicit, competition between them. Competing claims to the scriptures, which, as already noted, also belonged to the public sphere, rival interpretations of the Isaac narratives, of martyrdom, or of the Passover memory, have pointed to an encounter which was not merely a stage-piece or an academic exercise. Both the Apologies and the *Dialogue* of Justin suggest a real competition, whether over respectability or over potential adherents and supporters. This is not the place to return to the debate about whether there was active proselytising by Jews or by Christians;[26] it is to repeat the conviction, confirmed by our texts, that this was not a theoretical debate carried on in the minds of the Christians as an exercise in self-justification. How differently it might have been presented from the Jewish side, and what value might have been given to it, is beyond our knowledge. Yet there is here real encounter, positive and creative as well as passive or hostile.

Shaping the Image

Perhaps more than anything, especially as we look to the future, the Jews and Judaism represent that which Christianity has left behind, a foil to the universal claims that were to become characteristic of Christian rhetoric, a differentiation particularly noticeable in the Apologies. This is an image which has remained remarkably persistent, most notoriously in the now abandoned label 'late Judaism', and in the more enduring tendency to see, and to study, Judaism as a fossil from the first century, if not from the pages, particularly Torah and prophetic denunciation, of the 'Old Testament'.

It is as an extension of this that they are also the Jews of Palestine and of recent historical experience there. The fall of Jerusalem in 70 CE was engraved deep in Christian consciousness: it shapes decisively the argument of both Justin and of Melito. Merged with it, if only in part by the former, is the defeat under Bar Kochba. The Jews are those who should, but can no longer, sacrifice in their Temple in Jerusalem. They are defined by the loss of their city and Temple, and by the devastation of their land.[27] There is little hint that they could continue an authentic existence without these, either in Palestine or in the Diaspora, although both Trypho – who, we must remember, speaks only with the permission of Justin – and, by the implications of his silence regarding Temple or sacrifice, Aristides know that to be the case. Yet other aspects of that history are ignored; although the imposition of the *fiscus iudaicus* and its alleviation under Nerva have been seen as formative in the development of Jewish, and hence of a separate Christian, self-identity,[28] it is not until Origen in the next century that there is any mention of this by a Christian author. Any other experiences which might have shaped the contemporary Jewish communities of the cities, for example any backlash following the Trajanic revolts, are passed over in silence.

Jews in the World of the Christian Writers

Already it has become impossible to separate the threads which make up the construction of the image from the real context in which it was formed. Here we need not return again to the undoubted evidence for continuing Jewish–Christian meeting and sharing, friendly as well as polemical. Yet we may still ask whether exploring the Christian image allows us to glimpse something of the reality which lay behind it. At various points we have drawn on our other evidence of the Judaism of Asia Minor, finding it enriching our understanding of the genesis of the image, and often, perversely, confirmed by it. A good example would be all that has already been said about the significance of the scriptures and the continuing role of Greek versions, perhaps for far longer than the survival of the Septuagint at Christian hands would suggest.[29]

Yet this importance of scripture cannot be equated with the 'turning towards the ever finer interpretation of the Law' too often deduced from the character of rabbinic literature and from Christian polemics against Jewish literalism and legalism. As yet the very different ways in which Jews and Christians were to read scripture are not apparent; instead we find similar texts, similar exegetical techniques, diverging sharply in conclusion only because of the divergence between their initial presuppositions.

Yet if a focus on scripture tends towards a focus on separation, as confirmed by Trypho's objections to Christianity, there were also other dimensions to the 'sacred'; we have found hints, although they are to become stronger in later centuries, of the role of miracle or exorcism, and perhaps of the veneration of angels.[30] This is not the syncretism of older accounts; the Jews of our texts have clearly defined identities, although perhaps because only so do they meet our authors' needs. Justin is only able to 'prove' the persistent idolatrous weakness of his Jewish opponents by appeal to scripture and by rhetoric, not by contemporary evidence, whereas he is all too aware of those whom he, but not Trypho, perceives as false Christians who willingly eat food sacrificed to idols.

We have found other hints of attitudes to diaspora living, to proselytes, to apologetic, to scriptural or liturgical traditions. Where these find some confirmation only in traditions from Palestine or 'rabbinic' Judaism,[31] we can proceed only with caution. Yet, while it would be wrong to return to an imposition on the Diaspora of a picture drawn from our Hebrew and Aramaic sources, the vibrant and self-confident Judaism of the former now being regularly affirmed must have developed corresponding spiritual and intellectual structures, inevitably within an exegetical framework.[32] If the survival for the most part only of literary sources for early Christianity may distort our picture of their life and experience, so equally does their virtual absence for the diaspora Judaism of the same period. The Christian 'image' may offer us important traces of a lost world.

The image of the Jew shifts with author, context and, most important, with literary genre. Even more important, in exploring this theme we have not discovered a total explanation or characterisation of second-century Christianity. This goes a long way to qualify any argument that Christianity was decisively shaped by a formative battle with Judaism, the oft-repeated 'image' of the child who discovers her identity only through conflict with her mother, or the brother through the love–hate relationship with his all-too-similar sibling. We have had to go looking for the image of the Jew, and sometimes, as in the apocryphal *Acts*, have had but little success in finding it. The theme has not been demanded by the literature but has been imposed upon it, and it would have been possible to study a number of our texts with only cursory attention to it.[33]

This is not to deny that before long Christian authors constructed an image of the Jew which would meet their own needs, social, theological or political, or that this process is already at work in the second century and earlier. Yet for all the continuities, the process by which 'from neighbours came Jews'[34] was and remained shifting and fluid. So too, whether in dialogue and theological exploration today, or when we enter the Christian world of the second century, must we encounter those who are both neighbours and Jews.

Notes

[1] See above, pp. 183–4, 188, and, on Justin, Holfelder 1977.

[2] See above, pp. 8–9, and Lieu 1994c.

[3] Robert 1978: 245–9.

[4] Sheppard 1980–1; Kraabel 1969.

[5] See M. Taylor 1995, who warns that by reducing anti-Judaism to dependence on various historical circumstances, particularly the vibrancy of contemporary Judaism, scholars are able to avoid the pressing question how far it is intrinsic to Christian thinking.

[6] So Horbury 1992: 102.

[7] As the 'charter' see Smallwood 1981: 359; for their antiquity in apologetic debate see Josephus, *C. Apion.* I.37–43; Barton 1986: 59–60; for appeals to the curses of Deuteronomy on gravestones see n. 3 above.

[8] See his affirmation of the requirements for true reverence of God, pp. 114–15 above.

[9] For example, the significant role given exegesis among the Dead Sea scrolls.

[10] See Lieu 1996.

[11] Both Ignatius and *M. Poly.* witness to this.

[12] Perkins 1985.

[13] Goehring 1990.

[14] See above, pp. 112–13, 123–4.

[15] See above, pp. 251–2, 262.

[16] So Buschmann 1994.

[17] Grumel 1960.

[18] See above, pp. 42–7, on Ignatius.

[19] See pp. 138–9.

[20] See Stanton 1992a: 97–8.

[21] The term comes only at *Poly.* 4.2 in an exhortation for more frequent assemblies.

[22] Only at *Dial.* 134.3 is there a contrast with συναγωγή; see above, pp. 141–2.

[23] Chadwick 1965: 287.

[24] See pp. 136–7 for Justin, p. 252 for the Elder, and p. 242 for Polycarp.

[25] Gager 1983.

[26] See Goodman 1994a and above, pp. 106–8.

[27] See above, pp. 178, 217.

[28] Goodman 1994a: 121–5; Hemer 1986: 8–11.

[29] Treu 1973: 144.

[30] See Lightstone 1984: 125–40; 1988.

[31] See above pp. 111, 124 on Justin; pp. 222–8 on Passover traditions in Melito.

[32] We cannot generalise from Philo but neither can we reduce him to an aberrant exception.

[33] So Buschmann 1994 in his study of *M. Poly.* makes only passing reference to the 'antiJudaism' of the text which he largely attributes to the theme of 'according to the Gospel', while not excluding the possibility of a judaising threat (pp. 156–60, 259).

[34] The title of Rosenstrauch 1988, a study of how 'the Jew' became a symbol in the Germany of 1933–42.

BIBLIOGRAPHY

Texts and translations

Editions of texts have been listed in the full bibliography; those of writings discussed are listed here for ease of reference. For other ancient sources see index of references.

Ignatius
Lightfoot 1889 and 1891
Lindemann and Paulsen 1992
Schoedel 1985

Martyrdom of Polycarp
Dehandschutter 1979
Lindemann and Paulsen 1992
Musurillo 1972

Justin Martyr: Dialogue
Goodspeed 1914
A. Williams 1930

Apologists
Geffcken 1907
Goodspeed 1914
Harris 1891
Marcovich 1994
Otto 1872
Seeberg 1894

Melito
Bonner 1940
Hall 1979
Perler 1966

Apostolic Traditions
Elders (incl. Polycarp and Papias)
Harvey (1857) (Irenaeus)
Lightfoot 1891
Rousseau 1965 (Irenaeus)
Retelling the Story
Junod and Kaestli 1983
Schmidt 1904
Schneemelcher 1992
Vouaux 1913 and 1922
Marcion
Evans 1972 (Tertullian)
C. Mitchell 1921 (Ephraim)

Secondary Sources

Achetemeier, P. 1976. 'Jesus and the Disciples as Miracle Workers in the Apocryphal New Testament', in E. S. Fiorenza, ed., *Aspects of Religious Propaganda in Judaism and Early Christianity* (Notre Dame and London) 149–86.

Aland, B. 1973. 'Marcion. Versuch einer neuen Interpretation', *ZThK* 70: 420–47.

Aland, K. 1960. 'Bemerkungen zum Montanismus und zu frühchristlichen Eschatologie', in idem, *Kirchengeschichtliche Entwürfe* (Gütersloh) 105–48.

Alexander, P. 1984. 'Epistolary Literature', in M. E. Stone, ed., *Jewish Writings of the Second Temple Period. Apocrypha etc.* (The Literature of the Jewish People in the Period of the Second Temple and Talmud II. CRINT 2, Assen and Philadelphia) 579–96.

— 1992. '"The Parting of the Ways" from the Perspective of Rabbinic Judaism', in J. Dunn, ed., 1992: 1–25.

van Amersfoort, J. and van Oort, J., eds., 1990. *Juden und Christen in der Antike* (Kampen).

Amir, Y. 1982. 'The Term Ιουδαισμος (IOUDAISMOS). A Study in Jewish-Hellenistic Self- Definition', *Immanuel* 14: 34–41.

— 1985. 'Das jüdische Paradox auf dem Grunde der hellenistischen Judenfeindschaft', in idem, *Studien zum Antiken Judentum* (Frankfurt au Main) 114–21.

Anderson, G. 1994. *Sage, Saint and Sophist. Holy Men and their Associates in the Early Roman Empire* (London).

Andresen, C. 1965. 'Zum Formular frühchristlicher Gemeindebriefe', *ZNW* 56: 233–59.

Andriessen, P. 1947. 'The Authorship of the Epistula ad Diognetum', *VC* 16: 129–36.

Angerstorfer, I. 1985. 'Melito und das Judentum' (Diss., Regensburg).

Arazy, A. 1977. 'The Apellations of the Jews (IOUDAIOS, HEBRAIOS, ISRAEL) in the Literature from Alexander to Justinian' (Ph.D. New York, 1977. UM 78–3061).

Ashton, J. 1994. *Studying John: approaches to the fourth Gospel.* (Oxford).

Aziza, C. 1981. 'Juifs et Judaïsme dans le monde Romain: état des recherches (1976–80)', *REL* 59: 44–52.

Baeck, L. 1935. 'Das dritte Geschlecht', in S. Baron and A. Marx, eds., *Jewish Studies in Memory of G. A. Kohut* (New York) 40–6.

Bamberger, B. J. 1939. *Proselytism in the Talmudic Period* (New York. repr. KTAV, 1968).

Bammel, C. P. 1982. 'Ignatian Problems', *JTS* ns. 33: 62–97.

Bammel, E. 1987. 'Rückehr zum Judentum', *Augustinianum* 27: 317–29.

Baneth, E. 1968. *Mishnayot II Moed* (Basel).

Bardy, G. 1949. 'Sur l'apologiste Quadratus', *Mélanges H. Grégoire: Annuaire de l'Institut de Philologie et d'Histoire Orientales et Slaves* 9: 75–86.

Barnard, L. W. 1964a. 'Hadrian and Christianity', *CQR* 165: 277–89.

—— 1964b. 'The Old Testament and Judaism in the Writings of Justin Martyr', *VT* 14: 395–406.

—— 1970. 'In Defence of Pseudo-Pionius' account of Saint Polycarp's Martyrdom', in P. Granfield and J. Jungmann, eds., *Kyriakon* (Fs. J. Quasten, Münster) I, 192–204.

Barnes, T. 1967. 'A Note on Polycarp', *JTS* ns. 18: 433–7.

—— 1968. 'Pre-Decian *Acta Martyrorum*', *JTS* ns. 19: 509–31.

—— 1971. *Tertullian. A Historical and Literary Study* (Oxford, 2nd edn. 1985).

Barrett, C. K. 1976. 'Jews and Judaizers in the Epistles of Ignatius', in R. Hamerton-Kelly and R. Scroggs, eds., *Jews, Greeks and Christians. Religious Cultures in Late Antiquity* (Fs. W. D. Davies. SJLA 21, Leiden) 220–44.

Barton, J. 1986. *Oracles of God. Perceptions of Ancient Prophecy in Israel after the Exile* (London).

Bartsch, H. W. 1940. *Gnostisches Gut und Gemeindetradition bei Ignatius v. Antiochen* (Gütersloh).

Bastiaensen, A. A. R., et al.1987. *Atti e Passioni dei Martiri* (Milan 1990[2]).

Bauckham, R. 1993. 'The *Acts of Paul* as a Sequel to Acts', in B. W. Winter and A. D. Clarke, eds., *The Book of Acts in its Ancient Literary Setting* (The Book of Acts in its First Century Setting I, Grand Rapids and Carlisle) 105–52.

Bauer, W. 1971. *Orthodoxy and Heresy in Earliest Christianity* (ET R. Kraft. London).

Baumeister, T. 1980. *Die Anfänge der Theologie des Martyriums* (MBTh. 45, Münster).

Beaujeu, J. 1973. 'Les Apologètes et le culte du souverain', in W. den Boer, ed., *Le Culte des souverains dans l'empire romain* (Entretiens Hardt.19, Geneva).

Beckwith, R. 1985. *The Old Testament Canon of the New Testament Church, and its Background in Early Judaism* (London).

Berger, D., ed. 1986. *History and Hate* (Philad., New York, Jerusalem).

Berger, K. 1975. 'Jüdisch-Hellenistische Missionsliteratur und Apokryphe Apostelakten', *Kairos* 17: 233–48.

Bernays, J. 1885. 'Die Gottesfürchtigen bei Juvenal', in H. Usener, ed., *Gesammelte Abhandlungen von Jacob Bernays* (Berlin) 71–80.

Beyschlag, K. 1965. 'Das Jakobsmartyrium und seine Verwandten in der frühchristlichen Literatur', *ZNW* 56: 149–78.

   1966.   *Klemens Romanus und der Frühkatholizmus* (BHT 35, Tübingen).

Bickermann, E. 1980. 'The Altars of the Gentiles. A Note on the Jewish "Ius Sacrum"', in idem, *Studies in Jewish and Christian History* II (AGAJU 9, Leiden) 324–46.

Binyamin, B.-Z. 1987. '*Birkat ha minim* and the Ein Gedi Inscription', *Immanuel* 21: 68–79.

Birley, A. 1966. *Marcus Aurelius* (London).

Black, M. 1958-9. 'The Patristic Accounts of Jewish Sectarianism', *BJRL* 41: 285–303.

Blackman, P. 1952. *Mishnayoth II. Order Moed* (London).

Blanchetière, F. 1973. 'Aux sources de l'anti-judaisme chrétien', *RHPhR* 53: 354–98.

   1974.   'Juifs et non juifs. Essai sur la diaspora en Asie–Mineure', *RHPhR* 54: 367–82.

   1981.   'Le Christianisme Asiate aux IIème et IIème siècles' (Univ. Strasbourg Thesis. Service de reproduction des Theses Université de Lille III).

Blank, J., ed. 1963. *Meliton von Sardes: Vom Passa* (Freiburg im Breisgau).

Bloedhorn, H. 1990. 'Appendix' to M. Hengel, 1990: 64–72.

Blumenkranz, B. 1946. *Die Judenpredigt Augustins* (Basle).

den Boeft, J. and Bremmer, J. 1985. 'Notiunculae Martyrologicae III. Some observations on the Martyria of Polycarp and Pionius', *VC* 39: 110–70.

1991. 'Notiunculae Martyrologicae IV' *VC* 45: 105–22.

1995. 'Notiunculae Martyrologicae V' *VC* 49: 146–64.

Bokser, B. M. 1983. 'Rabbinic Responses to Catastrophe. From Continuity to Discontinuity', *PAAJR* 50: 37–61.

1984. *The Origins of the Seder* (California and London).

Bommes, K. 1976. *Weizen Gottes* (Theophaneia 27, Cologne, Bonn).

Bonner, C., ed. 1940. *The Homily on the Passion by Melito of Sardis* (Studies & Documents XII. London, Philadelphia).

Bonz, M. P. 1990. 'The Jewish Community of Ancient Sardis: A Reassessment of its Rise to Prominence', *HSCP* 93: 343–59.

1993. 'Differing Approaches to Religious Benefaction: The Late Third-Century Acquisition of the Sardis Synagogue', *HTR* 86: 139–54.

Borgen, P. 1987a. 'Debates on Cirumcision', in idem, *Philo, Paul and John. New Perspectives on Paul and Early Christianity* (BJS 131, Atlanta) 61–71.

1987b. 'The Early Church and the Hellenistic Synagogue', ibid.: 207–32.

Botermann, H. 1990. 'Die Synagoge von Sardes: Eine Synagoge aus dem 4. Jahrhundert?', *ZNW* 81: 103–121.

Bousset, W. 1915. *Jüdisch-Christlicher Schulbetrieb in Alexandria und Rom* (FRLANT nf. 6, Göttingen).

Bovon, F. and Junod, E. 1986. 'Reading the Apocryphal Acts of the Apostles', in D. R. McDonald, ed., *The Apocryphal Acts of the Apostles* (*Semeia* 38, Decatur) 161–71.

Bremmer, J. 1989. 'Why did Early Christianity attract Upper Class Women?', in A. Bastiaensen, A. Hilhorst and C. Kneepkens, eds., *Fructus Centesimus* (Mél. G. Bartelink. Instr. Patr. 19, Dordrecht) 37–48.

Brind' Amour, P. 1980. 'La Date du martyre de Saint Polycarp (le 23 février 167)', *AnBoll* 98: 456–62.

Brocke, M. D. 1977. 'On the Jewish Origin of the "Improperia"', *Immanuel* 7: 44–51.

van den Broek, R. 1988. '*Der Brief des Jakobus am Quadratus* und das Problem der judenchristliche Bischöfe von Jerusalem (Eusebius *HE* IV, 5, 1–3)' in T. Baarda et al., eds., *Text and Testimony* (Fs. A. F. J. Klijn, Kampen) 56–65.

Brooten, B. 1982. *Women Leaders in the Ancient Synagogue* (BJS 36, Chico).

Brown, R. E. 1979. *The Community of the Beloved Disciple* (New York and London).

Buschmann, G. 1994. *Martyrium Polycarpi – Eine formkritische Studie; ein Beitrag zur frage nach der Enstehung der Gattung Märtyrerakte* (BZNW 70, Berlin and New York).

    1995. '*Martyrium Polycarpi* 4 und der Montanismus', *VC* 49: 105–43.

Cadoux, C. 1938. *Ancient Smyrna* (Oxford).

Cameron, A. 1991. *Christianity and the Rhetoric of Empire. The Development of Christian Discourse* (Sather Classical Lectures 53, Berkeley, Los Angeles, Oxford).

von Campenhausen, H. 1951. *Polykarp v Smyrna und die Pastoralbriefe* (*SHAW* Ph-H Klasse 2, 1951, Heidelberg).

    1957. 'Bearbeitungen und Interpolationen des Polykarpmartyriums' (*SHAW* Ph-H Klasse 8, 1957, Heidelberg) [reprinted in idem, *Aus der Frühzeit des Christentums* (Tübingen, 1963) 253–301].

    1970. 'Die Enstehung der Heilsgeschichte. Der Aufbau des christlichen Geschichtesbildes in der Theologie des ersten und zweiten Jahrhunderts', *Saeculum* 21: 189–212.

Cantalamessa, R. 1967. *L'omelia "In S. Pascha" dello Pseudo-Ippolito di Roma* (Milan).

Carleton Paget, J. 1994. *The Epistle of Barnabas. Outlook and Background* (WUNT 2.64, Tübingen).

Carmichael, D. B. 1991. 'David Daube on the Eucharist and the Passover Seder', *JSNT* 42: 45–67.

Chadwick, H. 1965. 'Justin Martyr's Defence of Christianity', *BJRL* 47 (1965) 275–97 [reprinted in idem, *History and Thought of the Early Church* (London, 1982) ch. 7].

Childs, B. 1974. *Exodus* (OTL, London).

Clarke, G. W. 1966. 'Irenaeus, Ad. Haer. 4.30.1', *HTR* 59: 95–7.

Cohen, S. 1981–2/1987. 'Epigraphical Rabbis', *JQR* 72: 1–17; *JSS* 38: 102–6.

    1986. '"AntiSemitism" in Antiquity: The Problem of Definition', in D. Berger, 1986: 43–8.

    1987. 'Pagan and Christian Evidence on the Ancient Synagogue', in L. Levine, ed., *The Synagogue in Late Antiquity* (Philadelphia) 159–181.

    1989. 'Crossing the Boundary and Becoming a Jew', *HTR* 82: 13–33.

Colin, J. 1964. *L'Empire des Antonins et les martyrs gaulois de 177* (Antiquitas I, Bonn).

    1965. 'L'Importance de la comparaison des calendriers païens et chrétiens pour l'histoire des persécutions', *VC* 19: 233–6.

Collins, J. J. 1984. *Between Athens and Jerusalem. Jewish Identity in the Hellenistic Diaspora* (New York).

1985. 'A Symbol of Otherness: Circumcision and Salvation in the First Century', in J. Neusner and E. Frerichs, eds., 1985: 163–86.

Conzelmann, H. 1978. 'Bemerkungen zur Martyrium Polycarpus', *NAWG* Ph-H Klasse 1977. (Göttingen) 41–58.

Corwin, V. 1960. *St Ignatius and Christianity in Antioch* (Yale).

Cosgrove, C. H. 1982. 'Justin Martyr and the Emerging Christian Canon', *VC* 36: 209–32.

van Damme, D. 1976. 'ΜΑΡΤΥΣ-ΧΡΙΣΤΙΑΝΟΣ Überlegungen zur ursprünglichen Bedeutung des altkirchlichen Märtyretitels', *FZPhT* 23: 286–303.

Daniel, J. L. 1979. 'Anti-Semitism in the Hellenistic-Roman Period', *JBL* 98: 45–65.

Daniélou, J. 1964. *The Theology of Jewish Christianity* (ET J. A. Baker. London).

1969. 'Bulletin d'histoire des origenes chrétiennes. 1. Le christianisme asiate au second siècle', *RechSR* 57: 75–92.

Daube, D. 1966. *He that Cometh* (St Paul's Lecture, London).

1968. 'The Significance of the Afikoman', *Pointer* 3: 4–5.

Davids, A. 1973. 'Irrtum und Häresie', *Kairos* 15: 165–87.

1983 *Iustinus philosophus et martyr. Bibliographie* (Kath. Univ. Nijmegen).

Davies, A., ed. 1979. *Antisemitism and the Foundations of Christianity* (New York).

Davies, P. R. 1979. 'Passover and the Dating of the Aqedah', *JJS* 30: 59–67.

1982 'Martyrdom and Redemption; on the Development of Isaac Typology in the Early Church', in E. Livingstone, ed., *Studia Patristica* XVII.2 (Oxford) 652–8.

Davies, P. R. and Chilton, B. 1978. 'The Aqedah: A Revised Tradition History', *CBQ* 40: 514–46.

Davies, S. 1976. 'The Predicament of Ignatius of Antioch', *VC* 30: 175–80.

Le Deaut, R. 1970. 'Aspects de l'intercession dans le judaisme ancien', *JSJ* 1: 35–57.

Dehandschutter, B. 1979. *Martyrium Polycarpi. Een literair-kritische Studie* (BETL 52, Leuven).

1982. 'Le Martyre de Polycarpe et le dévelopment de la conception du martyre au deuxième siècle', in E. Livingstone, ed., *Studia Patristica* XVII.2 (Oxford) 659–68.

1989. 'Anti-judaism in the Apocrypha', in E. Livingstone, ed., *Studia Patristica* XIX (Leuven) 345–50.

1993. 'The Martyrdom of Polycarp: a Century of Research', *ANRW* II.27.1: 485–522.

Denker, J. 1975. *Die theologiegeschichtliche Stellung des Petrusevangeliums* (Bern and Frankfurt).

Donahue, P. 1973. 'Jewish-Christian Controveries in the Second Century. A Study in the Dialogue of Justin Martyr' (Ph.D. Yale, 1973. UM. Ann Arbor, 73–25,197).

1978. 'Jewish Christianity in the Letters of Ignatius of Antioch', *VC* 32: 81–93.

Dörrie, H. 1971. 'Was ist "spätantiker Platonismus"?', *TRu* 36: 285–302.

Drijvers, H. 1987–8. 'Marcionism in Syria: Principles, Problems, Polemics', *Second Century* 6: 153–77.

1989. 'Christ as Warrior and Merchant. Aspects of Marcion's Christology', in E. Livingstone, ed., *Studia Patristica* XXI (Leuven) 73–85.

Drobner, H. 1982. '15 Jahre Forschung zu Melito von Sardes (1965–1980)', *VC* 36: 313–33.

Droge, A.J. 1989. *Homer or Moses? Early Christian Interpretations of the History of Culture* (HUT 26, Tübingen).

Dunn, J., ed. 1992. *Jews and Christians. The Parting of the Ways* AD *70 to 135* (WUNT 66, Tübingen).

Eckert, W. P., Levinson, N. P., Stöhr, M. 1967. *Antijudaismus im Neuen Testament?* (Munich).

Efroymson, D. 1979. 'The Patristic Connection', in A. Davies, ed., 1979: 98–117.

Emerton, J. A. 1970. 'Were Greek Transliterations of the Old Testament used by Jews before the Time of Origen?', *JTS* ns. 21: 17–31.

1971. 'A Further Consideration of the Purpose of the Second Column of the Hexapla', *JTS* ns. 22: 15–28.

Essig, K.-G. 1986. 'Mutmassungen über den Anlass des Martyriums von Ignatius von Antiochien', *VC* 40: 105–17.

Evans, E. 1972. *Tertullian. Adversus Marcionem* (2 vols. OECT, Oxford).

Falls, T. B. 1946. *St. Justin Martyr* (FoC 6, Washington).

Feischer, E. 1964. 'Jerusalems Untergang in der urchristlichen und altkirchlichen Überlieferung', *TLZ* 89: 81–98.

Feldman, L. 1986. 'Anti-Semitism in the Ancient World', in D. Berger, ed., 1986: 15–42.

1993. *Jew and Gentile in the Ancient World* (Princeton).

Fischel, H. A. 1947. 'Martyr and Prophet', *JQR* 37: 265–80, 363–86.

Fischer, J. 1956. *Die Apostolischen Väter* (Munich).

Flusser, D. 1974. 'Hebrew Improperia', *Immanuel* 4: 51–4.

    1977. 'Some Notes on Easter and the Passover Haggadah', *Immanuel* 7: 52–60.

Frederiksen, P. 1991. 'Judaism, The Circumcision of the Gentiles, and Apocalyptic Hope: Another Look at Galatians 1 and 2', *JTS* ns. 42: 532–64.

Fredouille, J. C. 1972. *Tertullian et la conversion de la culture antique* (Paris).

Frend, W. H. C. 1964. 'A Note on the Chronology of Polycarp and the Outbreak of Martyrdom', in *Oikumene. Studi Paleochristiani pubblicati in onore del concilio Ecumenico Vaticano II* (Catania).

    1965. *Martyrdom and Persecution in the Early Church* (Oxford).

    1973. 'The Old Testament in the Age of the Greek Apologists', *SJT* 26: 129–50.

Freudenberger, R. 1967. 'Christenreskript. Ein umstrittenes Reskript des Antoninus Pius', *ZKG* 78: 1–14.

Friedländer, M. 1878. *Patristische und Talmudische Studien* (Vienna).

Friesen, S. 1993. *Twice Neokoros. Ephesus, Asia and the Cult of the Flavian Imperial Family* (Leiden).

Gabba, E. 1962. 'L'*Apologia* di Melitone di Sardi', *Critica Storica* 1: 469–82.

Gager, J. 1983. *The Origins of AntiSemitism. Attitudes Towards Judaism in Pagan and Christian Antiquity* (New York and Oxford).

Gaston, L. 1979. 'Paul and the Torah', in A. Davies, ed., 1979: 48–71.

    1986. 'Judaism of the Uncircumcised in Ignatius of Antioch and Related Writers', in S. Wilson, ed., 1986c: 33–44.

Geffcken, J. 1907. *Zwei Griechische Apologeten* (Leipzig and Berlin).

Georgi, D. 1967. 'Der Kampf um die reine Lehre im Urchristentum als Auseinandersetzung um das rechte Verständnis der an Israel ergangenen Offenbarung Gottes', in Eckert et al., ed., 1967: 82–94.

Gero, S. 1978. 'Jewish Polemic in the Martyrium Pionii and a "Jesus" Passage from the Talmud', *JJS* 29: 164–68.

Goehring, J. 1990. *The Crosby Schoyen Codex MS 193 in the Schoyen Collection* (CSCO 521. Subsidia 85, Louvain).

Goldfahn, A. 1883. 'Justinus Martyr und die Agada', *MGWJ* 22: 49–60, 104–15, 145–53, 193–202, 257–69.

Goldsten, H. 1979. *Gottesverächter und Menschenfeinde?* (Düsseldorf).

Goodenough, E. R. 1923. *The Theology of Justin Martyr* (Jena [Amsterdam, 1968 repr.]).

Goodman, M. 1989a. *Who was a Jew?* (Yarnton Trust for Oxford Centre for Postgraduate Hebrew Studies).

    1989b 'Proselytising in Rabbinic Judaism', *JJS* 40: 175–85.

1992. 'Jewish Proselytising in the First Century', in J. Lieu, J. North and T. Rajak, eds., 1992: 53–78.

1994a. *Mission and Conversion. Proselytizing in the Religious History of the Roman Empire* (Oxford).

1994b. 'Jews and Judaism in the Mediterranean Diaspora in the Late-Roman Period: The Limitations of Evidence', *JMedStuds.* 4: 208–24.

Goodspeed, E. 1914. *Die ältesten Apologeten. Texte mit kurzen Einleitungen* (Göttingen. repr. 1984).

Gordon, R. L. 1990. 'Religion in the Roman Empire', in M. Beard and J. L. North, eds., *Pagan Priests: Religion and Power in the Ancient World* (London) 233–55.

Goulder, M. D. 1994. 'Vision and Knowledge', *JSNT* 56: 53–71.

Grant, R. M. 1955. 'The Chronology of the Greek Apologists', *VC* 9: 25–33.

1963. 'Scripture and Tradition in Ignatius of Antioch', *CBQ* 25: 322–35.

1988. *Greek Apologists of the Second Century* (London).

Grégoire, H. and Orgels, P. 1951. 'La Veritable Date du martyre de S. Polycarpe (23 février 177) et le "Corpus Polycarpum"', *AnBoll* 69: 1–38.

Grégoire, H., Orgels, P., Moreau, J. and Maniq, A. 1964. *Les Persecutions dans l'Empire Romain* (Acad. royale de Belgique. Cl. de Lettres et des Sci. Mor. et Pol. Mémoires 56.5, Brussels).

Grumel, V. 1960. 'Le Problème de la date pascale aux IIIe et IVe siècles', *REByz* 18: 163–78.

Guillaumin, M.-L. 1975. 'En marge du "Martyre de Polcarpe". Le discernment des allusions scripturaires', in *Forma Futuris* (Fs. M. Pellegrino, Paris) 462–9.

Guy, F. 1964. '"The Lord's Day" in the Letter of Ignatius to the Magnesians', *AUSS* 2: 1–17.

Guyot, P. and Klein, R. 1993–4. *Das Frühe Christentum bis zum Ende der Verfolgungen* I & II. (TzF 60, 62, Darmstadt).

Hall, S. 1971. 'Melito in the Light of the Passover Haggadah', *JTS* ns. 22: 29–46.

1979. *Melito of Sardis On Pascha and Fragments* (OECT, Oxford).

1984. 'The Origins of Easter', in E. Livingstone, ed., *Studia Patristica* XV (TU 128, Berlin) 554–67.

Hanfmann, G. M. A. 1963. 'The Fifth Campaign at Sardis (1962)', *BASOR* 170: 1–62, 38–48.

1983. *Sardis from Prehistoric to Roman Times* (assisted by W. Mierse. Cambridge, Mass. and London).

Hanfmann, G. M. A., and Bloom, J. 1987. 'Samoe, Priest and Teacher of Wisdom', *Eretz Israel* (M. Avi Yonah Memorial Volume) 19: 10*–14*.

Hann, R. 1987. 'Judaism and Jewish Christianity in Antioch: Charisma and Conflict in the First Century', *JRH* 22: 341–60.

Hansen, A. 1968. 'The Sitz im Leben of the Paschal Homily of Melito of Sardis with special Reference to the Paschal Festival in Early Christianity' (Diss., N.W. Univ. 1968. DissAbstr. 29.2343A).

Harakas, S. S. 1967. 'The Relation of Church and Synagogue in the Apostolic Fathers', *St Vladimir's Seminary Quarterly* 11: 123–38.

Hare, D. 1967. *The Theme of Jewish Persecution of Christians in the Gospel according to St Matthew* (SNTSMS 6, Cambridge).

Harkins, P. 1979. *Saint John Chrysostom. Discourses Against Judaizing Christians* (FoC 68, Washington).

Harl, M. 1986. 'La "Ligature" d'Isaac (GEN 22,9) dans la Septante et chez les pères grecs', in A. Caquot, M. Hadas-Lebel, J. Riaud, eds., *Hellenica et Judaica* (Fs. V. Nikiprowetzky, Leuven and Paris) 457–72.

von Harnack, A. 1883. *Die Altercatio Simonis Iudaei et Theophilii Christiani* (TU 1.3, Leipzig).

— 1904. *The Expansion of Christianity in the First Three Centuries* (ET J. Moffatt. London).

— 1907. 'Der Presbyter-Prediger des Irenäus (IV,27,1 – 32,1)', in *Philotesia. Paul Kleinert zum 70 Geburtstag* (Berlin) 1–37.

— 1913. 'Judentum und Judenchristentum in Justins Dialog mit Trypho', TU 39.1 (Leipzig) 47–98.

— 1924. *Marcion. Das Evangeliums vom Fremden Gott; Neue Studien zu Marcion* (TU 45. Leipzig[2]).

Harris, J. Rendel 1891. *The Apology of Aristides on behalf of the Christians* (with an appendix by J. A. Robinson) (*Texts and Studies* I, Cambridge).

Harrison, P. N. 1936. *Polycarp's Two Epistles to the Philippians* (Cambridge).

Harvey, A. E. 1966. 'Melito and Jerusalem', *JTS* ns. 17: 401–4.

Harvey, W. W. 1957. *S. Irenaei. Libros quinque adversus haereses*. 2 vols. (Cambridge).

Hemer, C. 1986. *The Letters to the Seven Churches of Asia in their Local Setting* (JSNT.SS 11, Sheffield).

Hengel, M. 1966. 'Die Synagoge von Stobi', *ZNW* 57: 145–83.

— 1971. 'Proseuche und Synagoge. Jüdische Gemeinde, Gotteshaus und Gottesdienst in der Diaspora und in Palästina', in G. Jeremias, H.-W. Kuhn, H. Stegemann, eds., *Tradition und Glaube* (Fs. K. G. Kuhn, Göttingen) 157–84.

1984–5. 'Hadrians Politik gegenüber Juden und Christen', *JANES* 16–17: 153–81.

1990. 'Der Alte und der Neue 'Schürer'', *JSS* 35: 19–72.

1992. 'Die Septuaginta als von den Christen beanspruchte Schriftensammlung bei Justinus und den Vätern vor Origenes', in J. Dunn, ed., 1992: 39–84.

Henrichs, A. 1970. 'Pagan ritual and the Alleged Crimes of the Early Christians', in P. Granfield and J. Jungmann, eds., *Kyriakon* (Fs. J. Quasten, Münster) I, 18–35.

van Henten, J. 1986. 'Datierung und Herkunft des vierten Makkabäerbuches', in idem et al., ed., *Tradition and Reinterpretation in Jewish and Early Christian Literature* (Fs. J. Lebram. SPB 36, Leiden) 136–49.

1989a. ed., *Die Enstehung der Jüdischen Martyrologie* (SPB 38, Leiden).

1989b. 'Das Jüdische Selbstverständnis in den Ältesten Martyrien', in J. van Henten, ed., 1989a: 127–61.

1993. 'Zum Einfluss jüdischer Martyrien auf die Literatur des frühen Christentums, II. Die Apostolischen Väter', *ANRW* II.27.1: 700–23.

1994. 'A Jewish Epitaph in a Literary Text: 4 Macc. 17:8–10', in J. van Henten and P. van der Horst, 1994: 44–69.

van Henten, J. and van der Horst, P. W., eds. 1994. *Studies in Early Jewish Epigraphy* (AGAJU 21, Leiden).

Herr, M. D. 1972. 'Persecutions and Martyrdom in Hadrian's Days', *ScriptHier* 2: 85–125.

Higgins, A. J. B. 1967. 'Jewish Messianic Belief in Justin Martyr's *Dialogue with Trypho*', *NT* 9: 295–305.

Hilgenfeld, A. 1879. 'Das Martyrium Polykarp's von Smyrna', *ZWT* 22: 145–70.

Hirshman, M. 1992–3. 'Polemic Literary Units in the Classical Midrashim and Justin Martyr's *Dialogue with Trypho*', *JQR* 83: 369–84.

Hoffmann, L. A. 1981. 'Censoring in and Censoring Out: A Function of Liturgical Language', in J. Gutman, ed., *Ancient Synagogues* (BJS 22, Chico) 19–37.

Hoffmann, M. 1966. *Der Dialog bei den christlichen Schriftstellern der erstern vier Jahrhunderte* (TU 96, Berlin).

Hoffmann, R. J. 1984. *Marcion: On the Restitution of Christianity* (AAR Academy Series 46, Chico).

Hoheisel, K. 1978. *Das antike Judentum im christlicher Sicht* (Studies in Oriental Religions 2, Wiesbaden).

Holfelder, H. H. 1977. Ἐυσέβεια καὶ φιλοσοφία. Literarische Einheit und politischer Kontext von Justins Apologie', *ZNW* 68: 48–66, 231–51.

Holl, K. 1928. 'Die Vorstellung vom Märtyrer und die Märtyreracte in ihrer geschichtlichen Entwicklung', in *Gesammelte Aufsätze zur Kirchengeschichte* II (Tübingen) 68–102.

Horbury, W. 1982. 'The Benediction of the *Minim* and Early Jewish–Christian Controversy', *JTS* ns. 33: 19–61.

— 1985. 'Extirpation and Excommunication', *VT* 35: 13–38.

— 1992. 'Jews and Christians on the Bible: Demarcation and Convergence [325–451]', in J. van Oort and U. Wickert, eds., *Christliche Exegese zwischen Nicaea und Chalcedon* (Kampen) 72–103.

— 1994. 'Jewish Inscriptions and Jewish Literature in Egypt with Special Reference to Ecclesiasticus', in J. van Henten and P. van der Horst, eds., 1994: 9–43.

Horbury, W. and McNeil B., eds. 1981. *Suffering and Martyrdom in the New Testament* (Cambridge).

Horsley, G. H. R. 1992. 'The Inscriptions of Ephesus and Asia Minor', *NT* 34: 105–68.

van der Horst, P. W. 1989. 'Jews and Christians in Aphrodisias in the Light of their Relations in other Cities of Asia Minor', *NTT* 43: 106–21.

— 1992. 'A New Altar of a Godfearer?', *JJS* 43: 32–7.

Hruby, K. 1971. *Juden und Judentum bei den Kirchenvätern* (Zurich).

— 1973. 'Exégèse Rabbinique et Exégèse Patristique', *RevSciRel* 47: 341–69.

Huber, W. 1969. *Passa und Ostern* (BZNW 35, Berlin).

Hübner, R. M. 1989. 'Melito von Sardes und Noët von Smyrna', in D. Papandreou, W. Bienert, K. Schäferdiek, eds., *Oecumenica et Patristica* (Fs. W. Schneemelcher. Stuttgart, Berlin, Cologne) 219–40.

Hulen, A. B. 1932. 'The "Dialogues with the Jews" as Sources for the Early Jewish Argument against Christianity', *JBL* 51: 58–70.

Hurtado, L. 1988. *One God, One Lord* (London).

Hyldahl, N. 1956. 'Tryphon und Tarphon', *StTh* 10: 77–88.

— 1966. *Philosophie und Christentum* (Copenhagen).

Isaac, B. and Oppenheimer, A. 1985. 'The Revolt of Bar Kochba. Ideology and Modern Scholarship', *JJS* 36: 33–60.

Jackson, F. J. 1927. *The Rise of Gentile Christianity* (London).

Johnson, S. 1975. 'Asia Minor and Early Christianity', in J. Neusner, ed., *Christianity, Judaism and Other Greco-Roman Cults* (Fs. Morton Smith. SJLA 12, Leiden) II. 77–145.

304   *Image and Reality*

Joly, R. 1973. *Christianisme et philosophie* (Brussels).

     1979. *Le Dossier d'Ignace d'Antioche* (Ed. de l'Univ. Bruxelles).

Jonkers, E. J. 1943. 'Einige Bemerkungen über das Verhältnis der christlichen Kirche zum Judentum vom vierten bis auf das siebente Jahrhundert', *Mnemosyne* 11 (ser. 3): 304–20.

Junod, E. 1984. 'La Formation et la composition de l'ancien testament dans l'église grecque des quatres premiers siècles', in J. D. Kaestli and O. Wermlinger, eds., *Le Canon d'ancien testament* (La Monde de la Bible, Geneva) 105–51.

Junod, E. and Kaestli, J.D. 1983. *Acta Iohannis* (CC.SA. Turnhout).

Juster, J. 1914. *Les Juifs dans L'empire romain* I (Paris).

Kampling, R. 1984. *Das Blut Christi. Mt 27,25 bei den lateinischensprachigen christlichen Autoren bis zu Leo dem Großen* (NTAb, nf.16. Münster).

Karpp, H. 1954. 'Christennamen', *RAC* II: 1114–38.

Katz, P. 1957. 'Justin's O.T. Quotations and the Greek Dodekapropheton Scroll', in K. Aland and F. L. Cross, eds., *Studia Patristica* I (TU 63, Berlin) 343–53.

Katz, S. 1984. 'Issues in the Separation of Judaism and Christianity after 70 CE: A Reconsideration', *JBL* 103: 43–76.

Kearsley, R. A. 1987. 'Some Asiarchs of Ephesos', in G. H. R. Horsley, ed., *New Documents Illustrating Early Christianity IV. A Review of the Greek Inscriptions and Papyri Published in 1979* (Macquarie Univ.) 46–55.

Kellermann, U. 1980. 'Zum traditionsgeschichtlichen Problem des Stellvertretenden Sühnestodes in 2 Makk 7.37f.', *BibNot* 13: 63–83.

     1989. 'Das Danielbuch und die Martyrtheologie der Auferstehung', in J. van Henten, ed., 1989: 51–75.

Kimelmann, R. 1981. '*Birkat Ha-Minim* and the Lack of Evidence for an Anti-Christian Jewish Prayer in Late Antiquity', in E. P. Sanders with A. I. Baumgarten and A. Mendelson, eds., *Jewish and Christian Self-Definition* II *Aspects of Judaism in the Greco-Roman Period* (London) 226–44.

Kinzig, W. 1990. 'Der "Sitz im Leben" der Apologie in den Alten Kirche', *ZKG* 100: 291–317.

Kittel, G. 1944. 'Das kleinasiatischen Judentum in der hellenistisch-römischen Zeit', *TLZ* 64: 9–20.

Klauck, H. J. 1989. *4 Makkabäerbuch* (JSHRZ III.6, Gütersloh).

Klevinghaus, J. 1948. *Die theologische Stellung der Apostolischen Väter zur alttestamentlichen Offenbarung* (Gütersloh).

Klijn, A. F. J. 1963. 'The Apocryphal Correspondence between Paul and the Corinthians', *VC* 17: 2–23.

Kominiak, B. 1948. *The Theophanies of the OT in the Writings of St Justin* (Cath. Univ. of Amer. Studies in Sacred Theol. 2:14, Washington).

Körtner, U. 1983. *Papias von Hierapolis. Ein Beitrag zur Geschichte des frühen Christentum* (Göttingen).

Köster, H. 1959. 'Häretiker im Urchristentum', *RGG* III [3]: 18–21.

1965. 'ΓΝΩΜΑΙ ΔΙΑΦΟΡΑΙ', *HTR* 38: 279–318.

Kraabel A. T. 1968. 'Judaism in Western Asia Minor under the Roman Empire with a Preliminary Study of the Jewish Community at Sardis' (Harvard D. Th. Cambridge, Mass.).

1969. 'Υψιστος and the Synagogue at Sardis', *GRBS* 10: 81–93.

1971. 'Melito the Bishop and the Synagogue at Sardis: Text and Context', in D. G. Mitten, J. G. Pedley, J. A. Scott, eds., *Studies Presented to George M. A. Hanfmann* (Mainz) 77–85 (reprinted in J. Overman and R. MacLennan, eds., 1992: 197–205).

1978. 'Paganism and Judaism: The Sardis Evidence', in *Paganisme, Judaisme, Christianisme* (Mél. M. Simon, Paris) 13–33.

1981. 'Social Systems of Six Diaspora Synagogues', in J. Gutmann, ed., *Ancient Synagogues: The State of Research* (Chico, Calif.) 79–91 (reprinted in J. Overman and R. MacLennan, eds. 1992: 257–68).

1992. 'The Synagogue at Sardis: Jews and Christians', in J. Overman and R. MacLennan, eds., 1992: 225–36.

1994. 'Immigrants, Exiles, Expatriates and Missionaries', in L. Bormann, K. del Tredici, A. Standhartinger, eds., *Religious Propaganda and Missionary Competition in the New Testament World* (Fs. D. Georgi. NT.S. 74, Leiden) 71–88.

Kraeling, C. 1932. 'The Jewish Community at Antioch', *JBL* 33: 130–66.

Kraemer, R. 1991. 'Jewish Tuna and Christian Fish. Identifying Religious Affiliation in Epigraphic Sources', *HTR* 84: 141–62.

Kraft, R. 1965. 'Some Notes on Sabbath Oservance in Early Christianity', *AUSS* 3: 18–33.

Krauss, S. 1892–3. 'The Jews in the Works of the Church Fathers', *JQR* 5: 122–57; 6: 83–9, 225–61.

1922. *Synagogale Altertümer* (Berlin and Vienna).

Kretschmar, G. 1972. 'Christliches Passa im 2. Jahrhundert und die Ausbildung der Christlichen Theologie', *RechSR* 60: 287–323.

Kürzinger, J. 1983. *Papias von Hierapolis und die Evangelien des Neuen Testaments* (Eischstätter Materialen 4, Regensburg).

Lampe, G. W. H. 1973. '"Grievous wolves" (Acts 20: 29)', in B. Lindars and S. Smalley, eds., *Christ and Spirit in the New Testament* (Fs. C. F. D. Moule, Cambridge) 253–68.

1981. 'Martyrdom and Inspiration', in W. Horbury and B. McNeil, eds., 1981: 118–35.

Lampe, P. 1987. *Die Stadtrömischen Christen in den ersten beiden Jahrhunderten* (WUNT 2.18, Tübingen).

Laeuchli, S. 1972. 'The Drama of Replay', in M. Friedman, T. P. Burke, S. Laeuchli, eds., *Searching in the Syntax of Things* (Philadelphia) 69–126.

Lane Fox, R. 1986. *Pagans and Christians* (Harmondsworth).

de Lange, N. 1976. *Origen and the Jews. Studies in Jewish-Christian Relations in Third-Century Palestine* (Cambridge).

1978. 'Antisemitismus IV. Alte Kirche', *TRE* III, 128–37.

Langmuir, G. 1990. *Towards a Definition of Antisemitism* (Berkeley, Los Angeles, London).

Lerch, D. 1950. *Isaaks Opferung Christlich Gedeutet* (BHT 12, Tübingen).

Levenson, J. D. 1993. *The Death and Resurrection of the Beloved Son. The Transformation of Child Sacrifice in Judaism and Christianity* (New York and London).

Levi, I. 1912. 'La Dispute entre les égyptiens et les juifs', *REJ* 63: 211–16.

Levine, E. 1971. 'Some Characteristics of Pseudo-Jonathon Targum to Genesis', *Augustinianum* 11: 89–103.

Lewis, R.B. 1968. 'Ignatius and the "Lord's Day"', *AUSS* 6: 46–59.

Lieu, J. 1992. 'History and Theology in Early Christian Views of Judaism', in J. Lieu, J. North, T. Rajak, eds., 1992: 79–96.

1993. 'What was from the Beginning: Scripture and Tradition in the Johannine Epistles', *NTS* 39: 458–77.

1994a. 'Do God-fearers make Good Christians', in S. E. Porter, P. Joyce, D. E. Orton, *Crossing the Boundaries. Essays in Biblical Interpretation in Honour of Michael D. Goulder* (Bib. Interp. Series 8, Leiden) 329–45.

1994b. 'Circumcision, Women and Salvation', *NTS* 40: 358–70.

1994c. '"The Parting of the Ways": Theological Construct or Historical Reality', *JSNT* 56: 101–19.

1995a. 'Reading in Canon and Community: Deut. 21. 22–23, A Test Case for Dialogue', in M. D. Carroll, D. J. Clines, P. R. Davies, eds., *The Bible in Human Society* (Fs. J. Rogerson, Sheffield) 317–34.

1995b. 'The Race of the God-fearers', *JTS* ns. 46: 483–501.

1996. 'Accusations of Jewish Persecution in early Christian Sources', in G. N. Stanton and G. Stroumsa, eds., *Tolerance and its Lim-*

its in Early Judaism and Early Christianity (Cambridge, forth-coming).

Lieu, J., North, J., and Rajak, T., eds. 1992. *The Jews between Pagans and Christians in the Roman Empire* (London).

Lightfoot, J. B. 1889. *The Apostolic Fathers* (2 parts in 5 vols. Rev. edn., London).

— 1891. *The Apostolic Fathers. Revised Texts with Short Introductions and English Translations*, ed. and completed by J. R. Harmer (London).

Lightstone, J. 1984. *The Commerce of the Sacred: Mediation of the Divine among Jews in the Graeco-Roman Diaspora* (BJS 59, Chico).

— 1986. 'Christian Anti-Judaism in its Judaic Mirror: The Judaic Context of Early Christianity Revisited', in S. Wilson, ed, 1986c: 103–32.

— 1988. *Society, the Sacred and Scripture in Ancient Judaism* (Studies in Christianity & Judaism III, Ontario).

Lim, R. 1995. *Public Disputation, Power and Social Order in Late Antiquity* (Berkeley, Los Angeles, London).

Lincoln, A. T. 1995. Review of E. Faust, *Pax Christi et Pax Caesaris. Religionsgeshichtliche, traditionsgeschichtliche und sozialgeschichtliche Studien zum Epheserbrief* (NTOA 24. Freiburg and Göttingen, 1993), *JTS* ns. 45: 288–93.

Lindemann, A. 1979. *Paulus im ältesten Christentum. Das Bild des Apostels und die Rezeption der paulinische Theologie in der frühchristlichen Literatur bis Marcion* (BHT 58, Tübingen).

Lindemann, A. and Paulsen, H. 1992. Trans. and ed. *Die Apostolischen Väter* (Greichisch-deutsche Parallelausgabe auf der Grundlage der Ausgaben von F. X. Funk, K. Bihlmeyer und M. Whittaker mit Übersetzungen von M. Dibelius und D.-A. Koch) (Tübingen).

Linder, A. 1987. *The Jews in Roman Imperial Legislation* (Detroit and Jerusalem).

Lipsius, R. A. 1883–90. *Die Apokryphen Apostelgeschichten und Apostellegenden* (Braunschweig).

Lohse, B. 1953. *Das Passafest der Quartodecimaner* (BFCT 2.54, Gütersloh).

Loofs, F. 1930. *Theophilus von Antiochen Adversus Marcionem und die anderen theologischen Quellen bei Irenaeus* (TU 46.2, Leipzig).

Lowy, S. 1958. 'The Extent of Jewish Polygamy in Talmudic Times', *JJS* 9: 115–38.

— 1960. 'The Confutation of Judaism in the Epistle of Barnabas', *JJS* 11: 1–11.

Lucas, L. 1910. *Zur Geschichte der Juden im vierten Jahrhundert. Der Kampf zwischen Christentum und Judentum* (Berlin).

Lüderitz, G. 1983. *Corpus jüdischer Zeugnisse aus der Cyrenaika* mit einem Anhang von Joyce M. Reynolds (B.TAVO. Weisbaden: Reichert).

Lührmann, D. 1981. 'POx 2949: EvPt 3–5 in einer Handschrift des 2/3 Jahrhunderts', *ZNW* 72: 217–26.

1993. 'POx 4009. Ein Neues fragment des Petrusevangeliums?', *NT* 35: 390–410.

MacLennan, R. S. 1990. *Early Christian Texts on Jews and Judaism* (BJS 194, Atlanta).

MacMullen, R. 1983. 'Two Types of Conversion to Early Christianity', *VC* 37: 174–92.

Maier, H. 1991. *The Social Setting of the Ministry as Reflected in the Writings of Hermas, Clement and Ignatius* (Dissertations *SR* 1. Waterloo, Ontario).

Maier, J. 1978. *Jesus von Nazareth in der talmudischen Überlieferung* (ErFor 82, Darmstadt).

Malherbe, A. 1970. 'The Apologetic Theology of the *Preaching of Peter*', *Restoration Quarterly* 13: 205–23.

Manis, A. 1987. 'Melito of Sardis: Hermeneutic and Context', *Greek Orthodox Theological Review* 32: 387–401.

Marcovich, M. 1990. *Pseudo-Iustinus. Cohortatio ad Graecos. De Monarchia. Oratio ad Graecos* (PTS 32, Berlin and New York).

1994. *Iustini Martyri Apologiae pro Christianis* (PTS 38, Berlin and New York).

Marmorstein, A. 1919. 'Jews and Judaism in the Earliest Christian Apologies', *The Expositor* VIII. 17: 73–80, 100–16.

1926. 'Eine apologetische Mischna', *MGWJ* 70 (1926) 376–85.

1950. 'The Background of the Haggadah', in idem, *Studies in Jewish Theology – the Arthur Marmorstein Memorial Volume*, ed. J. Rabinowitz and M. S. Lew (London) 1–71 (originally published in *HUCA* 6 (1929)).

Les Martyrs de Lyon (177) 1978. (Coll. Int. CRNS 575, Paris).

Manns, F. 1979. *Bibliographie du Judéo-Christianisme* (Jerusalem).

Marcus, R. 1951. ' Appendix C. Alexander the Great and the Jews', in *Josephus VI* (LCL. London and Cambridge, Mass.) 512–32.

Marrou, H.-I. 1953. 'La Date du martyre de S. Polcarpe', *AnBoll* 71: 5–20.

May, G. 1986. 'Ein neues Marcionbild?', *TRu* 51: 404–13.

1987–8. 'Marcion in Contemporary Views: Results and Open Questions', *The Second Century* 6: 129–52.

Meeks, W. and Wilken, R. 1978. *Jews and Christians in Antioch in the First Four Centuries of the Christian Era* (Missoula).

Meijering, E. P. 1977. *Tertullian Contra Marcion. Gotteslehre in der Polemik Adversus Marcionem 1–11* (Philosophia Patrum III, Leiden).

Meinhold, P. 1952. 'Polykarpos' 1), PW 21.2 (Stuttgart) 1662–93.

1979a. 'Schweigende Bischöfe. Die Gegensätze in den kleinasiatischen Gemeinden nach den Ignatien', in idem, *Studien zu Ignatius von Antiochien* (Weisbaden) 19–37.

1979b. 'Die Geschichtstheologischen Konzeptionen bei Ignatius von Antioch', ibid.: 37–47.

Mélèze-Modrzejewski, J. 1990. 'L'Image du juif dans la pensée grecque vers 300 avant notre ère', in A. Kasher, U. Rappaport, G. Fuks, eds., *Greece and Rome in Eretz Israel. Collected Essays* (Jerusalem) 105–18.

Mendelson, A. 1988. *Philo's Jewish Identity* (BJS 161, Atlanta).

Merkelbach, R. 1975. 'Der griechische Wortschatz und die Christen', *ZPE* 18: 101–48.

Mildenberg, L. 1984. *The Coinage of the Bar Kochba War* (Typos VI, Sauerländer etc.).

Millar, F. 1992. 'The Jews of the Graeco-Roman Diaspora between Paganism and Christianity. AD 312–438', in J. Lieu, J. North, T. Rajak, eds., 1992: 97–123.

1993. *The Roman Near East, 31 BC– AD 337* (Cambridge, Mass. and London).

Mitchell, C. 1921. *S. Ephraim's Prose Refutations of Mani, Marcion and Bardaisan* Vol. 2 (London and Oxford).

Mitchell, S. 1990. 'Festivals, Games and Civic Life in Roman Asia Minor', *JRS* 80: 183–93.

1993. *Anatolia. Land, Men, and Gods in Asia Minor* (2 vols., Oxford).

Molland, E. 1954. 'The Heretics Combatted by Ignatius of Antioch', *JEH* 5: 1–6.

Mueller, J. 1993. 'Anti-Judaism in the New Testament Apocrypha. A Preliminary Survey', in C. A. Evans and D. A. Hagner, eds., *Anti-Semitism and Early Christianity. Issues of Polemic and Faith* (Minneapolis) 253–68.

Müller, H. 1908. 'Das Martyrium Polycarpi. Ein Beitrag zur altchristlichen Heiligengeschichte', *Römische Quartalschrift* 22: 1–16.

Müller, M. 1989. 'Graeca sive Hebraica Veritas? The Defense of the Septuagint in the Early Church', *SJOT* 1989/1: 103–24.

Müller, U.B. 1976. *Zur frühchristlichen Theologiegeschichte: Judenchristentum und Paulinismus im Kleinasien an der Wende vom ersten zum zweiten Jahrhundert n. Chr.* (Gütersloh).

Musurillo, H. 1972. *The Acts of the Christian Martyrs* (OECT, Oxford).

Nautin, P., ed. 1951. *Homélies Pascales I. Une homélie inspirée du Traité sur La Paque d'Hippolyte* (SC 27, Paris).

1974 'Les Citations de la "Prédication de Pierre" dans Clément d'Alexandrie', *JTS* ns. 25: 98–105.

Naveh, J. and Shaked, S. 1985. *Amulets and Magic Bowls* (Jerusalem and Leiden).

Neusner, J. 1971. *Aphrahat and Judaism* (SPB 19, Leiden).

Neusner, J. and Frerichs, E., eds. 1985. *'To See Ourselves as Others See Us'. Christians, Jews, 'Others' in Late Antiquity* (Chico).

Niebuhr, K.-W. 1994. '"Judentum" und "Christentum" bei Paulus und Ignatius', *ZNW* 85: 218–33.

Nikolai, K. 1963. 'Feiertage und Werktage in römischen Leben, besonders in den Zeit der ausgehenden Republik und in der frühen Kaiserzeit', *Saeculum* 14: 194–220.

Nikolasch, F. 1963. *Das Lamm als Christussymbol in den Schriften der Väter* (Wiener Beiträge zur Theologie III, Vienna).

Nilson, J. 1977. 'To whom is Justin's Dialogue with Trypho Addressed?', *TS* 38: 538–46.

Noakes, K. W. 1975. 'Melito of Sardis and the Jews', in E. Livingstone, ed., *Studia Patristica* XIII (TU 116, Berlin) 244–9.

Norris, F. 1986. 'Melito's Motivation', *ATR* 68: 16–24.

North, J. 1992. 'The Development of Religious Pluralism', in J. Lieu, J. North, T. Rajak, eds. 1992: 174–93.

O'Ceallaigh, G. C. 1958. '"Marcianus" Aristides, On the Worship of God', *HTR* 51: 227–54.

Olster, D. M. 1994. *Roman Defeat, Christian Response and the Literary Construction of the Jew* (Philadelphia).

Opelt, I. 1980. *Die Polemik in der christlichen lateinischen Literatur* (Bibl.der klass. Altertumswissenschaft nf. 2.63, Heidelberg).

Orbe, A. 1972. 'Ecclesia, sal terrae según San Ireneo', *RechSR* 60: 219–40.

Osborn, E. F. 1973. *Justin Martyr* (BHT 47, Tübingen).

Otto, J. C. T. 1872. *Corpus Apologetarum Christianorum Saeculi Secundi* IX (Jena).

Overman, J. A. and MacLennan, R. S., eds. 1992. *Diaspora Jews and Judaism. Essays in Honor of, and in Dialogue with A. Thomas Kraabel* (South Florida Studies in the History of Judaism 41, Atlanta).

Parke, H. W. 1985. *The Oracles of Apollo in Asia Minor* (London, Sydney, Dover, New Hampshire).

Parkes, J. 1934. *The Conflict of Church and Synagogue* (London).

Paulsen, H. 1977. 'Das Kerygma Petri und die urchristliche Apologie', *ZKG* 88: 1–37.

Penna, R. 1982. 'Les Juifs à Rome au temps de l'apôtre Paul', *NTS* 28: 321–47.

Perkins, J. 1985. 'The Apocryphal Acts of the Apostles and the Early Christian Martyrdom', *Arethusa* 18: 211–30.

Perler, O. 1949. 'Das vierte Makkabaerbuch, Ignatius von Antiochen und die ältesten Martyrerberichte', *Revista di Archeologia* 25: 47–72.

1963.   'Récherches sur le *Peri Pascha* de Méliton', *RechSR* 51: 407–21.

1964.   'L'Évangile de Pierre et Méliton de Sardes', *RBib* 71: 584–90.

1966.   *Méliton de Sardes. Sur la Pâque et Fragments* (SC 123, Paris).

Peterson, E. 1958. 'Das Praescritpum des 1. Clemens-briefes', in idem, *Frühkirche, Judentum und Gnosis* (Freiburg) 129–36 [reprinted from *Pro regno, pro sanctuario* (Fs. G. van der Leeuw. Nijkerk, 1950)].

Petuchowski, J. J. 1960. 'Diaspora Judaism – An Abnormality? The Testimony of History', *Judaism* 9: 17–28.

Petzl, G. 1982–7. *Die Inschriften von Smyrna* (Öst. Akad. der Wissenschaft. Rheinisch-Westfälisch Akad. der Wiss., Bonn).

Pines, S. 1974. 'From Darkness into Great Light', *Immanuel* 4: 47–51.

Porton, G. 1988. *GOYIM. Gentiles and Israelites in Mishnah – Tosefta* (BJS 155, Atlanta).

Potter, D.S. 1990. *Prophecy and History in the Crisis of the Roman Empire. A Historical Commentary on the Thirteenth Sibylline Oracle* (Oxford).

Price, S. 1984. *Rituals and Power. The Roman Imperial Cult in Asia Minor* (Cambridge).

Prigent, P. 1964. *Justin et l'ancien testament* (ÉtBib. Paris).

1977.   'L'Hérésie Asiate et l'église confessante de l'Apocalypse à Ignace', *VC* 31: 1–22.

Purves, G. 1889. *The Testimony of Justin Martyr to Early Christianity* (New York).

Rajak, T. 1985a. 'Jews and Christians as Groups in a Pagan World', in J. Neusner and E. Frerichs, eds., 1985: 247–62.

1985b.   'Jewish Rights in the Greek Cities Under Roman Rule: A New Approach', in W. S. Green, ed., *Approaches to Ancient Judaism* V (BJS 32, Atlanta) 19–35.

1992.   'The Jewish Community and its Boundaries', in J. Lieu, J. North, T. Rajak, eds., 1992: 9–28.

Rajak, T. and Noy, D. 1993. '*ARCHISYNAGOGOI:* Office, Title and Social Status in the Greco-Jewish Synagogue', *JRS* 83: 75–93.

Ramsay, W. M. 1902. 'The Jews in the Greco-Asiatic Cities', *The Expositor* VI.5 [55]: 19–33, 92–109.

Regul, J. 1969. *Die AntiMarcionitischen Evangelienprologe* (Vetus Latina. Aus der Geschichte der lateinischen Bibel 6, Freiburg).

Reinach, S. 1885. 'Saint Polycarpe et les juifs de Smyrne', *REJ* 11: 235–8.

Resnick, M. 1992. 'The Codex in Early Jewish and Christian Communities', *JRH* 17: 1–17.

Richardson, P. 1969. *Israel in the Apostolic Church* (SNTSMS 10, Cambridge).

Riesenfeld, H. 1961. 'Reflections on the Style and the Theology of St Ignatius of Antioch', in F. L. Cross, ed., *Studia Patristica* IV (TU 79, Berlin) 312–22.

Robert, L. 1960. *Hellenica XI–XII* (Limoges-Paris).

    1964. *Nouvelles inscriptions de Sardes I* (Paris).

    1966. *Documents de l'Asia Mineure méridionale* (Geneva and Paris).

    1978. 'Malédictions funéraires grecques', *CRAIBL* 1978: 241–89.

    1994. *Le Martyre de Pionios. Prêtre de Smyrne* (mis au point et complété G. W. Bowersock and C. P. Jones. Dumbarton Oaks Research Library & Collection, Washington).

Rogers, G. 1991. *The Sacred Identity of Ephesus. Foundation Myths of a Roman City* (London).

Rohde, J. 1968. 'Häresie und Schisma im ersten Clemensbrief und in den Ignatius-Briefen', *NT* 10: 217–33.

Rokeah, D. 1982. *Jews, Pagans and Christians in Conflict* (Jerusalem).

Root, M. 1984. 'Images of Liberation: Justin, Jesus and the Jews', *The Thomist* 48: 512–34.

Rordorf, W. 1966. *Sunday. The History of the Day of Rest and Worship in the Earliest Centuries of the Christian Church* (ET A. A. Graham, London).

    1972. 'Aux origenes du culte des martyrs', *Irénikon* 45: 315–31.

    1977. 'Zur Enstehung der christlichen Märtyrerverehrung', in H. Cancik, ed., *Aspekte Frühchristlicher Heiligenverehrung* (Oikonomia 6, Erlangen) 35–53.

    1980. 'Zum Problem des "grossen Sabbats" im Polykarp- und Pioniusmartyrium' in E. Dassmann and K. Frank, eds., *Pietas* (Fs. B. Kötting. JbAC Ergbd. 8, Münster) 245–9.

    1988. 'In welchem Verhältnis stehen die apokryphen Paulusakten zur kanonische Apostelgeschichte und zu den Pastoralbriefen', in T. Baarda et al., eds., *Text and Testimony* (Fs. A. F. J. Klijn, Kampen) 225–41.

1990. 'Wie steht es um den jüdischen Einfluss auf den christlichen Martÿrerkult', in J. van Amersfoort and J. van Oort, eds., 1990: 61–71.

Rosenstrauch, H. 1988. *Aus Nachbarn wurden Juden. Ausgrenzung und Selbstbehauptung 1933–1942* (Berlin).

Rossner, M. 1974. 'Asiarchen und Archiereis Asias', *Studi Clasice* 16: 101–42.

Rousseau, A. 1965. *Irenaeus. Contre les hérésies. Adversus haereses* IV (SC 100, 101. Paris).

Ruether, R. 1974. *Faith and Fratricide. The Theological Roots of Antisemitism* (New York).

Rutgers, L. 1992. 'Archaeological Evidence for the Interaction of Jews and Non-Jews in Late Antiquity', *AJA* 96: 101–18.

Salmon, G. 1877. 'Apolinaris', *Dictionary of Christian Biography* I (London) 132–3.

Sanders, E. P. 1992. *Judaism, Practice and Belief* (London).

Sanders, J. T. 1987. *The Jews in Luke-Acts* (London).

Sandmel, S. 1978. *Anti-semitism in the New Testament?* (Philadelphia).

Saxer, V. 1982. 'L'Authenticité du "Martyre de Polycarpe"; Bilan de 25 ans de critique', *Mélanges de l'École Française de Rome Antiquité* 94,2: 979–1001.

1986. *Bible et hagiographie. Textes et themes bibliques dans les Actes des martyrs authentiques des premiers siècles* (Berne, Frankfurt, New York).

Schäfke, W. 1979. 'Frühchristlicher Widerstand', *ANRW* II. 23.1: 460–723.

Schmidt, C., ed. 1904. *Acta Pauli aus der Heidelberger Koptischen Papyrushandscrift* (Veröffentlichungen aus der Heidelberger Papyrussammlung II, Leipzig).

Schneemelcher, W. 1974. 'Histoire du salut et empire romain: Méliton de Sardes et l'état', *BullLitEccl* 75: 81–98.

1992. ed. *New Testament Apocrypha* (Rev. edn. of coll. initiated by E. Henneke. ET ed. R. McL. Wilson. Cambridge and Louisville; [1965 edn. London]).

Schoedel, W. 1967. ed. *Polycarp, Martyrdom of Polycarp, Fragments of Papias* (*The Apostolic Fathers*, R. M. Grant, ed., Vol. 5, London and Toronto).

1978. 'Ignatius and the Archives', *HTR* 71: 97–106.

1980. 'Theological Norms and Social Perspectives in Ignatius of Antioch', in E. P. Sanders, ed. *Jewish and Christian Self-Definition* I *The Shaping of Christianity in the Second and Third Centuries* (London) 30–56.

1985. *Ignatius of Antioch* (Hermeneia, Philadelphia).

1989. 'Apologetic Literature and Ambassadorial Activities', *HTR* 82: 55–78.

1993. 'Polycarp of Smyrna and Ignatius of Antioch', in *ANRW* II.27.1: 272–358.

Scholer, D. M. 1982. 'Tertullian on Jewish Persecution of Christians', in E. Livingstone, ed., *Studia Patristica* XVII.2 (Oxford) 821–8.

Schreckenberg, H. 1990. *Die christlichen Adversus-Judaeos-Texte und ihr literarisches und historisches Umfeld (1.–11. Jh.)* (Europäische Hochschulschriften 23.172. 2nd edn., Frankfurt am Main).

Schürer, E. 1973–87. *The History of the Jewish People in the Age of Jesus Christ*, rev. edn., G. Vermes, F. Millar et al. (3 vols, Edinburgh).

Schulthess, O. 1918. 'Εἰρηνάρχαι', PW Suppl. III: 419–23.

Schwartz, E. 1906. 'Osterbetrachtungen', *ZNW* 7: 1–33 [reprinted in *Gesammelte Schriften* V (Berlin, 1963) 1–41].

Schwartz, J. 1972. 'Note sur le martyre de Polycarp de Smyrne', *RHPhR* 52: 331–5.

Schweizer, E. 1976. 'Christianity of the Circumcised and Judaism of the Uncircumcised', in R. Hamerton-Kelly and R. Scroggs, eds. 1976: 245–60.

Seager, A. R. 1972. 'The Building History of the Sardis Synagogue', *AJA* 76: 425–35.

Seager, A. R. and Kraabel, A. T. 1983. 'The Synagogue and the Jewish Community', in G. Hanfmann 1983: 168–90.

Seeberg, R. 1893. 'Die Apologie des Aristides', in T. Zahn, *Forschungen zur Geschichte des neutestamentlichen Kanons* V (Erlangen and Leipzig) 159–411.

1894. *Der Apologet Aristides. Der Text seiner uns erhaltenen Schriften* (Erlangen and Lepizig).

Seeley, D. 1990. *The Noble Death. Greco-Roman Martyrology and Paul's Concept of Salvation* (JSNT.SS 28, Sheffield).

Segal, A. 1977. *Two Powers in Heaven: Early Rabbinic Reports about Christianity and Gnosticism* (SJLA 25, Leiden).

1988. 'The Costs of Proselytism and Conversion', in D. J. Lull, ed., *SBL Seminar Papers 1988* (Atlanta) 336–69.

1990. *Paul the Convert. The Apostolate and Apostasy of Saul the Pharisee* (New Haven and London).

Sheppard, A. 1979. 'Jews, Christians and Heretics in Acmonia and Eumeneia', *AnatStuds* 29: 169–80.

1980–1. 'Pagan Cults of Angels in Roman Asia Minor', *Talanta* 12–13: 77–101.

Shotwell, W. A. 1965. *The Biblical Exegesis of Justin Martyr* (London).

Siegert, F. 1972–3. 'Gottesfürchtige und Sympathisanten', *JSJ* 3–4: 109–64.

Sigal, P. 1978–9. 'An Inquiry into Aspects of Judasim in Justin Martyr's Dialogue with Trypho', *Abr-Nahrain* 18: 74–100.

Siker, J. 1989. 'Gnostic Views on Jews and Christians in the Gospel of Philip', *NT* 31: 275–88.

    1991. *Disinheriting the Jews: Abraham in Early Christian Controversy* (Louisville).

Simon, M. 1957. 'Les sectes juives d'après les témoinages patristiques', in K. Aland and F. L. Cross, eds., *Studia Patristica* I (TU 63, Berlin) 526–39.

    1970. 'The Apostolic Decree and its Setting in the Ancient Church', *BJRL* 52: 437–60.

    1971. 'Remarques sur l'angélolâtrie juive au début de l'ére chrétien', *CRAIBL* 1971: 120–34.

    1986. *Verus Israel* (ET H. McKeating, Oxford [originally Paris, 1948/ 68]).

Skarsaune, O. 1976. 'The Conversion of Justin Martyr', *ST* 30: 53–73.

    1987. *The Proof from Prophecy. A Study in Justin Martyr's Proof-text Tradition* (NT.S 56, Leiden).

    1990. 'From Books to Testimonies. Remarks on the Transmission of the Old Testament in the Early Church', *Immanuel* 24–5: 207–19.

Slatter, F. 1985. 'The Restoration of Peace in Ignatius' Antioch', *JTS* ns. 35: 465–9.

Smallwood, E. M. 1976. *The Jews under Roman Rule from Pompey to Diocletian* (SJLA 20, Leiden).

Smith, J. D. 1986. 'The Ignatian Long Recension and Christian Communities in Fourth Century Syrian Antioch' (Harvard Univ. Th.D, 1986).

Smolar, L. and Aberbach, M. 1970. 'The Golden Calf Episode in Post-Biblical Literature', *HUCA* 39: 91–116.

Solin, H. 1983. 'Juden und Syrer im Westen Teil der römischen Welt. Eine ethnisch–demographische Studie mit besonderer Berücksichtigung der sprachliche Zustände', *ANRW* II.29.2: 587–789.

Sordi, M. 1962. 'Le polemiche intorno al cristianesimo nel II tecolo e la loro influenza sugli sviluppi della politica imperiale verso la chiesa', *Rivista di storia della chiesa in Italia* 16: 1–28.

Speigl, J. 1970. *Die Römische Staat und die Christen* (Amsterdam).

    1987. 'Ignatius in Philadelphia. Ereignisse und Anliegen in den Ignatiusbriefen', *VC* 41: 360–76.

Speyer, W. and Opelt, I. 1992. 'Barbar I', *RAC Suppl. Band I* (Stuttgart) 811–95.

Spiegel, S. 1967. *The Last Trial. On the Legends and Lore of the Command to Abraham to Offer Isaac as a Sacrifice: The Akedah* (ET J. Goldin, New York).

Staats, R. 1975. 'Die Sonntagnachtgottesdienst der christlichen Frühzeit', *ZNW* 66: 242–63.

1986. 'Die katholische Kirche des Ignatius von Antiochien und das Problem ihrer Normativität im zweiten Jahrhundert', *ZNW* 77: 242–54.

Stanton, G. N. 1992a *A Gospel for a New People. Studies in Matthew* (Edinburgh).

1992b. 'Aspects of Early Christian and Jewish Worship: Pliny and the *Kerygma Petri* ', in M. J. Wilkins and T. Paige, eds., *Worship, Theology and Ministry in the Early Church* (Fs. R. P. Martin. JSNT.SS 87, Sheffield) 84 – 98.

Stein, S. 1957. 'The Dietary Laws in Rabbinic and Patristic Literature', in. K. Aland and F. Cross, eds., *Studia Patristica* II (TU 64, Berlin) 141–54.

Stemberger, G. 1987. 'Pesachhaggadah und Abendmahlsberichte des Neuen Testaments', *Kairos* 29: 147–58.

Stern, M. 1974–84. *Greek and Latin Authors on Jews and Judaism* (3 vols. Jerusalem).

Stewart, Z. 1984. 'Greek Crowns and Christian Martyrs', in E. Lucchesi and H. D. Saffrey, eds., *Antiquité païenne et chrétienne* (Fs. A. J. Festugière, Geneva) 119–24.

Stoops, R.F. 1986. 'Patronage in the *Acts of Peter*', in D. R. McDonald, ed., *The Apocryphal Acts of the Apostles* (*Semeia* 38, Decatur) 91–100.

Stötzel, A. 1981. 'Warum Christus so spät erschien – die apologetische Argumentation bei des frühen Christentums', *ZKG* 92: 147–60.

Strobel, A. 1977. *Ursprung und Geschichte des Frühchristlichen Osterkalendars* (TU 121. Berlin).

Strubbe, J. H. M. 1989. 'Joden en Grieken: onverzoenlijke vijanden?', *Lampas* 22: 188–204.

1994. 'Curses against Violation of the Grave in Jewish Epitaphs from Asia Minor', in J. van Henten and P. van der Horst, eds., 1994: 70–128.

Stylianopoulos, T. 1975. *Justin Martyr and the Mosaic Law* (SBLDS 20, Montana).

Sumney, J. L. 1993. 'Those who "Ignorantly Deny Him": the Opponents of Ignatius of Antioch', *JECS* 1: 345–67.

Surkau, H.-W. 1938. *Martyrien in jüdischer und frühchristlicher Zeit* (FRLANT nf. 36, Göttingen).

Tarvainen, O. 1967. *Glaube und Liebe bei Ignatius von Antiochien* (Joensun).

Taylor, J. 1994. 'Why were the Disciples first called "Christians" at Antioch?', *RBib* 101: 75–94.

Taylor, M. 1995. *Anti-Judaism and Early Christian Identity. A Critique of the Scholarly Consensus* (SPB 46, Leiden).

Thompson, B. 1952. 'The Patristic Use of the Sibylline Oracles', *Review of Religion* 16: 115–36.

Thornton, T. C. G. 1986. 'The Crucifixion of Haman and the Scandal of the Cross', *JTS* ns. 37: 419–26.

1987. 'Christian Understandings of the *Birkath Ha-Minim* in the Eastern Roman Empire', *JTS* ns. 38: 419–31.

1989. 'Problematic Passovers. Difficulties for Diaspora Jews and Early Christians in determining Passover Dates in the first Three Centuries AD', in E. Livingstone, ed., *Studia Patristica* XX (Leuven) 402–8.

Tomson, P. J. 1986. 'The names Israel and Jew in Ancient Judaism and in the New Testament', *Bijdragen. Tijdschrift voor Filosophie en Theologie* 47: 120–40, 266–89.

Trakatellis, D. 1986. 'Justin Martyr's Trypho', in G. Nicklesburg and G. McRae, eds., *Christians among Jews and Gentiles* (Fs. K. Stendahl, Philadelphia) 286–97.

Tränkle, H. 1964. *QSF Tertulliani Adversus Iudaeos* (Weisbaden).

Trebilco, P. 1991. *Jewish Communities in Asia Minor* (SNTSMS 69, Cambridge).

Treu, K. 1973. 'Die Bedeutung des Griechischen für die Juden im Römischen Reich', *Kairos* 15: 123–44.

Trevett, C. 1983. 'Prophecy and Anti-Episcopal Activity; A Third Error Combatted by Ignatius?', *JEH* 34: 1–18.

1989a. 'Ignatius "To the Romans" and 1 Clement LIV-LVI', *VC* 43: 35–52.

1989b. 'Apocalypse, Ignatius, Montanism: Seeking the Seeds', *VC* 43: 313–38.

van Unnik, W. C. 1976. 'Irenaeus en de Pax Romana', in *Kerk en Vrede* (Fs. J. de Graaf. Baarn) 207–22.

1979. 'Der Fluch der Gekreuzigten: Dt 21,23 in der Deutung Justinus des Märtyrers', in C. Andresen and G. Klein, eds., *Theologia Crucis – Signum Crucis* (Fs. E. Dinkler. Tübingen) 483–99.

1983a. '"Diaspora" and "Church" in the first Centuries of the Christian Era', in *Sparsa Collecta* III (NT.S. 31. Leiden) 95–105.

1983b. 'A Note on the Dance of Jesus in the *Acts of John*', ibid.: 144–7.

1983c. 'An Unusal Formulation of the Redemption in the Homily on the Passion by Melito of Sardis', ibid.: 148–60.

Vermander, J. M. 1972. 'La Parution de l'ouvrage de Celse et la Satation de quelques Apologies', *REAug* 18: 27–42.

Vermes, G. 1973. 'Redemption and Genesis xxii – The Binding of Isaac and the Sacrifice of Jesus', in idem, *Scripture and Tradition in Judaism. Haggadic Studies* (SPB 4, 2nd edn., Leiden), 193–227.

Visotzky, B. L. 1989. 'Anti-Christian Polemic in Leviticus Rabbah', *PAAJR* 56: 83–100.

Vos, J. S. 1990. 'Legem statuimus. Rhetorische Aspekte der Gesetzesdebatte zwischen Juden und Christen', in J. van Amersfoort and J. van Oort, eds., 1990: 44–60.

Voss, B. 1970. *Der Dialog in der Frühchristlichen Literatur* (Munich).

Vouaux, L. 1913. *Les Actes de Paul* (Paris).

1922   *Les Actes de Pierre. Introduction, textes, traduction et commentaire* (Paris).

van der Waal, C. 1979. *Het Pascha van Onze Verlossing* (Johannesburg and Franeker).

Wardman, A. 1982. *Religion and Statecraft among the Romans* (London).

Weiner, E. and A. 1990. *The Martyr's Conviction. A Sociological Analysis* (BJS 203, Atlanta).

Werner, E. 1966. 'Melito of Sardes, The First Poet of Deicide', *HUCA* 37: 191–210.

White, L. M. 1987. 'The Delos Synagogue Revisited. Recent Fieldwork in the Greco-Roman Diaspora', *HTR* 80: 133–60.

1992.   'Finding the Ties that Bind: Issues from Social description', in idem, ed., *Social Networks in the Early Christian Movement. Issues and Methods for Social History* (*Semeia* 56, Atlanta) 3–22.

Wilde, R. 1949. *The Treatment of the Jews in Greek Christian Writings of the First Three Centuries* (Cath. Univ. Pat. Studs. 81, Washington).

Wilken, R. 1971. *Judaism and the Early Christian Mind* (Yale).

1976.   'Melito, the Jewish Community at Sardis, and the Sacrifice of Isaac', *TS* 37: 53–69.

1983.   *John Chrysostom and the Jews* (Berkeley).

Williams, A. L. 1909. 'The Cult of Angels at Colossae', *JTS* 10: 413–38.

1930.   *Justin Martyr. The Dialogue with Trypho* (London).

1935.   *Adversus Iudaeos. A Bird's-Eye View of Christian Apologiae until the Renaissance* (Cambridge).

Williams, M. H. 1992a. 'The Jews and Godfearers Inscription from Aphrodisias – A Case of Patriarchal Interference in Early Third Century Caria?', *Historia* 41: 297–310.

1992b. 'The Jewish Community of Corycus: Two More Inscriptions', *ZPE* 92: 248–52.

Williamson, R. 1989. *Jews in the Hellenistic World. Philo* (Cambridge Commentaries on Writings of the Jewish & Christian World 200BC to AD200, Cambridge).

Wilson, S. 1986a. 'Marcion and the Jews', in idem, 1986c: 45–58.

1986b. 'Melito and Israel', in idem, 1986c: 81–102.

1986c. ed., *Anti-Judaism in Early Christianity Vol. 2. Separation and Polemic* (Waterloo, Ontario).

1992. 'Gentile Judaizers', *NTS* 38: 605–16.

van Winden, J. C. M. 1971. *An Early Christian Philosopher. Justin Martyr's Dialogue with Trypho Chapters One to Nine* (Philosophia Patrum 1. Leiden).

Winslow, D. F. 1982. 'The Polemical Christology of Melito of Sardis', in E. Livingstone, ed., *Studia Patristica* XVII.2 (Oxford) 765–76.

Wright, D. F. 1985–6. 'Papyrus Egerton 2 (the *Unknown Gospel*) – Part of the *Gospel of Peter?*', *The Second Century* 5: 129–50.

Zahn, T. 1885–6. 'Studien zu Justinus Martyr', *ZKG* 8: 1–84.

Zeegers van der Vorst, N. 1972. *Les citations des poetes grecs chez les apologistes chrétiens du IIe siècle* (Rec. de travaux d'hist. et de phil. IV.47, Louvain).

INDEX OF SUBJECTS

References are given to footnotes only where these add substantially to the argument in the text. Italics indicate technical or Greek terms discussed in the text.

INDEX OF SOURCES

The use of English or latinized titles is eclectic, adopting the most familiar form.

A. Old Testament

Genesis

Exodus

Leviticus

Numbers

Deuteronomy

2 Kings

2 Chronicles

B. Other Jewish Sources

5 Ezra

Joseph and Aseneth

Josephus, Antiquitates

Bellum Iudaicum

Contra Apionem

Jubilees

Martyrdom of Isaiah

Philo, De cherubim

Kerygma Petri see **Clement of Alexandria**, *Stromateis*

Life of Polycarp

Martyrdom of Pionius

E. Pagan